VISUAL QUICKSTART GUIDE

EXCEL 2000

FOR WINDOWS

Maria Langer

Peachpit Press

Visual QuickStart Guide

Excel 2000 for Windows

Maria Langer

Peachpit Press
1249 Eighth Street
Berkeley, CA 94710
510-524-2178 • 800-283-9444
510-524-2221 (fax)

Find us on the World Wide Web at: http://www.peachpit.com/

Peachpit Press is a division of Addison Wesley Longman

Editor: Nancy Davis
Indexer: Emily Glossbrenner
Cover Design: The Visual Group
Production: Maria Langer, Kate Reber

Colophon

This book was produced with Adobe PageMaker 6.5 on a Power Macintosh G3/300. The fonts used were Kepler Multiple Master, Meta Plus, and PIXymbols Command. Screenshots were created using Hijaak Capture on a Gateway 2000 GP6-266.

ISBN 0-201-35427-6

9 8 7 6 5 4 3 2 1

Printed and bound in the United States of America.

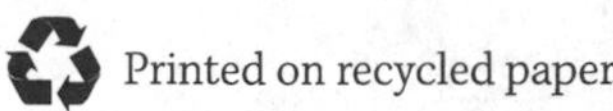
Printed on recycled paper.

Dedication

To Misty & Jake

Thanks!

To Nancy Davis, for her long-distance editing skills. It's always a pleasure to work with Nancy.

To Nancy Ruenzel, for letting me revise my *Excel 95 for Windows: Visual QuickStart Guide.*

To Kate Reber, for being so nice and patient while I laid out this book—and then tweaking it to perfection.

To the rest of the folks at Peachpit Press—especially Gary-Paul, Trish, Hannah, Paula, Zigi, Jimbo, and Keasley—for doing what they do so well.

To Emily Glossbrenner for applying her indexing skills.

To Microsoft Corporation's Office development team, for putting together a great revision to the world's best spreadsheet software package.

And to Mike, for the usual reasons.

http://www.gilesrd.com/mlanger/

TABLE OF CONTENTS

INTRODUCTION TO EXCEL 2000

Introduction

Excel, a component of Microsoft Office, is the most popular spreadsheet program for Windows users. Now more powerful and user friendly than ever, Excel 2000 enables users to create worksheets, charts, and Web pages that include a wide range of calculation features and formatting.

This Visual QuickStart Guide will help you learn the basics of Excel 2000 by providing step-by-step instructions, plenty of illustrations, and a generous helping of tips. On these pages, you'll find everything you need to know to get up and running quickly with Excel 2000—and more!

This book was designed for page flipping. Use the thumb tabs, index, or table of contents to find the topics for which you need help. If you're brand new to Excel or spreadsheets, however, I recommend that you begin by reading at least the first two chapters. **Chapter 1** provides basic information about Excel's interface while **Chapter 2** introduces worksheet concepts and explains exactly how they work in Excel.

If you've used other versions of Excel and are interested in information about new Excel 2000 features, be sure to browse through this **Introduction**. It'll give you a good idea of the new things Excel has in store for you. This book covers many, but not all, of the new features.

New & Improved Features in Excel 2000

Excel 2000 includes many brand new features, as well as major improvements to some existing features.

- The Open (**Figure 1**) and Save dialog boxes now display 50 percent more files.
- The Open (**Figure 1**) and Save dialog boxes include a Places bar, which provides quick and easy access to commonly used folders, files, and locations.
- The History folder on the Places bar in the Open (**Figure 1**) and Save dialog boxes contains links to the last 20 documents on which you have worked.
- The Back button in the Open (**Figure 1**) and Save dialog boxes makes it easy to backtrack through recently visited folders.
- Quick file switching can make it quicker and easier to switch from one open document to another by displaying a separate icon for each open document in the Windows Taskbar.

Editing

- Excel's new Collect and Paste feature enables you to copy multiple selections from Office 2000 documents and paste any combination of them, in any order, into your document.

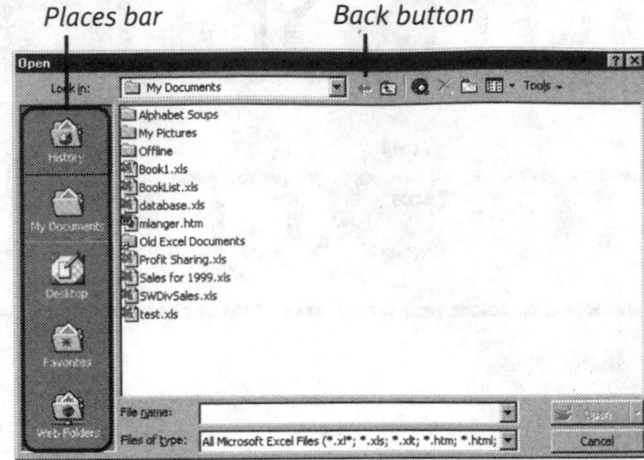

Figure 1 The Open dialog box has a whole new look.

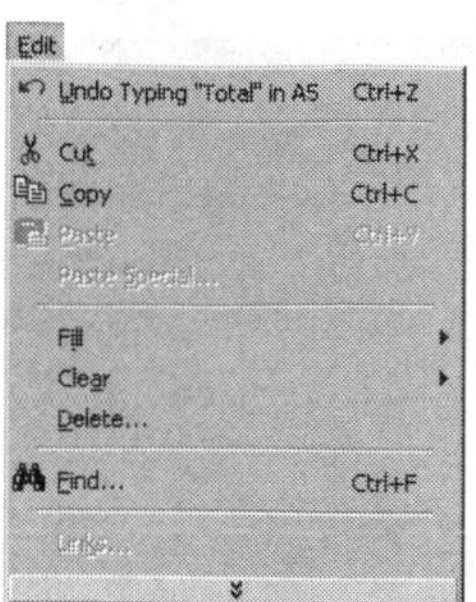

Figure 2
Commonly used commands appear on a personalized menu...

Figure 3
...but you can always display the full version of the menu.

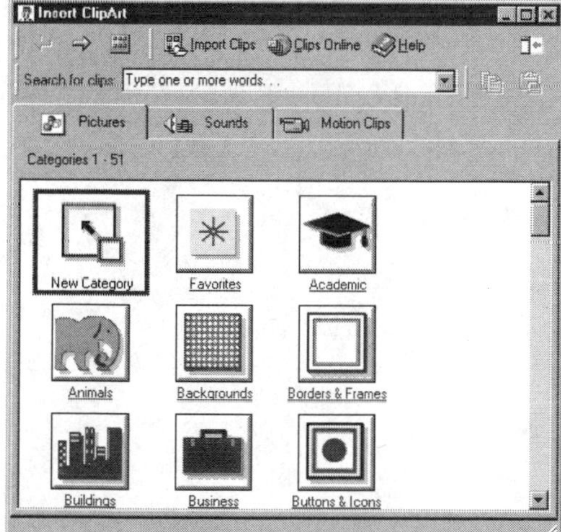

Figure 4 The Clip Art Gallery has many improvements.

Customization

- Excel automatically tracks the menu commands you use most and displays them on short, personalized menus (**Figure 2**), which can be expanded to show all commands (**Figure 3**).
- Excel automatically tracks the toolbar buttons you use most and can display them in a single row on the screen. Other toolbar buttons can be displayed when needed.
- It's now quicker and easier to customize toolbars.

Clip Art

- The Clip Art Gallery (**Figure 4**) is now searchable and includes more art and AutoShapes.
- Clip art can be organized into custom groups (**Figure 4**).
- Clip art can be dragged from the Clip Art Gallery window (**Figure 4**) into an Excel document.
- You can now leave the Clip Art Gallery window (**Figure 4**) open while working with Excel documents.
- Native clip art file formats are now passed to Excel when art is pasted or inserted into an Excel document.

Analysis Tools

- A new interface makes PivotTables easier to create and manipulate.
- You can now create charts based on PivotTable data.
- The new Data Access Pages feature enables you to create Web-enabled databases for sharing information.

Internet

- Excel can read and save to HTML format with greater fidelity than ever before.
- Documents can be saved in HTML format directly to the Web.
- The new Office Web Components, which include the Spreadsheet, Chart, and PivotTable components, enable you to create interactive Web pages (**Figure 5**) based on Excel worksheets, charts, and PivotTables.
- An improved interface for the Insert Hyperlink dialog box (**Figure 6**) makes it easier to insert hyperlinks into Excel documents.
- Excel automatically checks and attempts to repair broken hyperlinks when you save a document.
- Excel automatically selects the correct graphic format (GIF or JPEG) based on a graphic's contents when saving a graphic that's part of an HTML document.
- Web Queries has been enhanced to make it easier to bring data from the Web into an Excel document for tracking or analysis.
- Excel now includes many new and advanced Internet-based collaboration features.

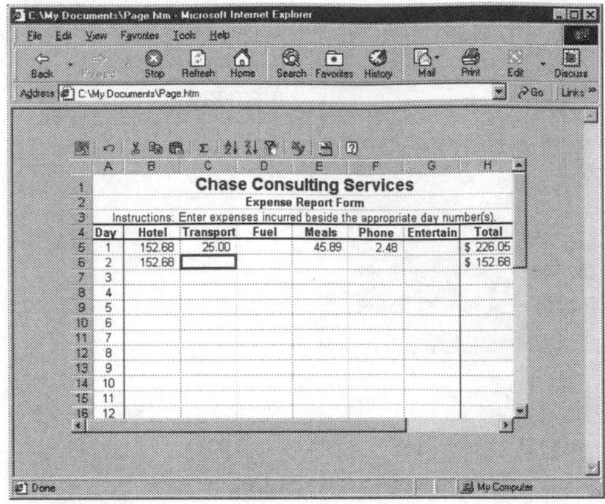

Figure 5 You can now publish worksheets as interactive Web pages.

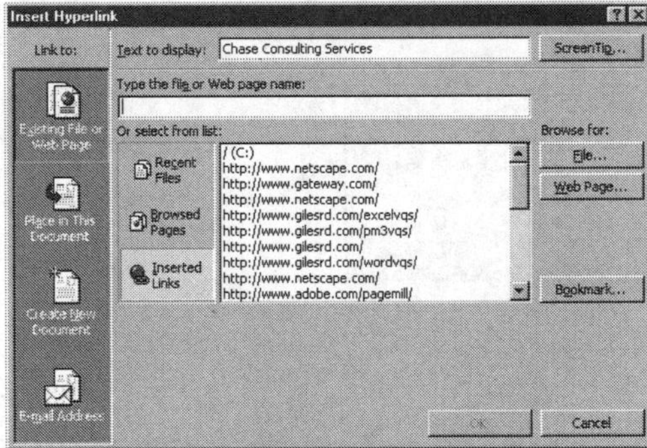

Figure 6 The Insert Hyperlink dialog box makes it easier than ever to insert hyperlinks into documents.

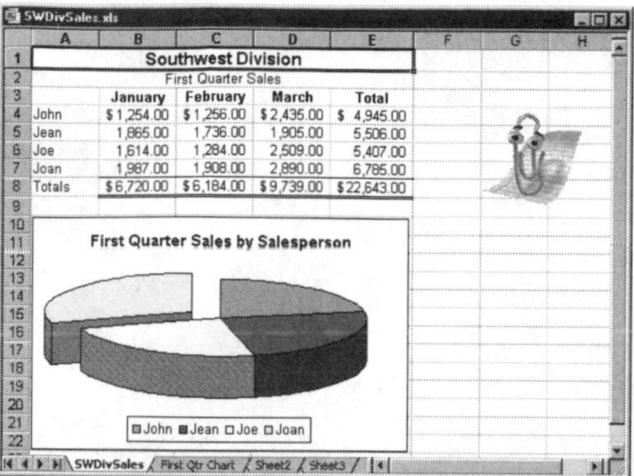

Figure 7 The Office Assistant now floats over the document window and does its best to stay out of your way.

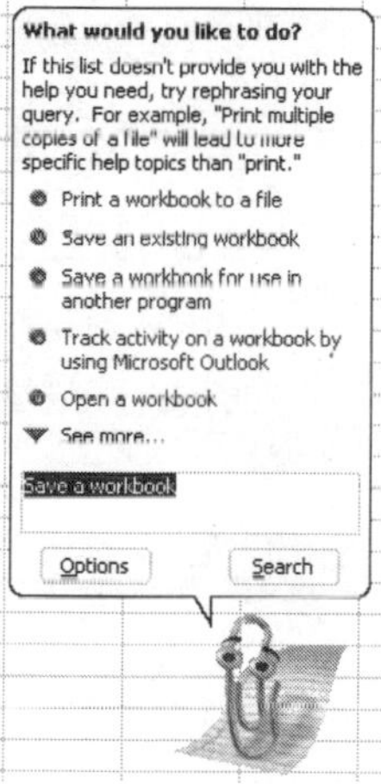

Figure 8 You can ask the Office Assistant for help in your own words.

Year 2000 Compliance

- Excel 2000 is Year 2000 compliant.
- Excel now includes advanced tools that system administrators can use to manage Year 2000 issues.

Online Help

- The Office Assistant no longer resides within its own window. Instead, it floats over the document window (**Figure 7**) to be less distracting.
- You can ask the Office Assistant for help in your own words (**Figure 8**).
- The Office Assistant now provides links to additional information on the Web.
- The Office Assistant can now be turned off.

The Excel Workplace

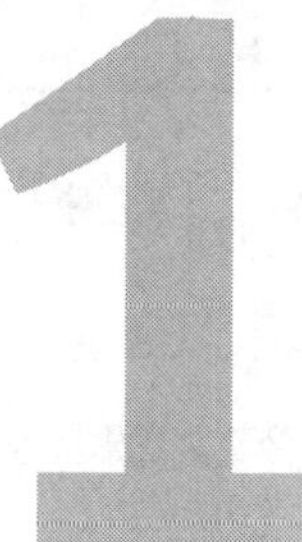

Meet Microsoft Excel

Microsoft Excel is a full-featured spreadsheet application that you can use to create worksheets, charts, lists, and even Web pages.

Excel's interface combines common Windows screen elements with buttons, commands, and controls that are specific to Excel. To use Excel effectively, you must have at least a basic understanding of these elements.

This chapter introduces the Excel workplace by illustrating and describing the following elements:

- The Excel screen, including window elements.
- Menus, shortcut keys, toolbars, and dialog boxes.
- Document scrolling techniques.
- Excel's Help feature, including the Office Assistant.

✔ Tips

- If you're brand new to Windows, don't skip this chapter. Many of the interface elements discussed in this chapter apply to all Windows programs, not just Excel.
- If you've used previous versions of Excel, browse through this chapter to learn about some of the interface elements that are new to this version of Excel.

The Excel Screen

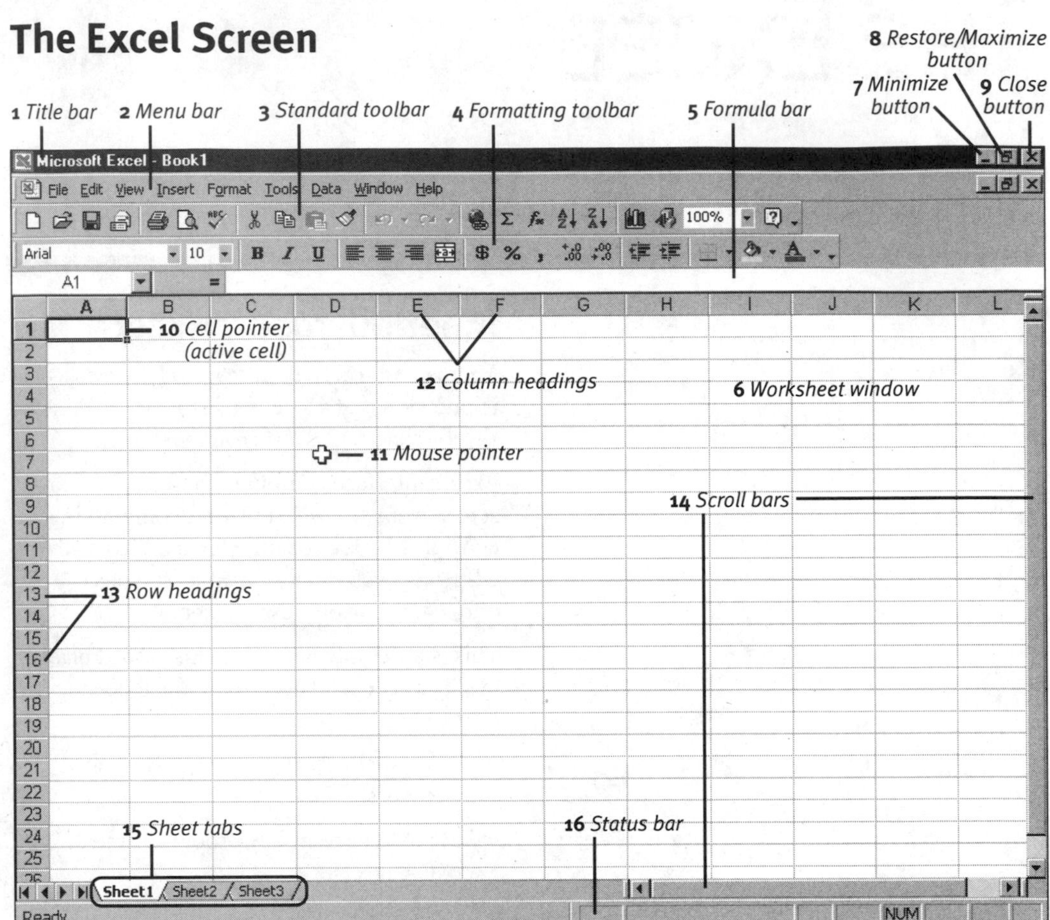

Figure 1 The Word screen in Normal view.

Key to the Excel Screen

1 *Title bar*

The title bar displays the document's title. You can drag the title bar to move the window.

2 *Menu bar*

The menu bar appears at the top of the screen and offers access to Excel's commands.

3 *Standard toolbar*

The Standard toolbar offers buttons for many basic Excel commands. This toolbar is similar in other Microsoft Office 2000 applications.

4 *Formatting toolbar*

The Formatting toolbar offers buttons for formatting commands.

5 *Formula bar*

The formula bar displays the contents of the active cell, as well as that cell's address or reference.

6 *Worksheet window*

The worksheet window is where you'll do most of your work with Excel. This window has columns and rows which intersect at cells. You enter data and formulas in the cells to build your spreadsheet.

7 *Minimize button*

The minimize button enables you to reduce the window to a button at the bottom of the screen. Clicking the button for a minimized window restores it to its normal size.

8 *Restore/Maximize button*

The restore button (shown here) resizes the window to a custom size that is smaller than the full size of the screen. (You can resize a window by dragging any of its edges when it is not maximized.) The maximize button increases the window's size so it fills the screen.

9 *Close button*

The close button offers one way to close the window.

10 *Cell pointer (active cell)*

The cell pointer is a heavy or colored border surrounding the active cell. The active cell is the cell in which text and numbers appear when you type.

11 *Mouse pointer*

When positioned within the worksheet window, the mouse pointer appears as a hollow plus sign. You can use the mouse pointer to select cells, enter data, choose menu commands, and click buttons.

12 *Column headings*

Column headings are the alphabetical labels that appear at the top of each column.

13 *Row headings*

Row headings are the numbered labels that appear on the left side of each row.

14 *Scroll bars*

Scroll bars enable you to shift the window's contents to view different parts of the document. To use a scroll bar, click an arrow at one end, click in the gray area between the arrows, or drag the scroll box.

15 *Sheet tabs*

Each Excel document has one or more sheets combined together in a workbook. The sheet tabs let you move from one sheet to another within the workbook. To use the sheet tabs, just click on the tab for the sheet that you want to view.

16 *Status bar*

The status bar displays information about the document.

The Mouse

As with most Windows programs, you use the mouse to select text, activate buttons, and choose menu commands.

Mouse pointer appearance

The appearance of the mouse pointer varies depending on its location and the item it is pointing to. Here are some examples:

- In the document window (**Figure 1**), the mouse pointer usually looks like a hollow plus sign.
- On a menu name (**Figure 2**) or on the border of a selection (**Figure 3**), the mouse pointer appears as an arrow pointing up and to the left.
- In the formula bar (**Figure 4**) or when positioned over a cell being edited (**Figure 5**), the mouse pointer appears as an I-beam pointer.

To use the mouse

There are four basic mouse techniques:

- **Pointing** means to position the mouse pointer so that its tip is on the item to which you are pointing (**Figures 2** and **3**).
- **Clicking** means to press the mouse button once and release it. You click to position the insertion point or to activate a button.
- **Double-clicking** means to press the mouse button twice in rapid succession. You double-click to open an item.
- **Dragging** means to press the mouse button down and hold it while moving the mouse. You drag to resize windows, select cells or text, choose menu commands, and draw shapes.

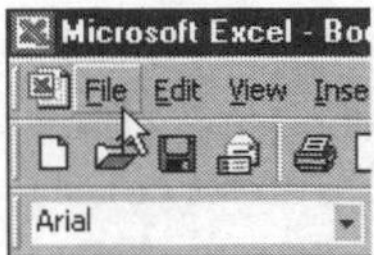

Figure 2 The mouse pointer looks like an arrow when pointing to a menu command...

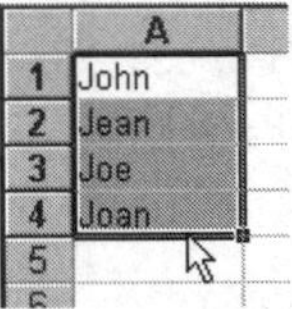

Figure 3 ...or selection border.

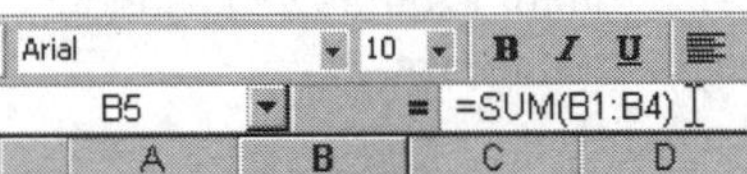

Figure 4 The mouse pointer looks like an I-beam pointer when positioned over the formula bar...

Figure 5 ...or the contents of a cell being edited.

✔ Tip

- Throughout this book, when I instruct you to simply *click*, press the left mouse button. When I instruct you to *right-click*, press the right mouse button.

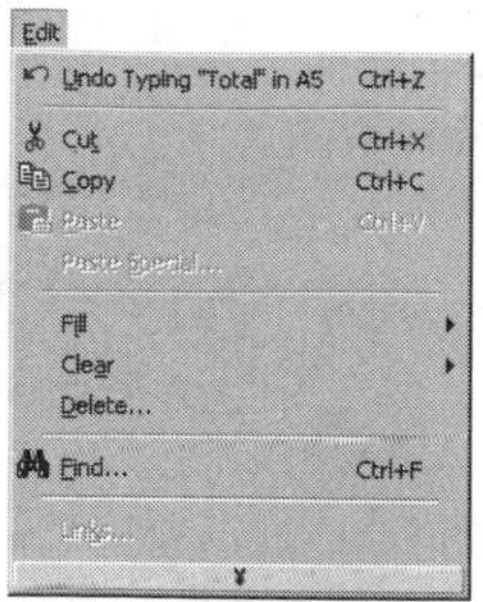

Figure 6 A personalized menu version of the Edit menu.

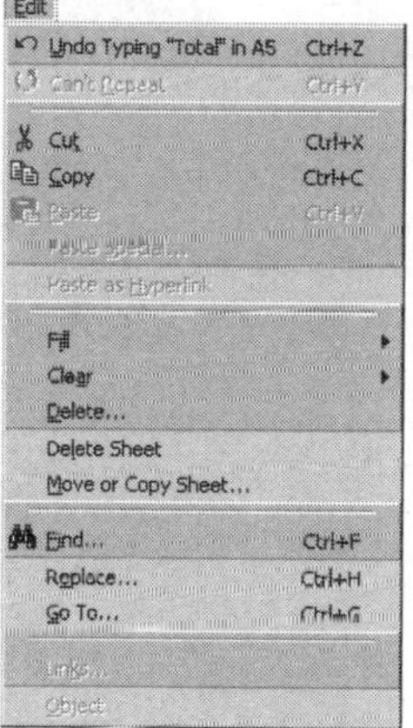

Figure 7 A full menu version of the Edit menu.

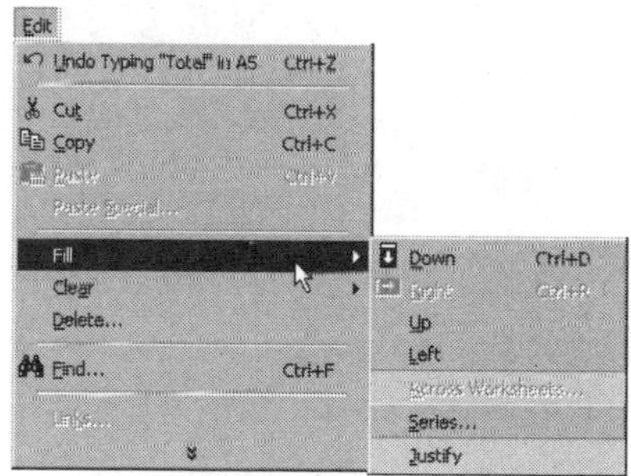

Figure 8 The Fill submenu under the Edit menu.

Menus

All of Excel's commands are accessible through its menus. Excel has three types of menus:

- **Personalized menus** appear on the menu bar near the top of the window. These menus automatically track and display only the commands you use most (**Figure 6**).
- **Full menus** also appear on the menu bar near the top of the window, but only when you either double-click the menu name, pause while displaying the menu, or click the arrows at the bottom of the menu. **Figure 7** shows the menu in **Figure 6** as a full menu with all commands displayed.
- **Shortcut menus** appear at the mouse pointer when you right-click on an item (**Figure 9**).

Here are some rules to keep in mind when working with menus:

- A menu command that appears in gray cannot be selected.
- A menu command followed by an ellipsis (...) displays a dialog box.
- A menu command followed by a triangle has a submenu. The submenu displays additional commands when the main command is chosen (**Figure 8**).
- A menu command followed by one or more keyboard characters can be chosen with a shortcut key.

✔ Tips

- Commands that appear on both personalized and full menus have a dark gray background while those that appear only on full menus have a light gray background. You can see this by comparing **Figures 6** and **7**.
- I discuss dialog boxes and shortcut keys later in this chapter.

To use a menu

1. Click on the name of the menu from which you want to choose a command. The personalized version of the menu appears (**Figure 6**).
2. If necessary, click the menu name again to display the full menu version of the menu (**Figure 7**).
3. If the command you want is on a submenu, click the name of the submenu to display it (**Figure 8**). Repeat this step if necessary to display submenus on submenus.
4. Click the command you want.

✔ Tips

- Throughout this book I use the following notation to indicate menu commands: *Menu Name* > *Submenu Name* (if necessary) > *Command Name*. For example, to instruct you to choose the Down command on the Fill submenu under the Edit menu (**Figure 8**), I'd say, "choose Edit > Fill > Down."
- You can also use mouseless menus. Press Alt, then use the letter and arrow keys to display and select menus and commands. Press Enter to activate a selected command.

To use a shortcut menu

1. Point to the item on which you want to use the shortcut menu.
2. Right-click to display the shortcut menu (**Figure 9**).
3. Click to choose the command you want.

✔ Tips

- The shortcut menu only displays the commands that can be applied to the item to which you are pointing.
- Shortcut menus are sometimes referred to as *context-sensitive* or *contextual menus*.

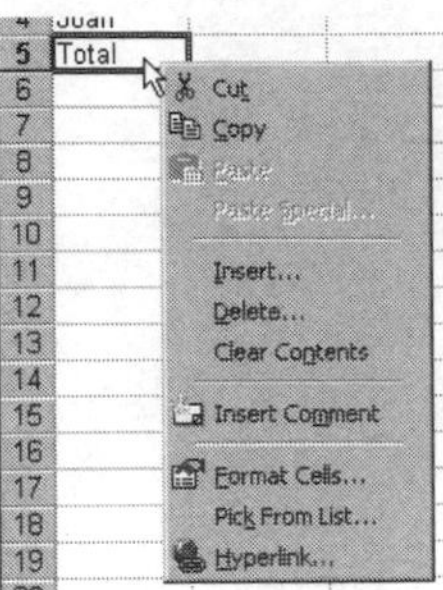

Figure 9 The shortcut menu for a cell containing a text value.

Shortcut Keys

Shortcut keys are combinations of keyboard keys that, when pressed, choose a menu command without displaying the menu. For example, the shortcut key for the Copy command under the Edit menu (**Figures 6** and **7**) is Ctrl C. Pressing this key combination chooses the command.

✔ Tips

- All shortcut keys use at least one of the following modifier keys:

Key Name	Keyboard Key
Control	Ctrl
Shift	Shift
Alt	Alt

- A menu command's shortcut key is displayed to its right on the menu (**Figures 6** and **7**).
- Many shortcut keys are standardized from one application to another. The Open, Save, and Print commands are three good examples; they're usually Ctrl O, Ctrl S, and Ctrl P.
- **Appendix A** includes a list of shortcut keys.

To use a shortcut key

1. Hold down the modifier key for the shortcut (normally Ctrl).
2. Press the letter or number key for the shortcut.

For example, to choose the Copy command, hold down Ctrl and press C.

Toolbars

Excel includes a number of toolbars for various purposes. Each toolbar has buttons or menus you can use to activate menu commands or set options.

By default, Excel automatically displays two toolbars beneath the menu bar (**Figure 1**):

- The **Standard toolbar** (**Figure 10**) offers buttons for a wide range of commonly used commands.
- The **Formatting toolbar** (**Figure 11**) offers buttons for formatting selected items.

When all of a toolbar's buttons cannot fit in the window, Excel displays the toolbar using its personalized toolbar feature (**Figure 12**). This feature keeps track of the buttons and options you use and displays the ones you use most on the toolbar. The other toolbar buttons are hidden; you can display them by clicking the More Buttons button at the end of the toolbar (**Figure 13**).

Figure 10 The Standard toolbar with all buttons displayed: New, Open, Save, E-mail, Print, Print Preview, Spelling Check, Copy, Paste, Format Painter, Undo, Redo, Insert Hyperlink, AutoSum, Paste Function, Sort Ascending, Sort Descending, Chart Wizard, Drawing, Zoom, and Microsoft Excel Help.

Figure 11 The Formatting toolbar with all buttons displayed: Font, Font Size, Bold, Italic, Underline, Align Left, Center, Align Right, Merge and Center, Currency Style, Percent Style, Comma Style, Increase Decimal, Decrease Decimal, Decrease Indent, Increase Indent, Borders, Fill Color, and Font Color.

Figure 12 Personalized toolbars show the buttons you use most.

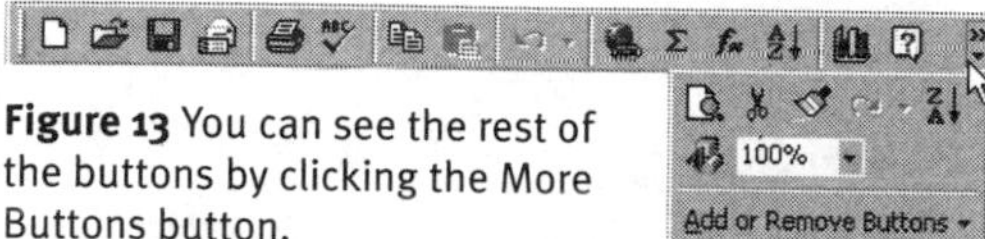

Figure 13 You can see the rest of the buttons by clicking the More Buttons button.

✔ Tips

- Other toolbars may appear automatically depending on the task you are performing with Excel.
- Toolbar buttons that are gray (for example, Paste in **Figure 10**) cannot be selected.
- Toolbar buttons that have a light gray background are "turned on" (**Figure 15**).
- A toolbar button that includes a triangle (for example, Undo and Zoom in **Figure 10**) displays a menu.
- You can identify a toolbar button by its ScreenTip.
- A toolbar can be *docked* or *floating*. A docked toolbar (**Figures 10** through **13**) is positioned against any edge of the screen. A floating toolbar can be moved anywhere within the screen.

To view ScreenTips

Point to a toolbar button. A tiny yellow box containing the name of the button appears (**Figure 14**).

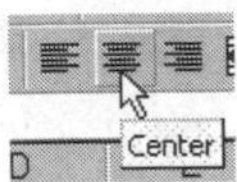

Figure 14 A ScreenTip appears when you point to a button.

To use a toolbar button

1. Point to the button for the command or option that you want (**Figure 14**).
2. Click once on the toolbar button to activate the command or select the option.

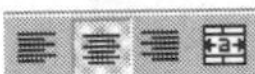

Figure 15 The Center button, turned on.

✔ Tip

- Some toolbar buttons, such as the alignment buttons on the Formatting toolbar, are "turned on" when you click them (**Figure 15**).

To use a toolbar menu

1. Point to the triangle to the right of the button.
2. Press the mouse button down to display the menu (**Figure 16**).
3. Choose an option from the menu.

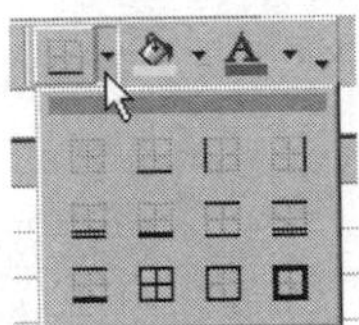

Figure 16 The Borders button menu has a gray bar at the top of it. Dragging the bar away from the toolbar...

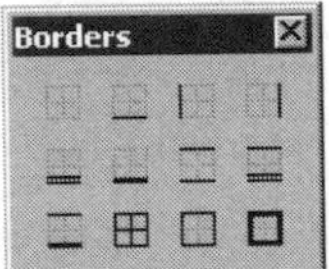

Figure 17 ...displays the menu as a floating toolbar.

✔ Tips

- Toolbar menus that display a gray bar along the top edge (**Figure 16**) can be "torn off" and used as floating menus or palettes. Simply display the menu, point to the gray bar, and drag it away from the toolbar. When the menu appears in a separate window, release the mouse button. The menu is displayed as a floating toolbar with a title bar that displays its name (**Figure 17**).
- Toolbar menus that include text boxes can be changed by typing a new value into the text box. Just click the contents of the text box to select it (**Figure 18**), then type in the new value and press Enter (**Figure 19**).

Figure 18 Select the contents of a text box...

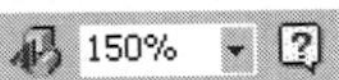

Figure 19 ...then type in a new value and press Enter.

Figure 20 By default, the Standard and Formatting toolbars are docked.

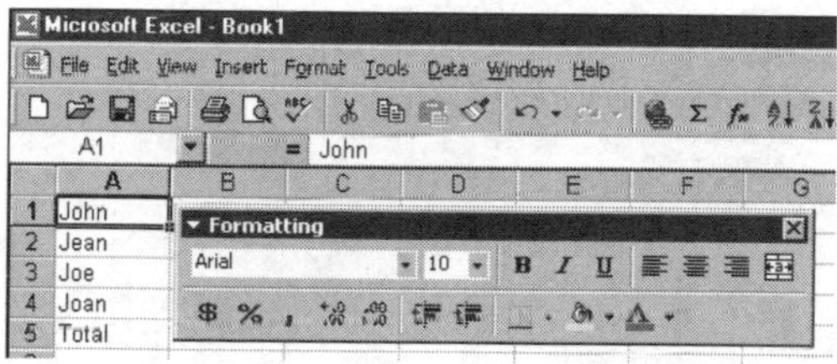

Figure 21 A floating toolbar.

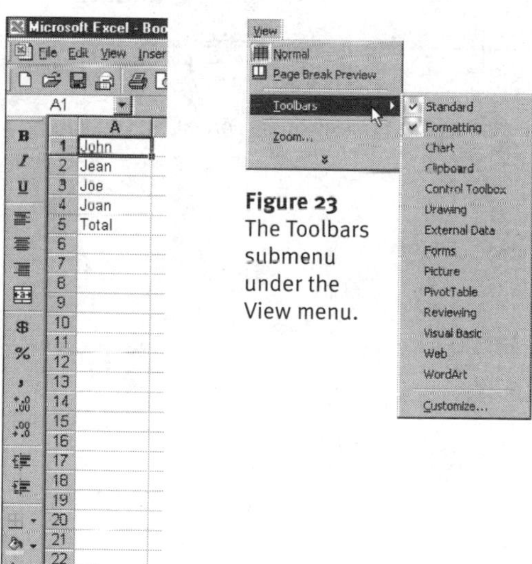

Figure 23 The Toolbars submenu under the View menu.

Figure 22 The Formatting toolbar docked on the left side of the screen.

To float a docked toolbar

Drag the toolbar's move handle (**Figure 20**) away from the toolbar's docked position (**Figure 21**).

To dock a floating toolbar

Drag the toolbar's title bar to the edge of the screen (**Figure 22**).

✔ Tip

- You can dock a toolbar against the top (**Figure 20**), either side (**Figure 22**), or the bottom of the screen. Buttons may change appearance when the toolbar is docked on the side of the screen.

To move a toolbar

- If the toolbar is docked, drag it by its move handle to a new position on the screen.
- If the toolbar is floating, drag it by its title bar to a new position on the screen.

To display or hide a toolbar

Choose the name of the toolbar that you want to display or hide from the Toolbars submenu under the View menu (**Figure 23**).

If the toolbar name has a check mark to its left, it is currently displayed and will be hidden.

or

If the toolbar name does not have a check mark to its left, it is currently hidden and will be displayed.

✔ Tip

- If a toolbar is floating (**Figure 21**), you can click its close button to hide it.

Dialog Boxes

Like most other Windows programs, Excel uses dialog boxes to communicate with you.

Excel can display many different dialog boxes, each with its own purpose. There are two basic types of dialog boxes:

- Dialog boxes that simply provide information (**Figure 24**).
- Dialog boxes that offer options to select (**Figure 25**) before Excel completes the execution of a command.

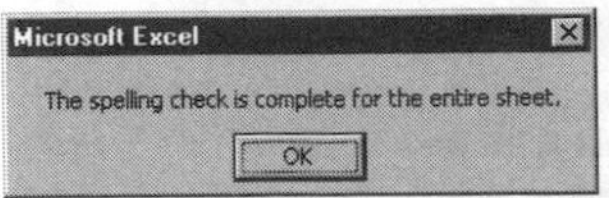

Figure 24 The dialog box that appears at the end of a spelling check simply displays a message.

✔ Tip

- Often, when a dialog box appears, you must dismiss it by clicking OK or Cancel before you can continue working with Excel.

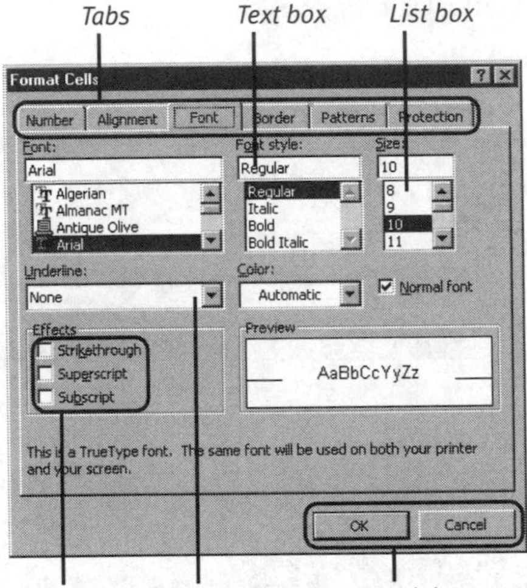

Figure 25 The Font tab of the Format Cells dialog box.

Anatomy of an Excel dialog box

Here are the components of many Excel dialog boxes, along with information about how they work.

- **Tabs** (**Figure 25**), which appear at the top of some dialog boxes, let you move from one group of options to another. To switch to another group of options, click its tab.
- **Text boxes** (**Figures 25** and **26**) let you enter information from the keyboard. You can press Tab to move from one text box to the next or click in a text box to position the insertion point within it. Then enter a new value.
- **List boxes** (**Figure 25**) offer a number of options. Use the scroll bar to view options that don't fit in the list window. Click an option to select it; it becomes highlighted and appears in the text box.
- **Check boxes** (**Figure 25**) let you turn options on or off. Click in a check box to toggle it. When a check mark or X appears in the check box, its option is turned on.

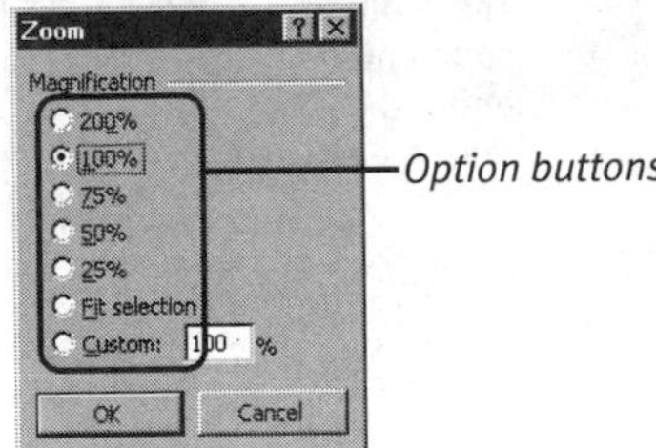

Figure 26 The Zoom dialog box.

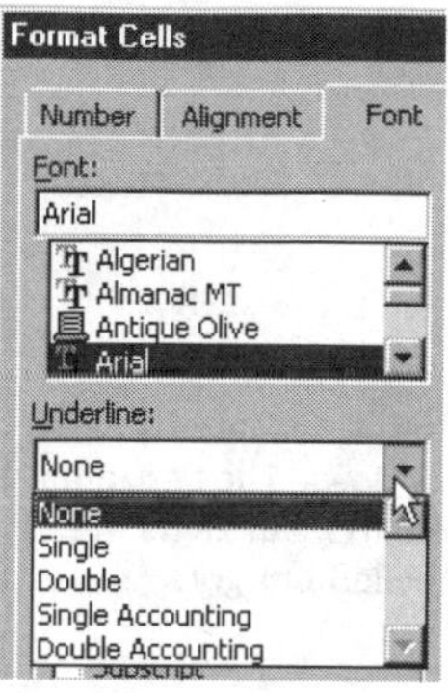

Figure 27 Displaying a menu within a dialog box.

- **Option buttons** (**Figure 26**) let you select only one option from a group. Click on an option to select it; the option that was selected before you clicked is deselected.
- **List box menus** (**Figure 25**) also let you select one option from a group. Display a list box menu as you would any other menu (**Figure 27**), then choose the option that you want.
- **Preview areas** (**Figure 25**), when available, illustrate the effects of your changes before you finalize them by clicking OK.
- **Push buttons** (**Figures 24**, **25**, and **26**) let you access other dialog boxes, accept the changes and close the dialog box (OK), or close the dialog box without making changes (Cancel). To select a button, click it.

✔ Tips

- When the contents of a text box are selected, whatever you type will replace the selection.
- Excel often uses text boxes and list boxes together (**Figure 25**). You can use either one to make a selection.
- If a pair of tiny triangles appear to the right of a text box, you can click a triangle to increase or decrease the value in the text box.
- In some list boxes, double-clicking an option selects it and dismisses the dialog box.
- You can turn on any number of check boxes in a group, but you can select only one option button in a group.
- The Excel 2000 documentation and online help system sometimes refer to list box menus as *drop-down lists* or *pop-up menus*.
- A push button with a black border around it is the button that will be "clicked" if you press Enter.
- You can usually "click" the Cancel button by pressing Esc.

Scrolling Window Contents

You can use Excel's scroll bars to shift the contents of a document window so you can see items that don't fit in the window.

✔ Tip

- I tell you more about working with document windows in **Chapter 4**.

To scroll the contents of the document window

Click the scroll arrow (**Figure 28**) for the direction that you want to view. For example, to scroll down to view the end of a document, click the down arrow.

or

Drag the scroll box (**Figure 28**) in the direction that you want to view. As you drag, a yellow box with a row or column heading appears on screen. It indicates the topmost row (**Figure 29**) or leftmost column (**Figure 30**) that will appear on screen when you release the mouse button. Release the mouse button to view the indicated part of the document.

or

Click in the scroll bar on either side of the scroll box (**Figure 28**). This shifts the window contents one screenful at a time.

✔ Tips

- Having trouble remembering which scroll arrow to click? Just remember this: click up to see up, click down to see down, click left to see left, and click right to see right.
- Although some keyboard keys change the portion of the document being viewed, they also move the cell pointer. I tell you about these keys in **Chapter 2**.

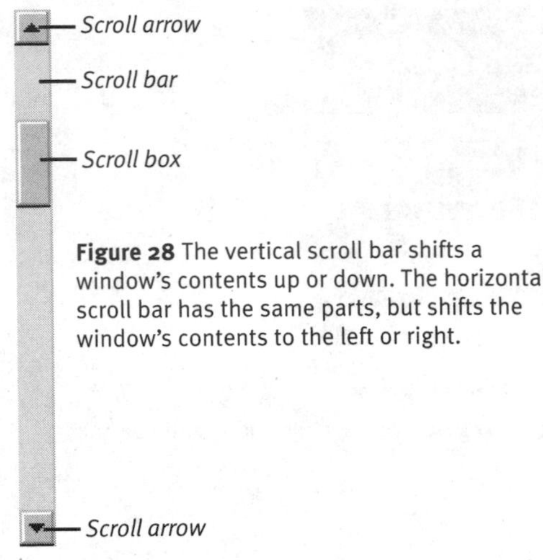

Figure 28 The vertical scroll bar shifts a window's contents up or down. The horizontal scroll bar has the same parts, but shifts the window's contents to the left or right.

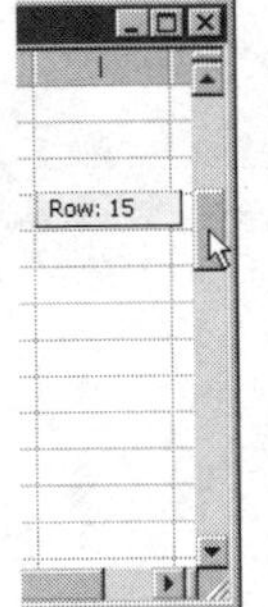

Column: C

Figures 29 & 30
When you drag the scroll box, a yellow box with the row heading number (left) or the column heading letter (right) appears.

Figure 31
The Office Assistant.

Figure 32
The Help menu.

Figure 33
The Office Assistant, with a tip.

The Office Assistant

The Office Assistant is an animated character (**Figure 31**) that appears on screen. It can provide tips and assistance while you work.

To display the Office Assistant

Choose Help > Show the Office Assistant (**Figure 32**).

or

Click the Microsoft Excel Help button on the Standard toolbar. (This technique will only work if the Office Assistant has not been disabled.)

To hide the Office Assistant

Choose Help > Hide the Office Assistant.

To move the Office Assistant

1. Position the mouse pointer on the Office Assistant.
2. Press the mouse button down and drag the Office Assistant to a new position on the screen.

✔ Tip

- The Office Assistant will automatically move out of the way if necessary as you work.

To read a tip

1. Click the light bulb that appears near the Office Assistant's head (**Figure 31**) when the Office Assistant has a tip for you. The tip appears in a balloon near the Office Assistant (**Figure 33**).
2. When you are finished reading the tip, click anywhere in the document window to dismiss it.

To ask a question

1. If necessary, click the Office Assistant to get its attention. A balloon with a text box containing instructions appears (**Figure 34**).
2. Type your question into the text box and click the Search button. A list of possible topics appears in another balloon (**Figure 35**).
3. Click a topic that interests you. The Microsoft Excel Help window appears (**Figure 36**). It provides detailed information and clickable links for the topic you selected.
4. When you are finished reading help information, click the Microsoft Excel Help window's close button to dismiss it.

To disable the Office Assistant

1. Display the Office Assistant and click it to display its balloon (**Figure 34**).
2. Click the Options button.
3. In the Office Assistant dialog box that appears (**Figure 37**), turn off the Use the Office Assistant check box.
4. Click OK. The Office Assistant disappears.

✔ Tips

- Once the Office Assistant has been disabled, it will not reappear unless you choose Help > Show the Office Assistant (**Figure 32**).
- You can also use the Office Assistant dialog box (**Figure 37**) to customize the way the Office Assistant looks and works.

Figure 34 The Office Assistant displays a balloon containing instructions.

Figure 35 The Office Assistant suggests several topics based on the question or words you enter. When you click a suggested topic...

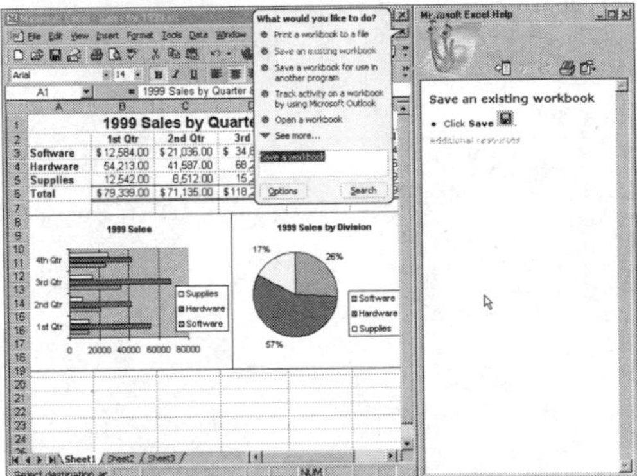

Figure 36 ...The Microsoft Excel Help window appears with information.

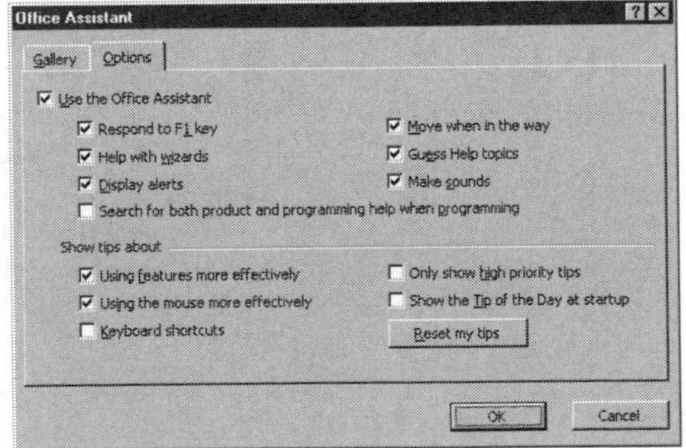

Figure 37 The Office Assistant dialog box lets you set its options—and disable it.

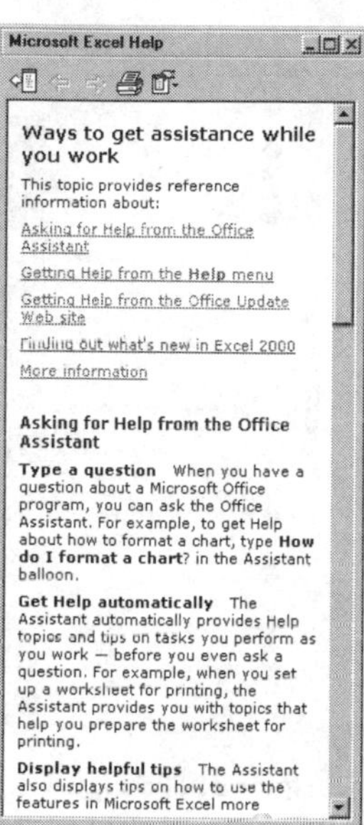

Figure 38 The Microsoft Excel Help window with the Help tabs hidden...

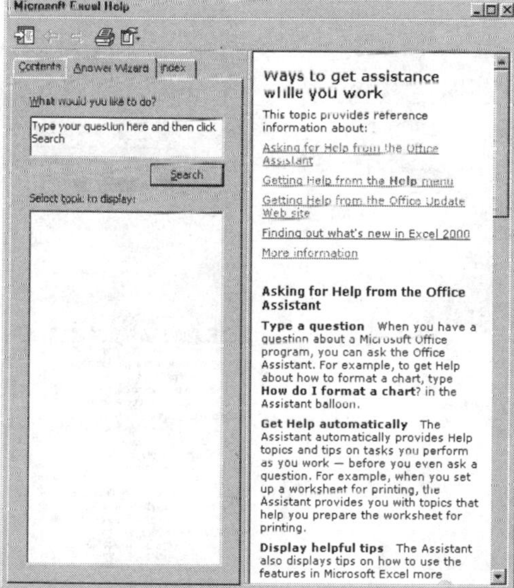

Figure 39 ...and with the Help tabs displayed.

Microsoft Excel Help

Excel has an extensive online help feature that provides information about using Excel to complete specific tasks. You access Microsoft Excel Help via the Office Assistant (as discussed on the previous page) or by using commands under the Help menu (**Figure 32**).

To open Microsoft Excel Help

1. If the Office Assistant is enabled, follow the steps on the previous page to display the Microsoft Excel Help window (**Figure 36**).

   or

   If the Office Assistant is disabled, choose Help > Microsoft Excel Help (**Figure 32**), press F1, or click the Microsoft Excel Help button on the Standard toolbar to display the Microsoft Excel Help window (**Figure 38** or **39**).
2. If necessary, click the Show button at the top of the window to expand the window and view the help tabs (**Figure 39**).

✔ Tip

- The Microsoft Excel Help window includes hyperlinks—blue, underlined words and phrases that, when clicked, display related information.

To ask a question

1. Open the Microsoft Excel Help window as instructed above.
2. If necessary, click the Answer Wizard tab (**Figure 39**).
3. Enter your question in the text box at the top of the tab and click Search. A list of help topics appears in the Select topic to display box.
4. Click a topic that interests you. Detailed information and instructions appear on the right side of the window.

To use the Table of Contents

1. Open the Microsoft Excel Help window as instructed on the previous page.
2. If necessary, click the Contents tab (**Figure 40**).
3. Click the plus sign to the left of a main topic to display its subtopics (**Figure 41**).
4. Click a subtopic that interests you. Detailed information and instructions appear on the right side of the window.

To use the Index

1. Open the Microsoft Excel Help window as instructed on the previous page.
2. If necessary, click the Index tab (**Figure 42**).
3. Type one or more keywords in the text box near the top of the window. Then click Search.

   or

   Scroll through the keywords list and click one that interests you.

   A list of topics appears in the Choose a topic box (**Figure 43**).
4. Click a topic. Detailed information and instructions appear on the right side of the window.

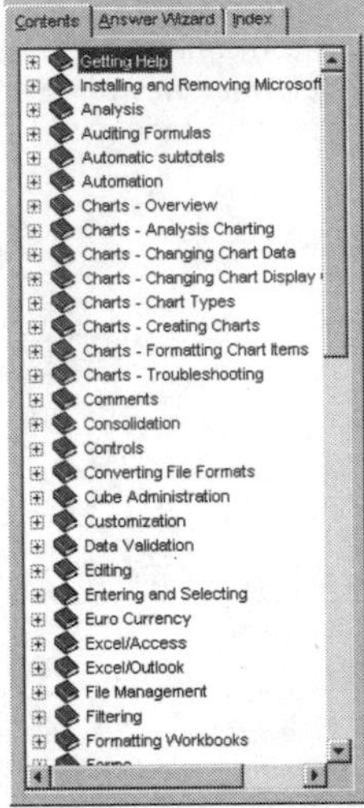

Figure 40 The Contents tab of the Microsoft Excel Help window.

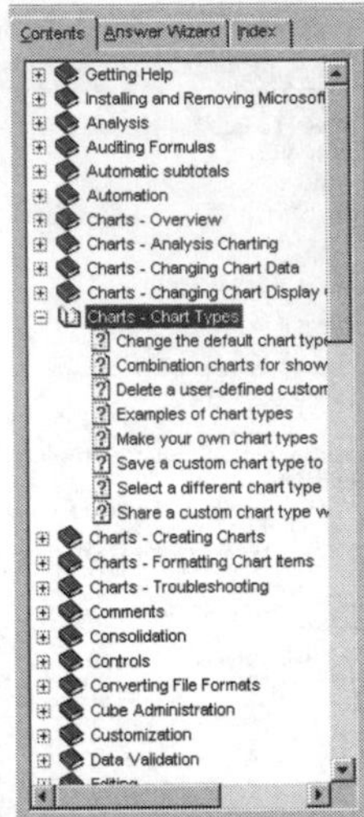

Figure 41 Clicking a plus sign beside a topic displays subtopics.

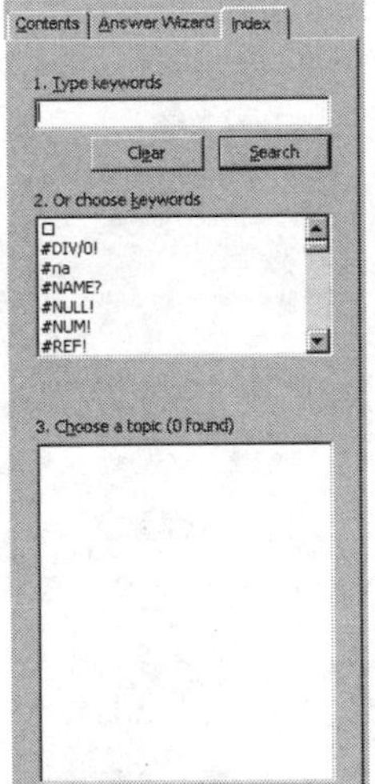

Figure 42 The Index tab of the Microsoft Excel Help window.

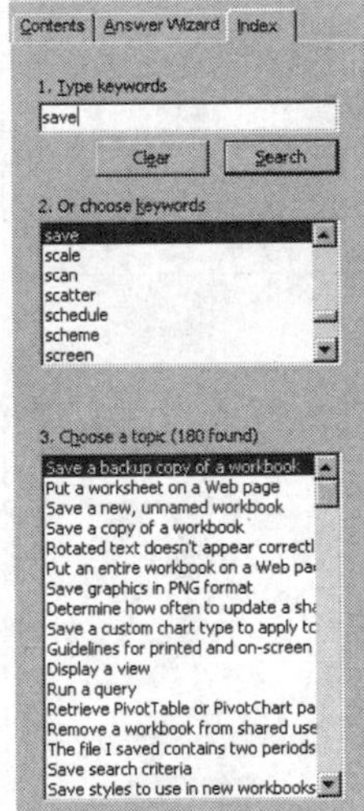

Figure 43 Use keywords to search for topics that interest you.

WORKSHEET BASICS

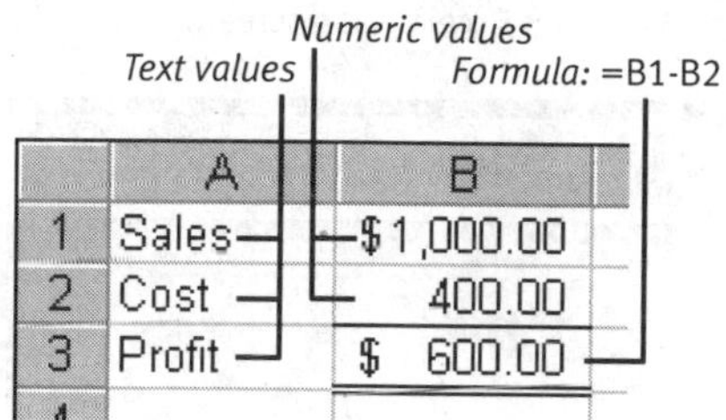

Figure 1 This very simple worksheet illustrates how a spreadsheet program like Excel works with values and formulas.

	A	B
1	Sales	$1,150.00
2	Cost	400.00
3	Profit	$ 750.00

Figure 2 When the value for Sales changes from $1,000 to $1,150, the Profit result changes automatically.

How Worksheets Work

Excel is most commonly used to create *worksheets*. A worksheet is a collection of information laid out in columns and rows. As illustrated in **Figure 1**, each worksheet cell can contain one of two kinds of input:

- A *value* is a piece of information that does not change. Values can be text, numbers, dates, or times. A cell containing a value usually displays the value.
- A *formula* is a collection of values, cell references, operators, and predefined functions that, when evaluated by Excel, produces a result. A cell containing a formula usually displays the results of the formula.

Although any information can be presented in a worksheet, spreadsheet programs like Excel are usually used to organize and calculate numerical or financial information. Why? Well, when properly prepared, a worksheet acts like a super calculator. You enter values and formulas and it calculates and displays the results. If you change one of the values, Excel recalculates the results almost instantaneously, without any additional effort on your part (**Figure 2**).

How does this work? By using cell *references* rather than actual numbers in formulas, Excel knows that it should use the contents of those cells in its calculations. Thus, changing one or more values affects the results of calculations that include references to the changed cells. As you can imagine, this makes worksheets powerful business planning and analysis tools!

Running Excel

To use Excel, you must run the Excel program. This loads Excel into RAM (Random Access Memory), so your computer can work with it.

Figure 3 The Microsoft Excel splash screen.

To run Excel from the Taskbar

Click Start > Programs > Microsoft Excel.

The Excel splash screen appears briefly (**Figure 3**), then an empty document window named *Book1* appears (**Figure 4**).

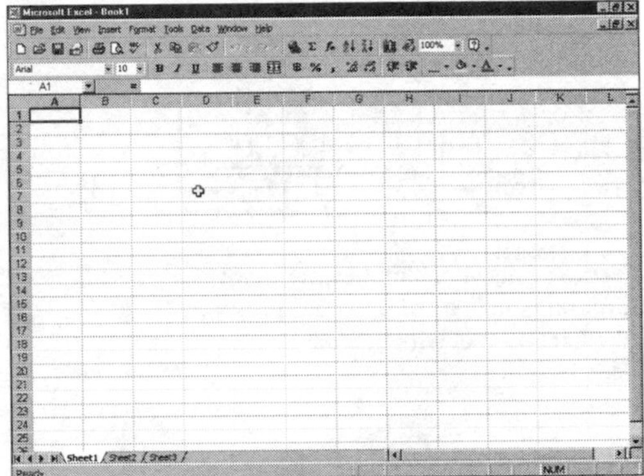

Figure 4 When you run Excel from the Windows Taskbar, it displays an empty document window.

To run Excel by opening an Excel document

1. In Windows Explorer, locate the icon for the document that you want to open (**Figure 5**).
2. Double-click the icon.

The Excel splash screen appears briefly (**Figure 3**), then a document window containing the document that you opened appears (**Figure 6**).

Figure 5 An Excel document icon.

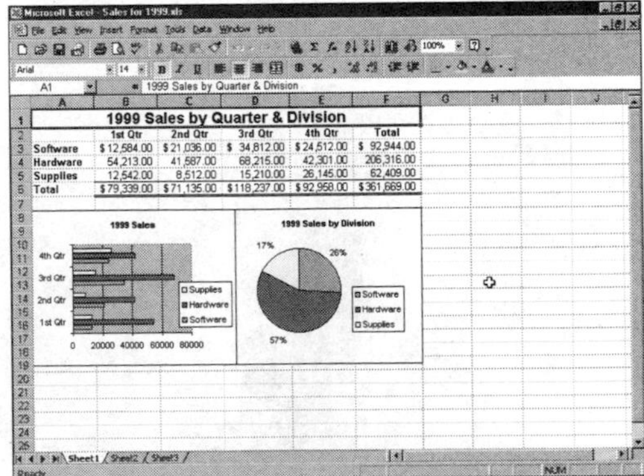

Figure 6 When you run Excel by opening an Excel document icon, it displays the document you opened.

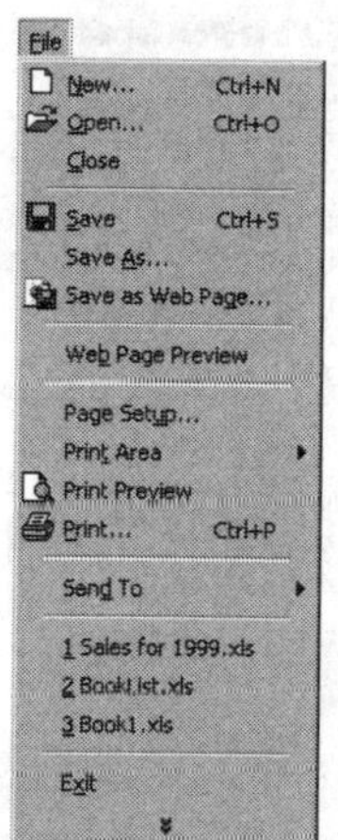

Figure 7
The File menu.

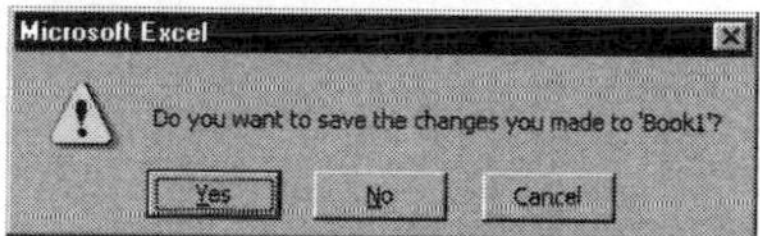

Figure 8 A dialog box like this appears when a document with unsaved changes is open when you exit Excel.

Exiting Excel

When you're finished using Excel, you should use the Exit command to close it. This completely clears Excel out of RAM, freeing up RAM for other programs.

✔ Tip

- Exiting Excel also instructs Excel to save preference settings.

To exit Excel

Choose File > Exit (**Figure 7**). Here's what happens:

- If any documents are open, they close.
- If an open document contains unsaved changes, a dialog box appears (**Figure 8**) so you can save the changes.
- The Excel program closes.

✔ Tip

- As you've probably guessed, Excel automatically exits when you restart or shut down your computer.

Creating a New Workbook

By default, the documents you create using Excel are Excel *workbook* files. Excel enables you to create two kinds of workbook files:

- A blank workbook file is an empty workbook file with Excel's default settings.
- A workbook file based on a *template* contains the values, formulas, formatting, custom toolbars, and macros included in a template file.

✔ Tips

- I tell you more about Excel workbook files in **Chapter 4**.
- Basing a workbook on a template can save a lot of time if you often need to create a standard document—such as a monthly report or invoice—repeatedly. I explain how to create templates in **Chapter 4**.

To create a blank workbook file

1. Choose File > New (**Figure 7**).
2. If necessary, click the General tab in the New dialog box that appears to display its options (**Figure 9**).
3. Click to select the Workbook icon.
4. Click OK.

   A new, empty workbook window appears (**Figure 4**).

or

Click the New button on the Standard toolbar or press Ctrl N.

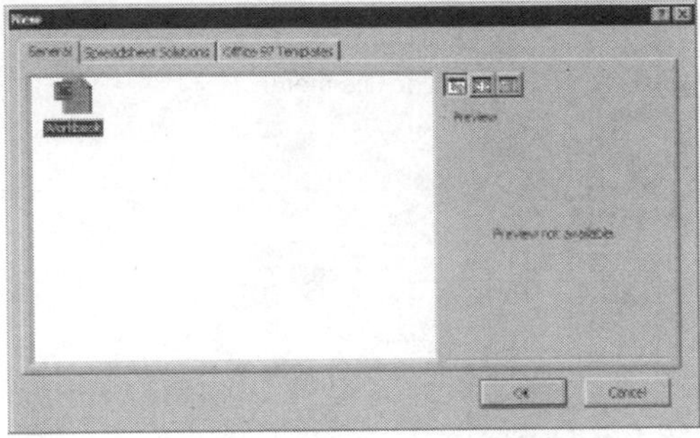

Figure 9 The General tab of the New dialog box.

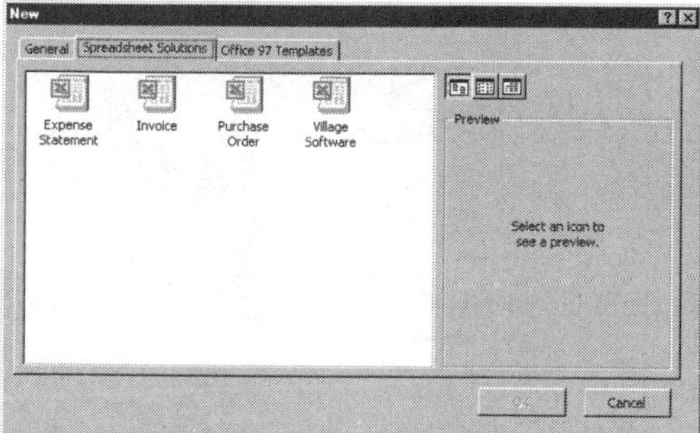

Figure 10 The Spreadsheet Solutions tab of the New dialog box offers a number of templates that come with Excel.

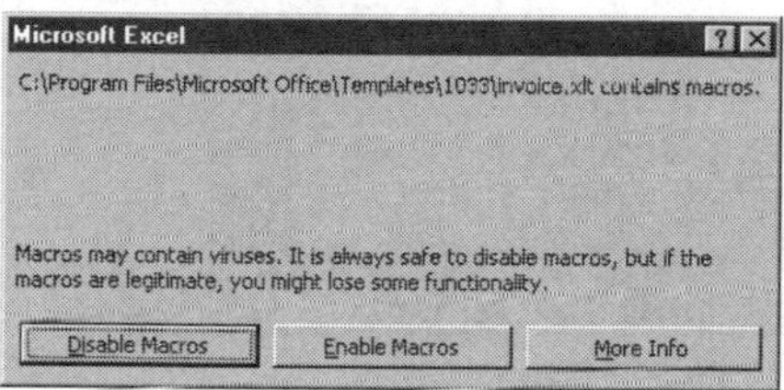

Figure 11 Excel's macro virus protection feature allows you to disable macros in a template file.

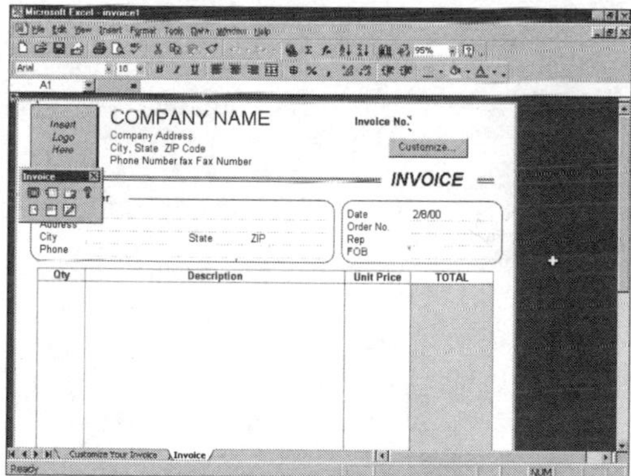

Figure 12 A new workbook file based on the Invoice template that comes with Excel. Note the custom Invoice toolbar.

To create a workbook file based on a template

1. Choose File > New (**Figure 7**).
2. In the New dialog box that appears, click the tab containing the template you want to use (**Figure 10**).
3. Click to select the icon for the template on which you want to base the new workbook file.
4. Click OK.
5. If macro virus protection is turned on, Excel may warn you that the template contains macros (**Figure 11**).
   - ▲ If you know the template is from a reliable source, click the Enable Macros button.
   - ▲ If you are not sure about the reliability of the template's source, click the Disable Macros button.

   A new workbook based on the template that you selected appears (**Figure 12**).

✔ Tips

- Excel comes with several sample templates (**Figure 10**) that you can experiment with.
- If you click the Disable Macros button in step 5, the template's macros will not be available for you to use.
- I tell you more about macros in **Chapter 11** and about macro virus protection in **Chapter 13**.

Activating & Selecting Cells

Worksheet information is entered into *cells*. A cell is the intersection of a column and a row. Each little "box" in the worksheet window is a cell.

Each cell has a unique *address* or *reference*. The reference uses the letter(s) of the column and the number of the row. Thus, cell *B6* would be at the intersection of column *B* and row *6*. The reference for the active cell appears in the Name Box at the far left end of the formula bar (**Figure 13**).

To enter information in a cell, you must make that cell *active*. A cell is active when there is a dark or colored border called the *cell pointer* around it. When a cell is active, anything you type is entered into it.

To use Excel commands on a cell or its contents, you must *select* the cell. The active cell is also a selected cell. If desired, however, you can select multiple cells or a *range* of cells. This enables you to use commands on all selected cells at once. A range (**Figure 14**) is a rectangular selection of cells defined by the top left and bottom right cell references.

✔ Tips

- Although the active cell is always part of a selection of multiple cells, it is never highlighted like the rest of the selection. You should, however, see a dark or colored border (the cell pointer) around it (**Figure 14**).
- Although you can select multiple cells, only one cell—the one referenced in the Name Box (**Figure 14**)—is active.
- The column and row headings for selected cells appear bold (**Figures 13** and **14**).
- Using the scroll bars does not change the active or selected cell(s). It merely changes your view of the worksheet's contents.

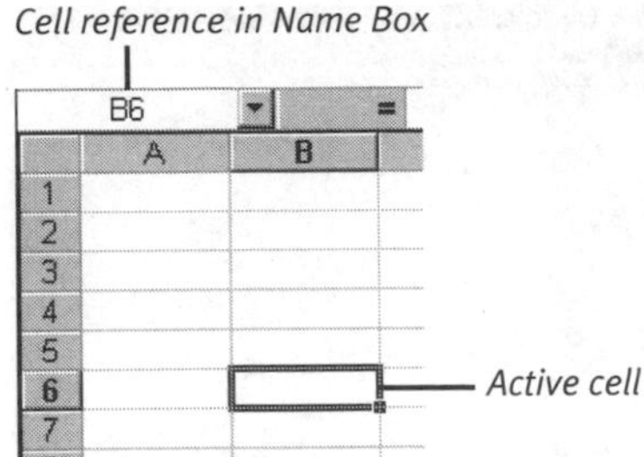

Figure 13 The reference for an active cell appears in the formula bar.

A3

	A	B	C	D	E
1		Southwest Division			
2		First Quarter Sales			
3		Jan	Feb	Mar	Total
4	John	$ 1,256.00	$ 1,254.00	$ 2,451.00	$ 4,961.00
5	Jean	1,846.00	1,726.00	2,105.00	5,677.00
6	Joe	1,601.00	1,575.00	2,569.00	5,745.00
7	Joan	1,954.00	1,864.00	2,248.00	6,066.00
8	Totals	$ 6,657.00	$ 6,419.00	$ 9,373.00	$ 22,449.00

Figure 14 In this illustration, the range A3:B8 is selected. Within that range, cell A3 is the active cell.

Table 1

Keys for Moving the Cell Pointer

Key	Movement
↑	Up one cell
↓	Down one cell
←	Left one cell
→	Right one cell
Tab	Right one cell
Home	First cell in row
Page Up	Up one window
Page Down	Down one window
Ctrl Home	Cell A1
Ctrl End	Cell at the intersection of the last column and last row containing data

	A	B	C	D	E
1	Southwest Division				
2	First Quarter Sales				
3		Jan	Feb	Mar	Total
4	John	$ 1,256.00	$ 1,254.00	$ 2,451.00	$ 4,961.00
5	Jean	1,846.00	1,726.00	2,105.00	5,677.00
6	Joe	1,601.00	1,575.00	2,569.00	5,745.00
7	Joan	1,954.00	1,864.00	2,248.00	6,066.00
8	Totals	$ 6,657.00	$ 6,419.00	$ 9,373.00	$ 22,449.00

Figure 15 To select cells, begin in one corner of the range,...

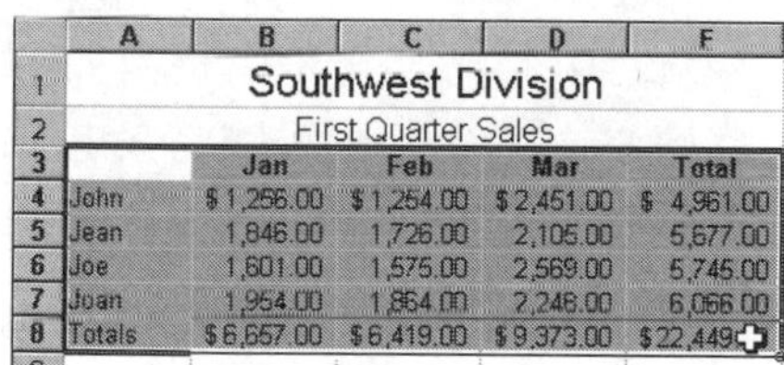

	A	B	C	D	E
1	Southwest Division				
2	First Quarter Sales				
3		Jan	Feb	Mar	Total
4	John	$ 1,256.00	$ 1,254.00	$ 2,451.00	$ 4,961.00
5	Jean	1,846.00	1,726.00	2,105.00	5,677.00
6	Joe	1,601.00	1,575.00	2,569.00	5,745.00
7	Joan	1,954.00	1,864.00	2,248.00	6,066.00
8	Totals	$ 6,657.00	$ 6,419.00	$ 9,373.00	$ 22,449

Figure 16 ...press the mouse button down, and drag to the opposite corner of the range.

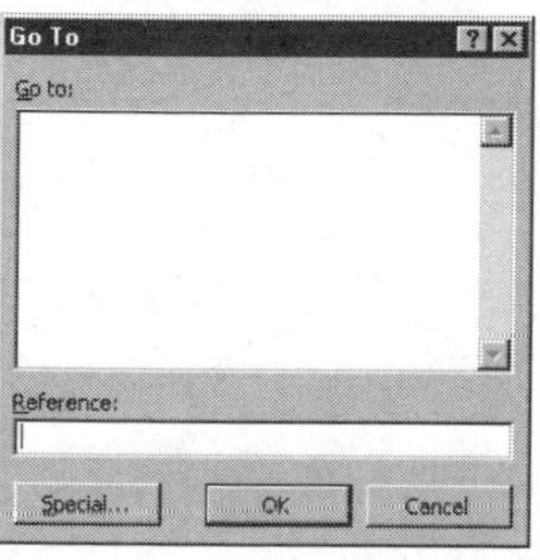

Figure 17 The Go To dialog box lets you move to any cell or select any range quickly.

To activate a cell

Use the mouse pointer to click in the cell you want to make active.

or

Press the appropriate keystroke (**Table 1**) to move the cell pointer to the cell you want to make active.

To select a range of cells with the mouse

1. Position the mouse pointer in the first cell you want to select (**Figure 15**).
2. Press the mouse button down and drag to highlight all the cells in the selection (**Figure 16**).

or

1. Click in the first cell of the range you want to select.
2. Hold down Shift and click in the last cell of the range. Everything between the first and second clicks is selected. This technique is known as "Shift-Click."

To go to a cell or range of cells

1. Choose Edit > Go To or press Ctrl G to display the Go To dialog box (**Figure 17**).
2. Enter the reference for the cell you want to activate or the range that you want to select in the Reference box.
3. Click OK.

   If you entered a single cell reference, the cell is activated. If you entered a range reference, the range is selected.

✔ Tip

- To specify a reference for a range, enter the addresses of the first and last cells of the range, separated with a colon (:). For example, **Figure 14** shows *A3:B8* selected and **Figure 16** shows *A3:E8* selected.

To select an entire column

Click on the column heading of the column you want to select (**Figure 18**).

or

Press [Ctrl][Spacebar] when the cell pointer is in any cell of the column you want to select.

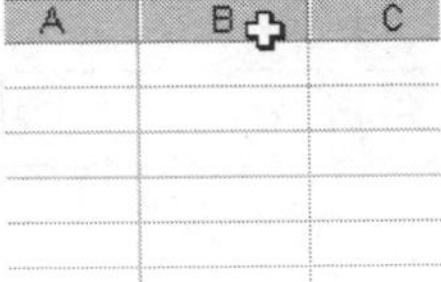

Figure 18 Click a column heading to select that column.

To select an entire row

Click on the row heading of the row you want to select (**Figure 19**).

or

Press [Shift][Spacebar] when the cell pointer is in any cell of the row you want to select.

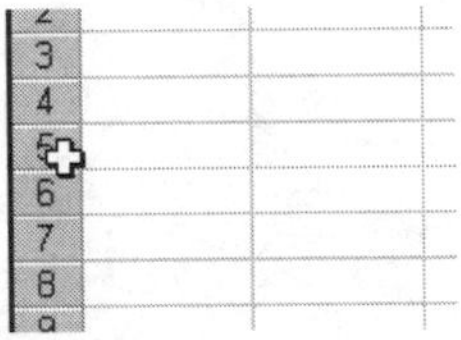

Figure 19 Click a row heading to select that row.

To select multiple columns or rows

1. Position the mouse pointer on the first column or row heading.
2. Press the mouse button down, and drag along the headings until all the desired columns or rows are selected.

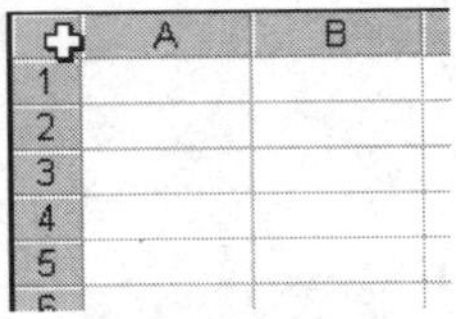

Figure 20 The Select All button is in the corner of the worksheet, where column and row headings meet.

✔ Tip

- When selecting multiple columns or rows, be careful to position the mouse pointer on the heading and not between two headings! If you drag the border of two columns or two rows, you will change a column's width or row's height rather than make a selection. I tell you about changing column width and row height in **Chapter 6**.

To select the entire worksheet

Click the Select All button at the upper-left corner of the worksheet window (**Figure 20**).

or

Press [Ctrl][A].

or

Press [Ctrl][Spacebar] and then [Shift][Spacebar].

	A	B	C	D	E
1		Southwest Division			
2		First Quarter Sales			
3		Jan	Feb	Mar	Total
4	John	$ 1,256.00	$ 1,254.00	$ 2,451.00	$ 4,961.00
5	Jean	1,846.00	1,726.00	2,105.00	5,677.00
6	Joe	1,601.00	1,575.00	2,569.00	5,745.00
7	Joan	1,954.00	1,864.00	2,248.00	6,066.00
8	Totals	$ 6,657.00	$ 6,419.00	$ 9,373.00	$ 22,449.00

Figure 21 To select two ranges of cells, start by selecting the first range...

	A	B	C	D	E
1		Southwest Division			
2		First Quarter Sales			
3		Jan	Feb	Mar	Total
4	John	$ 1,256.00	$ 1,254.00	$ 2,451.00	$ 4,961.00
5	Jean	1,846.00	1,726.00	2,105.00	5,677.00
6	Joe	1,601.00	1,575.00	2,569.00	5,745.00
7	Joan	1,954.00	1,864.00	2,248.00	6,066.00
8	Totals	$ 6,657.00	$ 6,419.00	$ 9,373.00	$ 22,449

Figure 22 ...then hold down Ctrl and select the second range.

To select multiple ranges

1. Use any selection technique to select the first cell or range of cells (**Figure 21**).
2. Hold down Ctrl and drag to select the second cell or range of cells (**Figure 22**).
3. Repeat step 2 until all desired ranges are selected.

✔ Tips

- Selecting multiple ranges can be tricky. It takes practice. Don't be frustrated if you can't do it on the first few tries!
- To add ranges that are not visible in the worksheet window, be sure to use the scroll bars to view them. Using the keyboard to move to other cells while selecting multiple ranges will remove the selections you've made so far or add undesired selections.
- Do not click in the worksheet window or use the movement keys while multiple ranges are selected unless you are finished working with them. Doing so will deselect all the cells.

To deselect cells

Click anywhere in the worksheet.

or

Press any of the keys in **Table 1**.

✔ Tip

- Remember, at least one cell must be selected at all times—that's the active cell.

Entering Values & Formulas

To enter a value or formula into a cell, you begin by making the cell active. As you type or click to enter information, the information appears in both the cell and in the formula bar just above the window's title bar. You complete the entry by pressing Enter or clicking the Enter button on the formula bar.

While you are entering information into a cell, the formula bar is *active*. You can tell that it's active because the Name Box on the far left end of the formula bar turns into a Functions list (when you enter a formula) and two additional buttons appear between it and the cell contents area (**Figure 23**).

There are two important things to remember when the formula bar is active:

- Anything you type or click on may be included in the active cell.
- Many Excel options and menu commands are unavailable (**Figures 24** and **25**).

You deactivate the formula bar by accepting or cancelling the current entry.

✔ Tips

- Pressing Enter to complete a formula entry accepts the entry and moves the cell pointer one cell down. Clicking the Enter button accepts the entry without moving the cell pointer.
- To cancel an entry before it has been completed, press Esc or click the Cancel button on the formula bar. This restores the cell to the way it was before you began.
- If you include formatting notation such as dollar signs, commas, and percent symbols when you enter numbers, you may apply formatting styles. I tell you about formatting the contents of cells in **Chapter 6**.

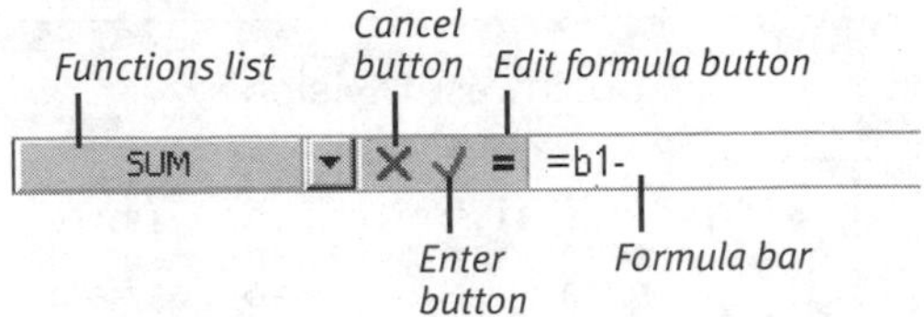

Figure 23 The individual components of an active formula bar.

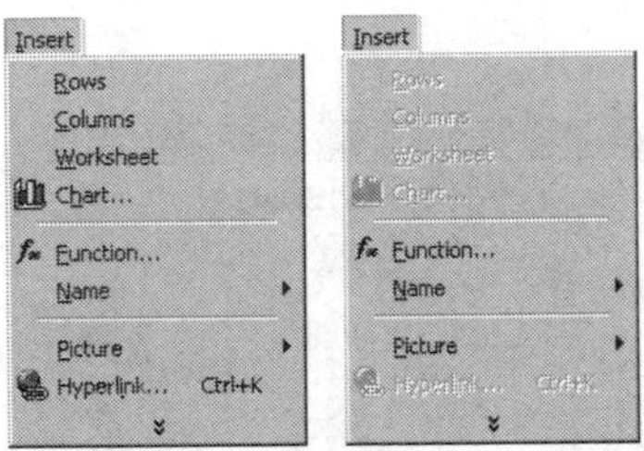

Figures 24 & 25 The Insert menu when the formula bar is inactive (left) and when the formula bar is active (right).

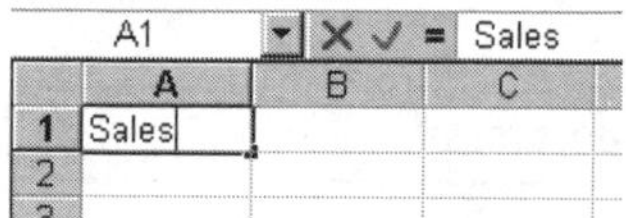

Figure 26 As data is entered into a cell, it appears in the cell and the formula bar.

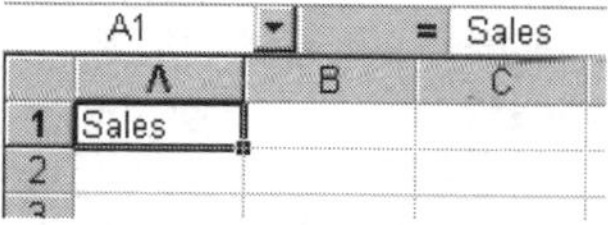

Figure 27 A completed entry. The insertion point and Cancel and Enter buttons are gone.

Values

As discussed at the beginning of this chapter, a value is any text, number, date, or time you enter into a cell. Values are constant—they don't change unless you change them.

To enter a value

1. Activate the cell in which you want to enter the value.
2. Type in the value. As you type, the information appears in two places: the active cell and the formula bar, which becomes active (**Figure 26**).
3. To complete and accept the entry (**Figure 27**), press Enter or click the Enter button ✓ on the formula bar.

✔ Tips

- Although you can often use the arrow keys or other movement keys in **Table 1** to complete an entry by moving to another cell, it's a bad habit because it won't always work.
- Excel aligns text against the left side of the cell and aligns numbers against the right side of the cell. I explain how to change alignment in **Chapter 6**.
- Don't worry if the data you put into a cell doesn't seem to fit. You can always change the column width or use the AutoSize Text feature to make it fit. I tell you how in **Chapter 6**.

Formula Basics

Excel makes calculations based on formulas you enter into cells. When you complete the entry of a formula, Excel displays the results of the formula rather than the formula you entered.

Here are some important things to keep in mind when writing formulas:

- If a formula uses cell references to refer to other cells and the contents of one or more of those cells changes, the result of the formula changes, too.
- All formulas begin with an equal (=) sign. This is how Excel knows that a cell entry is a formula and not a value.
- Formulas can contain any combination of values, references, operators (**Table 2**), and functions. I tell you about using operators in formulas in this chapter and about using functions in **Chapter 5**.
- Formulas are not case sensitive. This means that *=A1+B10* is the same as *=a1+b10*. Excel automatically converts characters in cell references and functions to uppercase.

When calculating the results of expressions with a variety of operators, Excel makes calculations in the following order:

1. Negation
2. Expressions in parentheses
3. Percentages
4. Exponentials
5. Multiplication or division
6. Addition or subtraction

Table 3 shows some examples of formulas and their results to illustrate this. As you can see, the inclusion of parentheses can really make a difference when you write a formula!

Table 2

Mathematical Operators

Operator	Use	Example
+	Addition	=A1+B10
-	Subtraction	=A1-B10
-	Negation	=-A1
*	Multiplication	=A1*B10
/	Division	=A1/B10
^	Exponential	=A1^3
%	Percentage	=20%

Table 3

How Excel Evaluates Expressions

Assumptions

A1=5
B10=7
C3=4

Formula	Evaluation	Result
=A1+B10*C3	=5+7*4	33
=C3*B10+A1	=4*7+5	33
=(A1+B10)*C3	=(5+7)*4	48
=A1+10%	=5+10%	5.1
=(A1+10)%	=(5+10)%	0.15
=A1^2-B10/C3	=5^2-7/4	23.25
=(A1^2-B10)/C3	=(5^2-7)/4	4.5
=A1^(2-B10)/C3	=5^(2-7)/4	0.00008

	A	B	
1	Sales	1000	
2	Cost	400	
3	Profit	600	=1000-400
4			
5	Commission	90	=600*15%

Figure 28 If any of the values in this example change, the formulas will have to be rewritten!

	A	B	
1	Sales	1000	
2	Cost	400	
3	Profit	600	=B1-B2
4			
5	Rate	15%	
6			
7	Commission	90	=B3*B5

Figure 29 But if the formulas reference cells containing the values, when the values change, the formulas will not need to be rewritten to show correct results.

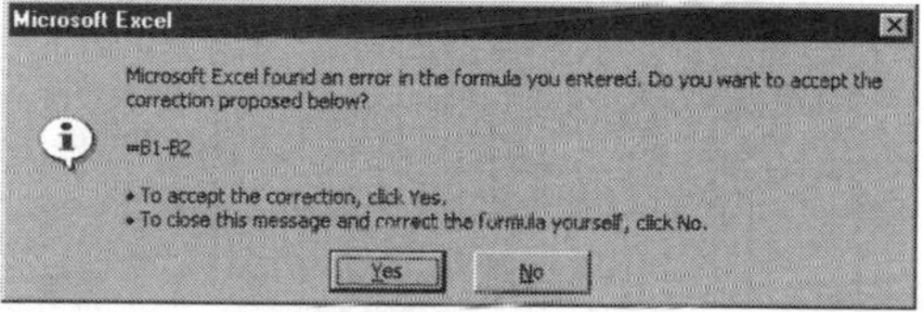

Figure 30 Excel tells you when you make an error in a formula. Sometimes it can fix it...

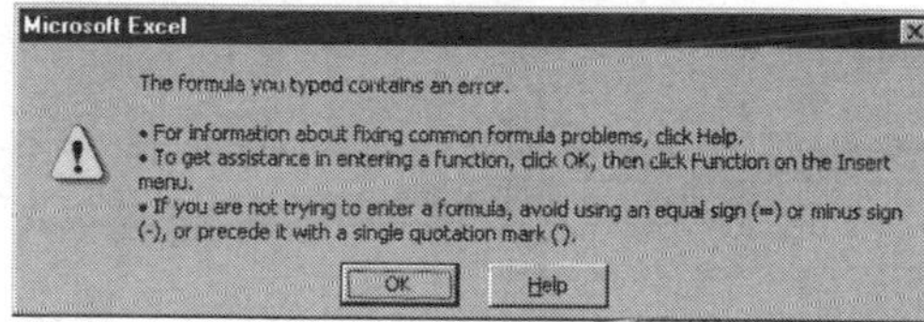

Figure 31 ...and sometimes it can't.

✔ Tips

- Do not use the arrow keys or other movement keys to complete an entry by moving to another cell. Doing so may add cells to the formula!
- Whenever possible, use references rather than values in formulas. This way, you won't have to rewrite formulas when values change. **Figures 28** and **29** illustrate this.
- A reference can be a cell reference, a range reference, or a cell or range name. I tell you about name references a little later in this chapter and in **Chapter 11**.
- To add a range of cells to a formula, type the first cell in the range followed by a colon (:) and then the last cell in the range. For example: *B1:B10* references the cells from *B1* straight down through *B10*.
- If you make a syntax error in a formula, Excel tells you (**Figures 30** and **31**). If the error is one of the common errors programmed into Excel's Formula AutoCorrect feature, Excel offers to correct the formula for you (**Figure 30**). Otherwise, you will have to troubleshoot the formula and correct it yourself.
- I tell you how to edit formulas in **Chapter 3** and how to include functions in formulas in **Chapter 5**.

To enter a formula by typing

1. Activate the cell in which you want to enter the formula.
2. Type in the formula. As you type, the formula appears in two places: the active cell and the formula bar, which becomes active (**Figure 32**).
3. To complete the entry (**Figure 33**), press Enter or click the Enter button ✓ on the formula bar.

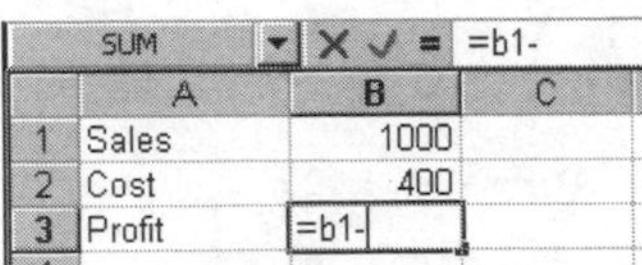

Figure 32 To enter a formula, simply type it into the cell.

Figure 33 A completed formula entry.

To enter a formula by clicking

1. Activate the cell in which you want to enter the formula.
2. Type an equal (=) sign to begin the formula (**Figure 34**).
3. To enter a constant value or operator, type it in (**Figure 36**).

   or

   To enter a cell reference, click on the cell you want to reference (**Figures 35** and **37**).
4. Repeat step 3 until the entire formula appears in the formula bar.
5. To complete the entry (**Figure 38**), press Enter or click the Enter button ✓ on the formula bar.

Figure 34 To enter a formula by clicking, type = to begin the formula,...

Figure 35 ...click a cell to enter its reference to the formula,...

Figure 36 ...type an operator,...

Figure 37 ...click a cell to enter its reference to the formula,...

Figure 38 ...and finally click the Enter button to complete the formula.

✔ Tips

- If you click a cell reference without typing an operator, Excel assumes you want to add that reference to the formula.
- Be careful where you click when writing a formula! Each click adds a reference to the formula. If you add an incorrect reference, press Backspace until it has been deleted or click the Cancel button ✕ to start the entry from scratch. I tell you more about editing a cell's contents in **Chapter 3**.
- You can add a range of cells to a formula by dragging over the cells.

EDITING WORKSHEETS

Editing Worksheets

Excel offers a number of features and techniques that you can use to modify your worksheets.

- Use standard editing techniques and the Clear command to change or clear the contents of cells.
- Use Insert and Edit menu commands to insert or delete cells, columns, and rows.
- Use Edit menu commands, the fill handle, and drag-and-drop editing to copy cells from one location to another, including cells containing formulas.
- Use the fill handle and Fill submenu commands to copy cell contents to multiple cells or create a series.
- Modify formulas so they are properly updated by Excel when copied.
- Use Edit menu commands and drag-and-drop editing to move cells from one location to another.
- Undo, redo, and repeat multiple actions.

This chapter covers all of these techniques.

Editing Cell Contents

You can use standard editing techniques to edit the contents of cells either as you enter values or formulas or after you have completed an entry. You can also clear a cell's contents, leaving the cell empty.

To edit as you enter

1. If necessary, click to position the blinking insertion point cursor in the cell (**Figure 1**) or formula bar (**Figure 2**).
2. Press Backspace to delete the character to the left of the insertion point.

   or

   Type the characters that you want to insert at the insertion point.

To edit a completed entry

1. Double-click the cell containing the incorrect entry to activate it for editing.
2. If the cell contains a value, follow the instructions in the previous section to insert or delete characters as desired.

   or

   If the cell contains a formula, color-coded *Range Finder* frames appear, to graphically identify cell references (**Figures 3** and **5**). You have three options for editing cell references:

   ▲ Edit the reference as discussed in the previous section.

   ▲ Drag a frame border to move the frame over another cell (**Figure 4**).

   ▲ Drag a frame handle to expand or contract it so the frame includes more (**Figure 6**) or fewer cells.

Figure 1 To edit a cell's contents while entering information, click to reposition the insertion point in the cell...

Figure 2 ...or in the formula bar and make changes as desired.

	A	B
1	Sales	1000
2	Cost	400
3	Profit	=A1-B2

Figure 3 The Range Finder frames clearly indicate the problem with this formula.

	A	B
1	Sales	1000
2	Cost	400
3	Profit	=B1-B2

Figure 4 You can drag a Range Finder frame to correct the cell reference.

	A	B
1		Jan
2	John	1254
3	Jean	1865
4	Joe	1614
5	Joan	1987
6	Totals	=SUM(B2:B4)

Figure 5 In this example, the Range Finder indicates that the range of cells in the formula excludes a cell.

	A	B
1		Jan
2	John	1254
3	Jean	1865
4	Joe	1614
5	Joan	1987
6	Totals	=SUM(B2:B5)

Figure 6 You can drag a Range Finder frame handle to expand the range and correct the reference in the formula.

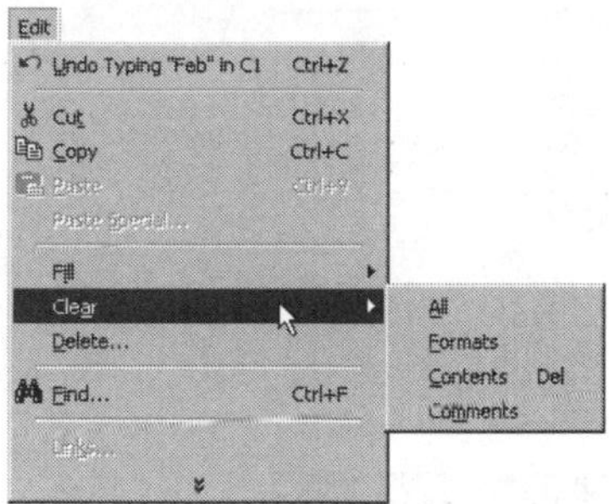

Figure 7 The Edit menu's Clear submenu offers four commands for clearing selected cell(s).

To clear cell contents

1. Select the cell(s) you want to clear.
2. Choose Edit > Clear > Contents (**Figure 7**) or press Delete.

✔ Tips

- Another way to clear the contents of just one cell is to activate the cell, press Backspace, and then press Enter.
- Do not press Spacebar to clear a cell's contents! Doing so inserts a space character into the cell. Although the contents seem to disappear, they are just replaced by an invisible character.
- Clearing a cell is very different from deleting a cell. When you clear a cell, the cell remains in the worksheet—only its contents are removed. When you delete a cell, the entire cell is removed from the worksheet and other cells shift to fill the gap. I tell you about inserting and deleting cells next.
- The Contents command clears only the values or formulas entered into a cell. The other Clear submenu commands (**Figure 7**) work as follows:
  - **All** clears everything, including formatting and comments.
  - **Formats** clears only cell formatting.
  - **Comments** clears only cell comments.

  I tell you about formatting cells and adding cell comments in **Chapter 6**.

Inserting & Deleting Cells

Excel offers an Insert command and a Delete command to insert and delete columns, rows, or cells.

- When you use the Insert command, Excel shifts cells down or to the right to make room for the new cells.
- When you use the Delete command, Excel shifts cells up or to the left to fill the gap left by the missing cells.

Figures 8, **11**, and **14** show examples of how inserting a column or deleting a row affects the addresses or references of the cells in a worksheet. Fortunately, Excel is smart enough to know how to adjust cell references in formulas so that the formulas you write remain correct.

To insert a column or row

1. Select a column (**Figure 9**) or row.
2. Choose Insert > Columns, or Insert > Rows, or Insert > Cells (**Figure 10**).

   The column (**Figure 11**) or row is inserted.

✔ Tips

- To insert multiple columns or rows, in step 1, select the number of columns or rows you want to insert. For example, if you want to insert three columns before column *B*, select columns *B*, *C*, and *D*.
- If a complete column or row is not selected when you choose the Cells command in step 2, the Insert dialog box appears (**Figure 17**). Select the appropriate option (Entire row or Entire column) for what you want to insert, then click OK. I tell you about inserting cells a little later in this chapter.

	A	B	C	D
1		Jan	Feb	Mar
2	John	1254	1256	2435
3	Jean	1865	1736	1905
4	Joe	1614	1284	2509
5	Joan	1987	1908	2890

Figure 8 A simple worksheet.

	A	B	C	D
1		Jan	Feb	Mar
2	John	1254	1256	2435
3	Jean	1865	1736	1905
4	Joe	1614	1284	2509
5	Joan	1987	1908	2890

Figure 9 Selecting a column.

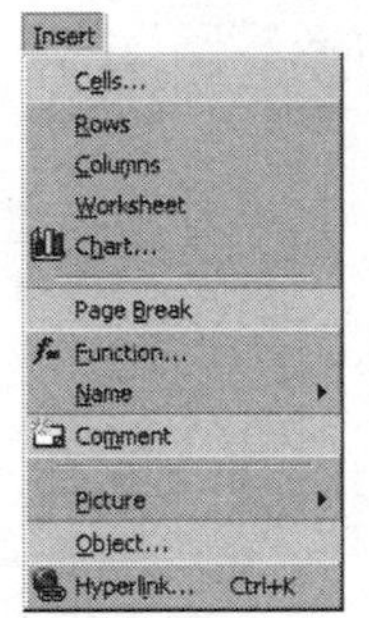

Figure 10 The Insert menu.

	A	B	C	D	E
1			Jan	Feb	Mar
2	John		1254	1256	2435
3	Jean		1865	1736	1905
4	Joe		1614	1284	2509
5	Joan		1987	1908	2890

Figure 11 An inserted column.

	A	B	C	D
1		Jan	Feb	Mar
2	John	1254	1256	2435
3	Jean	1865	1736	1905
4	Joe	1614	1284	2509
5	Joan	1987	1908	2890

Figure 12 Selecting a row.

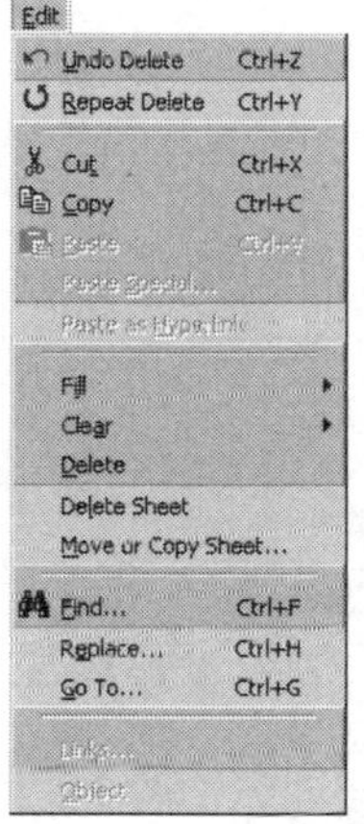

Figure 13 The Edit menu.

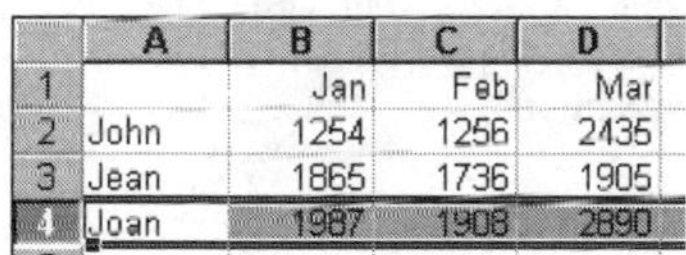

	A	B	C	D
1		Jan	Feb	Mar
2	John	1254	1256	2435
3	Jean	1865	1736	1905
4	Joan	1987	1908	2890

Figure 14 The row selected in **Figure 12** is deleted.

	A	B
1	Sales	1000
2	Cost	400
3	Profit	600
4		
5	Commissions	#REF!

Figure 15 In this example, I deleted a row containing a value referenced in the formula in B5. Because Excel can't find one of the references it needs, it displays a #REF! error.

To delete a column or row

1. Select a column or row (**Figure 12**).
2. Choose Edit > Delete (**Figure 13**).

   The column or row (**Figure 14**)—along with all of its contents—disappears.

✔ Tips

- To delete more than one column or row at a time, in step 1, select all of the columns or rows you want to delete.
- If a complete column or row is not selected when you choose the Delete command in step 2, the Delete dialog box appears (**Figure 19**). Select the appropriate option (Entire row or Entire column) for what you want to delete, then click OK.
- If you delete a column or row that contains referenced cells, the formulas that reference the cells may display a #REF! error message (**Figure 15**). This means that Excel can't find a referenced cell. If this happens, you'll have to rewrite any formulas in cells displaying the error.

To insert cells

1. Select a cell or range of cells (**Figure 16**).
2. Choose Insert > Cells (**Figure 10**).
3. In the Insert dialog box that appears (**Figure 17**), select the appropriate option to tell Excel how to shift the selected cells to make room for new cells—Shift cells right or Shift cells down.
4. Click OK.

   The cell(s) are inserted (**Figure 18**).

✔ Tip

- Excel always inserts the number of cells that is selected when you use the Cells command (**Figures 16** and **18**).

To delete cells

1. Select a cell or range of cells to delete (**Figure 16**).
2. Choose Edit > Delete (**Figure 13**).
3. In the Delete dialog box that appears (**Figure 19**), select the appropriate option to tell Excel how to shift the other cells when the selected cells are deleted—Shift cells left or Shift cells up.
4. Click OK.

   The cell(s) are deleted (**Figure 20**).

✔ Tip

- If you delete a cell that contains referenced cells, the formulas that reference the cells may display a #REF! error message (**Figure 15**). If this happens, you'll have to rewrite any formulas in cells displaying the error.

	A	B	C	D
1		Jan	Feb	Mar
2	John	1254	1256	2435
3	Jean	1865	1736	1905
4	Joe	1614	1284	2509
5	Joan	1987	1908	2890

Figure 16 Select a range of cells.

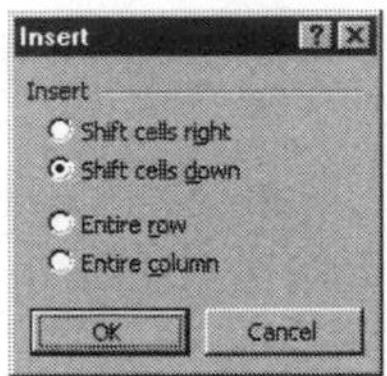

Figure 17 The Insert dialog box.

	A	B	C	D
1		Jan	Feb	Mar
2	John	1254	1256	2435
3	Jean	1865	1736	1905
4	Joe			
5	Joan	1614	1284	2509
6		1987	1908	2890

Figure 18 Here's what happens when you insert cells as selected in **Figure 16**, using the Shift cells down option.

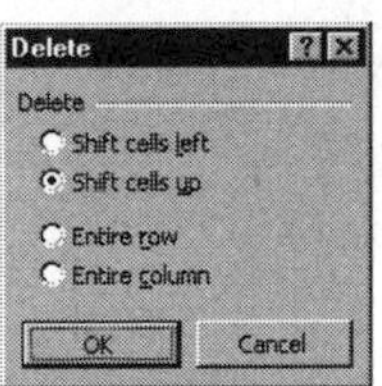

Figure 19 The Delete dialog box.

	A	B	C	D
1		Jan	Feb	Mar
2	John	1254	1256	2435
3	Jean	1865	1736	1905
4	Joe	1987	1908	2890
5	Joan			

Figure 20 Here's what happens when you delete the cells selected in **Figure 16**, using the Shift cells up option.

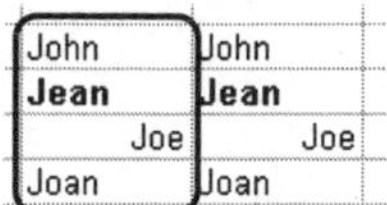

Figure 21 The Copy and Paste commands can make an exact copy.

Figure 22 Using the fill handle on a cell containing the word *Monday* generates a list of the days of the week.

	A	B	C	D
1		Jan	Feb	Mar
2	John	1254	1256	2435
3	Jean	1865	1736	1905
4	Joe	1614	1284	2509
5	Joan	1987	1900	2890
6	Totals	6720	6184	9739
7				

Figure 23 Copying a formula that totals a column automatically writes correctly referenced formulas to total similar columns.

Copying Cells

Excel offers several ways to copy the contents of one cell to another: the Copy and Paste commands, the fill handle, and the Fill command.

How Excel copies depends not only on the method used, but on the contents of the cell(s) being copied.

- When you use the Copy and Paste commands to copy a cell containing a value, Excel makes an exact copy of the cell, including any formatting (**Figure 21**). I tell you about formatting cells in **Chapter 6**.
- When you use the fill handle or Fill command to copy a cell containing a value, Excel either makes an exact copy of the cell, including any formatting, or creates a series based on the original cell's contents (**Figure 22**).
- When you copy a cell containing a formula, Excel copies the formula, changing any relative references in the formula so they're relative to the destination cell(s) (**Figure 23**).

✔ Tip

- Copy cells that contain formulas whenever possible to save time and ensure consistency.

Copy & Paste

The Copy and Paste commands in Excel work very much the same way they do in other applications. Begin by selecting the source cells and using the Copy command to copy them. Then select the destination cells and use the Paste command to paste the copied selection in.

To copy with Copy and Paste

1. Select the cell(s) you want to copy (**Figure 24**).
2. Choose Edit > Copy (**Figure 13**), press Ctrl C, or click the Copy button on the Standard toolbar.

   An animated marquee appears around the selection (**Figure 25**).
3. Select the cell(s) into which you want to paste the selection (**Figure 26**). If more than one cell was copied, you can select either the first cell of the destination range or the entire range.
4. Choose Edit > Paste (**Figure 27**), press Ctrl V or Enter, or click the Paste button on the Standard toolbar.

   The originally selected cells are copied to the new location (**Figure 28**).

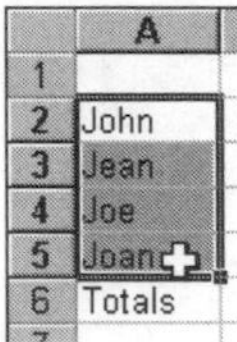

Figure 24
Begin by selecting the cell(s) that you want to copy.

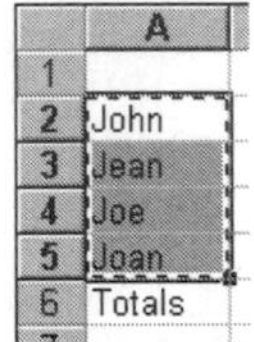

Figure 25
A marquee appears around the selection when it has been copied.

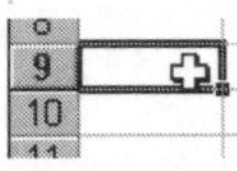

Figure 26
Select the destination cell(s).

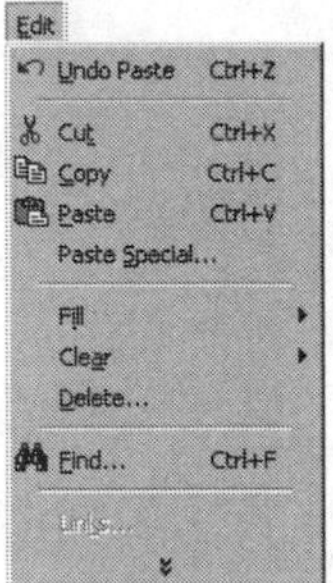

Figure 27
The Edit menu with the Paste command available. The Paste command is only available when something has been cut or copied.

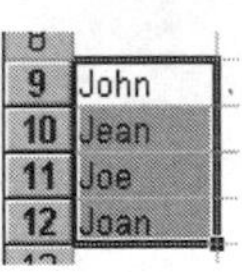

Figure 28
The contents of the copied cells appear in the destination cells.

✔ Tips

- If the destination cell(s) contain information, Excel may overwrite them without warning you.
- If you choose the Paste command, press Ctrl V, or click the Paste button, the marquee remains around the copied range, indicating that it may be pasted elsewhere. The marquee disappears automatically as you work, but if you want to remove it manually, press Esc.
- The Edit menu's Paste Special command (**Figure 27**) offers additional options over the regular Paste command. For example, you can use it to paste only the formatting of a copied selection, convert formulas in the selection into values, or add the contents of the source cells to the destination cells.

Figure 29 The Microsoft Office Clipboard with two items copied.

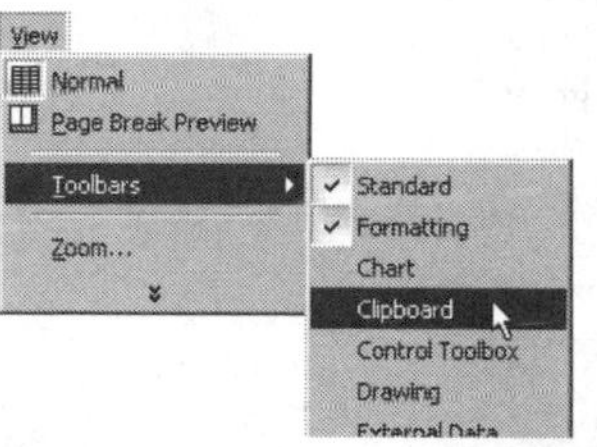

Figure 30 To open the Clipboard toolbar, choose Clipboard from the Toolbars submenu under the View menu.

	A	B	C	D	E	F
1		Jan	Feb	Mar		
2	John	1254	1256	2435		
3	Jean	1865	1736			
4	Joe	1614	1284			
5	Joan	1987	1908			
6	Totals	6720	6184			
7						
8						

Clipboard (1 of 12)
Paste All

Figure 31 When you click the Copy button on the Clipboard toolbar, an icon for the copied selection appears on the toolbar.

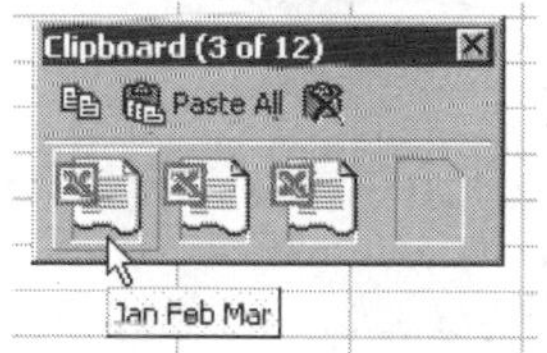

Figure 32 You can point to a Clipboard toolbar item to see its contents.

✔ Tips

- To learn what's in a collected item, point to its icon. The beginning of its contents appears as a screen tip below it (**Figure 32**).
- If you collect a cell containing a formula, the result of the formula—not the formula itself—is collected.
- To clear all collected items from the Microsoft Office Clipboard, click the Clear Clipboard button on the Clipboard toolbar.

Collect & Paste

Collect and Paste enables you to copy up to 12 selections at a time and paste any combination of them—or all of them—into a document. This feature utilizes the Clipboard toolbar (**Figure 29**), which gives you access to the Microsoft Office Clipboard.

✔ Tip

- The Microsoft Office Clipboard is shared by all Office 2000 programs. This means you can use Collect and Paste to copy selections in multiple documents created with any combination of Office programs and paste them in any other Office document.

To open the Clipboard toolbar

Choose View > Toolbars > Clipboard (**Figure 30**).

To use Collect and Paste

1. Select a cell or range of cells you want to collect.
2. Click the Copy button on the Clipboard toolbar. An icon for the current application appears in one of the wells at the bottom of the toolbar (**Figure 31**).
3. Repeat steps 1 and 2 for each cell or range of cells you want to collect. You can collect up to 12 items.
4. Position the insertion point where you want to paste one or more collected items.
5. To paste in one item, click its icon in the Clipboard toolbar. You can repeat this step to paste multiple items in any order.

   or

   To paste in all items in the order in which they were collected, click the Paste All button Paste All on the Clipboard toolbar.
6. Repeat steps 4 and 5 to paste in items as desired.

The Fill Handle

The *fill handle* is a small black or colored box in the lower-right corner of the cell pointer (**Figure 33**) or selection (**Figure 34**). You can use the fill handle to copy the contents of one or more cells to adjacent cells.

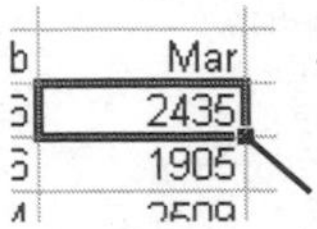

Figure 33 The fill handle on a single cell.

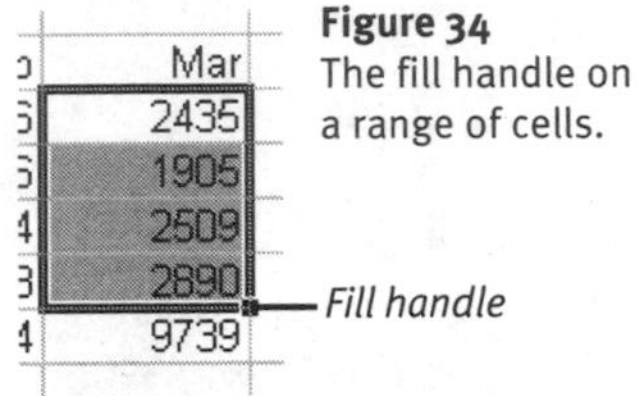

Figure 34 The fill handle on a range of cells.

To copy with the fill handle

1. Select the cell(s) containing the information you want to copy (**Figure 34**).
2. Position the mouse pointer on the fill handle. The mouse pointer turns into a crosshairs (**Figure 35**).
3. Press the mouse button down and drag to the adjacent cells. A gray border surrounds the destination cells (**Figure 36**).
4. When all the destination cells are surrounded by the gray border, release the mouse button. The cells are filled (**Figure 37**).

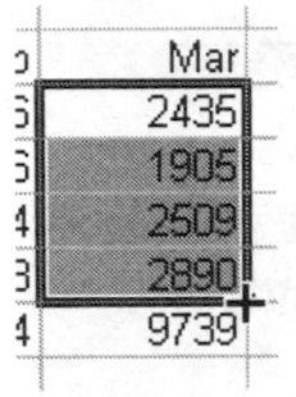

Figure 35 When the mouse pointer is over a fill handle, it turns into a thick crosshairs pointer.

✔ Tips

- You can use the fill handle to copy any number of cells. The destination cells, however, must be adjacent to the original cells.
- When using the fill handle, you can only copy in one direction (up, down, left, or right) at a time.
- If the destination cells contain information, Excel will overwrite them without warning you.

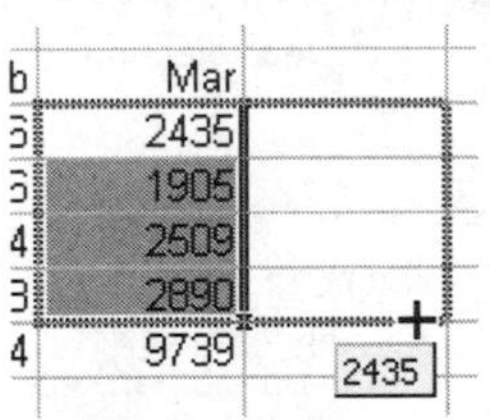

Figure 36 As you drag the fill handle, a gray border indicates the destination cell(s).

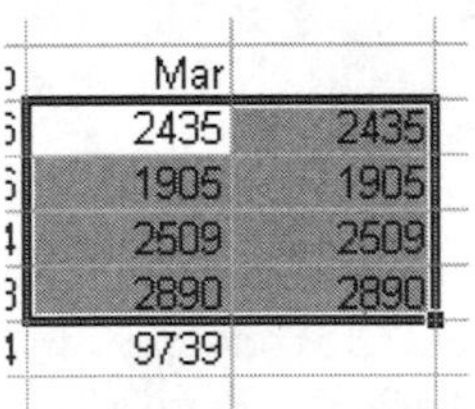

Figure 37 The destination cells fill with the contents of the source cells.

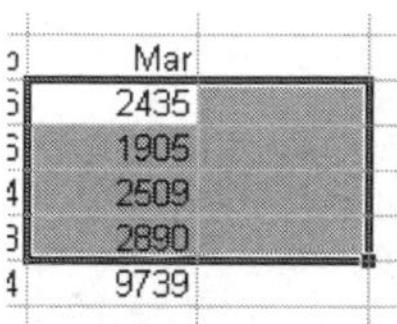

Figure 38 To use the Fill command, begin by selecting the source and destination cells.

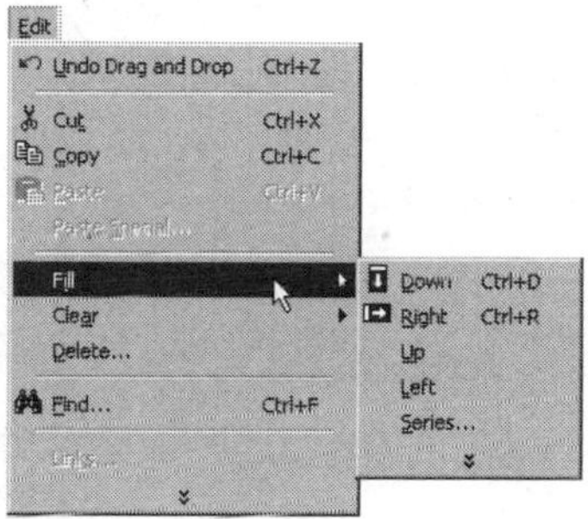

Figure 39 The Fill submenu under the Edit menu.

The Fill Command

The Fill command works a lot like the fill handle in that it copies information to adjacent cells. But rather than dragging to copy, you select the source and destination cells at the same time (**Figure 38**) and then use the Fill command to complete the copy. The Fill submenu (**Figure 39**) offers several options for copying to adjacent selected cells:

- **Down** copies the contents of the top cell(s) in the selection to the selected cells beneath it.
- **Right** copies the contents of the left cell(s) in the selection to the selected cells to the right of it.
- **Up** copies the contents of the bottom cell(s) in the selection to the selected cells above it.
- **Left** copies the contents of the right cell(s) in the selection to the selected cells to the left of it.

To copy with the Fill command

1. Select the cell(s) you want to copy along with the adjacent destination cell(s) (**Figure 38**).
2. Choose the appropriate command from the Fill submenu under the Edit menu (**Figure 39**): Down, Right, Up, Left.

   The cells are filled as specified (**Figure 37**).

✔ Tips

- You must select both the source and destination cells when using the Fill command. If you select just the destination cells, Excel won't copy the correct cells.
- I tell you about the Fill submenu's Series command on the next page.

Series & AutoFill

A *series* is a sequence of cells that form a logical progression. Excel's AutoFill feature can generate a series of numbers, months, days, dates, and quarters.

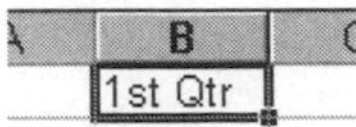

Figure 40 To create an AutoFill series, start by entering the first value in a cell.

To create a series with the fill handle

1. Enter the first item of the series in a cell (**Figure 40**). Be sure to complete the entry by pressing Enter.
2. Position your mouse pointer on the fill handle and drag. All the cells that will be part of the series are surrounded by a gray border and a yellow box indicates the value that will be in the last cell in the range (**Figure 41**).
3. Release the mouse button to complete the series (**Figure 42**).

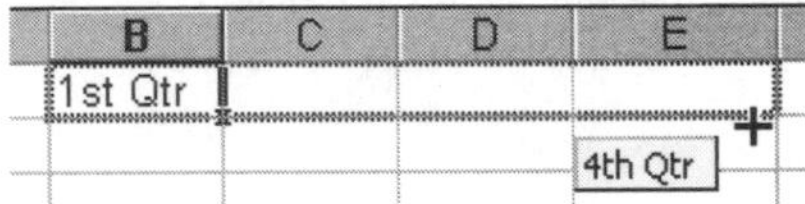

Figure 41 Drag the fill handle to include all cells that will be part of the series.

Figure 42 Excel creates the series automatically.

To create a series with the Series command

1. Enter the first item in the series in a cell (**Figure 40**).
2. Select all cells that will be part of the series, including the first cell (**Figure 43**).
3. Choose Edit > Fill > Series (**Figure 39**).
4. In the Series dialog box that appears (**Figure 44**), select the AutoFill option.
5. Click OK to complete the series (**Figure 42**).

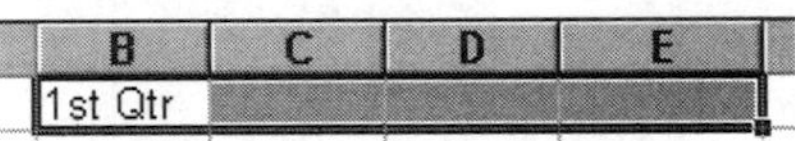

Figure 43 To use the Fill command, select the source and destination cells.

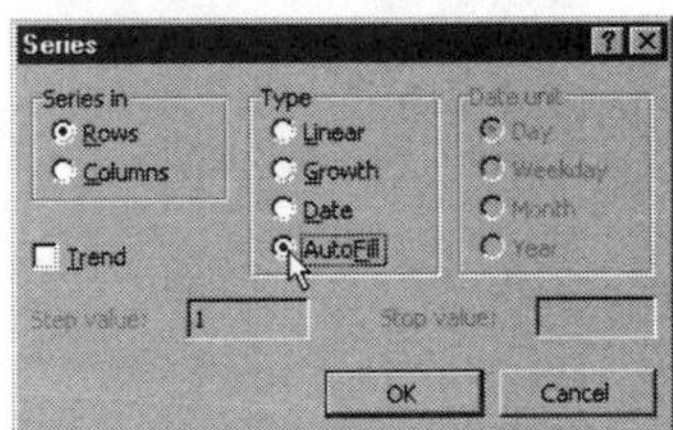

Figure 44 Select the AutoFill option in the Series dialog box.

✔ Tip

- To generate a series that skips values, enter the first two values of the series in adjoining cells, then use the fill handle or Fill command to create the series, including both cells as part of the source (**Figures 45** and **46**).

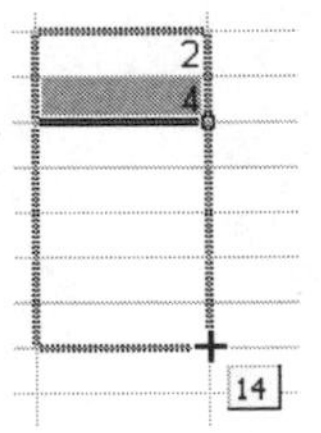

Figures 45 & 46 Enter the first two values in the series, then select them and drag the fill handle (left) to complete the series (right).

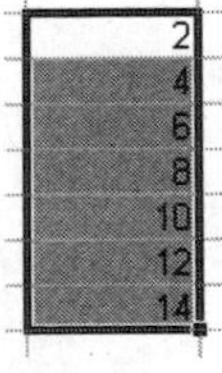

	A	B	C	D
1	Item	Price	Cost	Markup
2	Product A	24.95	15.36	=(B2-C2)/C2
3	Product B	16.95	12.48	
4	Product C	18.95	9.58	
5	Product D	59.95	30.48	

Figure 47 Here's a formula to calculate markup percentage. If the company has 763 products, would you want to write the same basic formula 762 more times? Of course not!

	A	B	C	D
1	Item	Price	Cost	Markup
2	Product A	24.95	15.36	62%
3	Product B	16.95	12.48	36%
4	Product C	18.95	9.58	98%
5	Product D	59.95	30.48	97%

=(B2-C2)/C2
=(B3-C3)/C3
=(B4-C4)/C4
=(B5-C5)/C5

Figure 48 Copying formulas can save time. If the original formula is properly written, the results of the copied formula should also be correct.

	A	B	C	D	E	F
1			Jan	Feb	Mar	
2		Sales	1000	1250	1485	
3		Cost	400	395	412	
4		Profit	600	855	1073	
5						
6	Owner	Percent	Jan	Feb	Mar	Totals
7	John	50%	300	427.5	536.5	0
8	Jean	20%	120	171	214.6	
9	Joe	15%	90	128.25	160.95	
10	Joan	15%	90	128.25	160.95	
11	Totals	100%	600	855	1073	

=SUM(C7:C10)   =SUM(F3:F6)

Figure 49 In this illustration, the formula in cell *C11* was copied to cell *F7*. This doesn't work because the two cells don't add up similar ranges. The formula in cell *F7* would have to be rewritten from scratch. It could then be copied to *F8* through *F10*. (I tell you about the SUM function in **Chapter 5**.)

Copying Formulas

You copy a cell containing a formula the same way you copy any other cell in Excel: with the Copy and Paste commands, with the fill handle, or with the Fill command. These methods are discussed earlier in this chapter.

Generally speaking, Excel does not make an exact copy of a formula. Instead, it copies the formula based on the kinds of references used within it. If relative references are used, Excel changes them based on the location of the destination cell in relation to the source cell. You can see an example of this in **Figures 47** and **48**.

✔ Tips

- It is usually much quicker to copy formulas rather than to write each and every formula from scratch.
- Not all formulas can be copied with accurate results. For example, you can't copy a formula that sums up a column of numbers to a cell that should represent a sum of cells in a row (**Figure 49**).
- I explain the various types of cell references—relative, absolute, and mixed—beginning on the next page.

Relative vs. Absolute Cell References

There are two primary types of cell references:

- A *relative cell reference* is the address of a cell relative to the cell the reference is in. For example, a reference to cell *B1* in cell *B3*, tells Excel to look at the cell two cells above *B3*. Most of the references you use in Excel are relative references.
- An *absolute cell reference* is the exact location of a cell. To indicate an absolute reference, enter a dollar sign ($) in front of the column letter(s) and row number of the reference. An absolute reference to cell *B1*, for example, would be written *$B$1*.

As **Figures 50** and **51** illustrate, relative cell references change when you copy them to other cells. Although in many cases, you might want the references to change, sometimes you don't. That's when you use absolute references (**Figures 52** and **53**).

✔ Tips

- Here's a trick for remembering the meaning of the notation for absolute cell references: in your mind, replace the dollar sign with the word *always*. Then you'll read *$B$1* as *always B always 1—always B1*!
- If you're having trouble understanding how these two kinds of references work and differ, don't worry. This is one of the most difficult spreadsheet concepts that you'll encounter. Try creating a worksheet like the one illustrated on this page and working your way through the figures one at a time. Pay close attention to how Excel copies the formulas you write!

	A	B	C
1	Sales	1000	
2	Cost	400	
3	Profit	600	
4			
5	**Owner**	**Percent**	**Share**
6	John	50%	=B3*B6
7	Jean	20%	
8	Joe	15%	
9	Joan	15%	

Figure 50 This formula correctly calculates a partner's share of profit.

	A	B	C	
1	Sales	1000		
2	Cost	400		
3	Profit	600		
4				
5	**Owner**	**Percent**	**Share**	
6	John	50%	300	=B3*B6
7	Jean	20%	0	=B4*B7
8	Joe	15%	#VALUE!	=B5*B8
9	Joan	15%	0.075	=B6*B9

Figure 51 But when the formula is copied for the other partners, the relative references to the cell *B3* is changed, causing incorrect results and an error message!

	A	B	C
1	Sales	1000	
2	Cost	400	
3	Profit	600	
4			
5	**Owner**	**Percent**	**Share**
6	John	50%	=$B$3*B6
7	Jean	20%	
8	Joe	15%	
9	Joan	15%	

Figure 52 Rewrite the original formula so it includes an absolute reference to cell *B3*, which all the formulas must reference.

	A	B	C	
1	Sales	1000		
2	Cost	400		
3	Profit	600		
4				
5	**Owner**	**Percent**	**Share**	
6	John	50%	300	=$B$3*B6
7	Jean	20%	120	=$B$3*B7
8	Joe	15%	90	=$B$3*B8
9	Joan	15%	90	=$B$3*B9

Figure 53 When the formula is copied for the other partners, only the relative reference (to the percentages) changes. The results are correct.

=$B$3

Figure 54 To create an absolute reference, simply insert dollar signs in the cell reference.

C7 = =$B7*C$4

	A	B	C	D	E
1			**Jan**	**Feb**	**Mar**
2		Sales	1000	1250	1485
3		Cost	400	395	412
4		Profit	600	855	1073
5					
6	**Owner**	**Percent**	**Jan**	**Feb**	**Mar**
7	John	50%	300		
8	Jean	20%			
9	Joe	15%			
10	Joan	15%			

Figure 55 The formula in cell *C7* includes two different kinds of mixed references. It can be copied to cells *C8* through *C10* and *C7* through *E10* for correct results in all cells. Try it for yourself and see!

To include an absolute cell reference in a formula

1. Enter the formula by typing or clicking as discussed in **Chapter 2**.
2. Insert a dollar sign before the column and row references for the cell reference you want to make absolute (**Figure 54**).
3. Complete the entry by pressing Enter.

✔ Tips

- You can edit an existing formula to include absolute references by inserting dollar signs where needed in a selected reference. I tell you how to edit cell contents earlier in this chapter.
- Do not use a dollar sign in a formula to indicate currency formatting. I explain how to apply formatting to cell contents, including currency format, in **Chapter 6**.

About Mixed References

Once you've mastered the concept of relative vs. absolute cell references, consider the third type of reference: a *mixed cell reference*.

In a mixed cell reference, either the column or row reference is absolute while the other reference remains relative. Thus, you can use cell references like *A$1* or *$A1*. Use this when a column reference must remain constant but a row reference changes or vice versa. **Figure 55** shows a good example.

Moving Cells

Excel offers two ways to move the contents of one cell to another: the Cut and Paste commands and dragging the border of a selection. Either way, Excel moves the contents of the cell.

✔ Tip

- When you move a cell, Excel searches the worksheet for any cells that contain references to it and changes the references to reflect the cell's new location (**Figures 56** and **57**).

To move with Cut & Paste

1. Select the cell(s) you want to move (**Figure 58**).
2. Choose Edit > Cut (**Figure 13**), press Ctrl X, or click the Cut button on the Standard toolbar.

   An animated marquee appears around the selection (**Figure 59**).
3. Select the cell(s) into which you want to paste the selection. If more than one cell was cut, you can select either the first cell of the destination range (**Figure 60**) or the entire range.
4. Choose Edit > Paste (**Figure 27**), press Ctrl V or Enter, or click the Paste button on the Standard toolbar.

   The cell contents are moved to the new location (**Figure 61**).

✔ Tip

- Consult the tips at the bottom of **page 40** for Paste command warnings and tips.

C6 = =$B$3*B6

	A	B	C
1	Sales	1000	
2	Cost	400	
3	Profit	600	
4			
5	Owner	Percent	Share
6	John	50%	300
7	Jean	20%	120
8	Joe	15%	90
9	Joan	15%	90

Figure 56 Note the formula in cell *C6*.

C6 = =$C$3*B6

	A	B	C
1		Sales	1000
2		Cost	400
3		Profit	600
4			
5	Owner	Percent	Share
6	John	50%	300
7	Jean	20%	120
8	Joe	15%	90
9	Joan	15%	90

Figure 57 See how it changes when one of the cells it references is moved?

	A
1	
2	John
3	Jean
4	Joe
5	Joan
6	Totals

Figure 58 Select the cell(s) you want to move.

	A
1	
2	John
3	Jean
4	Joe
5	Joan
6	Totals

Figure 59 When you use the Cut command, a marquee appears around the selection, but the selected cells do not disappear.

	A
1	
2	John
3	Jean
4	Joe
5	Joan
6	Totals
7	
8	
9	
10	

Figure 60 Select the destination cell(s).

	A
1	
2	
3	
4	
5	
6	Totals
7	
8	
9	John
10	Jean
11	Joe
12	Joan

Figure 61 When you use the Paste command, the selection moves.

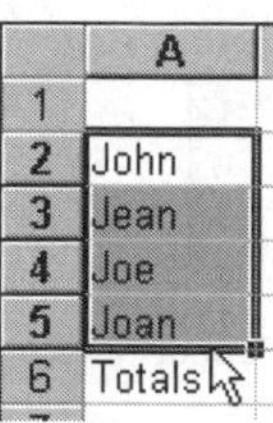

Figure 62 When you position the mouse pointer on the border of a selection, it turns into an arrow.

	A	B
1		Jan
2	John	1254
3	Jean	1865
4	Joe	1614
5	Joan	1987
6	Totals	6720
7		
8		
9		
10		
11		
12		A9:A12
13		

Figure 63 As you drag, a gray border moves with the mouse pointer.

To move with drag & drop

1. Select the cell(s) you want to move (**Figure 60**).
2. Position the mouse pointer on the border of the selection. It turns into an arrow pointing up and to the left (**Figure 62**).
3. Press the mouse button down and drag toward the new location. As you move the mouse, a gray border the same shape as the selection moves along with it and a yellow box indicates the range where the cells will move (**Figure 63**).
4. Release the mouse button. The selection moves to its new location (**Figure 61**).

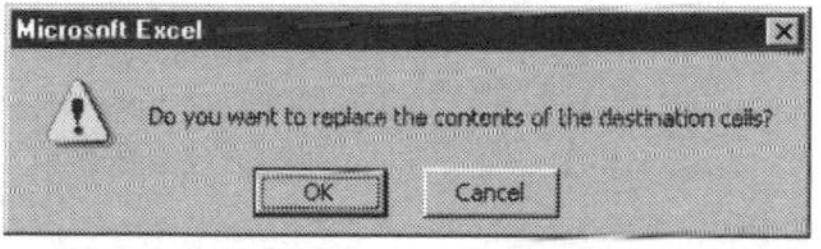

Figure 64 Excel warns you when you will overwrite cells with a selection you drag.

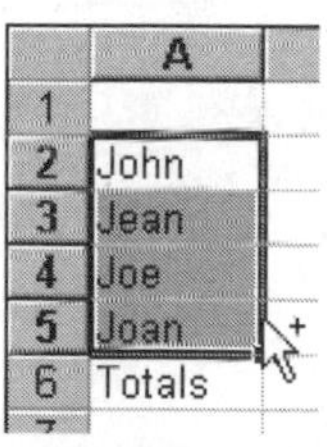

Figure 65
Hold down Ctrl to copy a selection by dragging it. A plus sign appears beside the mouse pointer.

	A	B	C
1		Jan	Feb
2	John	1254	1256
3	Jean	1865	1736
4	Joe	1614	1284
5	Joan	1987	C2:C5
6	Totals	6720	6184

Figure 66
Hold down Shift to insert a selection between other cells. A bar indicates where the cells will be inserted.

	A	B
1		Jan
2	1254	John
3	1865	Jean
4	1614	Joe
5	1987	Joan
6	Totals	6720

Figure 67
This makes it possible to rearrange the cells in a worksheet.

✓ Tips

- If you try to drag a selection to cells already containing information, Excel warns you (**Figure 64**). If you click OK to complete the move, the destination cells will be overwritten with the contents of the cells you are moving.
- To copy using drag and drop, hold down Ctrl as you press the mouse button down. The mouse pointer turns into an arrow with a tiny plus sign (+) beside it (**Figure 65**). When you release the mouse button, the selection is copied.
- To insert cells using drag and drop, hold down Shift as you press the mouse button down. As you drag, a gray bar moves along with the mouse pointer and a yellow box indicates where the cells will be inserted (**Figure 66**). When you release the mouse button, the cells are inserted (**Figure 67**).

Undoing, Redoing, & Repeating Actions

Excel's Edit menu offers a trio of commands that enable you to undo, redo, or repeat the last thing you did.

- **Undo** (**Figures 68** and **69**) reverses your last action. Excel supports multiple levels of undo, enabling you to reverse more than just the very last action.
- **Redo** (**Figure 68**) reverses the Undo command. This command is only available if the last thing you did was use the Undo command.
- **Repeat** (**Figure 69**) performs your last action again. This command is only available when you performed any action other than use the Undo or Redo command.

✔ Tips

- The exact wording of these commands on the Edit menu (**Figures 68** and **69**) varies depending on the last action performed. The Undo command is always the first command under the Edit menu; the Redo or Repeat command (whichever appears on the menu) is always the second command under the Edit menu.
- The Redo and Repeat commands are never both available at the same time.
- Think of the Undo command as the Oops command—anytime you say "Oops," you'll probably want to use it.

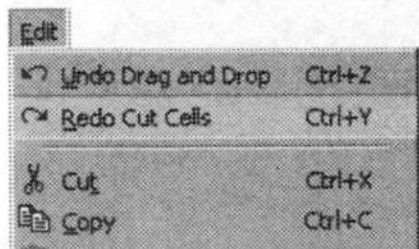

Figures 68 & 69 The Undo, Redo, and Repeat commands on the Edit menu.

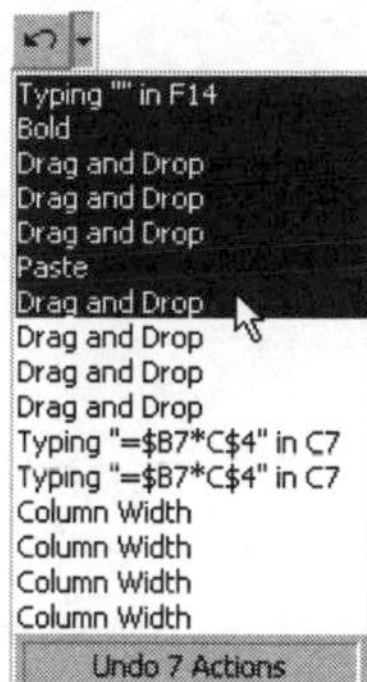

Figure 70
You can use the Undo button's menu to select multiple actions to undo.

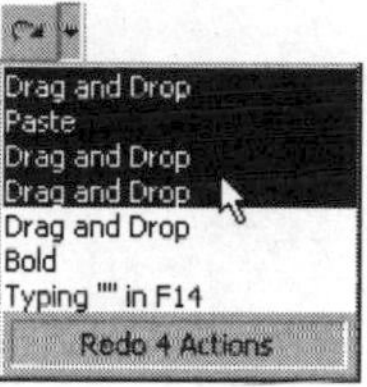

Figure 71
You can also use the Redo button's menu to select multiple actions to redo.

To undo the last action

Choose Edit > Undo (**Figures 68** or **69**), press Ctrl Z, or click the Undo button on the Standard toolbar.

To undo multiple actions

Choose Edit > Undo (**Figures 68** or **69**) or press Ctrl Z repeatedly.

or

1. Click the triangle beside the Undo button on the standard toolbar to display a menu of recent actions.
2. Drag down to select all the actions that you want to undo (**Figure 70**).
3. Release the mouse button to undo all selected actions.

To reverse the last undo

Choose Edit > Redo (**Figure 68**), press Ctrl Y, or click the Redo button on the Standard toolbar.

To reverse multiple undos

Choose Edit > Redo (**Figure 68**) or press Ctrl Y repeatedly.

or

1. Click the triangle beside the Redo button on the standard toolbar to display a menu of recently undone actions.
2. Drag down to select all the actions that you want to redo (**Figure 71**).
3. Release the mouse button to reverse all selected undos.

To repeat the last action

Choose the Repeat command from the Edit menu (**Figure 69**) or press Ctrl Y.

WORKING WITH FILES

SWDivSales.xls

	A	B	C	D	E
1	Southwest Division				
2	First Quarter Sales				
3		January	February	March	Total
4	John	$ 1,254.00	$ 1,256.00	$ 2,435.00	$ 4,945.00
5	Jean	1,865.00	1,736.00	1,905.00	5,506.00
6	Joe	1,614.00	1,284.00	2,509.00	5,407.00
7	Joan	1,987.00	1,908.00	2,800.00	6,785.00
8	Totals	$ 6,720.00	$ 6,184.00	$ 9,739.00	$ 22,643.00

Sheet1 / Chart1 / Sheet2 / Sheet3

Figure 1 Here's a worksheet.

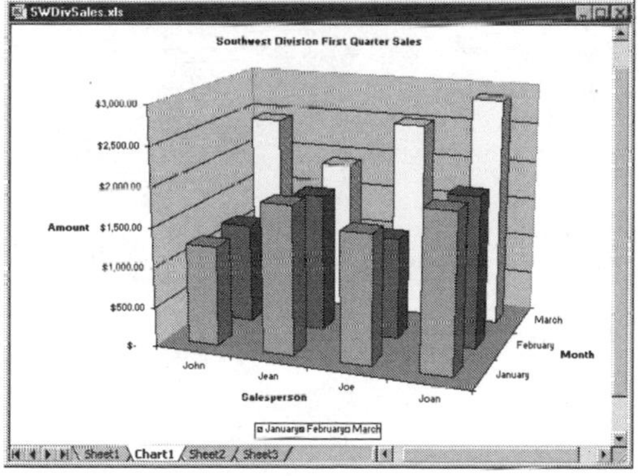

Figure 2 And here's a chart sheet in the same workbook file.

Excel Files

Excel 2000 document files are called *workbooks*.

- Each workbook file consists of multiple sheets.
- Workbook files appear in document windows.
- Workbook files can be saved on disk and reopened for editing and printing.

In this chapter, I tell you how to perform a variety of tasks with workbook sheets, windows, and files.

Workbook Sheets

Excel workbook files can include up to 255 individual *sheets*, which are like pages in the workbook. Each workbook, by default, includes three sheets named *Sheet1* through *Sheet3*.

In Excel 2000, there are two kinds of sheets:

- A *worksheet* (**Figure 1**) is for entering information and performing calculations. You can also embed charts in a worksheet.
- A *chart sheet* (**Figure 2**) is for creating charts that aren't embedded in a worksheet.

✔ Tips

- Use the multiple sheet capabilities of workbook files to keep sheets for the same project together. This is an excellent way to organize related work.
- I tell you about worksheets throughout this book and about charts and chart sheets in **Chapter 8**.

To switch between sheets

Click the sheet tab at the bottom of the workbook window (**Figure 3**) for the sheet you want.

or

Press Ctrl Page Down or Ctrl Page Up to scroll through all the sheets in a workbook, one at a time.

✔ Tips

- If the sheet tab for the sheet you want is not displayed, use the tab scrolling buttons (**Figure 4**) to scroll through the sheet tabs.
- To display more or fewer sheet tabs, drag the tab split box (**Figure 5**) to increase or decrease the size of the sheet tab area. As you change the size of the sheet tab area, you'll also change the size of the bottom scroll bar for the workbook window.

To select multiple sheets

1. Click the sheet tab for the first sheet you want to select.
2. Hold down Ctrl and click the sheet tab(s) for the other sheet(s) you want to select. The sheet tabs for each sheet you include in the selection turn white (**Figure 6**).

✔ Tips

- To select multiple adjacent sheets, click the sheet tab for the first sheet, then hold down Shift and click on the sheet tab for the last sheet you want to select. All sheet tabs in between also become selected.
- Selecting multiple sheets makes it quick and easy to print, delete, edit, format, or perform other tasks with more than one sheet at a time.

Sheet1 Sheet2 Sheet3

Figure 3 Sheet tabs enable you to move from one sheet to another within a workbook.

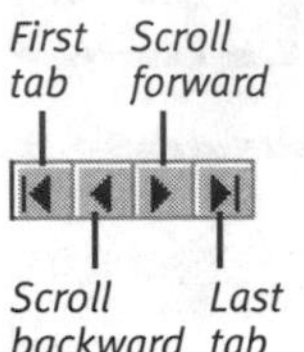

Figure 4 Use the tab scrolling buttons to view sheet tabs that are not displayed.

Figure 5 Drag the tab split box to change the size of the sheet tab area and display more or fewer sheet tabs.

Figure 6 To select multiple sheets, hold down Ctrl while clicking each sheet tab.

Figure 7 Begin by selecting the sheet you want the new sheet inserted before.

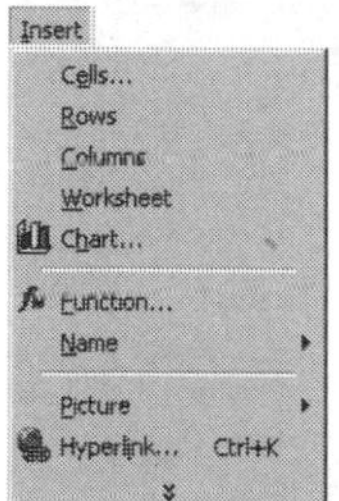

Figure 8 You can use the Insert menu to insert a new worksheet or chart sheet.

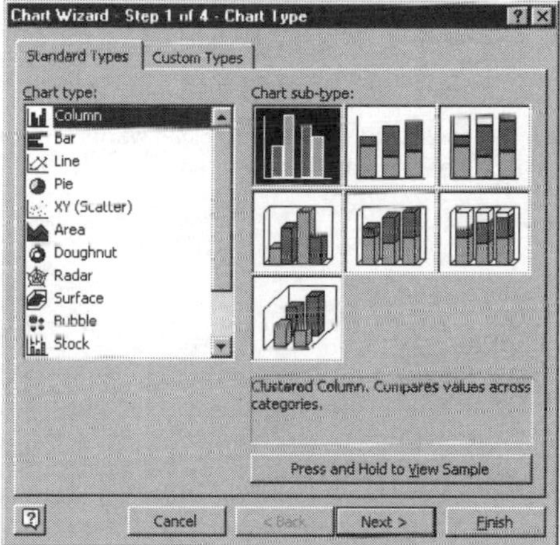

Figure 9 An inserted worksheet.

Figure 10 The first step of the Chart Wizard.

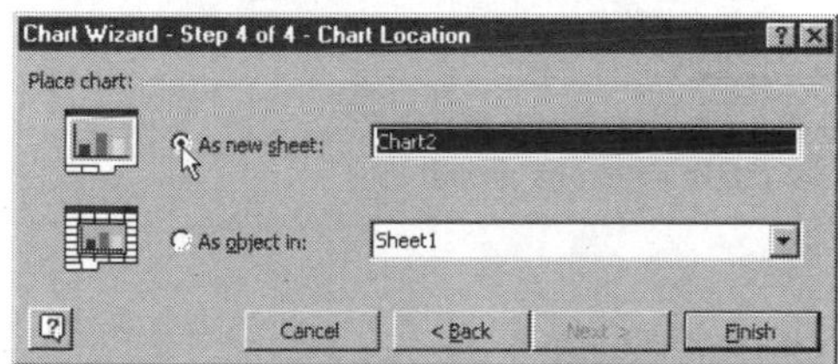

Figure 11 The last step of the Chart Wizard enables you to insert the chart as a new sheet.

Figure 12 An inserted chart sheet.

To insert a worksheet

1. Click the tab for the sheet you want to insert a new sheet before (**Figure 7**).
2. Choose Insert > Worksheet (**Figure 8**) or press Shift F11.

   A new worksheet is inserted before the one you originally selected (**Figure 9**).

✔ Tip

- By default, the new worksheet is named with the word *Sheet* followed by a number. I explain how to rename sheets on the next page.

To insert a chart sheet

1. Click the tab for the sheet you want to insert a new sheet before (**Figure 7**).
2. Choose Insert > Chart (**Figure 8**).
3. The Chart Wizard - Step 1 of 4 dialog box appears (**Figure 10**). Follow the steps in the Chart Wizard (as discussed in **Chapter 8**) to create a chart.
4. In the Chart Wizard - Step 4 of 4 dialog box, select the As new sheet option (**Figure 11**) and enter a name for the sheet beside it. Then click Finish.

   A new chart sheet is inserted before the worksheet you originally selected (**Figure 12**).

To delete a sheet

1. Click on the sheet tab for the sheet you want to delete to select it.
2. Choose Edit > Delete Sheet (**Figure 13**).
3. A warning appears (**Figure 14**). Click OK to confirm that you want to delete the sheet.

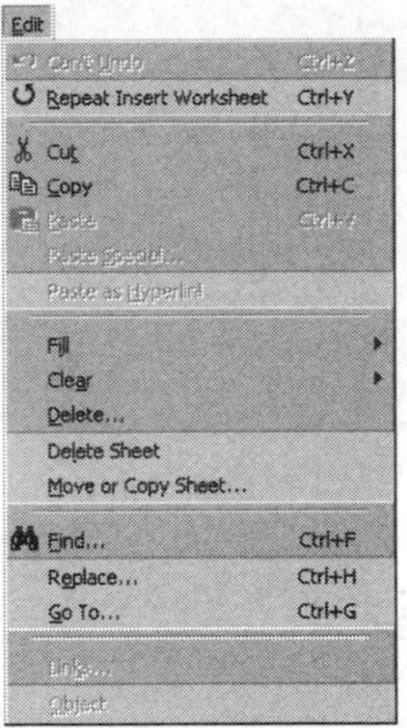

Figure 13 The Edit menu.

✔ Tips

- As Excel warns you (**Figure 14**), sheets are permanently deleted. That means even the Undo command won't get a deleted sheet back.
- If another cell in the workbook contains a reference to a cell on the sheet you deleted, that cell will display a #REF! error message. The formula in that cell will have to be rewritten.

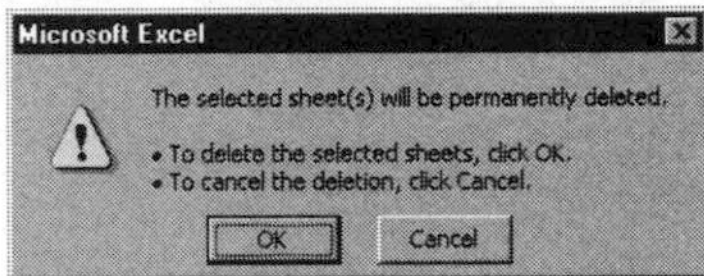

Figure 14 When you delete a sheet, Excel warns you that it will be permanently deleted.

To rename a sheet

1. Click on the sheet tab for the sheet you want to rename to make it active.
2. Choose Format > Sheet > Rename (**Figure 15**) or double-click the sheet tab.
3. The sheet tab becomes highlighted (**Figure 16**). Enter a new name for the sheet (**Figure 17**) and press Enter.

   The sheet tab displays the new name you gave it (**Figure 18**).

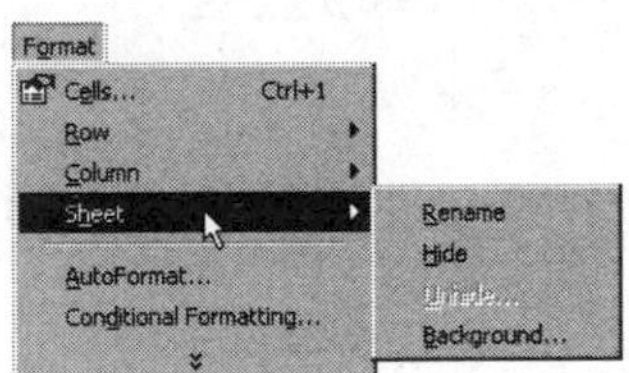

Figure 15 The Sheet submenu under the Format menu.

Sheet1

Figure 16 Double-click the sheet tab to select its name.

SW Div Sales

Figure 17 Enter a new name for the sheet.

Figure 18 Press Enter to complete the entry.

✔ Tips

- The appearance of the Format menu (**Figure 15**) varies depending on the type of sheet.
- Sheet names can be up to 31 characters long and can contain any character you can type from your keyboard.

Chart1 Sheet2 Sheet3

Figure 19 When you hide a sheet, its tab disappears.

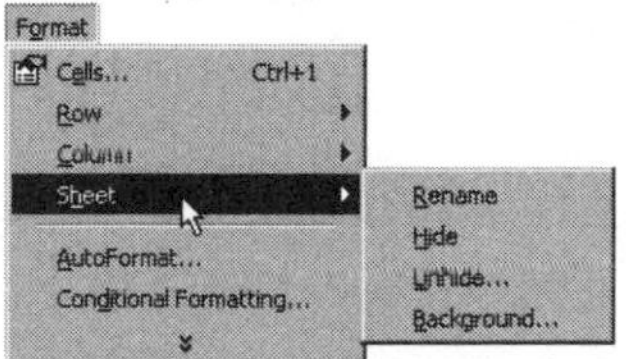

Figure 20 When a sheet is hidden, the Unhide command is available on the Sheet submenu.

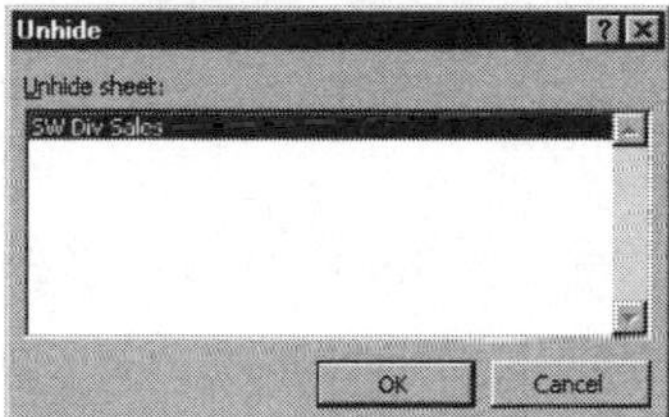

Figure 21 The Unhide dialog box lists all hidden sheets.

To hide a sheet

1. Select the sheet(s) you want to hide (**Figure 18**).
2. Choose Format > Sheet > Hide (**Figure 15**).

   The sheet and its sheet tab disappear (**Figure 19**), just as if the sheet were deleted! But don't worry—the sheet still exists in the workbook file.

✔ Tips

- You cannot hide a sheet if it is the only sheet in a workbook.
- Don't confuse this command with the Hide command under the Window menu. These commands do two different things. I tell you about the Window menu's Hide command later in this chapter.

To unhide a sheet

1. Choose Format > Sheet > Unhide (**Figure 20**).
2. In the Unhide dialog box that appears (**Figure 21**), select the sheet you want to unhide.
3. Click OK.

   The sheet and its sheet tab reappear.

✔ Tips

- You can only unhide one sheet at a time.
- If the Unhide command is gray (**Figure 15**), no sheets are hidden.
- Don't confuse this command with the Unhide command under the Window menu. I tell you about the Window menu's Unhide command later in this chapter.

To move or copy a sheet

1. Select the tabs for the sheet(s) you want to move or copy.
2. Choose Edit > Move or Copy Sheet (**Figure 13**). The Move or Copy dialog box appears (**Figure 22**).
3. Use the To book menu (**Figure 23**) to choose the workbook you want to move or copy the sheet(s) to.
4. Use the Before sheet list to select the sheet you want the sheet(s) to be copied before.
5. If you want to copy or duplicate the sheet rather than move it, turn on the Create a copy check box.
6. Click OK.

✔ Tips

- To move or copy sheets to another workbook, make sure that workbook is open (but not active) before you choose the Move or Copy Sheet command. Otherwise, it will not be listed in the To book menu (**Figure 23**).
- If you choose (new book) from the To book menu (**Figure 23**) Excel creates a brand new, empty workbook file and places the selected sheet(s) into it.
- You can use the Move or Copy Sheet command to change the order of sheets in a workbook. Just make sure the current workbook is selected in the To book menu (**Figure 23**). Then select the appropriate sheet from the Before sheet scrolling list or select (move to end).
- You can also move or copy a sheet within a workbook by dragging. To move the sheet, simply drag the sheet tab to the new position (**Figure 24**). To copy the sheet, hold down Ctrl while dragging the sheet tab (**Figure 25**).

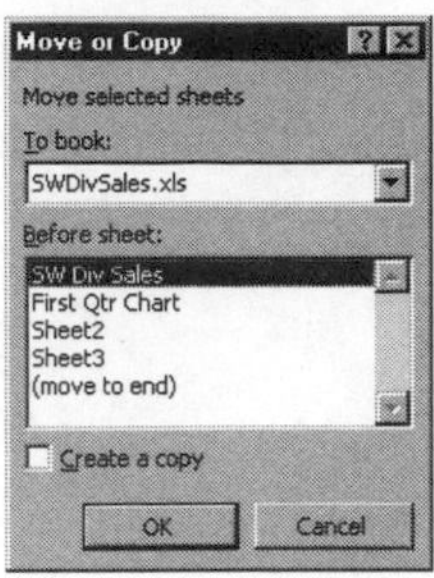

Figure 22 Use the Move or Copy dialog box to pick a destination for the selected sheet(s).

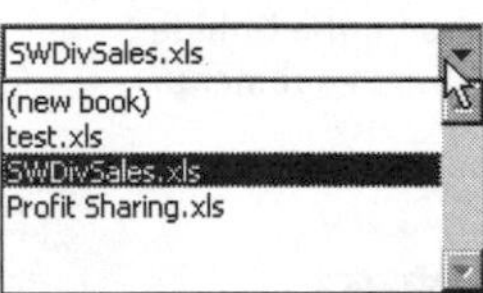

Figure 23 The To book menu lists all of the workbook files that are currently open.

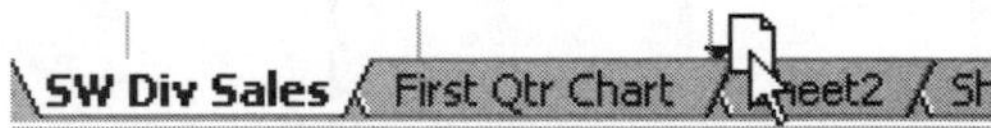

Figure 24 You can also drag a sheet tab to move it...

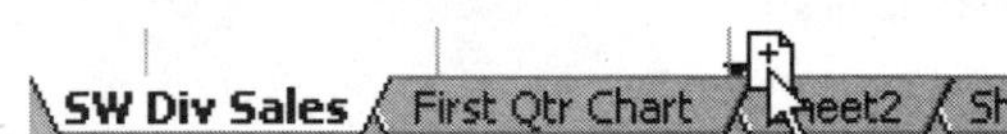

Figure 25 ...or hold down Ctrl while dragging a sheet tab to copy it.

Moving & Copying Sheets

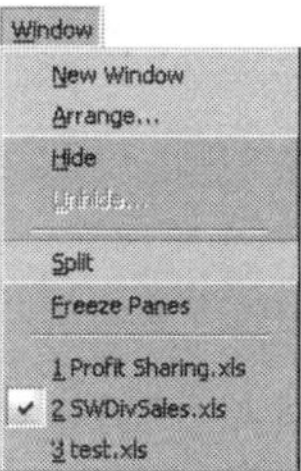

Figure 26 The Window menu offers commands for working with open document windows.

SWDivSales.xls:2

	A	B	C	D	E
1	Southwest Division				
2	First Quarter Sales				
3		January	February	March	Total
4	John	$1,254.00	$1,256.00	$2,435.00	$ 4,945.00
5	Jean	1,866.00	1,736.00	1,905.00	5,506.00
6	Joe	1,614.00	1,284.00	2,509.00	5,407.00
7	Joan	1,987.00	1,908.00	2,890.00	6,785.00
8	Totals	$6,720.00	$6,184.00	$9,739.00	$22,643.00

SW Div Sales / First Qtr Chart / Sheet2 / Sheet3

Figure 27 When you open more than one window for a file, the window number appears in the title bar...

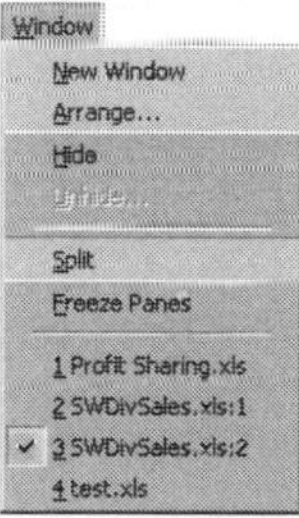

Figure 28 ...and both windows are listed on the Window menu.

Workbook Windows

Like most Windows programs, Excel lets you have more than one document open at a time. But Excel also goes a step further by enabling you to open multiple windows for the same workbook. Then, by arranging the windows on screen, you can see and work with more than one sheet in the same workbook.

✔ Tip

- I tell you how to create a new workbook in **Chapter 2** and how to open an existing workbook later in this chapter.

To activate another window

Choose the name of the window you want to make active from the list of open windows at the bottom of the Window menu (**Figure 26**).

To create a new window

1. Activate the workbook for which you want to create another window.
2. Choose Window > New Window (**Figure 26**).

   A new window for that workbook appears (**Figure 27**) and the new window's name appears at the bottom of the Window menu (**Figure 28**).

✔ Tip

- If more than one window is open for a workbook and you close one of them, the workbook does not close—just that window. I tell you about closing windows later in this section.

To arrange windows

1. Choose Window > Arrange (**Figure 26**).
2. In the Arrange Windows dialog box that appears (**Figure 29**), select an Arrange option. **Figures 30** through **33** illustrate all of them.
3. To arrange only the windows of the active workbook (rather than all open windows), turn on the Windows of active workbook check box.
4. Click OK.

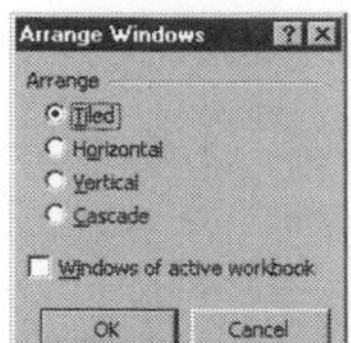

Figure 29 The Arrange Windows dialog box.

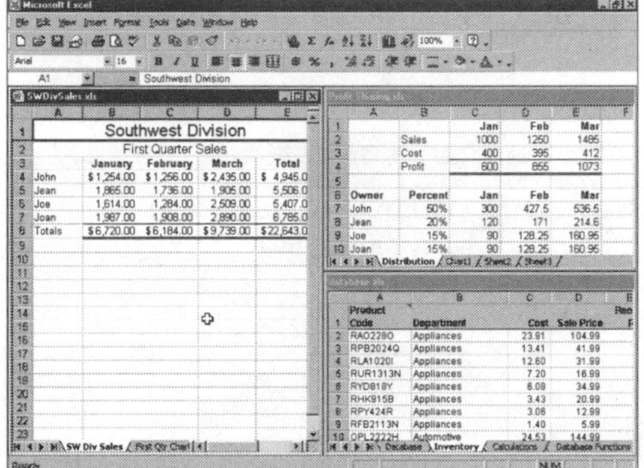

Figure 30 Tiled windows.

✔ Tips

- To work with one of the arranged windows, click in it to make it active.
- The window with the striped title bar is the active window.
- To make one of the arranged windows full size again, click on it to make it active and then click the window's zoom box. The window fills the screen while the other windows remain arranged behind it. Click the zoom box again to shrink it back down to its arranged size.

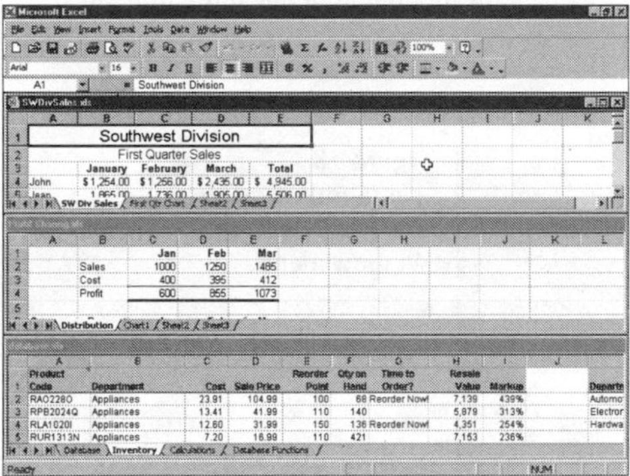

Figure 31 Horizontally arranged windows.

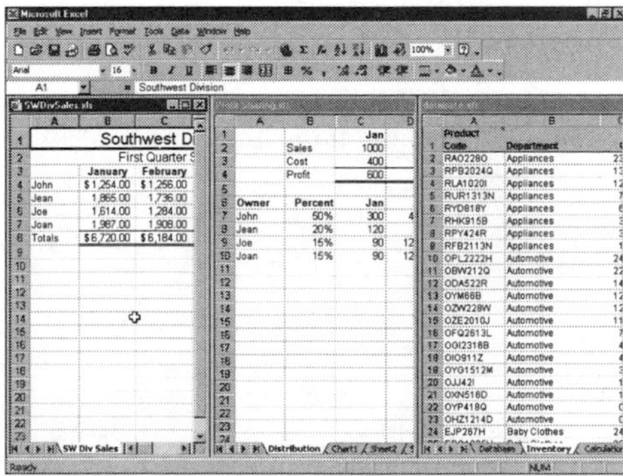

Figure 32 Vertically arranged windows.

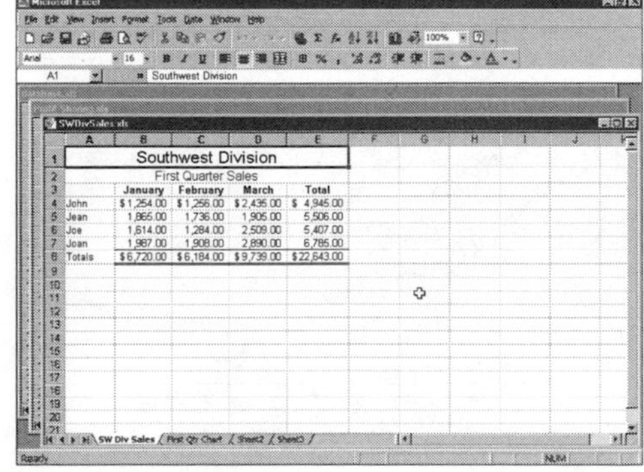

Figure 33 Cascading windows.

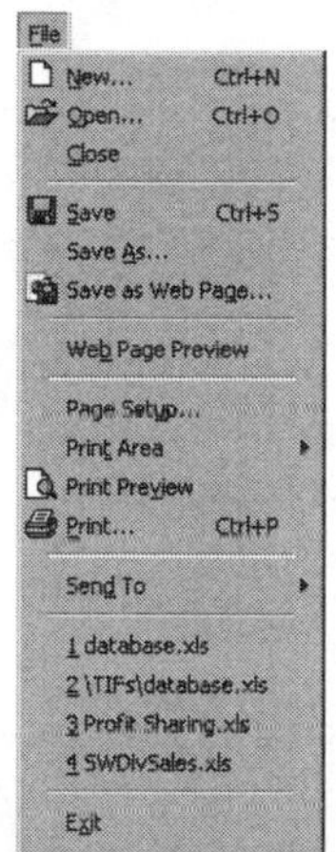

Figure 34
The File menu.

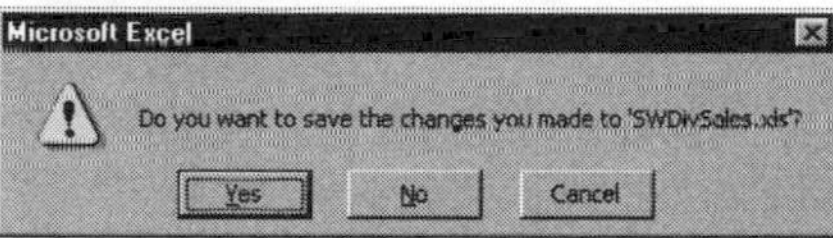

Figure 35 Excel warns you when you attempt to close an unsaved document and gives you an opportunity to save it.

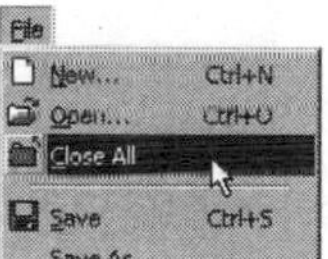

Figure 36
Hold down [Shift] to display the Close All command.

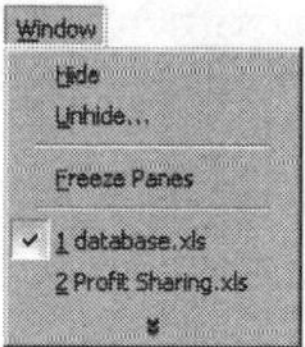

Figure 37
When a window is hidden, the Unhide command is available on the Window menu.

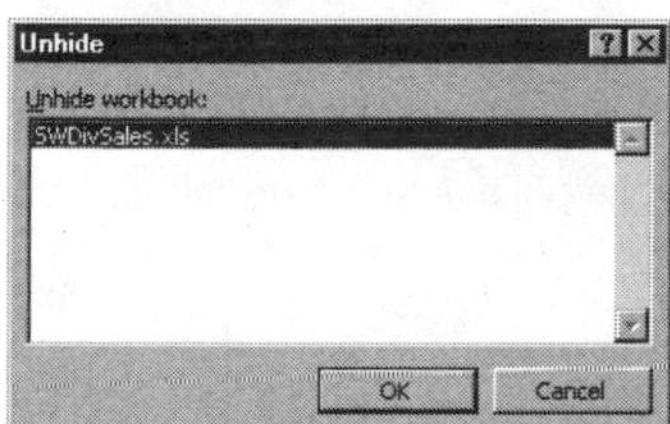

Figure 38 Use the Unhide dialog box to select the window you want to unhide.

To close a window

Click the document window's close box.

or

Choose File > Close (**Figure 34**) or press [Ctrl][W].

✔ Tips

- If the file you are closing has unsaved changes, Excel warns you (**Figure 35**). Click Yes to save changes. I tell you about saving files later in this chapter.
- To close all open windows, hold down [Shift] and choose File> Close All (**Figure 36**).

To hide a window

1. Activate the window you want to hide.
2. Choose Window > Hide (**Figure 26**).

✔ Tips

- Hiding a window is not the same as closing it. A hidden window remains open, even though it is not listed at the bottom of the Window menu.
- Hiding a window is not the same as hiding a sheet in a workbook. I tell you about hiding sheets earlier in this chapter.

To unhide a window

1. Choose Window > Unhide (**Figure 37**).
2. In the Unhide dialog box that appears (**Figure 38**), choose the window you want to unhide.
3. Click OK.

✔ Tip

- If the Unhide command is gray (**Figures 26** and **28**), no windows are hidden.

To change a window's magnification

1. Choose View > Zoom (**Figure 39**).
2. In the Zoom dialog box that appears (**Figure 40**), select the option for the magnification you want.
3. Click OK.

or

1. Click the arrow beside the Zoom control 100% on the Standard toolbar to display a menu of magnifications (**Figure 41**).
2. Choose the magnification you want from the menu.

✔ Tips

- To zoom selected cells so they fill the window, select the Fit selection option in the Zoom dialog box (**Figure 40**) or choose the Selection command on the Zoom control's menu (**Figure 41**).
- You can enter a custom magnification in the Zoom dialog box (**Figure 40**) by selecting the Custom option and entering a value of your choice.
- You can enter a custom magnification in the Zoom box 100% on the Standard toolbar by clicking the value in the box to select it, typing in a new value (**Figure 42**), and pressing Enter.
- Custom zoom percentages must be between 10% and 400%.
- Zooming the window using techniques discussed here does not affect the way a worksheet will print.
- A "zoomed" window's sheet works just like any other worksheet.
- When you save a workbook, the magnification settings of its sheets are saved. When you reopen the workbook, the sheets appear with the last used zoom magnification.

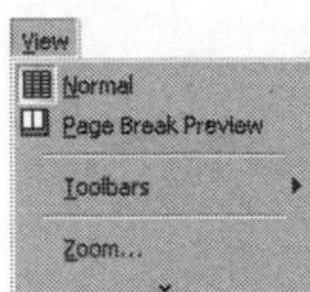

Figure 39 The View menu.

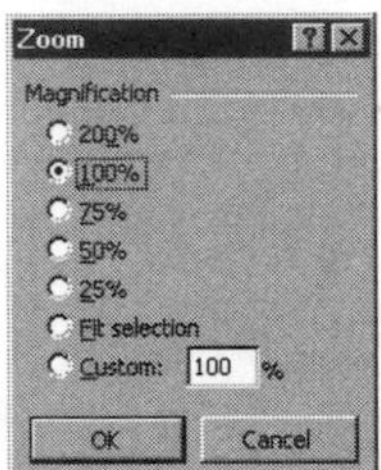

Figure 40 Use the Zoom dialog box to set the window's magnification.

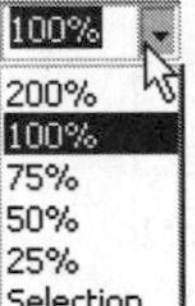

Figure 41 You can also choose a magnification option from the Zoom menu on the Standard toolbar.

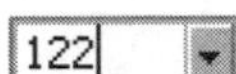

Figure 42 You can enter a custom zoom percentage in the Zoom box on the Standard toolbar.

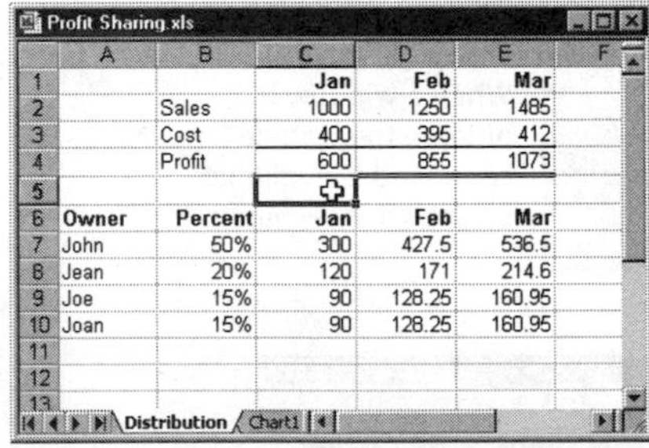

Profit Sharing.xls

	A	B	C	D	E	F
1			Jan	Feb	Mar	
2		Sales	1000	1250	1485	
3		Cost	400	395	412	
4		Profit	600	855	1073	
5						
6	Owner	Percent	Jan	Feb	Mar	
7	John	50%	300	427.5	536.5	
8	Jean	20%	120	171	214.6	
9	Joe	15%	90	128.25	160.95	
10	Joan	15%	90	128.25	160.95	
11						
12						

Distribution / Chart1

Figure 43 Position the cell pointer where you want the split to occur.

Profit Sharing.xls

	A	B	C	D	E	F
1			Jan	Feb	Mar	
2		Sales	1000	1250	1485	
3		Cost	400	395	412	
4		Profit	600	855	1073	
5						
6	Owner	Percent	Jan	Feb	Mar	
7	John	50%	300	427.5	536.5	
8	Jean	20%	120	171	214.6	
9	Joe	15%	90	128.25	160.95	
10	Joan	15%	90	128.25	160.95	
11						
12						

Figure 44 The window splits.

Figure 45 Position the mouse pointer on the split bar at the end of the scroll bar.

Profit Sharing.xls

	A	B	C	D	E	F
1			Jan	Feb	Mar	
2		Sales	1000	1250	1485	
3		Cost	400	395	412	
4		Profit	600	855	1073	
5						
6	Owner	Percent	Jan	Feb	Mar	
7	John	50%	300	427.5	536.5	
8	Jean	20%	120	171	214.6	
9	Joe	15%	90	128.25	160.95	
10	Joan	15%	90	128.25	160.95	
11						
12						

Distribution / Chart1

Figure 46 Drag the split bar into the window.

Profit Sharing.xls

	A	B	C	D	E	F
1			Jan	Feb	Mar	
2		Sales	1000	1250	1485	
3		Cost	400	395	412	
4		Profit	600	855	1073	
5						
6	Owner	Percent	Jan	Feb	Mar	
7	John	50%	300	427.5	536.5	
8	Jean	20%	120	171	214.6	
9	Joe	15%	90	128.25	160.95	
10	Joan	15%	90	128.25	160.95	
11						
12						

Distribution / Chart1

Figure 47 When you release the mouse button, the window splits.

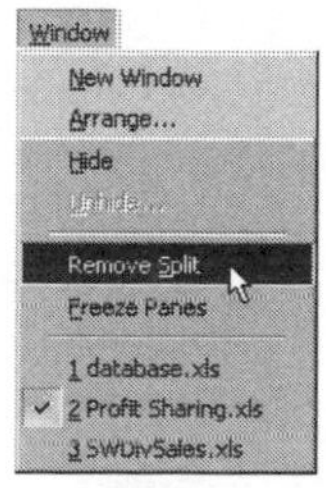

Figure 48 You can use the Remove Split command to remove a window split.

To split a window

1. Position the cell pointer in the cell immediately below and to the right of where you want the split(s) to occur (**Figure 43**).
2. Choose Window > Split (**Figure 26**).

   The window splits at the location you specified (**Figure 44**).

or

1. Position the mouse pointer on the split bar at the top of the vertical scroll bar or right end of the horizontal scroll bar. The mouse pointer turns into a double line with arrows coming out of it (**Figure 45**).
2. Press the mouse button down and drag. A gray split bar moves along with the mouse pointer (**Figure 46**).
3. Release the mouse button.

   The window splits at the bar (**Figure 47**).

✔ Tip

- Splitting a window enables you to see and work with two or more parts of a sheet at a time.

To adjust the size of panes

1. Position the mouse pointer on a split bar.
2. Press the mouse button down and drag until the split bar is in the desired position.
3. Release the mouse button.

   The window split moves.

To remove a window split

Choose Window > Remove Split (**Figure 48**).

or

Double-click a split bar.

The window split disappears.

Saving Files

As you work with a file, everything you do is stored in only one place: *random access memory* or *RAM*. The contents of RAM are a lot like the light in a lightbulb—as soon as you turn it off or pull the plug, it's gone. Your hard disk or a floppy disk provides a much more permanent type of storage area. You use the Save command to copy the workbook file in RAM to disk.

✔ Tip

- It's a very good idea to save documents frequently as you work to prevent data loss in the event of a computer problem.

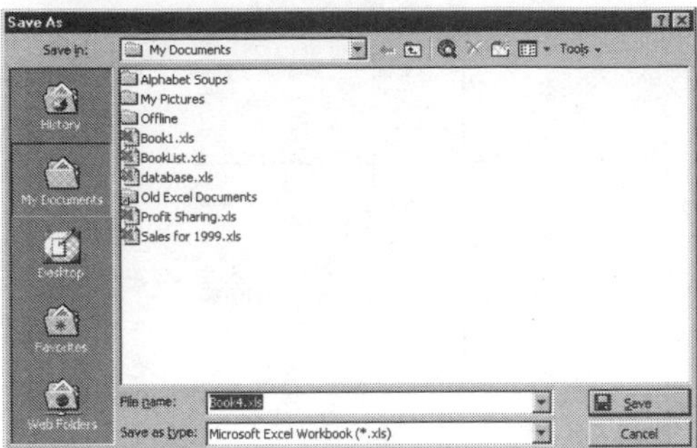

Figure 49 The Save As dialog box.

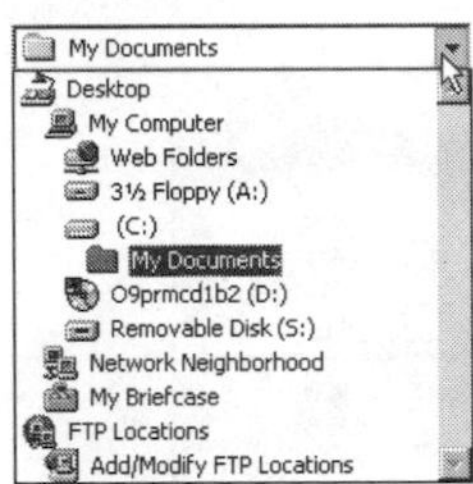

Figure 50 Use the Save in menu to navigate to another location on your computer or network.

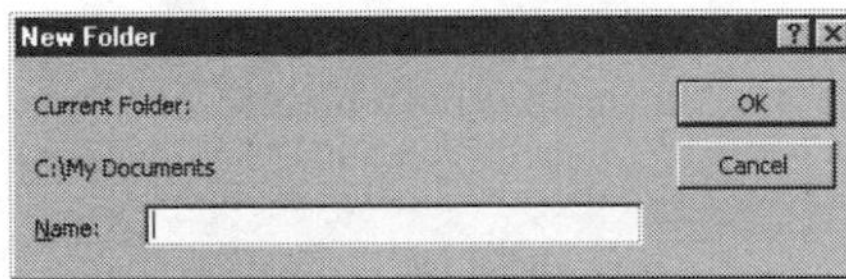

Figure 51 You can use the New Folder dialog box to create a new folder within the current disk location.

Figure 52 The name of a file appears in the workbook's title bar.

To save a workbook for the first time

1. Choose File > Save or File > Save As (**Figure 34**) or press Ctrl S.

   or

   Click the Save button on the Standard toolbar.

2. Use the Save As dialog box that appears (**Figure 49**) to navigate to the folder (and disk, if necessary) in which you want to save the file:
   - Use the Save in menu near the top of the dialog box (**Figure 50**) to go to another location.
   - Double-click a folder to open it.
   - Click the Create New Folder button on the command bar to create a new folder within the current folder. Enter a name for the folder in the New Folder dialog box (**Figure 51**) and click OK.

3. Enter a name for the file in the File name box.

4. Click the Save button.

The file is saved to disk. Its name appears on the workbook window's title bar (**Figure 52**).

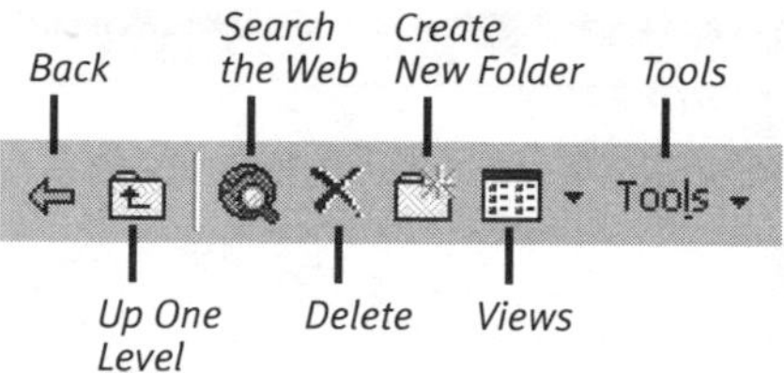

Figure 53 The command bar in the Save As and Open dialog boxes.

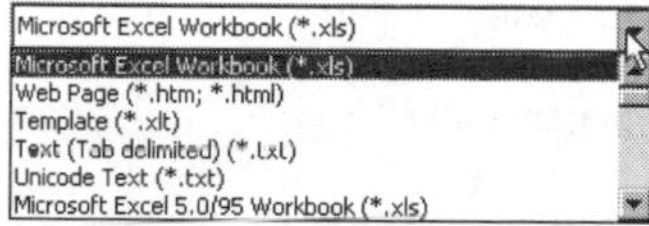

Figure 54 Use the Save as type menu to save the document as a template or another type of file.

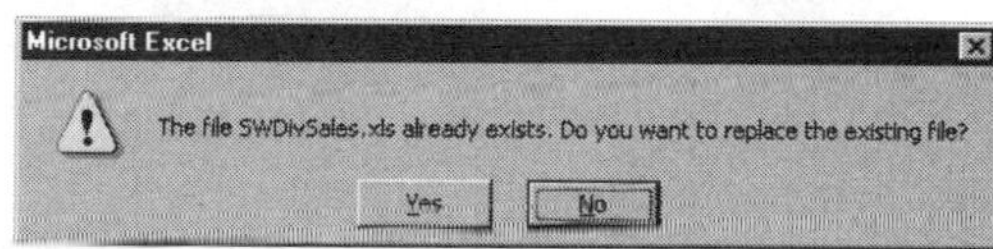

Figure 55 Excel double-checks to make sure you want to overwrite a file with the same name.

- If you save a file with the same name and same disk location as another file, a dialog box appears, asking if you want to replace the file (**Figure 55**).
  - Click Yes to replace the file already on disk with the file you are saving.
  - Click No to return to the Save As dialog box where you can enter a new name or specify a new location.

✔ Tips

- The Places bar, a series of buttons along the left side of the Save As dialog box (**Figure 49**), enables you to quickly go to certain locations:
  - **History** maintains a list of the 20 most recent locations where you accessed files.
  - **My Documents** opens the My Documents folder on your hard disk.
  - **Desktop** displays items on your Windows desktop.
  - **Favorites** displays items you added to your Favorites.
  - **Web Folders** displays folders you access on the Web.
- You can use buttons on the command bar (**Figure 53**) in the Save As dialog box to work with the files and folders listed in the dialog box.
- You can use the Save as type menu at the bottom of the Save dialog box (**Figure 54**) to specify a format for the file. This enables you to save the document in a format that can be opened and read by other versions of Excel or other applications.
- Windows file names can be almost any length, as long as the complete path to the file (including drive letter, all folder names, and the file name with extension) does not exceed 255 characters. File names cannot include any of the following characters: /, \, >, <, *, ?, ", |, :, or ;. It is not necessary to include the three-character extension when you enter a file name; Excel does it for you based on the file type selected from the Save as type menu (**Figure 54**).

To save changes to a workbook

Choose File > Save (**Figure 34**), press Ctrl S, or click the Save button on the Standard toolbar.

The workbook is saved with the same name in the same location on disk.

To save a workbook with a different name or in a different disk location

1. Choose File > Save As (**Figure 34**).
2. Follow steps 2 and/or 3 on page 64 to select a new disk location and/or enter a different name for the workbook.
3. Click the Save button.

To save a workbook as a template

1. Choose File > Save As (**Figure 34**).
2. Enter a name for the workbook in the File name box.
3. Choose Template from the Save as type menu (**Figure 54**). The directory portion of the dialog box automatically displays the contents of the Templates folder (**Figure 56**).
4. To store the template in a specific folder, double-click the name of the folder to open it.
5. Click the Save button.

The file is saved as a template. Its name appears in the document title bar.

✔ Tips

- To begin using a template right after you created it, close it, then follow the instructions in **Chapter 2** to open a new file based on a template. The template appears in the New dialog box (**Figure 57**). I tell you more about templates in **Chapter 2**.
- I tell you more about templates near the beginning of this chapter.

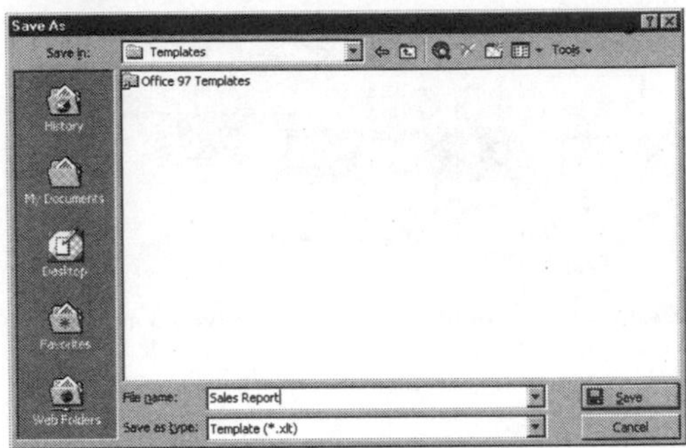

Figure 56 When you choose Template from the Save as type menu, Excel automatically displays the contents of the Templates folder.

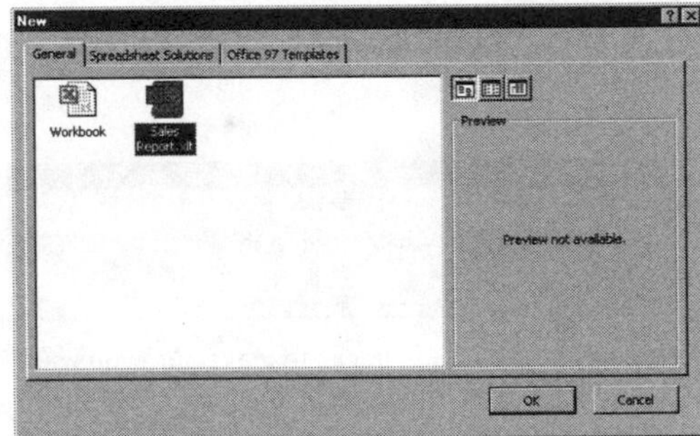

Figure 57 The template appears in the New dialog box.

SAVING FILES

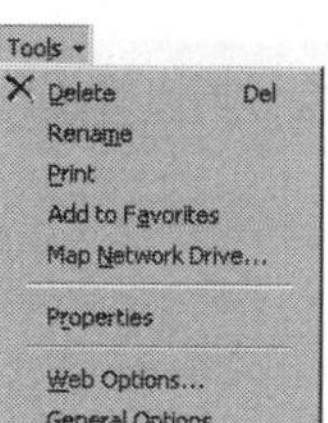

Figure 58 The Tools menu in the command bar of the Save As dialog box.

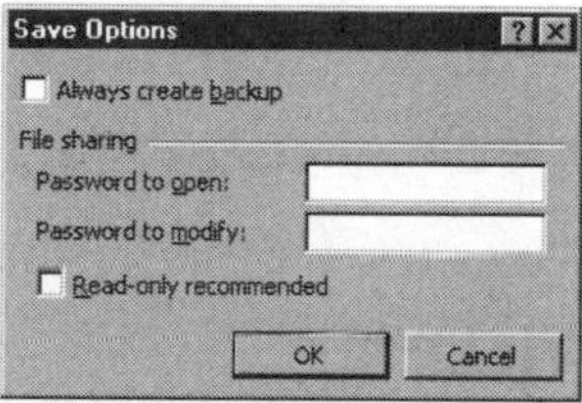

Figure 59 The Save Options dialog box.

Figure 60 This dialog box appears when you attempt to open a file that requires a password to open.

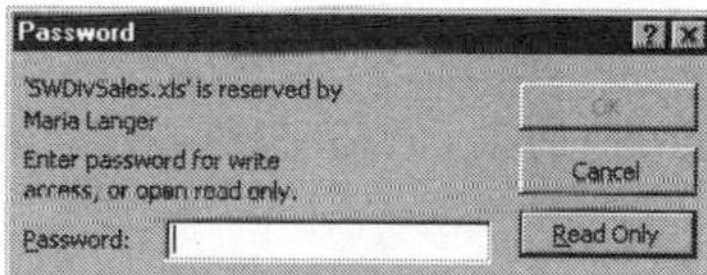

Figure 61 This dialog box appears when you attempt to open a file that requires a password to modify.

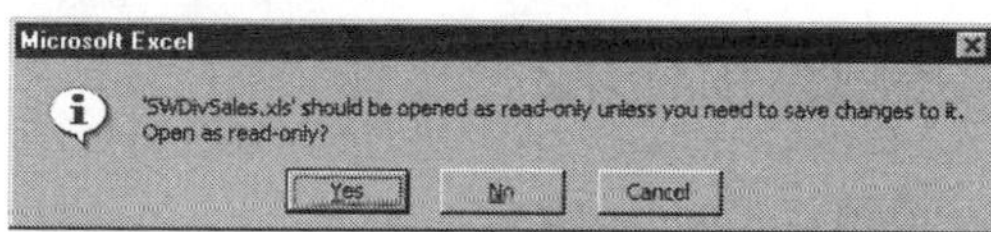

Figure 62 This dialog box appears when you attempt to open a file that has the Read-only recommended option enabled.

To set save options

1. Choose General Options from the Tools menu in the command bar of the Save As dialog box (**Figure 58**) to display the Save Options dialog box (**Figure 59**).
2. To tell Excel to always save the previous version of the file as a backup copy every time you save the file, turn on the Always create backup check box.
3. Set File sharing options as desired:
   - ▲ **Password to open** enables you to specify a password that must be entered to open the file. **Figure 60** shows the dialog box that appears when you attempt to open a file with this option set.
   - ▲ **Password to modify** enables you to specify a password that must be entered to save modifications to the file. **Figure 61** shows the dialog box that appears when you attempt to open a file with this option set.
   - ▲ **Read-only recommended** tells Excel to recommend that the file be opened as a read-only file (**Figure 62**). If the file is opened as read-only, changes to the file must be saved in a file with a different name or in a different disk location.
4. Click OK to save your settings.

✔ Tip

- If you set a password in the File sharing options, don't forget the password or you may be locked out of the file!

Opening Existing Workbook Files

Once a workbook has been saved on disk, you can reopen it to read it, modify it, or print it.

To open an existing document

1. Choose File > Open (**Figure 34**), press Ctrl O, or click the Open button on the Standard toolbar.
2. Use the Open dialog box that appears (**Figure 63**) to locate the file that you want to open:
   - Use the Look in menu near the top of the dialog box (**Figure 64**) to go to another location.
   - Double-click a folder to open it.
3. Select the file that you want to open and click the Open button.

   or

   Double-click the file that you want to open.

✔ Tips

- The Places bar in the Open dialog box (**Figure 63**), which I tell you about on page 65, enables you to quickly go to certain locations.
- To view only specific types of files in the Open dialog box, select a format from the Files of type menu at the bottom of the dialog box (**Figure 65**).
- If you select All Files from the Files of type menu (**Figure 65**), you can open just about any kind of file. This makes it easy to import files into Excel. A document in an incompatible format, however, may not appear the way you expect when opened.
- You can use buttons on the command bar (**Figure 53**) in the Open dialog box to work with listed files and folders.

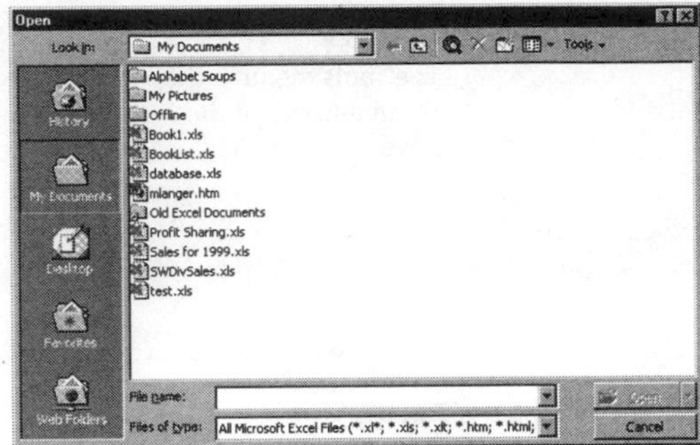

Figure 63 The Open dialog box.

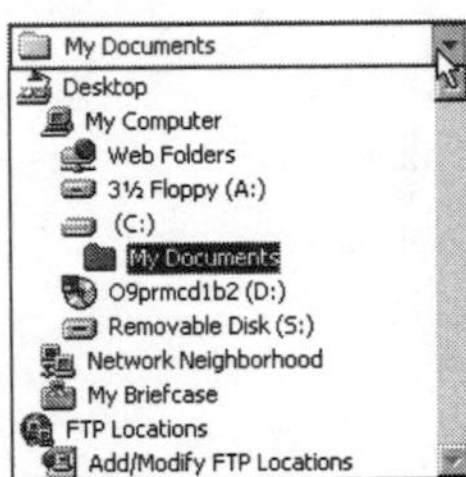

Figure 64 Use the Look in menu to navigate to another location on your computer or network.

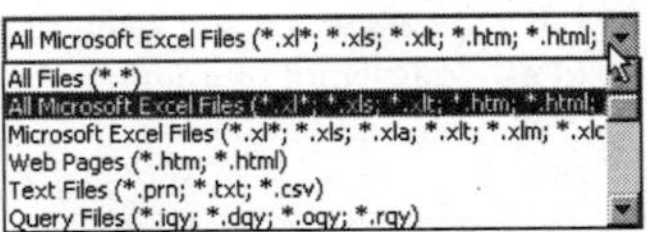

Figure 65 You can narrow down or expand the list of files shown by choosing an option from the Files of type menu.

Using Functions in Formulas

5

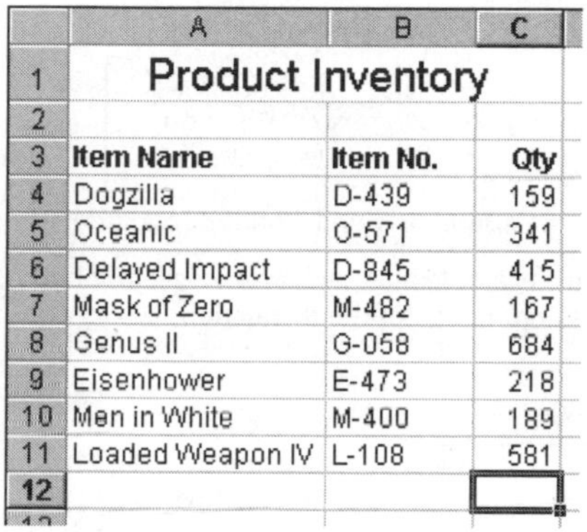

	A	B	C
1	Product Inventory		
2			
3	**Item Name**	**Item No.**	**Qty**
4	Dogzilla	D-439	159
5	Oceanic	O-571	341
6	Delayed Impact	D-845	415
7	Mask of Zero	M-482	167
8	Genus II	G-058	684
9	Eisenhower	E-473	218
10	Men in White	M-400	189
11	Loaded Weapon IV	L-108	581
12			

Figure 1 Using the SUM function makes it easier to add up a column of numbers.

Function name

Arguments

SUM(number1,number2,...)

Figure 2 The parts of a function. The components shown in bold are required.

✔ Tips

- If a function comes at the beginning of a formula, it must begin with an equal sign (=).
- Some arguments are optional. In the SUM function, for example, you can have only one argument, like a reference to a single range of cells.

Functions

A function is a predefined formula for making a specific kind of calculation. Functions make it quicker and easier to write formulas.

For example, say you need to add up a column of numbers like the one in **Figure 1**. It's perfectly acceptable to write a formula using cell references separated by the addition operator (+), like this:

=C4+C5+C6+C7+C8+C9+C10+C11

But rather than enter a lengthy formula, you can use the SUM function to add up the same numbers, like this:

=SUM(C4:C11)

The SUM function is only one of over 200 functions built into Excel. I list all functions in **Appendix B**.

Anatomy of a Function

As shown in **Figure 2**, each function has two main parts.

- The *function name* determines what the function does.
- The *arguments* determine what values or cell references the function should use in its calculation. Arguments are enclosed in parentheses and, if there's more than one, separated by commas.

Arguments

The argument component of a function can consist of any of the following:

- **Numbers (Figure 3).** Like any other formula, the result of a function that uses values for arguments will not change unless the formula is changed.
- **Text (Figure 4).** Excel includes a number of functions just for text. I tell you about them later in this chapter.
- **Cell references (Figures 4 through 8).** This is a practical way to write functions, since when you change cell contents, the results of functions that reference them change automatically.
- **Formulas (Figures 6 and 7).** This lets you create complex formulas that perform a series of calculations at once.
- **Functions (Figures 7 and 8).** When a function includes another function as one of its arguments, it's called *nesting functions.*
- **Error values (Figure 8).** You may find this useful to "flag" errors or missing information in a worksheet.
- **Logical values.** Some function arguments require TRUE or FALSE values.

	A
1	6/30/00

=DATE(2000,6,30)

Figure 3 This example uses numbers as arguments for the DATE function.

	A	B	C	D
1		Rates		
2	Over $400	15%		
3	Up to $400	10%		
4				
5		**Sales**	**Amt. Due**	**Comment**
6	John	443.16	66.47	Good Work!
7	Jean	512.84	76.93	Good Work!
8	Joe	328.69	32.87	Try harder.
9	Joan	401.98	60.3	Good Work!

=IF(B6>400,"Good Work!","Try Harder.")

Figure 4 This example uses cell references, numbers, and text as arguments for the IF function.

	A	B
1		Rates
2	Over $400	15%
3	Up to $400	10%
4		
5		**Sales**
6	John	443.16
7	Jean	512.84
8	Joe	328.69
9	Joan	401.98
10	**Total**	1686.67

=SUM(B6:B9) *or*
=SUM(B6,B7,B8,B9)

Figure 5 This example shows two different ways to use cell references as arguments for the SUM function.

	A	B	C	D
1	Commissions Report			
2				
3		**Sales**	**Rate**	**Amt. Due**
4	John	443.16	15%	66.47

=ROUND(B4*C4,2)

Figure 6 This example uses a formula as an argument for the ROUND function.

	A	B	C
1		Rates	
2	Over $400	15%	
3	Up to $400	10%	
4			
5		**Sales**	**Amt. Due**
6	John	443.16	66.47

=ROUND(IF(B6>400,B6*B2,B6*B3),2)

Figure 7 This example uses the ROUND and IF functions to calculate commissions based on a rate that changes according to sales.

	A	B
1		Rates
2	Over $400	15%
3	Up to $400	10%
4		
5		**Sales**
6	John	443.16
7	Jean	512.84
8	Joe	
9	Joan	401.98
10		#N/A

=IF(COUNTBLANK(B6:B9)>0,#N/A,SUM(B6:B9))

Figure 8 This example uses three functions (IF, COUNTBLANK, and SUM), cell references, and an error value to indicate missing information or add a column of numbers.

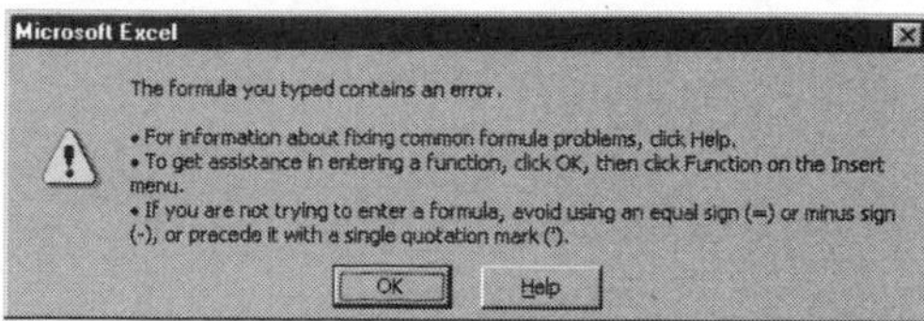

Figure 9 If you make an error in a formula containing a function, Excel displays an error message like this.

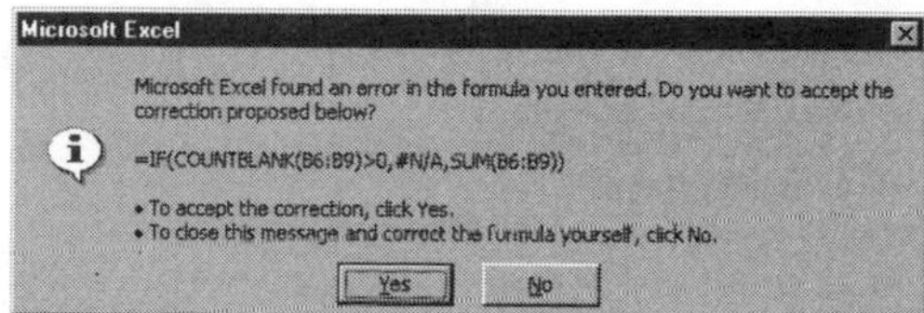

Figure 10 Sometimes, Excel knows just what the problem is.

	A	B
1	Commissions Re	
2		
3		**Sales**
4	John	443.16
5	Jean	512.84
6	Joe	328.69
7	Joan	401.98
8	**Total**	=SUM(B4:B7)

Figure 11 You can type in a function just like you type in any other formula.

	A	B
1	Commissions R	
2		
3		**Sales**
4	John	443.16
5	Jean	512.84
6	Joe	328.69
7	Joan	401.98
8	**Total**	1686.67

Figure 12 When you press Enter, the cell containing the function displays the result of the formula.

Entering Functions

Excel offers several ways to enter a function:

- typing
- typing and clicking
- using the Formula Palette

There is no "best" way—use the methods that you like most.

✔ Tips

- Function names are not case sensitive. *Sum* or *sum* is the same as *SUM*. Excel converts all function names to uppercase characters.
- Do not include spaces when writing formulas.
- When writing formulas with nested functions, it's important that you properly match parentheses. Excel helps you by boldfacing parentheses as you type them. If parentheses don't match, Excel either displays an error message (**Figure 9**) or offers to correct the error for you (**Figure 10**). Sometimes Excel will simply fix the error without displaying a message.

To enter a function by typing

1. Begin the formula by typing an equal sign (=).
2. Type in the function name.
3. Type an open parenthesis character.
4. Type in the value or cell reference for the first argument.
5. If entering more than one argument, type each of them in with commas between them.
6. Type a closed parenthesis character (**Figure 11**).
7. Press Enter or click the Enter button ✔ on the formula bar.

   The result of the function is displayed in the cell (**Figure 12**).

To enter a function by typing & clicking

1. Begin the formula by typing an equal sign (=).
2. Type in the function name.
3. Type an open parenthesis character.
4. Type in a value or click on the cell whose reference you want to include as the first argument (**Figure 13**).
5. If entering more than one argument, type a comma, then type in a value or click on the cell for the next reference (**Figure 14**). Repeat this step for each argument in the function.
6. Type a closed parenthesis character (**Figure 15**).
7. Press [Enter] or click the Enter button ✓ on the formula bar.

   The result of the function is displayed in the cell (**Figure 12**).

✔ Tips

- To include a range by clicking, in step 4 or 5 above, drag the mouse pointer over the cells you want to include (**Figure 16**).
- Be careful where you click or drag when entering a function or any formula. Each click or drag may add references to the formula! If you click on a cell by mistake, you can press [Backspace] to delete each character of the incorrectly added reference or click the Cancel button ✖ on the formula bar to start over from scratch.

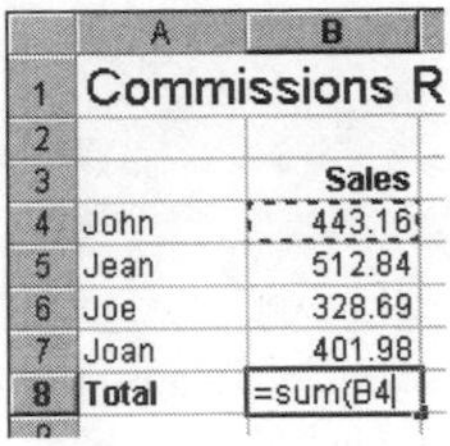

	A	B
1	Commissions R	
2		
3		Sales
4	John	443.16
5	Jean	512.84
6	Joe	328.69
7	Joan	401.98
8	Total	=sum(B4

Figure 13 After typing the beginning of the function, you can click on cell references for arguments.

	A	B
1	Commissions R	
2		
3		Sales
4	John	443.16
5	Jean	512.84
6	Joe	328.69
7	Joan	401.98
8	Total	=sum(B4,B5

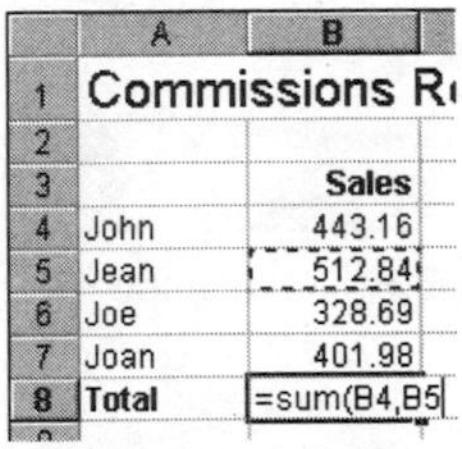

Figure 14 Type a comma before clicking to enter additional cell references for arguments.

	A	B	C
1	Commissions Repor		
2			
3		Sales	
4	John	443.16	
5	Jean	512.84	
6	Joe	328.69	
7	Joan	401.98	
8	Total	=sum(B4,B5,B6,B7)	

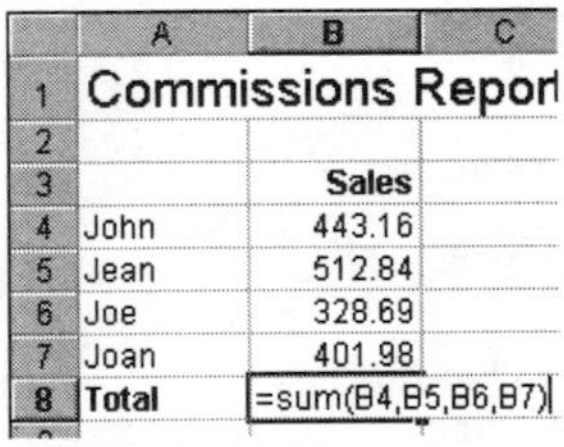

Figure 15 Be sure to type a closed parenthesis character at the end of the function.

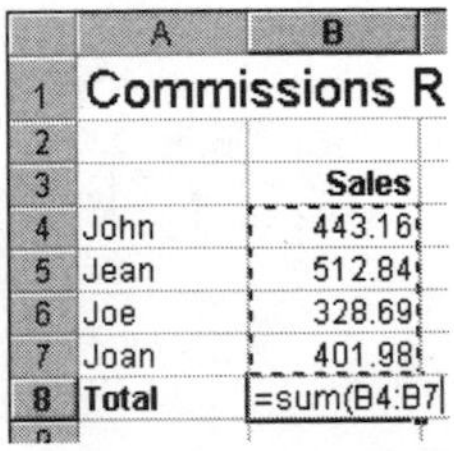

	A	B
1	Commissions R	
2		
3		Sales
4	John	443.16
5	Jean	512.84
6	Joe	328.69
7	Joan	401.98
8	Total	=sum(B4:B7

Figure 16 You can always enter a range in a formula by dragging, even when the range is an argument for a function.

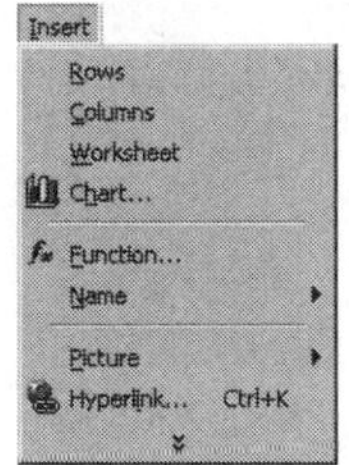

Figure 17
The Insert menu.

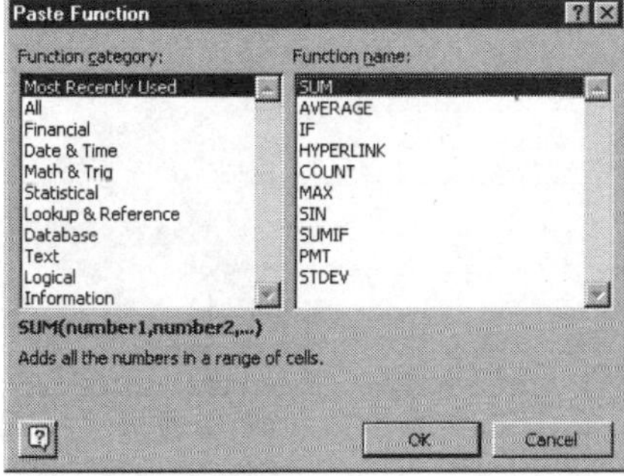

Figure 18 The Paste Function dialog box lists all of Excel's functions.

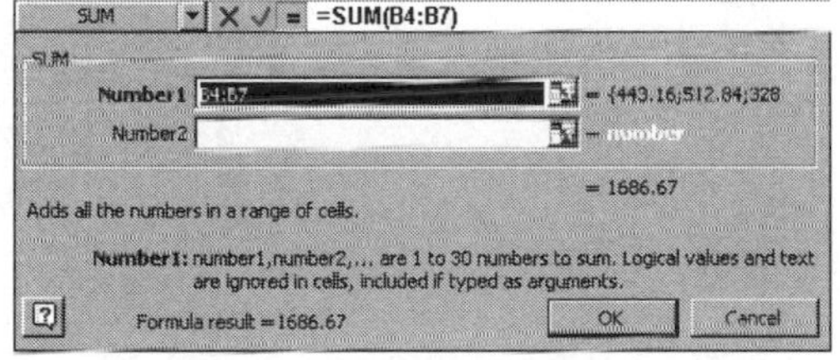

Figure 19 The Formula Palette enables you to write a formula by entering values or references in text boxes for each of a function's arguments.

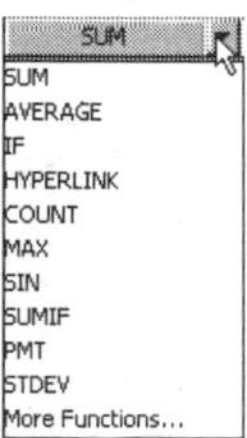

Figure 20
The Functions menu at the far left end of the formula bar.

To enter a function with the Formula Palette

1. Choose Insert > Function (**Figure 17**) or click the Paste Function button on the Standard toolbar.
2. In the Paste Function dialog box that appears (**Figure 18**), click to select a category in the Function category list on the left side of the dialog box.
3. Click to select a function from the Function name scrolling list on the right side of the dialog box. You may have to use the scroll bar to locate the function you want.
4. Click OK.

   The Formula Palette appears beneath the formula bar (**Figure 19**). It provides information about the function you selected and may include one or more entries for the argument(s).
5. Enter a value or cell reference in the appropriate box for each required argument.
6. When you are finished entering function arguments, click OK.

   The Formula Palette closes and the result of the function is displayed in the cell (**Figure 12**).

✔ Tips

- You can also open the Formula Palette by clicking the Edit Formula button on the formula bar. (This enables you to use the Formula Palette to enter or edit any formula, even if it doesn't include a function.) To paste a function into the Formula Palette, choose a specific function or More Functions from the Functions menu at the far left end of the formula bar (**Figure 20**).

Continued on next page...

Continued from previous page.

- In step 2, if you're not sure what category a function is in, select All. The Function name list displays all the functions Excel has to offer.
- In step 5, you can click or drag in the worksheet window to enter a cell reference or range. To see obstructed worksheet cells, click the Hide Formula Palette button to collapse the Formula Palette (**Figure 21**). When you're finished selecting the cell or range, click the Display Formula Palette button to expand the Formula Palette and continue working with it.
- In step 5, you can enter a function as an argument by clicking in the text box for the argument (**Figure 19**) and choosing a specific function or More Functions from the Functions menu at the far left end of the formula bar (**Figure 20**). Although the Formula Palette only shows function options for one function at a time, you can view and edit the entire formula in the formula bar (**Figure 22**).
- As you enter arguments in the Formula Palette, the calculated value of your entries appears at the bottom of the Formula Palette (**Figure 19**).

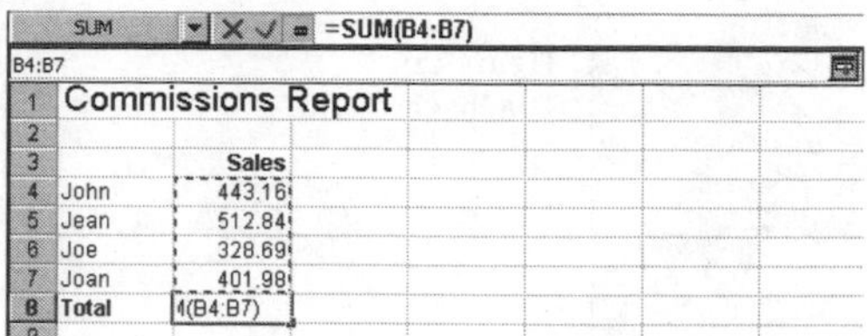

Figure 21 You can collapse the Formula Palette to see and select cell references in the worksheet window.

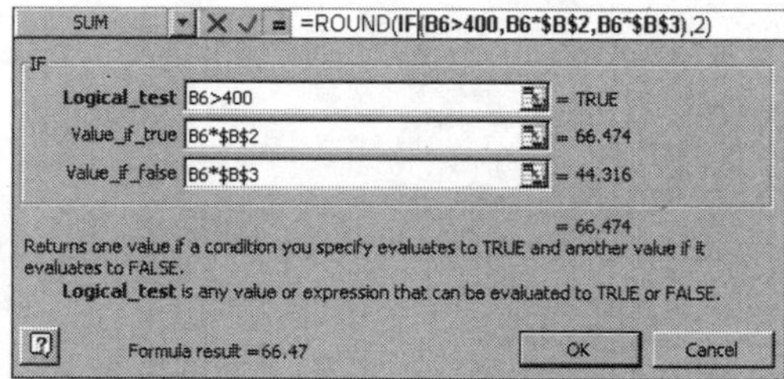

Figure 22 Only one function's options appear in the Formula Palette at a time, but you can view and edit the entire formula in the formula bar.

	A	B
1	Commissions Re	
2		
3		Sales
4	John	443.16
5	Jean	512.84
6	Joe	328.69
7	Joan	401.98
8	Total	=SUM(B4:B7)

Figure 23 When you click the AutoSum button, Excel "guesses" which cells you want to sum and writes the formula.

Math & Trig Functions

Excel's math and trig functions perform standard mathematical and trigonometric calculations. On the next few pages, I tell you about the most commonly used functions, starting with the most popular one: SUM.

The SUM Function

The SUM function (**Figure 5**) adds up numbers. It uses the following syntax:

SUM(number1,number2,...)

Although the SUM function can accept up to 30 arguments separated by commas, only one is required.

To use the AutoSum button

1. Select the cell below the column or to the right of the row of numbers you want to add.
2. Click the AutoSum button Σ on the Standard toolbar once.

   Excel examines the worksheet and makes a "guess" about which cells you want to add. It writes the corresponding formula and puts a marquee around the range of cells it used (**Figure 23**).
3. If the range in the formula is incorrect, type or select the correct range. Since the reference for the range of cells is selected in the formula, anything you type or select will automatically replace it.
4. When the formula is correct, press Enter, click the Enter button ✓ on the formula bar, or click the AutoSum button Σ on the Standard toolbar a second time.

   The formula is entered and its results appear in the cell (**Figure 12**).

To use the AutoSum button on multiple cells

1. Select a range of cells adjacent to the columns or rows you want to add (**Figure 24**).
2. Click the AutoSum button Σ once.

   Excel writes the formulas in the cells you selected (**Figure 25**).

or

1. Select the cells containing the columns you want to add (**Figure 26**).
2. Click the AutoSum button Σ once.

   Excel writes all the formulas in the row of cells immediately below the ones you selected (**Figure 27**).

or

1. Select the cells containing the columns and rows you want to add, along with the empty row beneath them and the empty column to the right of them (**Figure 28**).
2. Click the AutoSum button Σ once.

   Excel writes all the formulas in the bottom and rightmost cells (**Figure 29**).

✔ Tip

- Be sure to check the formulas Excel writes when you use the AutoSum button. Excel is smart, but it's no mind-reader. The cells it includes may not be the ones you had in mind!

	A	B	C	D
1		Southwest Division		
2		First Quarter Sales		
3		Jan	Feb	Mar
4	John	1254	1256	2435
5	Jean	1865	1736	1905
6	Joan	1614	1284	2509
7	Joe	1987	1908	2890
8	Totals			

Figure 24 Select the cells adjacent to the columns (or rows) of cells that you want to add.

	A	B	C	D
1		Southwest Division		
2		First Quarter Sales		
3		Jan	Feb	Mar
4	John	1254	1256	2435
5	Jean	1865	1736	1905
6	Joan	1614	1284	2509
7	Joe	1987	1908	2890
8	Totals	6720	6184	9739

Figure 25 When you click the AutoSum button, Excel enters the appropriate formulas in the selected cells.

	A	B	C	D
1		Southwest Division		
2		First Quarter Sales		
3		Jan	Feb	Mar
4	John	1254	1256	2435
5	Jean	1865	1736	1905
6	Joan	1614	1284	2509
7	Joe	1987	1908	2890
8	Totals			

Figure 26 Select the cells containing the columns that you want to add.

	A	B	C	D
1		Southwest Division		
2		First Quarter Sales		
3		Jan	Feb	Mar
4	John	1254	1256	2435
5	Jean	1865	1736	1905
6	Joan	1614	1284	2509
7	Joe	1987	1908	2890
8	Totals	6720	6184	9739

Figure 27 When you click the AutoSum button, Excel enters the appropriate formulas in the cells beneath the selected cells.

	A	B	C	D	E
1		Southwest Division			
2		First Quarter Sales			
3		Jan	Feb	Mar	Total
4	John	1254	1256	2435	
5	Jean	1865	1736	1905	
6	Joan	1614	1284	2509	
7	Joe	1987	1908	2890	
8	Totals				

Figure 28 Select the cells you want to add, along with the cells in which you want the totals to appear.

	A	B	C	D	E
1		Southwest Division			
2		First Quarter Sales			
3		Jan	Feb	Mar	Total
4	John	1254	1256	2435	4945
5	Jean	1865	1736	1905	5506
6	Joan	1614	1284	2509	5407
7	Joe	1987	1908	2890	6785
8	Totals	6720	6184	9739	22643

Figure 29 When you click the AutoSum button, Excel enters the appropriate formulas in the empty cells of the selection.

	A	B	C	D	E	F
1	Item	Cost	Markup	Qty	Value	
2	Product A	1.54	115%	152	269.192	=PRODUCT(B2:D2)
3	Product B	3.58	250%	142	1270.9	=PRODUCT(B3,C3,D3)

Figure 30 Two ways to use the PRODUCT function. The formulas in column *E* are shown in column *F*.

	A	B	C	D	E	F
1		Sales	Rate	Amount Due	Rounded	
2	John	14528.16	15%	2179.224	2179.22	=ROUND(D2,2)
3	Jean	45204.48	20%	9056.896	9056.9	=ROUND(D3,2)
4	Joe	36547.19	15%	5482.0785	5482.08	=ROUND(D4,2)
5	Joan	27582.43	15%	4137.3645	4137.36	=ROUND(D5,2)

Figure 31 Use the ROUND function to round numbers to the number of decimal places you specify. The formulas in column *E* are shown in column *F*.

	A	E	F	G
1		Total	Rounded	
2	Sales	154258.65	154300	=ROUND(E2,-2)

Figure 32 You can also use the ROUND function to round numbers to the left of the decimal point. The formula in cell *F2* is shown in cell *G2*.

	A	B	C	D	E
1		Sales	Rate	Amount Due	
2	John	14528.16	15%	2179.22	=ROUND(B2*C2,2)
3	Jean	45284.48	20%	9056.9	=ROUND(B3*C3,2)
4	Joe	36547.19	15%	5482.08	=ROUND(B4*C4,2)
5	Joan	27582.43	15%	4137.36	=ROUND(B5*C5,2)

Figure 33 You can use the ROUND function to round the results of another formula or function. The formulas in column *D* are shown in column *E*.

The PRODUCT Function

The PRODUCT function (**Figure 30**) multiplies its arguments much like the SUM function adds them. It uses the following syntax:

PRODUCT(number1,number2,...)

Although the PRODUCT function can accept up to 30 arguments separated by commas, only one is required.

The ROUND Function

The ROUND function (**Figure 31**) rounds a number to the number of decimal places you specify. It uses the following syntax:

ROUND(number,num_digits)

Both arguments are required. The num_digits argument specifies how many decimal places the number should be rounded to. If 0, the number is rounded to a whole number. If less than 0, the number is rounded on the left side of the decimal point (**Figure 32**).

✔ Tips

- Rather than make a calculation in one cell and round it in another as shown in **Figures 31** and **32**, combine the two formulas in one cell (**Figure 33**).
- The ROUNDUP function works like the ROUND function, but it always rounds up to the next higher number. The num_digits argument is not required; if omitted, the number is rounded to the next highest whole number.
- The ROUNDDOWN function works just like the ROUNDUP function, but it always rounds down.

The EVEN & ODD Functions

The EVEN function (**Figure 34**) rounds a number up to the next even number. It uses the following syntax:

EVEN(number)

The number argument, which is required, is the number you want to round.

The ODD function works exactly the same way, but rounds a number up to the next odd number.

	A	B	C	D	E
1	Number	Even		Odd	
2	159.487	160	=EVEN(A2)	161	=ODD(A2)
3	1647.1	1648	=EVEN(A3)	1649	=ODD(A3)
4	-14.48	-16	=EVEN(A4)	-15	=ODD(A4)

Figure 34 Use the EVEN and ODD functions to round a number up to the next even or odd number. The formulas in columns *B* and *D* are shown in columns *C* and *E*.

The INT Function

The INT function (**Figure 35**) rounds a number down to the nearest whole number or integer. It uses the following syntax:

INT(number)

The number argument, which is required, is the number you want to convert to an integer.

	A	B	C
1	Number	Integer	
2	159.487	159	=INT(A2)
3	1647.1	1647	=INT(A3)
4	-14.48	-15	=INT(A4)

Figure 35 Use the INT function to round a number down to the next whole number. The formulas in column *B* are shown in column *C*.

✔ Tip

- INT and ROUND are not the same. INT always rounds down to the nearest whole number. ROUND rounds a number up or down to whatever decimal place you desire. I tell you about ROUND on the previous page.

The ABS Function

The ABS function (**Figure 36**) returns the absolute value of a number—it leaves positive numbers alone but turns negative numbers into positive numbers. (Is that high school math coming back to you yet?) It uses the following syntax:

ABS(number)

The number argument, which is required, is the number you want to convert to an absolute value.

	A	B	C
1	Number	Absolute Value	
2	159.487	159.487	=ABS(A2)
3	1647.1	1647.1	=ABS(A3)
4	-14.48	14.48	=ABS(A4)

Figure 36 Use the ABS function to get the absolute value of a number. The formulas in column *B* are shown in column *C*.

	A	B	C
1	Number	Square Root	
2	36	6	=SQRT(A2)
3	22	4.69041576	=SQRT(A3)
4	-10	#NUM!	=SQRT(A4)

Figure 37 Use the SQRT function to find the square root of a number. The formulas in column *B* are shown in column *C*.

	A	B	C
1	Number	Square Root	
2	36	6	=SQRT(ABS(A2))
3	22	4.69041576	=SQRT(ABS(A3))
4	-10	3.16227766	=SQRT(ABS(A4))

Figure 38 By combining the SQRT and ABS functions, you can prevent #NUM! errors when calculating the square root of a negative number. The formulas in column *B* are shown in column *C*.

Figure 39 The PI function calculates π to 14 decimal places.

	A	B	C	D
1	Low	High	Random	
2	0	1	0.16268243	=RAND()
3	0	1000	924.450281	=RAND()*(B3-A3)+A3
4	36	42	36.6261794	=RAND()*(B4-A4)+A4
5	3458	4835	3785.09436	=RAND()*(B5-A5)+A5

Figure 40 The RAND function can be used alone or as part of a formula to generate a random number within a range. The formulas in column *C* are shown in column *D*.

The SQRT Function

The SQRT function (**Figure 37**) calculates the square root of a number. It uses the following syntax:

SQRT(number)

The number argument, which is required, is the number you want to find the square root of.

✔ Tip

- You'll get a #NUM! error message if you try to use the SQRT function to calculate the square root of a negative number (**Figure 37**). Prevent the error by using the ABS function in the formula (**Figure 38**).

The PI Function

The PI function (**Figure 39**) returns the value of . It uses the following syntax:

PI()

The RAND Function

The RAND (**Figure 40**) function generates a random number greater than or equal to 0 and less than 1 each time the worksheet is calculated. It uses the following syntax:

RAND()

✔ Tips

- Although there is no argument in either the PI or RAND function, if you fail to include the parentheses characters, you'll get a #NAME? error.
- To generate a random number between two numbers (low and high), write a formula like this:

  =*RAND()**(high-low*)*+low

  See **Figure 40** for some examples.
- The calculated value of a formula using the RAND function will change each time the worksheet is recalculated.

The RADIANS & DEGREES Functions

The RADIANS function converts degrees to radians. The DEGREES function converts radians to degrees. They use the following syntax:

RADIANS(angle)

DEGREES(angle)

The angle argument, which is required, is the angle you want converted. Use degrees in the RADIANS function and radians in the DEGREES function. Both functions are illustrated in **Figure 41**.

The SIN Function

The SIN function (**Figure 41**) calculates the sine of an angle. It uses the following syntax:

SIN(number)

The number argument, which is required, is the angle, in radians, for which you want the sine calculated.

The COS Function

The COS function (**Figure 41**) calculates the cosine of an angle. It uses the following syntax:

COS(number)

The number argument, which is required, is the angle, in radians, for which you want the cosine calculated.

The TAN Function

The TAN function (**Figure 41**) calculates the tangent of an angle. It uses the following syntax:

TAN(number)

The number argument, which is required, is the angle, in radians, for which you want the tangent calculated.

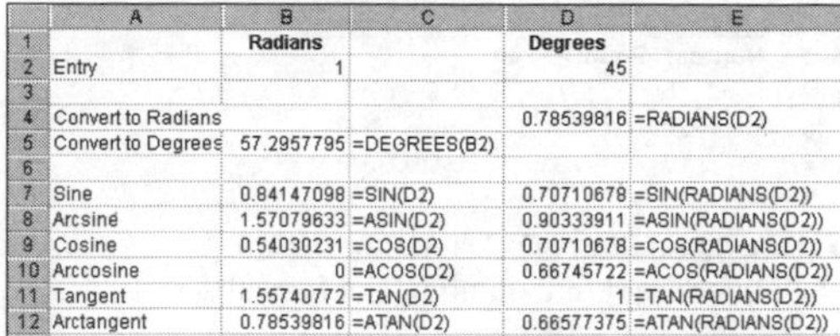

	A	B	C	D	E
1		Radians		Degrees	
2	Entry	1		45	
3					
4	Convert to Radians			0.78539816	=RADIANS(D2)
5	Convert to Degrees	57.2957795	=DEGREES(B2)		
6					
7	Sine	0.84147098	=SIN(D2)	0.70710678	=SIN(RADIANS(D2))
8	Arcsine	1.57079633	=ASIN(D2)	0.90333911	=ASIN(RADIANS(D2))
9	Cosine	0.54030231	=COS(D2)	0.70710678	=COS(RADIANS(D2))
10	Arccosine	0	=ACOS(D2)	0.66745722	=ACOS(RADIANS(D2))
11	Tangent	1.55740772	=TAN(D2)	1	=TAN(RADIANS(D2))
12	Arctangent	0.78539816	=ATAN(D2)	0.66577375	=ATAN(RADIANS(D2))

Figure 41 This example shows several trig functions in action. The formulas in columns *B* and *D* are shown in columns *C* and *E*.

✔ Tip

- To calculate the arcsine, arccosine, or arctangent of an angle, use the ASIN, ACOS, or ATAN function (**Figure 41**). Each works the same as its counterpart.

	A	B	C
1	*Product Inventory*		
2			
3	**Item Name**	**Price**	
4	Dogzilla	14.99	
5	Oceanic	15.99	
6	Delayed Impact	8.99	
7	Mask of Zero	24.99	
8	Genus II	19.99	
9	Eisenhower	19.99	
10	Men in White	22.99	
11	Loaded Weapon I	13.99	
12			
13	**Average**	17.74	=AVERAGE(B4:B11)
14	**Median**	17.99	=MEDIAN(B4:B11)
15	**Mode**	19.99	=MODE(B4:B11)
16	**Minimum**	8.99	=MAX(B4:B11)
17	**Maximum**	24.99	=MIN(B4:B11)

Figure 42 This example shows a few of Excel's statistical functions at work. The formulas in column *B* are shown in column *C*.

Statistical Functions

Excel's statistical functions make it easy to perform complex statistical analyses. Here's a handful of the functions I think you'll use most.

The AVERAGE Function

The AVERAGE function (**Figure 42**) calculates the average or mean of its arguments. It uses the following syntax:

AVERAGE(number1,number2,...)

The MEDIAN Function

The MEDIAN function (**Figure 42**) calculates the median of its arguments. The median is the "halfway point" of the numbers—half the numbers have higher values and half have lower values. The MEDIAN function uses the following syntax:

MEDIAN(number1,number2,...)

The MODE Function

The MODE function (**Figure 42**) returns the mode of its arguments. The mode is the most common value. The MODE function uses the following syntax:

MODE(number1,number2,...)

If there are no repeated values, Excel returns a #NUM! error.

The MIN & MAX Functions

The MIN function (**Figure 42**) returns the minimum value of its arguments while the MAX function returns the maximum value of its arguments. They use the following syntax:

MIN(number1,number2,...)

MAX(number1,number2,...)

✔ Tips

- Excel's AVERAGE function does not include empty cells when calculating the average for a range of cells.
- Although the AVERAGE, MEDIAN, MODE, MIN, and MAX functions can each accept up to 30 arguments separated by commas, only one argument is required.

The COUNT & COUNTA Functions

The COUNT function counts how many numbers are referenced by its arguments. The COUNTA function counts how many values are referenced by its arguments. Although this may sound like the same thing, it isn't—COUNT includes only numbers or formulas resulting in numbers while COUNTA includes any non-blank cell. **Figure 43** shows an example that clarifies the difference.

The COUNT and COUNTA functions use the following syntax:

COUNT(number1,number2,...)

COUNTA(number1,number2,...)

Although either function can accept up to 30 arguments separated by commas, only one is required.

	A	B	C
1			
2		6/30/99	
3		154.69	
4		chocolate	
5			
6		-475.69852	
7		45	
8		ice cream	
9		$ 75.00	
10			
11	**Blank Cells**	5	=COUNT(B2:B9)
12	**Values**	7	=COUNTA(B2:B9)

Figure 43 This example of the COUNT and COUNTA functions illustrates that while the COUNT function counts only cells containing numbers (including dates and times), the COUNTA function counts all non-blank cells. The formulas in column *B* are shown in column *C*.

The STDEV & STDEVP Functions

Standard deviation is a statistical measurement of how much values vary from the average or mean for the group. The STDEV function calculates the standard deviation based on a random sample of the entire population. The STDEVP function calculates the standard deviation based on the entire population. **Figure 44** shows an example of each.

The STDEV and STDEVP functions use the following syntax:

STDEV(number1,number2,......)

STDEVP(number1,number2,...)

Although either function can accept up to 30 arguments separated by commas, only one is required.

	A	B	C
1	*Product Inventory*		
2			
3	**Item Name**	**Price**	
4	Dogzilla	14.99	
5	Oceanic	15.99	
6	Delayed Impact	8.99	
7	Mask of Zero	24.99	
8	Genus II	19.99	
9	Eisenhower	19.99	
10	Men in White	22.99	
11	Loaded Weapon I	13.99	
12			
13	**Average**	17.74	=AVERAGE(B4:B11)
14	**STDEV**	5.230406	=STDEV(B4:B11)
15	**STDVP**	4.892596	=STDEVP(B4:B11)

Figure 44 In this example, the STDEV function assumes that the range is a random sample from a larger population of information. The STDEVP function assumes that the same data is the entire population. That's why the results differ. The formulas in column *B* are shown in column *C*.

✔ Tip

- To get accurate results from the STDEVP function, the arguments must include data for the entire population.

	A	B	C
1	*Depreciation Comparison*		
2			
3	Cost	$ 5,000.00	
4	Salvage Value	$ 250.00	
5	Life (in years)	5	
6			
7	Year	1	
8	Straight Line	$950.00	=SLN(B3,B4,B5)
9	Declining Balance	$2,255.00	=DB(B3,B4,B5,B7)
10	Double Declining Balan	$2,000.00	=DDB(B3,B4,B5,B7)
11	Sum of the Year's Digits	$1,583.33	=SYD(B3,B4,B5,B7)

Figure 45 A simple worksheet lets you compare different methods of depreciation using the SLN, DB, DDB, and SYD functions. The formulas in column *B* are shown in column *C*.

Financial Functions

Excel's financial functions enable you to calculate depreciation, evaluate investment opportunities, or calculate the monthly payments on a loan. On the next few pages, I tell you about a few of the functions I think you'll find useful.

The SLN Function

The SLN function (**Figure 45**) calculates straight line depreciation for an asset. It uses the following syntax:

SLN(cost,salvage,life)

Cost is the acquisition cost of the asset, salvage is the salvage or scrap value, and life is the useful life expressed in years or months. All three arguments are required.

The DB Function

The DB function (**Figure 45**) calculates declining balance depreciation for an asset. It uses the following syntax:

DB(cost,salvage,life,period,month)

The cost, salvage, and life arguments are the same as for the SLN function. Period, which must be expressed in the same units as life, is the period for which you want to calculate depreciation. These first four arguments are required. Month is the number of months in the first year of the asset's life. If omitted, 12 is assumed.

The DDB Function

The DDB function (**Figure 45**) calculates the double-declining balance depreciation for an asset. It uses the following syntax:

DDB(cost,salvage,life,period,factor)

The cost, salvage, life, and period arguments are the same as for the DB function and are required. Factor is the rate at which the balance declines. If omitted, 2 is assumed.

The SYD Function

The SYD function (**Figure 45**) calculates the sum-of-years' digits depreciation for an asset. It uses the following syntax:

SYD(cost,salvage,life,period)

The cost, salvage, life, and period arguments are the same as for the DB and DDB functions. All arguments are required.

The PMT Function

The PMT function calculates the periodic payment for an annuity based on constant payments and interest rate. This function is commonly used for two purposes: to calculate the monthly payments on a loan and to calculate the monthly contribution necessary to reach a specific savings goal.

The PMT function uses the following syntax:

PMT(rate,nper,pv,fv,type)

Rate is the interest rate per period, nper is the total number of periods, and pv is the present value or current worth of the total payments. These three arguments are required. The fv argument is the future value or balance desired at the end of the payments. If omitted, 0 is assumed. Type indicates when payments are due: use 0 for payments at the end of the period and 1 for payments at the beginning of the period. If omitted, 0 is assumed.

	A	B
1	Loan Amount	20000
2	Annual Interest Rate	11.50%
3	Loan Term (in Months)	48
4		
5	Monthly Payment	

Figure 46 A basic structure for a worksheet that calculates loan payments.

	A	B
1	Loan Amount	20000
2	Annual Interest Rate	11.50%
3	Loan Term (in Months)	48
4		
5	Monthly Payment	($521.78)

Figure 47 The loan payment worksheet after entering a formula with the PMT function.

	A	B
1	Loan Amount	25000
2	Annual Interest Rate	11.50%
3	Loan Term (in Months)	48
4		
5	Monthly Payment	($652.23)

Figure 48 Playing "what-if." In this example, I increased the loan amount to see how much more the monthly payment would be.

To calculate loan payments

1. Enter the text and number values shown in **Figure 46** in a worksheet. If desired, use your own amounts.
2. Enter the following formula in cell *B5*: *=PMT(B2/12,B3,B1)*

   This formula uses only the first three arguments of the PMT function. The rate argument is divided by 12 to arrive at a monthly interest rate since the number of periods is expressed in months and payments will be made monthly (all time units must match).
3. Press Enter or click the Enter button on the formula bar.

The result of the formula appears in the cell as a negative number (**Figure 47**) because it is an outgoing cash flow. (A minus sign or parentheses indicates a negative number.)

✔ Tips

- If you prefer, you can use the Formula Palette to write the formula in step 2. Be sure to include the formula *B2/12* in the rate box. Leave the fv and type boxes blank.
- You can calculate loan payments without creating a whole worksheet—simply enter values rather than cell references as arguments for the PMT function. But using cell references makes it easy to play "what-if"—see how payments change when the loan amount, rate, and number of periods changes. **Figure 48** shows an example.

PMT & Calculating Loan Payments

	A	B	C	D
1	Loan Amount	20000		
2	Annual Interest Rate	11.50%		
3	Loan Term (in Months)	48		
4				
5	Monthly Payment	($521.78)		
6				
7	Payment Number	Beg Balance	Interest	Principal
8	1			
9	2			
10	3			
11	4			

Figure 49 To create an amortization table, start with this simple worksheet.

	A	B	C	D
1	Loan Amount	20000		
2	Annual Interest Rate	11.50%		
3	Loan Term (in Months)	48		
4				
5	Monthly Payment	($521.78)		
6				
7	Payment Number	Beg Balance	Interest	Principal
8	1	20000	191.67	$330.11
9	2	$19,669.89		
10	3			
11	4			

Figure 50 Add formulas to calculate interest, principal, and beginning balance.

	A	B	C	D
1	Loan Amount	20000		
2	Annual Interest Rate	11.50%		
3	Loan Term (in Months)	48		
4				
5	Monthly Payment	($521.78)		
6				
7	Payment Number	Beg Balance	Interest	Principal
8	1	20000	191.67	$330.11
9	2	$19,669.89	188.5	$333.28
10	3	$19,336.61	185.31	$336.47
11	4	$19,000.14	182.08	$339.70
12	5	$18,660.44	178.83	$342.95
13	6	$18,317.49	175.54	$346.24
14	7	$17,971.25	172.22	$349.56
15	8	$17,621.69	168.87	$352.91
16	9	$17,268.78	165.49	$356.29

Figure 51 Then copy the formulas down each column for all months in the loan term.

To create an amortization table

1. Create a loan payment worksheet following the steps on the previous page.
2. Enter text and number values for headings as shown in **Figure 49**. Make sure there is a row with a payment number for each month of the loan term indicated in cell *B3*.
3. In cell *B8*, enter *=B1*.
4. In cell *C8*, enter the following formula: *=ROUND(B8*$B$2/12,2)*

   This formula calculates the interest for the period and rounds it to two decimal places.
5. In cell *D8*, enter the following formula: *=-$B$5–C8*

   This formula calculates the amount of principal paid for the current month.
6. In cell *B9*, enter the following formula: *=ROUND(B8–D8,2)*

   This formula calculates the current month's beginning balance, rounded to two decimal places.

   At this point, your worksheet should look like the one in **Figure 50**.
7. Use the fill handle to copy the formula in cell *B9* down the column for each month.
8. Use the Fill handle to copy the formulas in cells *C8* and *D8* down the columns for each month.

   Your amortization table is complete. It should look like the one in **Figure 51**.

✔ Tip

- If desired, you can add column totals at the bottom of columns *C* and *D* to total interest (you may be shocked) and principal (which should match cell *B1*).

To calculate contributions to reach a savings goal

1. Enter the text and number values shown in **Figure 52** in a worksheet. If desired, use your own amounts.
2. Enter the following formula in cell *B5*: *=PMT(B2/12,B3,,B1)*

   This formula uses the first four arguments of the PMT function, although the pv argument is left blank—that's why there are two commas after *B3*. The rate argument is divided by 12 to arrive at a monthly interest rate.
3. Press Enter or click the Enter button ✓ on the formula bar.

   The result of the formula is expressed as a negative number (**Figure 53**) because it is an outgoing cash flow. (A minus sign or parentheses indicates a negative number.)

✔ Tips

- If you prefer, you can use the Formula Palette to write the formula in step 2. Be sure to include the formula *B2/12* in the rate box. Leave the pv and type boxes blank.
- You can calculate the amount of a monthly contribution to reach a savings goal without creating a whole worksheet—simply enter values rather than cell references as arguments for the PMT function. But using cell references makes it easy to play "what-if"—see how contributions change when the desired amount, rate, and number of periods changes. **Figure 54** shows an example.
- To force an outgoing cash flow to be expressed as a positive number, simply include a minus sign (-) right after the equals sign (=) at the beginning of the formula.

	A	B
1	Desired Amount	30000
2	Annual Interest Rate	8.25%
3	Months	120
4		
5	Monthly Contribution	

Figure 52 A basic structure for a worksheet to calculate contributions to reach a savings goal.

	A	B
1	Desired Amount	30000
2	Annual Interest Rate	8.25%
3	Months	120
4		
5	Monthly Contribution	($161.71)

Figure 53 The PMT function calculates the monthly contribution.

	A	B
1	Desired Amount	50000
2	Annual Interest Rate	8.25%
3	Months	120
4		
5	Monthly Contribution	($269.51)

Figure 54 Change one value and the result of the formula changes.

	A	B
1	Monthly Payment	150
2	Annual Interest Rate	8.50%
3	Number of Months	12
4		
5	Future Value	($1,871.81)
6		=FV(B@/12,B3,B1)
7		

Figure 55 Use the FV function to calculate the future value of constant cash flows, like those of periodic payroll savings deductions. The formula in cell *B5* is shown in cell *B6*.

	A	B
1	Initial Investment	-25000
2		
3	Monthly Cash In	200
4	Annual Interest Rate	9%
5	Number of Months	360
6		
7	Present Value	($24,856.37)
8		=PV(B4/12,B5,B3)
9		

Figure 56 This example uses the PV function to determine whether an investment is a good one. (It isn't, because the present value is less than the initial investment.) The formula in cell *B7* is shown in cell *B8*.

	A	B
1	Year 1	-500
2	Year 2	150
3	Year 3	100
4	Year 4	125
5	Year 5	135
6	Year 6	200
7		
8	Internal Rate of Return	12%
9		=IRR(B1:B6)
10		

Figure 57 This worksheet calculates the internal rate of return of an initial $500 investment that pays out cash over the next few years. The formula in cell *B8* is shown in cell *B9*.

The FV Function

The FV function (**Figure 55**) calculates the future value of an investment with constant cash flows and a constant interest rate. It uses the following syntax:

FV(rate,nper,pmt,pv,type)

Rate is the interest rate per period, nper is the total number of periods, and pmt is the amount of the periodic payments. These three arguments are required. The pv argument is the present value of the payments. Type indicates when payments are due: use 0 for payments at the end of the period and 1 for payments at the beginning of the period. If either optional argument is omitted, 0 is assumed.

The PV Function

The PV function (**Figure 56**) calculates the total amount that a series of payments in the future is worth now. It uses the following syntax:

PV(rate,nper,pmt,fv,type)

The rate, nper, pmt, and type arguments are the same in the FV function. Only the first three are required. The fv argument is the amount left after the payments have been made. If omitted, 0 is assumed.

The IRR Function

The IRR Function (**Figure 57**) calculates the internal rate of return for a series of periodic cash flows. It uses the following syntax:

IRR(values,guess)

The values argument, which is required, is a range of cells containing the cash flows. The guess argument, which is optional, is for your guess of what the result could be. Although seldom necessary, guess could help Excel come up with an answer when performing complex calculations.

Logical Functions

You can use Excel's logical functions to evaluate conditions and act accordingly. Here's the most useful one: IF.

The IF Function

The IF function evaluates a condition and returns one of two different values depending on whether the condition is met (true) or not met (false). It uses the following syntax:

IF(logical_test,value_if_true,value_if_false)

The logical_test argument is the condition you want to meet. This argument is required. The value_if_true and value_if_false arguments are the values to return if the condition is met or not met. If omitted, the values TRUE and FALSE are returned.

The following example uses the IF function to calculate commissions based on two different commission rates.

To use the IF function

1. Create a worksheet with text and number values as shown in **Figure 58**.
2. In cell *C6*, enter the following formula: *=IF(B6>400,$B$2*B6,$B$3*B6)*

   This formula begins by evaluating the sales amount to see if it's over $400. If it is, it moves to the value_if_true argument and multiplies the higher commission rate by the sales amount. If it isn't, it moves on to the value_if_false argument and multiplies the lower commission rate by the sales amount.
3. Press Enter or click the Enter button on the formula bar to complete the formula (**Figure 59**).
4. Use the fill handle to copy the formula down the column for the rest of the salespeople (**Figure 60**).

	A	B	C
1		Rates	
2	Over $400	15%	
3	Up to $400	10%	
4			
5		Sales	Amt. Due
6	John	443.16	
7	Jean	512.84	
8	Joe	328.69	
9	Joan	401.98	

Figure 58 To try the IF function for yourself, start with a basic worksheet like this one.

	A	B	C
1		Rates	
2	Over $400	15%	
3	Up to $400	10%	
4			
5		Sales	Amt. Due
6	John	443.16	66.47
7	Jean	512.84	
8	Joe	328.69	
9	Joan	401.98	

Figure 59 Enter the formula with the IF function in cell *C6*.

	A	B	C
1		Rates	
2	Over $400	15%	
3	Up to $400	10%	
4			
5		Sales	Amt. Due
6	John	443.16	66.47
7	Jean	512.84	76.93
8	Joe	328.69	32.87
9	Joan	401.98	60.3

Figure 60 Then use the fill handle to copy the formula to the other cells.

	A	B	C	D
1	Item Number:	L-108		
2	Price:	13.99	=VLOOKUP(B1,A5:D12,4,FALSE)	
3				
4	**Item Number**	**Qty**	**Item Name**	**Price**
5	D-439	159	Dogzilla	14.99
6	D-845	341	Delayed Impact	8.99
7	E-473	415	Eisenhower	19.99
8	G-058	167	Genus II	19.99
9	L-108	684	Loaded Weapon IV	13.99
10	M-400	218	Men in White	22.99
11	M-482	189	Mask of Zero	24.99
12	O-571	581	Oceanic	15.99
13				

Figure 61 This example illustrates the VLOOKUP function. When you enter an item number in cell *B1*, the formula in *B2* attempts to match it to a value in the first column of the lookup table below it (*A5:D12*). If it finds a match, it returns the value in the fourth column of the same row as the match. The formula in cell *B2* is shown in cell *C2*.

	A	B	C	D
1	Item Number:	M-15		
2	Price:	#N/A	=VLOOKUP(B1,A5:D12,4,FALSE)	
3				
4	**Item Number**	**Qty**	**Item Name**	**Price**
5	D-439	159	Dogzilla	14.99
6	D-045	341	Delayed Impact	8.99
7	E-473	415	Eisenhower	19.99
8	G-058	167	Genus II	19.99
9	L-108	684	Loaded Weapon IV	13.99
10	M-400	218	Men In White	22.99
11	M-482	189	Mask of Zero	24.99
12	O-571	581	Oceanic	15.99
13				

Figure 62 If the formula in *B2* doesn't find a match, it returns the *#N/A* error value, since the optional range_lookup argument is set to *FALSE*.

Lookup and Reference Functions

Excel's lookup and reference functions return values based on information stored elsewhere in the workbook or in a linked worksheet.

The VLOOKUP & HLOOKUP Functions

The VLOOKUP (**Figures 61** and **62**) and HLOOKUP functions return information based on data stored in a *lookup table*—a range of cells containing lookup and result values. The function attempts to match a value in one of its arguments to values in the first column (VLOOKUP) or first row (HLOOKUP) of the lookup table. If it finds a match, it returns the associated value.

The VLOOKUP and HLOOKUP functions use the following syntax:

VLOOKUP(lookup_value,table_array, col_index_num,range_lookup)

HLOOKUP(lookup_value,table_array, row_index_num,range_lookup)

Lookup_value is the value you want to match in the table. Table_array is the range reference for the lookup table. Col_index_num or row_index_num is the number of the column or row, relative to the table, that contains the values you want returned. These three arguments are required. Range_lookup, which is not required, tells Excel what it should do if it can't match the lookup_value. There are two options for this argument: TRUE tells Excel to return the value associated with the next lowest value; FALSE tells Excel to return the #N/A error value. If omitted, TRUE is assumed.

✔ Tip

- The first column or row of the lookup table must be sorted in ascending order for the VLOOKUP or HLOOKUP function to work properly.

Information Functions

Excel's information functions return information about other cells.

The IS Functions

Excel's IS functions (**Figure 63**) use the following syntax:

ISBLANK(value)

ISERR(value)

ISERROR(value)

ISLOGICAL(value)

ISNA(value)

ISNONTEXT(value)

ISNUMBER(value)

ISREF(value)

ISTEXT(value)

In each case, Excel tests for a different thing. The value argument is the value or cell reference to be tested.

✔ Tip

- Use an IS function in conjunction with the IF function to return a value based on the condition of a cell (**Figures 64** and **65**).

	A	B	C	D	E
1	Values / Test	673.24	anchovy		#N/A
2	Blank Cell	FALSE	FALSE	TRUE	FALSE
3	Error other than #N/A	FALSE	FALSE	FALSE	FALSE
4	Any Error	FALSE	FALSE	FALSE	TRUE
5	Logical Value	FALSE	FALSE	FALSE	FALSE
6	#N/A Error	FALSE	FALSE	FALSE	TRUE
7	Not Text	TRUE	FALSE	TRUE	TRUE
8	Number	TRUE	FALSE	FALSE	FALSE
9	Cell Reference	TRUE	TRUE	TRUE	TRUE
10	Text	FALSE	TRUE	FALSE	FALSE

Figure 63 In this example, the IS functions were used to evaluate the contents of the cells in row *1* of the worksheet. The results of each function appear below the value.

	A	B
1	**Enter Your Name:**	
2		
3	**Message:**	You did not enter your name.

Figures 64 & 65 In this silly example, the formula in cell B3, =IF(ISTEXT(B1),"Hello "&B1,"You did not enter your name."), scolds the user for not entering a name (above), then greets her by name when she does enter it (below).

	A	B
1	**Enter Your Name:**	Maria
2		
3	**Message:**	Hello Maria

Table 1

How Excel Interprets Dates and Times

You Enter	Excel "Sees"
10/15/00	35352
6/30/61	21000
2:45 PM	0.61458333
10:02:56 AM	0.4187037
1/1/1900	0
12:00 AM	0

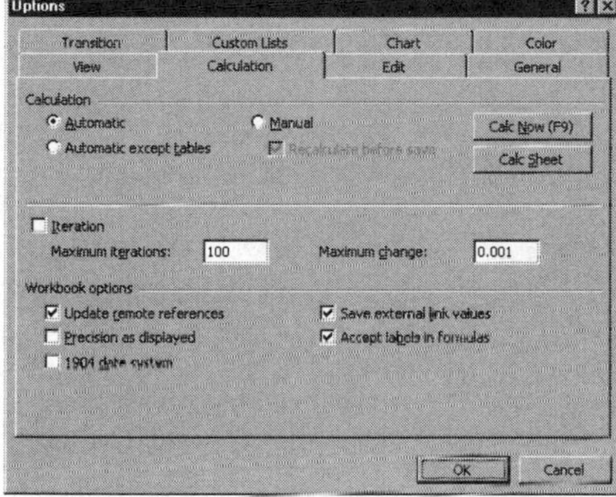

Figure 66 The Options dialog box enables you to switch between the Windows 1900 date system and the Mac OS 1904 date system.

Date and Time Functions

Excel's date and time functions are designed specifically to work with dates and times. I tell you about the most useful ones here.

✔ Tips

- Excel treats dates and times as serial numbers. This means that although you may enter information as a date or time—like 10/15/00 or 2:45 PM—Excel converts what you type into a number for its own internal use (**Table 1**). A date is the number of days since January 1, 1900. A time is the portion of a day since midnight. Excel's formatting makes the number look like a date or time. I tell you about cell formatting in **Chapter 6**.
- You can change Excel's date system from the Windows 1900 system to the Mac OS 1904 system. Choose Tools > Options, click the Calculation tab in the Options dialog box that appears (**Figure 66**), and turn on the 1904 date system check box. This will change the serial numbers for dates for all worksheets in the current workbook, thus enhancing compatibility with Mac OS spreadsheet programs. I tell you more about the Options dialog box in **Chapter 13**.
- Excel is Year 2000-ready. In fact, if you enter a date early in the 21st century, such as *5/15/03*, Excel assumes the year is 2003, not 1903. To ensure that Excel always has the right year for a date, be sure to enter all four digits of the year number.

The DATE Function

The DATE function (**Figure 3**) returns the serial number for a date. It uses the following syntax:

=DATE(year,month,day)

The year argument is the year number, the month argument is the month number, and the day argument is the day number. All arguments are required.

To calculate the number of days between two dates

Enter the two dates into separate cells of a worksheet, then write a formula using the subtraction operator (-) to subtract the earlier date from the later date (**Figure 67**).

or

In a worksheet cell, write a formula using the date function, like this:
=DATE(2000,10,15)-DATE(1999,5,8)

	A	B
1	First Date	5/8/99
2	Second Date	10/15/00
3	Days Between	526
4		=B2-B1

Figure 67 Calculating the number of days between two dates is as simple as subtracting the contents of one cell from another. The formula in cell *B3* is shown in cell *B4*.

2/14/00 14:37	=NOW()
2/14/00	=TODAY()

Figure 68 The NOW function returns the current date and time while the TODAY function returns just the current date.

The NOW & TODAY Functions

The NOW and TODAY functions (**Figure 68**) return the serial number for the current date and time (NOW) or current date (TODAY). Results are automatically formatted and will change each time the worksheet is recalculated or opened. They use the following syntax:

NOW()

TODAY()

Although there are no arguments, the parentheses characters must be included.

The DAY, WEEKDAY, MONTH, & YEAR Functions

The DAY, WEEKDAY, MONTH, and YEAR functions (**Figure 69**) return the day of the month, the day of the week, the month number, or the year number for a serial number. They use the following syntax:

DAY(serial_number)

WEEKDAY(serial_number)

MONTH(serial_number)

YEAR(serial_number)

The serial_number argument can be a cell reference, number, or date written as text, like *10/15/00* or *15-Apr-04*.

	A	B	C
1		**6/30/01**	
2	Day	30	=DAY(B1)
3	Weekday	7	=WEEKDAY(B1)
4	Month	6	=MONTH(B1)
5	Year	2001	=YEAR(B1)

Figure 69 The DAY, WEEKDAY, MONTH, and YEAR functions extract portions of a date. The formulas in column *B* are shown in column *C*.

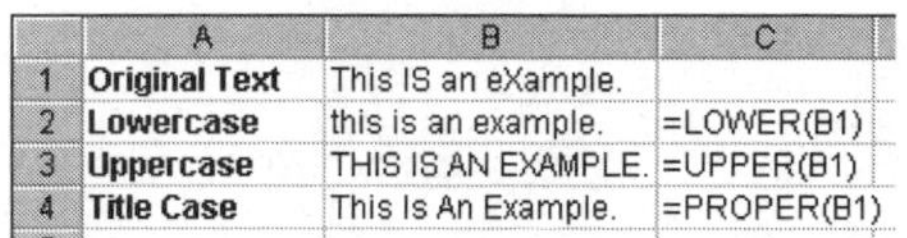

	A	B	C
1	**Original Text**	This IS an eXample.	
2	**Lowercase**	this is an example.	=LOWER(B1)
3	**Uppercase**	THIS IS AN EXAMPLE.	=UPPER(B1)
4	**Title Case**	This Is An Example.	=PROPER(B1)

Figure 70 Use the LOWER, UPPER, and PROPER functions to change the case of text. The formulas in column *B* are shown in column *C*.

	A	B	C
1	**Original Text**	Mississippi	
2	**First 4 characters**	Miss	=LEFT(B1,4)
3	**Last 4 characters**	ippi	=RIGHT(B1,4)
4	**4 characters starting with 3rd character**	ssis	=MID(B1,3,4)

Figure 71 Use the LEFT, RIGHT, and MID functions to extract characters from text. The formulas in column *B* are shown in column *C*.

Text Functions

Excel's text functions enable you to extract, convert, concatenate, and get information about text. I tell you about a few of the more commonly used ones here.

The LOWER, UPPER, & PROPER Functions

The LOWER, UPPER, and PROPER functions (**Figure 70**) convert text to lowercase, uppercase, and title case. They use the following syntax:

LOWER(text)

UPPER(text)

PROPER(text)

The text argument, which is required, is the text you want converted.

The LEFT, RIGHT, & MID Functions

The LEFT, RIGHT, and MID functions (**Figure 71**) return the leftmost, rightmost, or middle characters of a text string. They use the following syntax:

LEFT(text,num_chars)

RIGHT(text,num_chars)

MID(text,start_num,num_chars)

The text argument, which is required, is the text from which characters should be extracted. The num_chars argument is the number of characters you want extracted. If omitted from the LEFT or RIGHT function, 1 is assumed. The MID function has an additional argument, start_num, which is the number of the first character from which you want to extract text. The MID function requires all arguments.

The CONCATENATE Function

The CONCATENATE function (**Figure 72**) joins or concatenates two or more strings of text. It uses the following syntax:

CONCATENATE(text1,text2,...)

Each text argument can include single cell references, text, or numbers you want to join. The CONCATENATE function can accept up to 30 arguments, but only two are required.

✔ Tips

- Excel recognizes the ampersand character (&) as a concatenation operator in formulas. You can concatenate text by including an ampersand between cells or text strings in a formula, like this: *=B2&" "&A2*
- If you want spaces between the strings, be sure to include the space character, between double quote characters, as an argument (**Figure 72**).
- Creative use of the CONCATENATE function or operator makes it possible to give documents a personal touch. **Figure 73** shows an example.

	A	B	C
1	Last Name	First Name	Full Name
2	Twain	Mark	Twain Mark
3			=CONCATENATE(A2," ",B2)

Figure 72 Use the CONCATENATE function to join strings of text. The formula in cell *C2* is shown in cell *C3*.

	A	B	C	D
1	Amount Due	124.95		
2	Date Due	8/16/98		
3				
4	The total amount due is $124.95. Please pay by 08/16/98.			

Figure 73 The formula in cell *A4*, *="The total due is "&DOLLAR(B1)&". Please pay by "&TEXT(B2,"mm/dd/yy")&"."*, writes a sentence using the contents of two cells, the concatenate operator, and two text functions.

Formatting Worksheet Cells

Southwest Division				
First Quarter Sales				
	January	February	March	Total
John	1254	1256	2435	4945
Jean	1865	1736	1905	5506
Joe	1614	1284	2509	5407
Joan	1987	1908	2890	6785
Totals	6720	6184	9739	22643

Figure 1 While content should be more important than appearance, you can bet that this worksheet won't get as much attention...

Southwest Division				
First Quarter Sales				
	January	February	March	Total
John	$ 1,254	$ 1,256	$ 2,435	$ 4,945
Jean	1,865	1,736	1,905	5,506
Joe	1,614	1,284	2,509	5,407
Joan	1,987	1,908	2,890	6,785
Totals	$ 6,720	$ 6,184	$ 9,739	$ 22,643

Figure 2 ...as this one.

Formatting Basics

To paraphrase an old Excel mentor of mine, formatting a worksheet is like putting on its makeup. The worksheet's contents may be perfectly correct, but by applying formatting, you can increase its impact to make an impression on the people who see it (**Figures 1** and **2**).

Excel offers a wide range of formatting options you can use to beautify your worksheets:

- **Number formatting** lets you change the appearance of numbers, dates, and times.
- **Alignment** lets you change the way cell contents are aligned within the cell.
- **Font formatting** lets you change the appearance of text and number characters.
- **Borders** let you add lines around cells.
- **Patterns** let you add color, shading, and patterns to cells.
- **Column and row formatting** let you change column width and row height.

You can apply formatting to cells using a variety of techniques: with toolbar buttons, shortcut keys, menu commands, or the Conditional Formatting or AutoFormat features.

✔ Tip

- Excel may automatically apply formatting to cells, depending on what you enter. For example, if you use a date function, Excel formats the results of the function as a date. You can change Excel's formatting at any time to best meet your needs.

Number Formatting

By default, Excel applies the General number format to numerical values entered in worksheet cells. This format displays numbers just as they're entered (**Figure 3**).

1548.36
12458
14.2
-354.85
116.028
0.2
12563587695

Figure 3 General formatting displays the numbers just as they're typed in.

Excel offers a wide variety of predefined number formatting options for different purposes:

- **Number** formats are used for general number display.
- **Currency** formats are used for monetary values.
- **Accounting** formats are used to line up columns of monetary values.
- **Date** formats are used to display dates.
- **Time** formats are used to display times.
- **Percentage** formats are used to display percentages.
- **Fraction** formats are used to display decimal values as fractions.
- **Scientific** format is used to display values in scientific notation.
- **Text** format is used to display cell contents as text, the way it was entered.
- **Special** formats include a variety of special purpose formatting options.
- **Custom** lets you create your own number format using formatting codes.

You can change number formatting with toolbar buttons or the Format Cells dialog box.

Number 1	1.5049	$ 1.50
Number 2	3.504	$ 3.50
Total	5.0089	$ 5.01

Figure 4 The two columns contain identical values, but the column on the right is formatted with the Currency style. Because Excel performs calculations with the numbers underlying any formatting, the total on the right appears incorrect!

General	0.15	163.2	-12.785
Currency	$ 0.15	$ 163.20	$ (12.79)
Percent	15%	16320%	-1279%
Comma	0.15	163.20	(12.79)
Increase Decimal	0.150	163.200	-12.785
Decrease Decimal	0.2	163.2	-12.8

Figure 5 Three different numbers, each with one of the Formatting toolbar's number formats applied.

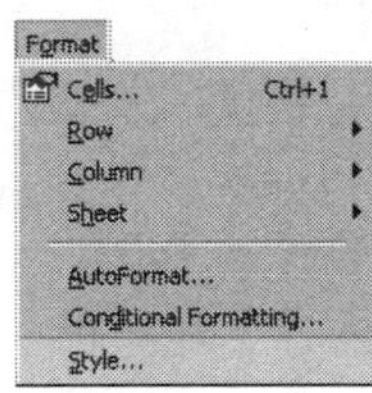

Figure 6 The Format menu offers access to most of the formatting commands discussed in this chapter.

✔ Tips

- If the integer part of a number is longer than the width of the cell, Excel automatically resizes the column so it will fit.
- Number formatting changes only the appearance of a number. Although formatting may remove decimal places from displayed numbers, it does not round numbers. **Figure 4** illustrates this. Use the ROUND function, which I discuss in **Chapter 5**, to round numbers in formulas.
- If you include characters like dollar signs or percent symbols with a number you enter, Excel automatically assigns an appropriate built-in format to the cell.

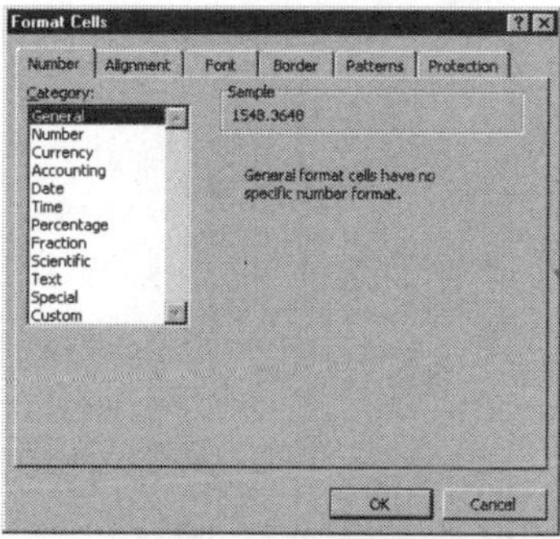

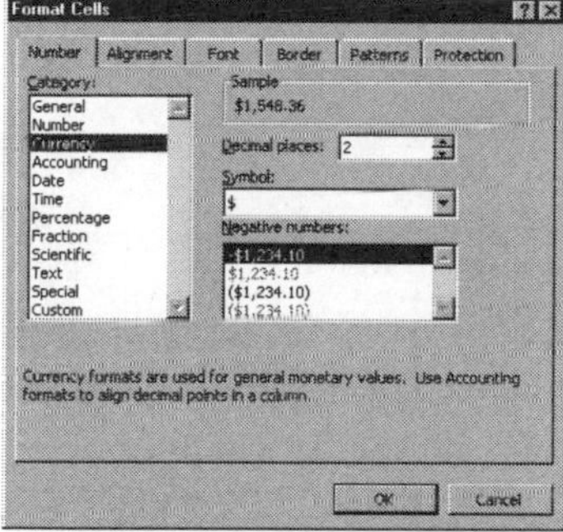

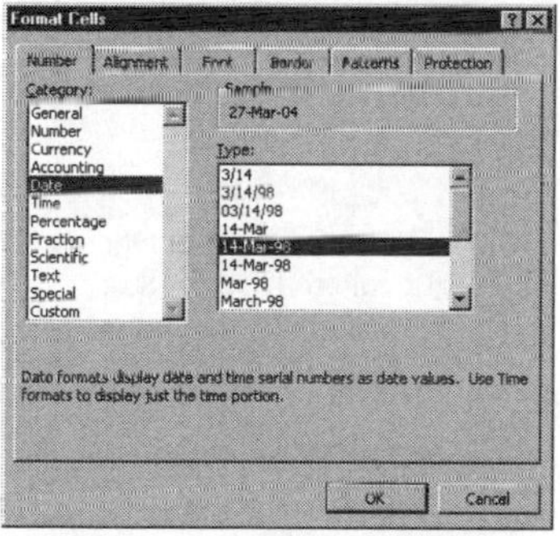

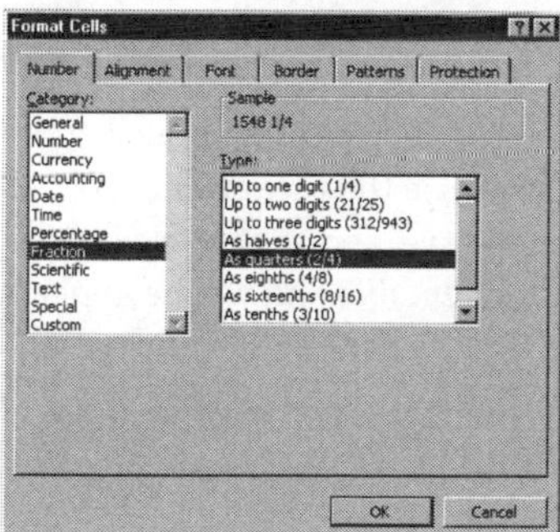

Figures 7, 8, 9, & 10 Examples of options in the Number tab of the Format Cells dialog box.

To format numbers with toolbar buttons

1. Select the cell(s) containing the number(s) you want to format.
2. Click the Formatting toolbar button for the number format you want to apply:
   - ▲ **Currency Style** $ displays the number as currency, with a dollar sign, commas, and two decimal places.
   - ▲ **Percent Style** % displays the number as a percentage with a percent symbol.
   - ▲ **Comma Style** , displays the number with commas and two decimal places.
   - ▲ **Increase Decimal** displays an additional digit after the decimal point.
   - ▲ **Decrease Decimal** displays one less digit after the decimal point.

   Figure 5 shows examples of these formats.

To format numbers with the Format Cells dialog box

1. Select the cell(s) containing the number(s) you want to format.
2. Choose Format > Cells (**Figure 6**) or press Ctrl 1.
3. In the Format Cells dialog box that appears, click the Number tab to display its options (**Figure 7**).
4. Choose a number format category from the Category scrolling list.
5. Set options in the dialog box. The options vary for each category; **Figures 8, 9**, and **10** show examples. Check the Sample area to see the number in the active cell with the formatting options you selected applied.
6. Click OK to apply the formatting.

Alignment

Excel offers a wide variety of options to set the way characters are positioned within a cell (**Figure 11**):

- **Text alignment** controls the alignment of cell contents in relation to the edge of a cell:
  - **Horizontal** positions the text between the left and right sides of the cell or selection.
  - **Vertical** positions the text between the top and bottom of the cell.
  - **Indent** determines the amount of space between the cell contents and the left side of the cell.
- **Orientation** controls the angle at which text appears within the cell.
- **Text control** offers other options for text in cells:
  - **Wrap text** allows word wrap between the cell's left and right sides. (This may increase the height of the cell's row.)
  - **Shrink to fit** reduces the size of characters to fit within the cell.
  - **Merge cells** combines multiple selected cells into one cell.

You can change alignment options with toolbar buttons or the Format Cells dialog box.

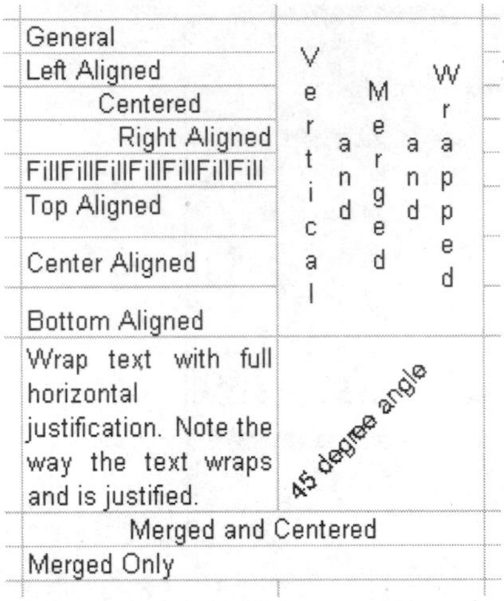

General	Vertical / Merged and / Wrapped and
Left Aligned	
Centered	
Right Aligned	
FillFillFillFillFillFillFill	
Top Aligned	
Center Aligned	
Bottom Aligned	
Wrap text with full horizontal justification. Note the way the text wraps and is justified.	45 degree angle
Merged and Centered	
Merged Only	

Figure 11 Examples of cells with different alignment options applied.

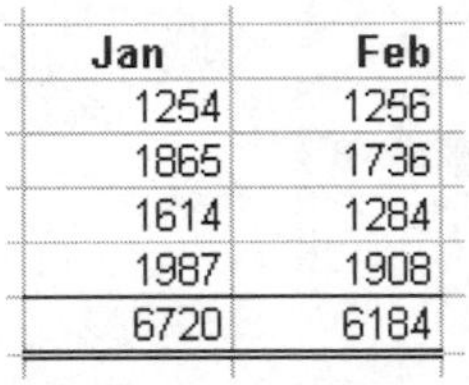

Jan	Feb
1254	1256
1865	1736
1614	1284
1987	1908
6720	6184

Figure 12 Headings sometimes look better when they're right aligned (right column) rather than centered (left column) over columns of numbers.

✔ Tips

- By default, within each cell, Excel left aligns text and right aligns numbers. This is called General alignment.
- Although it's common to center headings over columns containing numbers, the worksheet may actually look better with headings right aligned. **Figure 12** shows an example.
- Alignment is applied to cells, not cell contents. If you use the Clear Contents command or Delete shortcut to clear a cell, the formatting remains and will be applied to whatever data is next entered into it. I tell you about the Clear Contents command in **Chapter 3**.

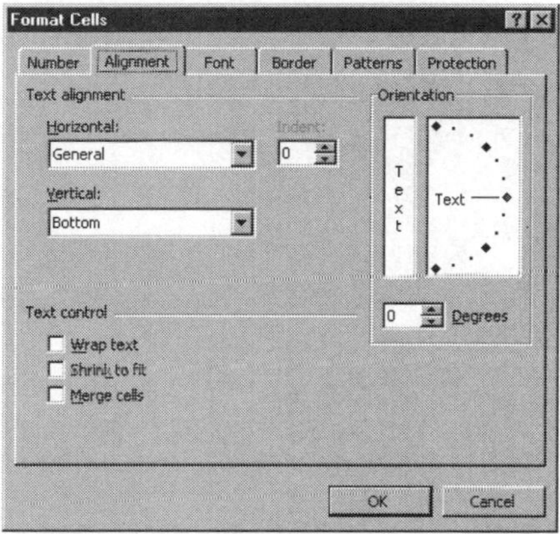

Figure 13 The Alignment tab of the Format Cells dialog box.

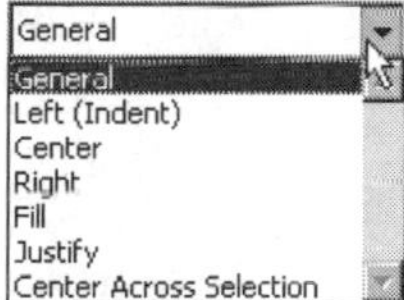

Figure 14 Options on the Horizontal menu.

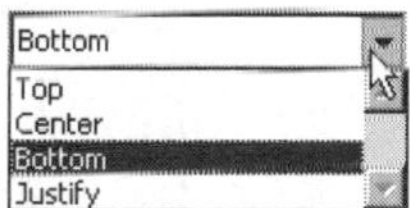

Figure 15 Options on the Vertical menu.

To align cell contents with toolbar buttons

1. Select the cell(s) whose contents you want to align.
2. Click the Formatting toolbar button for the alignment you want to apply:
   - ▲ **Align Left** aligns cell contents against the left side of the cell.
   - ▲ **Center** centers cell contents between the left and right sides of the cell.
   - ▲ **Align Right** aligns cell contents against the right side of the cell.

   The cell contents shift accordingly.

To align cell contents with the Format Cells dialog box

1. Select the cell(s) whose contents you want to align.
2. Choose Format > Cells (**Figure 6**) or press Ctrl 1.
3. The Format Cells dialog box appears. If necessary, click the Alignment tab to display its options (**Figure 13**).
4. Select options from the Horizontal (**Figure 14**) and Vertical (**Figure 15**) menus to set alignment as desired.
5. Click OK.

To indent cell contents

1. Select the cell(s) whose contents you want to indent (**Figure 16**).
2. Click one of the indentation buttons on the Formatting toolbar:
   - ▲ **Decrease Indent** reduces the amount of indentation.
   - ▲ **Increase Indent** increases the amount of indentation.

or

1. Select the cell(s) whose contents you want to indent (**Figure 16**).
2. Choose Format > Cells (**Figure 6**) or press Ctrl 1.
3. In the Format Cells dialog box, click the Alignment tab (**Figure 13**).
4. Choose Left (Indent) from the Horizontal menu (**Figure 14**).
5. In the Indent text box, enter the number of characters by which you want to indent cell contents (**Figure 17**).
6. Click OK.

The cell's contents are indented (**Figure 18**).

	A	B
1	Southwest Division	
2	First Quarter Sales	
3		January
4	John	$ 1,254
5	Jean	1,865
6	Joe	1,614
7	Joan	1,987
8	Totals	$ 6,720

Figure 16 Select the cell whose contents you want to indent.

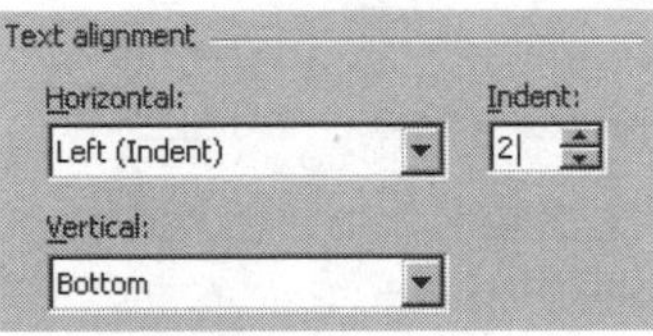

Figure 17 To indent text, set Text alignment options like this.

	A	B
1	Southwest Division	
2	First Quarter Sales	
3		January
4	John	$ 1,254
5	Jean	1,865
6	Joe	1,614
7	Joan	1,987
8	Totals	$ 6,720

Figure 18 The cell's contents are indented.

	A	B	C	D	E
1	Southwest Division				
2	First Quarter Sales				
3		January	February	March	Total
4	John	$ 1,254	$ 1,256	$ 2,435	$ 4,945

Figure 19 Select the cells you want to merge and center.

	A	B	C	D	E
1			Southwest Division		
2	First Quarter Sales				
3		January	February	March	Total
4	John	$ 1,254	$ 1,256	$ 2,435	$ 4,945

Figure 20 The cells are merged together and the cell contents are centered in the merged cell.

To merge & center cells

1. Select the cell(s) whose contents you want to center, along with the cells of the columns to the right that you want to center across (**Figure 19**).
2. Click the Merge and Center button on the Formatting toolbar.

or

1. Select the cell(s) whose contents you want to center, along with the cells of the columns to the right that you want to center across (**Figure 19**).
2. Choose Format > Cells (**Figure 6**) or press Ctrl 1.
3. In the Format Cells dialog box, click the Alignment tab (**Figure 13**).
4. Choose Center from the Horizontal menu (**Figure 14**).
5. Turn on the Merge cells check box.
6. Click OK.

The cell contents shift so they're centered between the left and right sides of the selected area (**Figure 20**).

✔ Tip

- You can get similar results by choosing Center Across Selection from the Horizontal menu (**Figure 14**) in step 4 and skipping step 5. The cells, however, are not merged, so an entry into one of the adjacent cells could obscure the centered contents.

To change the orientation or rotation of cell contents

1. Select the cell(s) whose orientation you want to change (**Figure 21**).
2. Choose Format > Cells (**Figure 6**) or press Ctrl 1.
3. In the Format Cells dialog box, click the Alignment tab (**Figure 13**).
4. Set Options in the Orientation area (**Figure 22**) using one of these methods:
   - ▲ To display text characters one above the other, click the Vertical Orientation button.
   - ▲ To display text characters at an angle, drag the red diamond in the rotation area to match the angle you want or enter an angle value in the Degrees box.
5. Click OK.

   The cell's contents change orientation (**Figure 23**). If necessary, the entire row's height changes to accommodate the shifted characters.

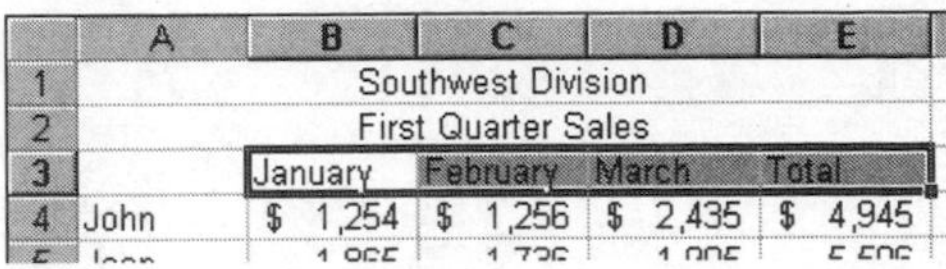

Figure 21 Select the cells for which you want to change orientation.

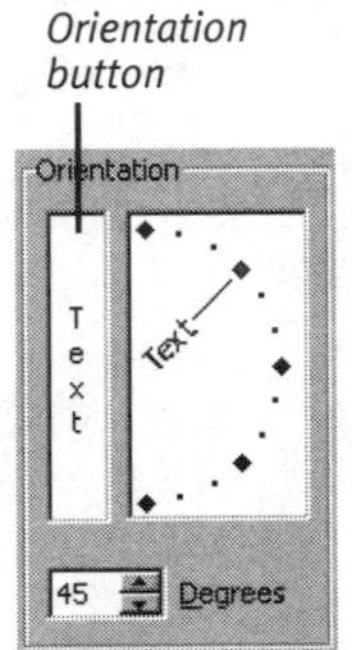

Figure 22 Set options using the orientation area of the Format Cells dialog box.

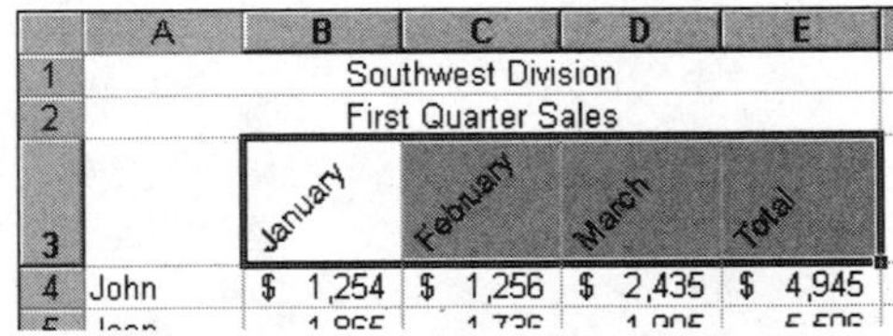

Figure 23 The orientation of selected cells changes.

✔ Tips

- You cannot set orientation options if Center Across Selection is chosen from the Horizontal menu (**Figure 14**). Choose another option before you set orientation.
- You can enter either a positive or negative value in the Degrees box (**Figure 22**).
- Rotated text appears much better when printed than it does on screen.
- Rotating the text in column headings often enables you to decrease column width, thus enabling you to fit more information on screen or on paper. I tell you how to change column width later in this chapter.

To fit cell contents within a cell

1. Select the cell(s) whose contents you want to fit within the cell (**Figure 24**).
2. Choose Format > Cells (**Figure 6**) or press Ctrl 1.
3. In the Format Cells dialog box, click the Alignment tab (**Figure 13**).
4. Turn on one of the following check boxes:
   - ▲ **Wrap text** forces word wrap to occur within the cell. This increases the row height (**Figure 25**).
   - ▲ **Shrink to fit** reduces the size of font characters to squeeze them into the cell. This may make cell contents difficult to read (**Figure 26**).
5. Click OK.

Figure 24 Select a cell whose contents do not fit in the cell.

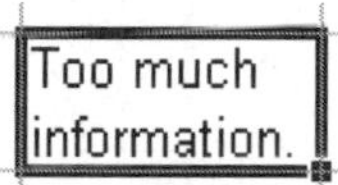

Figure 25 Here's the cell from Figure 24 with Wrap text applied.

Figure 26 Here's the cell from Figure 24 with Shrink to fit applied.

✔ Tips

- To benefit from either of these options, the text within the cell must be too wide to fit into the cell. I tell you how to change column width and row height later in this chapter.
- You cannot use the Wrap text and Shrink to fit options together.

To merge cells

1. Select the cells you want to merge into one cell.
2. Choose Format > Cells (**Figure 6**) or press Ctrl 1.
3. In the Format Cells dialog box, click the Alignment tab (**Figure 13**).
4. Turn on the Merge cells check box.
5. Click OK.
6. If more than one of the cells is not empty, Excel warns you that only the upper-left cell will retain its data (**Figure 27**). If this is OK, click OK to merge the cells. Otherwise, click Cancel and reconsider the merge.

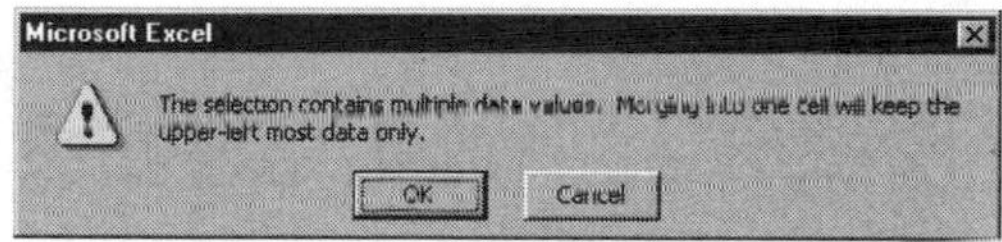

Figure 27 Excel warns you when merging cells could result in data loss.

✔ Tip

- The cell reference for merged cells is the cell reference for the upper-left cell in the original selection.

Font Formatting

Excel uses 10 point Arial as the default font or typeface for worksheets. You can apply a variety of font formatting options to cells, some of which are shown in **Figure 28**:

- **Font** is the typeface used to display characters. This includes all fonts properly installed in your system.
- **Font style** is the weight or angle of characters. Options usually include Regular, Bold, Italic, and Bold Italic.
- **Size** is the size of characters, expressed in points. (A point is 1/72 inch.)
- **Underline** is character underlining. Don't confuse this with borders, which can be applied to the bottom of a cell, regardless of its contents.
- **Color** is character color.
- **Effects** are special effects applied to characters.

You can apply font formatting with toolbar buttons, shortcut keys, and the Format Cells dialog box.

✔ Tip

- You can change the formatting of individual characters within a cell by double-clicking the cell to make it active, selecting the characters you want to change (**Figure 29**), and then using the appropriate font formatting technique to change the characters (**Figure 30**).

	A	B	C	D	E
1	Southwest Division				
2	First Quarter Sales				
3		*January*	*February*	*March*	*Total*
4	John	$ 1,254	$ 1,256	$ 2,435	$ 4,945
5	Jean	1,865	1,736	1,905	5,506
6	Joe	1,614	1,284	2,509	5,407
7	Joan	1,987	1,908	2,890	6,785
8	Totals	$ 6,720	$ 6,184	$ 9,739	$ 22,643

Figure 28 This example shows font, font size, and font style applied to the contents of some cells.

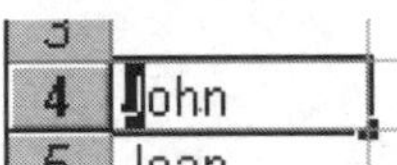

Figure 29 You can also select individual characters within a cell...

Figure 30 ...and apply formatting to them.

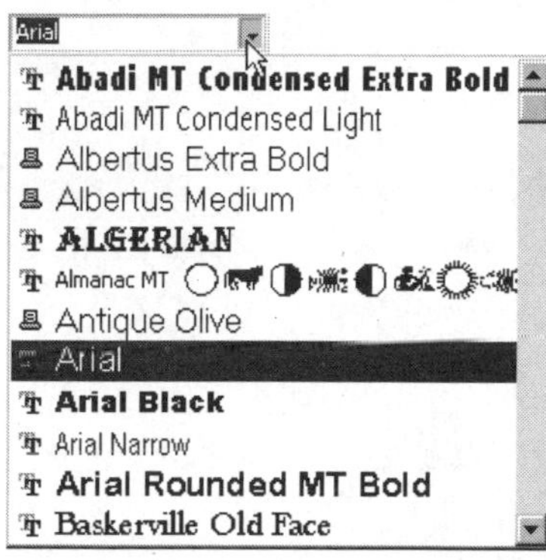

Figure 31 The Font menu on the Formatting toolbar lists all of the fonts properly installed in your system.

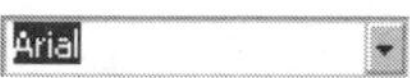

Figure 32 Click the font name to select it...

Figure 33 ...then type in the name of the font that you want to apply.

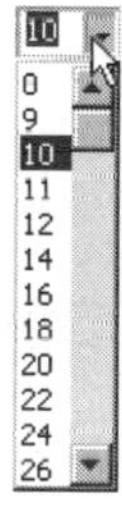

Figure 34 You can choose a font size from the Font Size menu on the Formatting toolbar...

Figure 35 ...or enter any size you like in the Font Size box.

To change a font with the Formatting toolbar

1. Select the cell(s) or character(s) whose font you want to change.
2. Click on the arrow beside the Font box on the Formatting toolbar to display a menu of all fonts installed in your system (**Figure 31**) and choose the font you want to apply.

   or

   Click on the Font box to select its contents (**Figure 32**), type in the name of the font you want to apply (**Figure 33**), and press Enter.

   The font you chose is applied to the selected cell(s).

To change font size with the Formatting toolbar

1. Select the cell(s) or character(s) whose font size you want to change.
2. Click on the arrow beside the Font Size box on the Formatting toolbar to display a menu of sizes (**Figure 34**) and choose the size you want to apply.

   or

   Click on the Font Size box to select its contents, type in a size (**Figure 35**), and press Enter.

   The font size you chose is applied to the selected cell(s).

✔ Tip

- Font size must be between 1 and 409 points in half-point increments.

To change font style with the Formatting toolbar or shortcut keys

1. Select the cell(s) whose font style you want to change.
2. Click the Formatting toolbar button for the style you want to apply:
   - ▲ **Bold** **B** (or Ctrl B) makes characters in the selected cell(s) appear in a bold style.
   - ▲ **Italic** *I* (or Ctrl I) makes characters in the selected cell(s) appear in an italic style.
   - ▲ **Underline** U (or Ctrl U) puts a single underline under characters in the selected cell(s).
3. The button you click turns dark to indicate that it's selected and the formatting changes accordingly.

✔ Tips

- You can apply more than one style to selected cells or characters.
- Use border formatting or accounting underlines rather than the Underline button to put lines at the bottom of columns being totalled. I tell you about border formatting and accounting underlines later in this chapter.

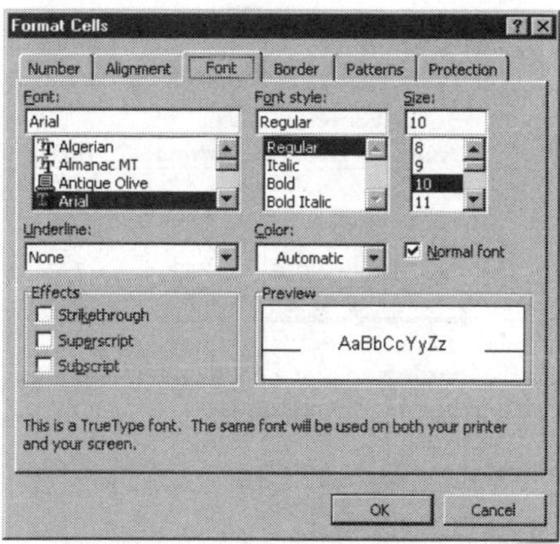

Figure 36 The Font tab of the Format Cells dialog box.

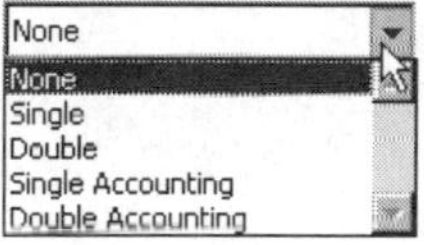

Figure 37 Excel offers several underlining options.

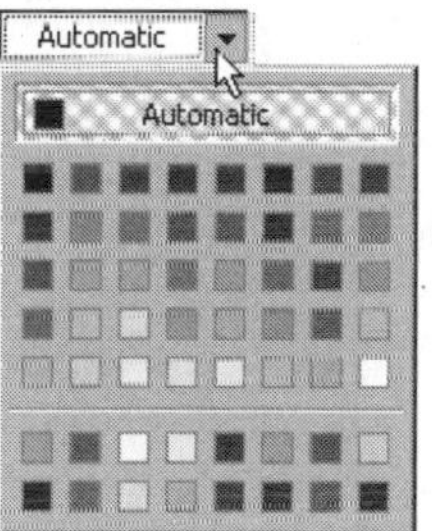

Figure 38 The Color menu in the Format Cells dialog box...

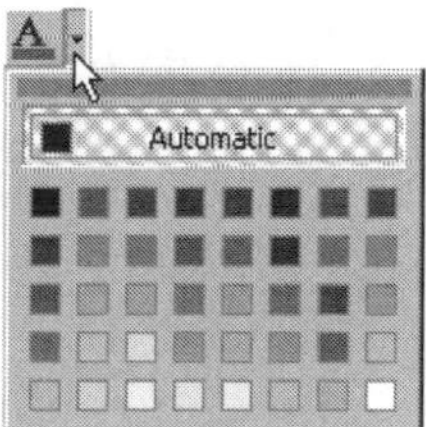

Figure 39 ...and the Font Color menu on the Formatting toolbar offer two ways to apply color to font characters.

To change font formatting with the Format Cells dialog box

1. Select the cell(s) or character(s) whose font you want to change.
2. Choose Format > Cells (**Figure 6**) or press Ctrl 1.
3. In the Format Cells dialog box that appears, click the Font tab to display its options (**Figure 36**).
4. Set options as desired:
   - ▲ Select a font from the Font list or type a font name into the box above the list.
   - ▲ Select a style from the Font style list or type a style name into the box above the list.
   - ▲ Select a size from the Size list or type a size into the box above the list.
   - ▲ Choose an underline option from the Underline menu (**Figure 37**).
   - ▲ Choose a font color from the Color menu (**Figure 38**).
   - ▲ Turn on check boxes in the Effects area to apply font effects.
5. When the sample text in the Preview area looks just the way you want, click OK.

✔ Tips

- To return a selection to the default font, turn on the Normal font check box in the Format Cells dialog box (**Figure 36**).
- The accounting underline options in the Underline menu (**Figure 37**) stretch almost the entire width of the cell.
- The Automatic color option in the Color menu (**Figure 38**) allows color to be determined by other formatting options.
- You can also change font color with the Font Color menu on the Formatting toolbar (**Figure 39**).

Borders

Excel offers a number of different border styles that you can apply to separate cells or a selection of cells (**Figure 40**). Use the Formatting toolbar or the Format Cells dialog box to add borders.

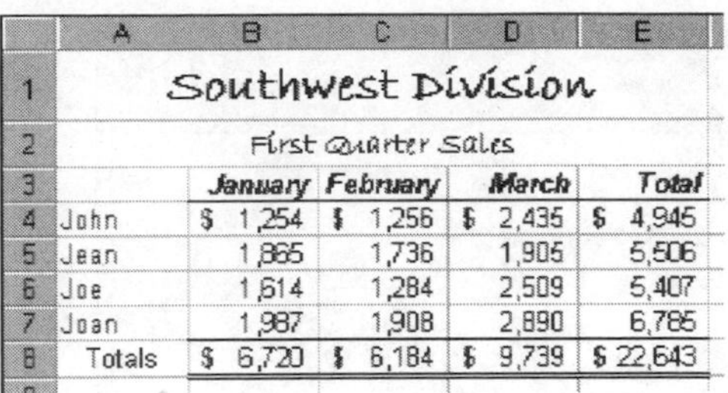

	A	B	C	D	E
1	Southwest Division				
2	First Quarter Sales				
3		*January*	*February*	*March*	*Total*
4	John	$ 1,254	$ 1,256	$ 2,435	$ 4,945
5	Jean	1,865	1,736	1,905	5,506
6	Joe	1,614	1,284	2,509	5,407
7	Joan	1,987	1,908	2,890	6,785
8	Totals	$ 6,720	$ 6,184	$ 9,739	$ 22,643

Figure 40 Use borders to place lines under headings and above and below column totals.

To add borders with the Borders button

1. Select the cell(s) to which you want to add borders.
2. Click on the Borders button on the Formatting toolbar to apply the border style illustrated on the button.

   or

   Click on the triangle on the right side of the Borders button on the Formatting toolbar to display a menu of border styles (**Figure 41**) and choose the style you want.

   The border is applied.

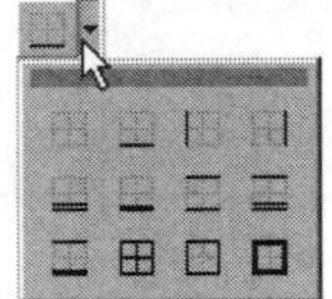

Figure 41 The Borders menu on the Formatting toolbar.

✔ Tips

- Most border styles on the Borders menu apply borders to each cell in the selection. The last two styles apply borders around just the outside of the selection.
- The Borders button displays the last border selection you made from the Borders menu, making it easy to apply the same border style again.
- To remove borders from a selection, choose the first (top left) border style. If the border does not disappear, it may be applied to a cell adjoining the one you selected.
- The underline options on the Underline menu in the Format Cells dialog box (**Figure 37**) are not the same as borders. They do not stretch the entire width of the cell and they only appear when the cell is not blank.

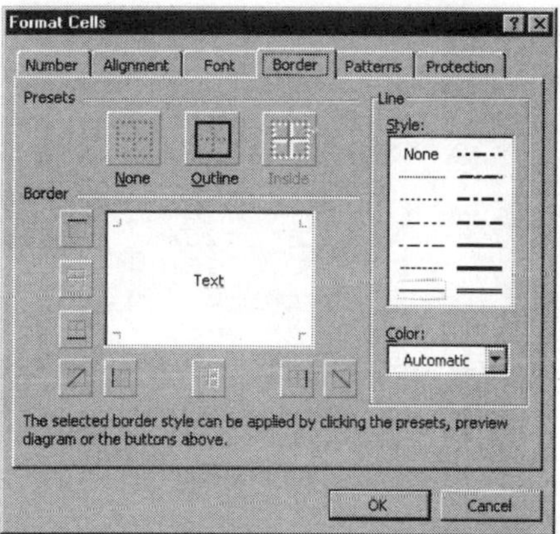

Figure 42 The Border tab of the Format Cells dialog box.

To add borders with the Format Cells dialog box

1. Select the cell(s) to which you want to add borders.
2. Choose Format > Cells (**Figure 6**) or press Ctrl 1.
3. In the Format Cells dialog box that appears, click the Border tab to display its options (**Figure 42**).
4. Select a line style in the Line area.
5. If desired, select a color from the Color menu, which looks just like the one in **Figure 38**.
6. Set individual borders for the selected cells using one of these methods:
   - ▲ Click one of the buttons in the Presets area to apply a predefined border. (None removes all borders from the selection.)
   - ▲ Click a button in the Border area to add a border to the corresponding area.
   - ▲ Click between the lines in the illustration in the Border area to place corresponding borders.
7. Repeat steps 4, 5, and 6 until all the desired borders for the selection are set.
8. Click OK.

   The borders are applied.

✔ Tip

- To get the borders in your worksheet to look just the way you want, be prepared to make several cell selections and trips to either the Borders button on the Formatting toolbar or the Border tab of the Format Cells dialog box.

Fill Colors & Patterns

Excel's pattern feature lets you add color to cells (**Figure 43**), either with or without patterns. Although the Fill Color menu on the Formatting toolbar lets you add color to cell backgrounds, the Format Cells dialog box offers far more flexibility.

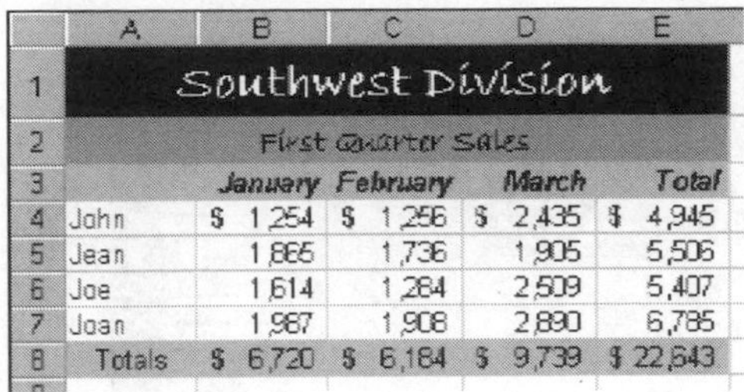

	A	B	C	D	E
1	Southwest Division				
2	First Quarter Sales				
3		January	February	March	Total
4	John	$ 1,254	$ 1,256	$ 2,435	$ 4,945
5	Jean	1,865	1,736	1,905	5,506
6	Joe	1,614	1,284	2,509	5,407
7	Joan	1,987	1,908	2,890	6,785
8	Totals	$ 6,720	$ 6,184	$ 9,739	$ 22,643

Figure 43 Use Excel's pattern feature to add fill colors and patterns to cells.

✔ Tips

- By combining two colors with a pattern, you can create various colors and levels of shading.
- Be careful when adding colors to cells! If the color is too dark, cell contents may not be legible.
- To improve the legibility of cell contents in colored cells, try making the characters bold.
- For a different look, use a dark color for the cell and make its characters white.

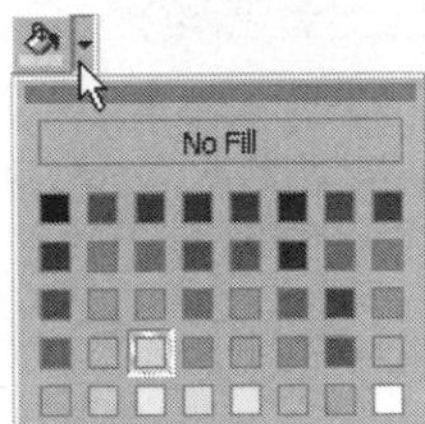

Figure 44 The Fill Color menu on the Formatting toolbar.

To add color with the Fill Color button

1. Select the cell(s) to which you want to add color.
2. Click on the Fill Color button on the Formatting toolbar to apply the color shown on the button.

   or

   Click on the triangle on the right side of the Fill Color button on the Formatting toolbar to display a menu of colors (**Figure 44**) and choose the color you want.

   The color is applied.

✔ Tips

- The Fill Color button displays the last color selection you made from the Fill Color menu, making it easy to apply the same color again.
- To remove colors from a selection, choose No Fill from the Fill Color menu (**Figure 44**).

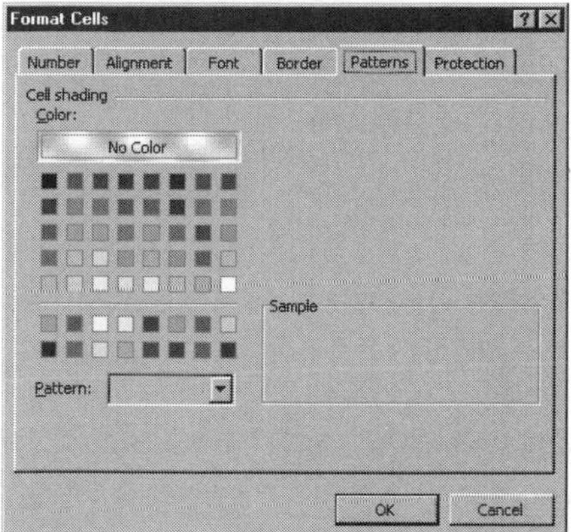

Figure 45 The Patterns tab of the Format Cells dialog box.

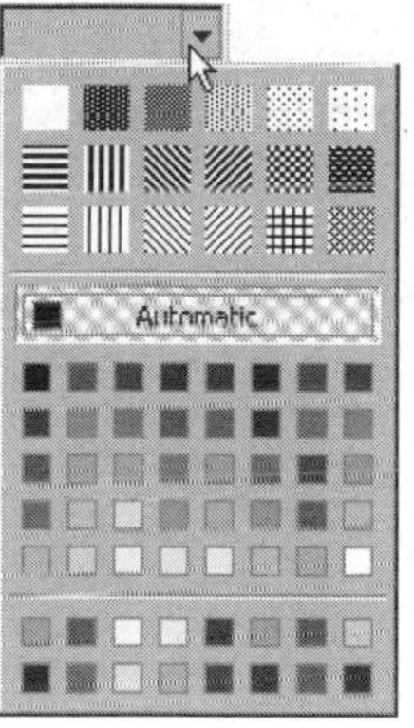

Figure 46
Use the Pattern menu to choose a pattern and a foreground color.

To add fill color & pattern with the Format Cells dialog box

1. Select the cell(s) to which you want to add colors, patterns, or shading.
2. Choose Format > Cells (**Figure 6**) or press Ctrl 1.
3. In the Format Cells dialog box that appears, click the Patterns tab to display its options (**Figure 45**).
4. Select a color from the Color palette in the Cell shading area of the dialog box. This is the background color.
5. If desired, choose a foreground color and pattern from the Pattern menu (**Figure 46**).
6. When the Sample area of the dialog box looks just the way you want your selection to look, click OK.

   The options you selected are applied.

Styles

Once you get the hang of using Excel's formatting options, check out its Style feature. This advanced feature, which is beyond the scope of this book, lets you combine formats into named styles that you can apply to any cell in the workbook. This can save time and ensure consistency.

✔ Tips

- Excel's style feature works a lot like Word's style feature.
- You can access the style feature by choosing Format > Style (**Figure 6**).

Conditional Formatting

Excel's Conditional Formatting feature enables you to set up special formatting that is automatically applied by Excel only when cell contents meet certain criteria.

For example, say you have a worksheet containing the total sales for each member of your company's sales staff. You want to display all sales over $5,000 in bold, blue type with a yellow background. You can use Conditional Formatting to automatically apply the desired formatting in cells containing values over $5,000 (**Figure 47**).

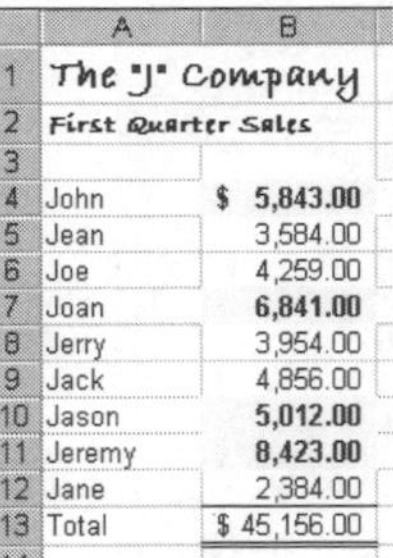

	A	B
1	The "J" Company	
2	First Quarter Sales	
3		
4	John	**$ 5,843.00**
5	Jean	3,584.00
6	Joe	4,259.00
7	Joan	**6,841.00**
8	Jerry	3,954.00
9	Jack	4,856.00
10	Jason	**5,012.00**
11	Jeremy	**8,423.00**
12	Jane	2,384.00
13	Total	$ 45,156.00

Figure 47 Conditional Formatting instructs Excel to format cells based on their contents.

To apply Conditional Formatting

1. Select the cells to which you want to apply conditional formatting.
2. Choose Format > Conditional Formatting (**Figure 6**) to display the Conditional Formatting dialog box (**Figure 48**).
3. Use the menus and text boxes in the Condition 1 part of the dialog box to set up the criteria for applying formatting. **Figure 49** shows an example.
4. Click the Format button to display a special version of the Format Cells dialog box that offers tabs for Font, Border, and Patterns only (**Figure 50**). Use the dialog box to set formatting options for cells meeting the condition, then click OK.
5. To add another condition for applying the formatting, click the Add button. The dialog box expands to offer an additional condition set (**Figure 51**). Repeat steps 3 and 4.
6. Repeat step 5 for each condition you want to add.
7. When you're finished specifying conditions and formatting, click OK.

   If any cells meet the condition(s) you specified, the formatting you specified is applied (**Figure 47**).

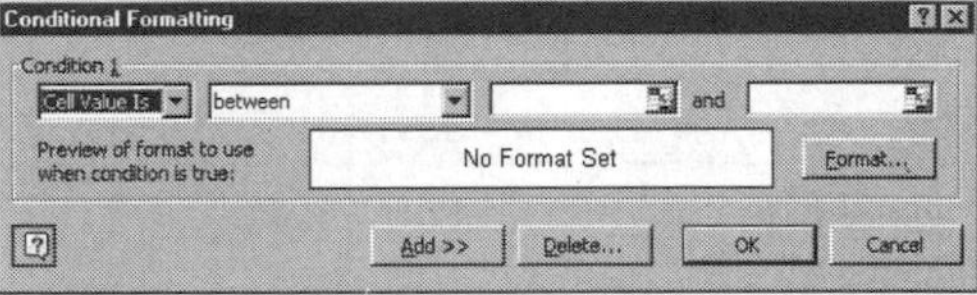

Figure 48 The Conditional Formatting dialog box.

Figure 49 This condition set applies formatting to selected cells containing values greater than 5000.

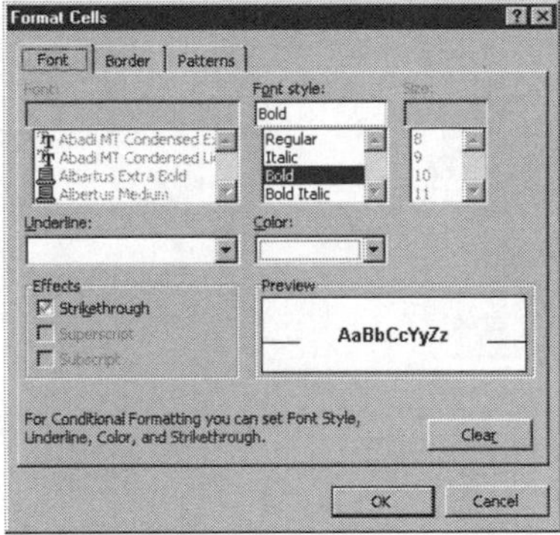

Figure 50 Formatting options for Conditional Formatting are limited.

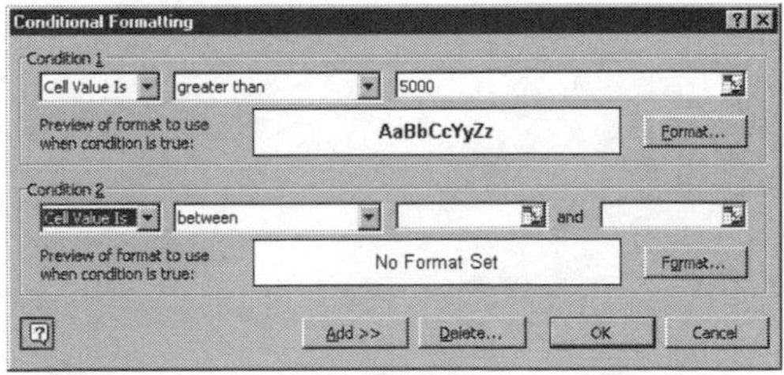

Figure 51 The Conditional Formatting dialog box expands so you can add more conditions.

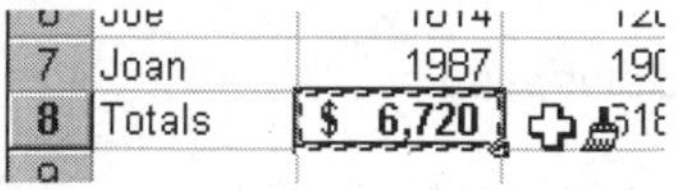

7	Joan	1987	190
8	Totals	$ 6,720	618

Figure 52 When you click the Format Painter button, a marquee appears around the original selection and the mouse pointer turns into the Format Painter pointer.

7	Joan	1987	1908	2890	6785
8	Totals	$ 6,720	6184	9739	22643

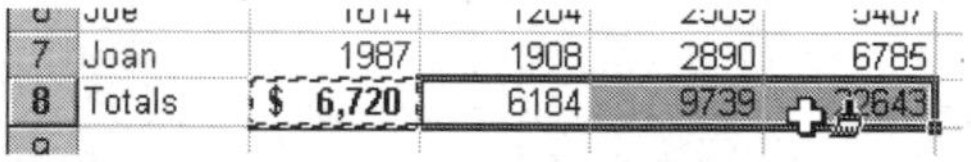

Figure 53 Drag to select the cells to which you want to apply the copied formats.

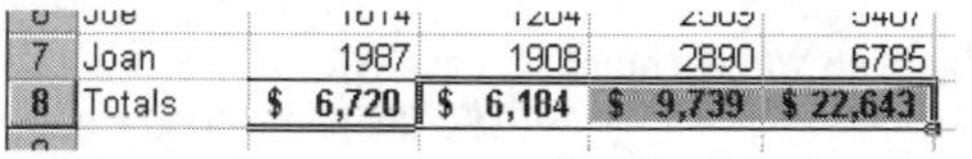

7	Joan	1987	1908	2890	6785
8	Totals	$ 6,720	$ 6,184	$ 9,739	$ 22,643

Figure 54 When you release the mouse button, the formatting is applied.

Figure 55 You can also use the Copy and Paste Special commands to copy and paste formatting.

The Format Painter

The Format Painter lets you copy cell formatting and apply it to other cells. This can help you format worksheets quickly and consistently.

To use the Format Painter

1. Select a cell with the formatting you want to copy.
2. Click the Format Painter button on the Standard toolbar. The mouse pointer turns into a little plus sign with a paintbrush beside it and a marquee appears around the original selection (**Figure 52**).
3. Use the Format Painter pointer to select the cells you want to apply the formatting to (**Figure 53**). When you release the mouse button, the formatting is applied (**Figure 54**).

✔ Tips

- You can double-click the Format Painter button in step 1 to keep applying a copied format throughout the worksheet. Press Esc or click the Format Painter button again to stop applying the format and return the mouse pointer to normal.
- You can also use the Copy and Paste Special commands under the Edit menu (**Figure 55**) to copy the formatting of selected cells and paste it into other cells.

Column Width & Row Height

If the data you enter into a cell doesn't fit, you can make the column wider to accommodate all the characters. You can also make columns narrower to use worksheet space more efficiently. And although Excel automatically adjusts row height when you increase the font size of cells within the row, you can increase or decrease row height as desired.

Excel offers two ways to change column width and row height: with the mouse and with Format menu commands.

✔ Tips

- If text typed into a cell does not fit, it appears to overlap into the cell to its right (**Figure 56**). Even though the text may appear to be in more than one cell, all of the text is really in the cell in which you typed it. (You can see for yourself by clicking in the cell to the right and looking at the formula bar—it will not contain any part of the text!) If the cell to the right of the text is not blank, the text appears truncated (**Figure 57**). Don't let appearances fool you. The text is still all there. The missing part is just hidden by the contents of the cell beside it.
- If a number doesn't fit in a cell, the cell fills up with pound signs (#) (**Figure 58**). To display the number, make the column wider (**Figure 59**) or change the number formatting to omit symbols and decimal places (**Figure 60**). I tell you how to make columns wider on the next page and how to change number formatting earlier in this chapter.
- Setting column width or row height to 0 (zero) hides the column or row.

Figure 56 When text doesn't fit in a cell, it appears to overlap into the cell beside it...

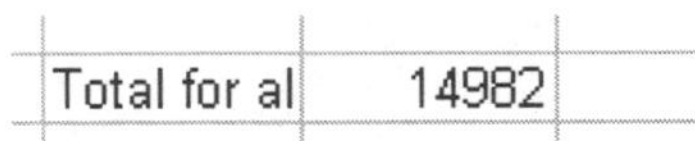

Figure 57 ...unless the cell beside it isn't blank.

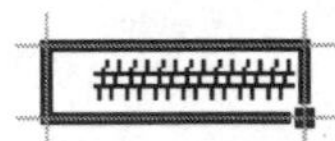

Figure 58 When a number doesn't fit into a cell, the cell fills with # signs.

Figure 59 You can display the number by making the cell wider...

Figure 60 ...or by changing the number's formatting to remove decimal places.

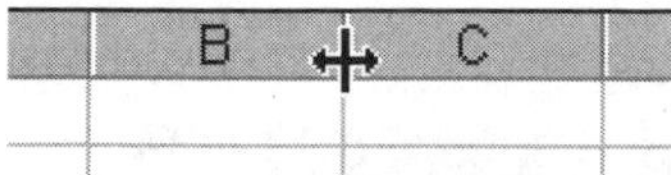

Figure 61 Position the mouse pointer on the right border of a column heading...

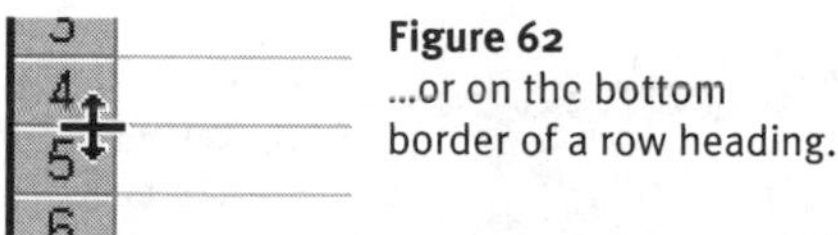

Figure 62 ...or on the bottom border of a row heading.

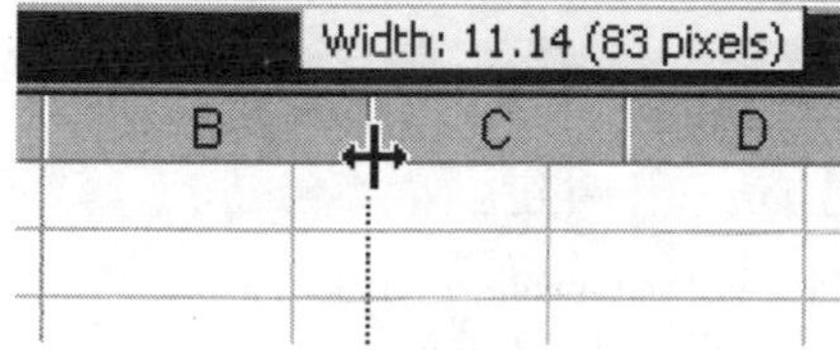

Figure 63 Drag to reposition the border.

To change column width or row height by dragging

1. Position the mouse pointer on the line right after the column letter(s) (**Figure 61**) or right below the row number (**Figure 62**) of the column or row you want to change. The mouse pointer turns into a line with two arrows coming out of it.
2. Press the mouse button down and drag.
   - ▲ To make a column narrower or wider, drag to the left or to the right.
   - ▲ To make a row taller or shorter, drag down or up.

   As you drag, a dotted line moves along with the mouse pointer and the width or height of the column or row appears in a yellow box (**Figure 63**).
3. Release the mouse button. The column width or row height changes.

✔ Tips

- When you change column width or row height, you change the width or height for the entire column or row, not just selected cells.
- To change column width or row height for more than one column or row at a time, select multiple columns or rows and drag the border of one of them.
- If you drag a column or row border all the way to the left or all the way up, you set the column width or row height to 0. The column or row disappears from view. I tell you more about hiding columns and rows on the next page.
- To quickly set the width or height of a column or row to fit its contents, double-click the column or row heading border. I tell you more about this AutoFit feature later in this chapter.

To change column width or row height with menu commands

1. Select the column(s) or row(s) whose width or height you want to change.
2. Choose Format > Column > Width (**Figure 64**) or Format > Row > Height (**Figure 65**).
3. In the Column Width dialog box (**Figure 66**) or Row Height dialog box (**Figure 67**), enter a new value. Column width is expressed in the number of standard font characters while row height is expressed in the number of points.
4. Click OK.

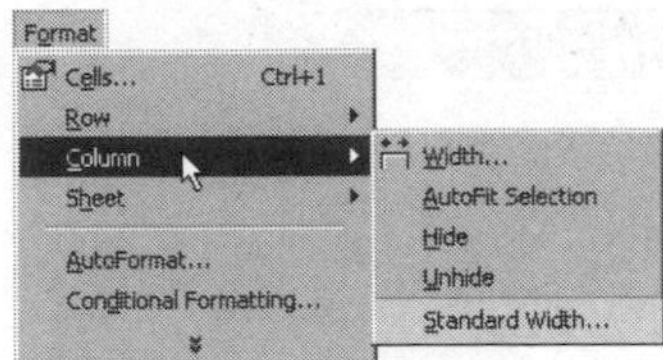

Figure 64 The Column submenu under the Format menu.

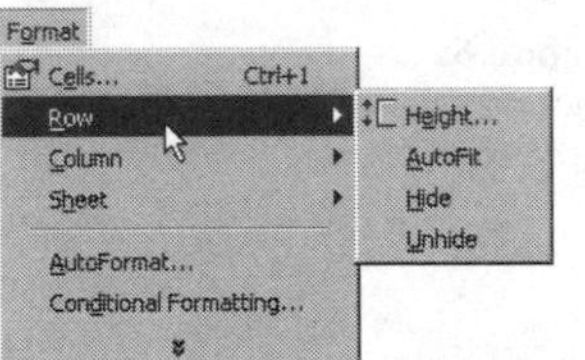

Figure 65 The Row submenu under the Format menu.

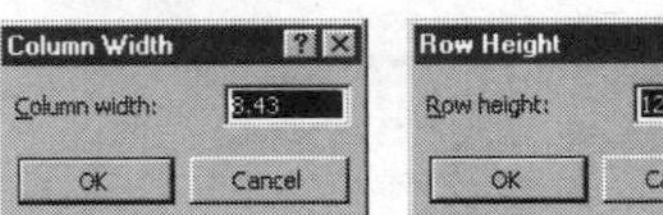

Figures 66 & 67 The Column Width (left) and Row Height (right) dialog boxes.

To hide columns or rows

1. Select the column(s) (**Figure 68**) or row(s) you want to hide.
2. Choose Format > Column > Hide (**Figure 64**) or Format > Row > Hide (**Figure 65**).

   The selected column(s) or row(s) disappear (**Figure 69**).

	A	B	C	D	
1	Southwest Division				
2	First Quarter Sales				
3		January	February	March	
4	John	$ 1,254	$ 1,256	$ 2,435	$
5	Jean	1,865	1,736	1,905	
6	Joe	1,614	1,284	2,509	
7	Joan	1,987	1,908	2,890	
8	Totals	$ 6,720	$ 6,184	$ 9,739	$

Figure 68 Select the column that you want to hide.

	A	B	D	
1	Southwest Division			
2	First Quarter Sales			
3		January	March	
4	John	$ 1,254	$ 2,435	$
5	Jean	1,865	1,905	
6	Joe	1,614	2,509	
7	Joan	1,987	2,890	
8	Totals	$ 6,720	$ 9,739	$

Figure 69 When you choose the Hide command, the column disappears.

✔ Tips

- Hiding a column or row is not the same as deleting it. Data in a hidden column or row still exists in the worksheet and can be referenced by formulas.
- Hiding a column or row enables you to reduce the size of a worksheet without permanently removing data. You may find this handy when printing reports.

To unhide columns or rows

1. Select the columns or rows on both sides of the hidden column(s) or row(s) (**Figure 70**).
2. Choose Format > Column > Unhide (**Figure 64**) or Format > Row > Unhide (**Figure 65**).

   The hidden columns(s) or rows(s) reappear (**Figure 71**).

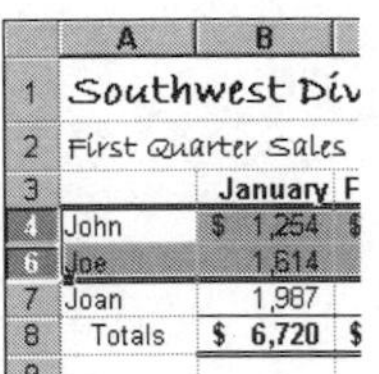

	A	B	
1	Southwest Div		
2	First Quarter Sales		
3		January	F
4	John	$ 1,254	$
6	Joe	1,614	
7	Joan	1,987	
8	Totals	$ 6,720	$

Figure 70 Select the rows above and below the hidden row.

	A	B	
1	Southwest Div		
2	First Quarter Sales		
3		January	F
4	John	$ 1,254	$
5	Jean	1,865	
6	Joe	1,614	
7	Joan	1,987	
8	Totals	$ 6,720	$

Figure 71 When you choose the Unhide command, the hidden row reappears.

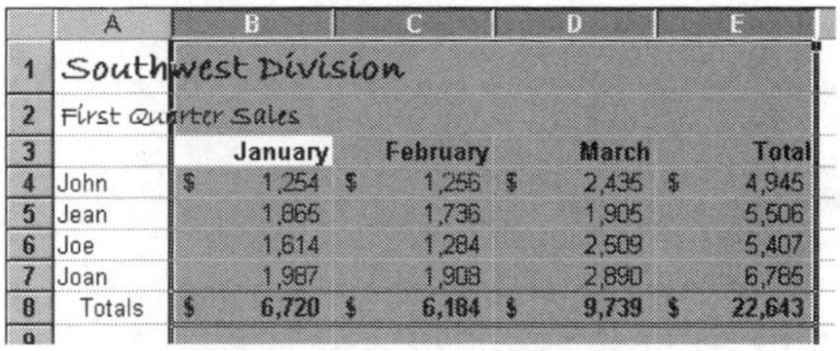

Figure 72 Select the columns for which you want to change the width.

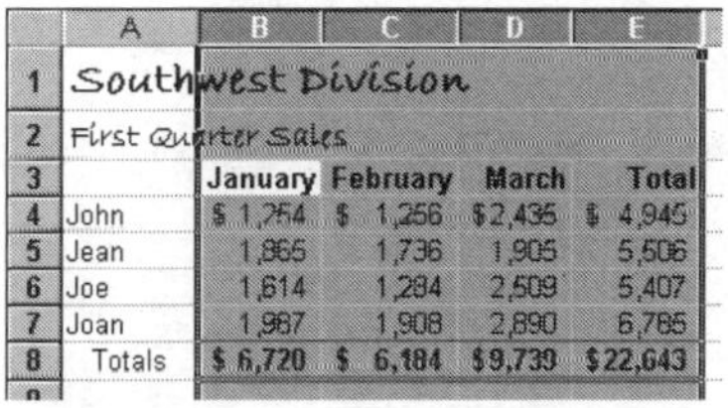

Figure 73 When you choose the AutoFit Selection command, the width of the columns changes so they're only as wide as they need to be to fit cell contents.

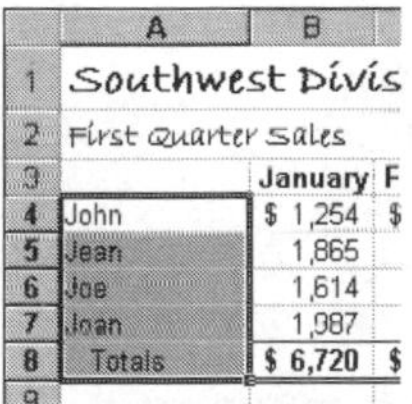

	A	B
1	Southwest Divis	
2	First Quarter Sales	
3		January F
4	John	$ 1,254 $
5	Jean	1,865
6	Joe	1,614
7	Joan	1,987
8	Totals	$ 6,720 $

Figure 74 Select the cells that you want Excel to measure for the AutoFit feature.

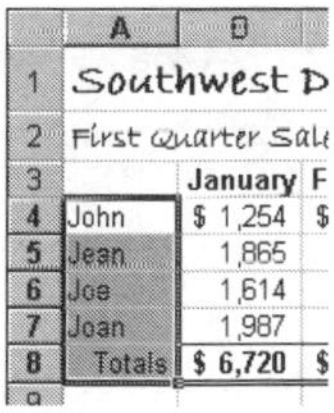

Figure 75 When you choose the AutoFit Selection command, Excel resizes the entire column based on the width of the contents in the selected cells.

AutoFit

Excel's AutoFit feature automatically adjusts a column's width or a row's height so it's only as wide or as high as it needs to be to display the information within it. This is a great way to adjust columns and rows to use worksheet space more efficiently.

To use AutoFit

1. Select the column(s) or row(s) for which you want to change the width or height (**Figure 72**).
2. Choose Format > Column > AutoFit Selection (**Figure 64**) or Format > Row > AutoFit (**Figures 65**).

   or

   Double-click on the border to the right of the column heading (**Figure 61**) or below the row heading (**Figure 62**).

   The column width or row height changes to fit cell contents (**Figure 73**).

✔ Tips

- To adjust a column's width without taking every cell into consideration—for example, to exclude a cell containing a lot of text—select only the cells for which you want to adjust the column (**Figure 74**). When you choose Format > Column > AutoFit Selection (**Figure 64**), only the cells you selected are measured for the AutoFit adjustment (**Figure 75**).
- Use the Wrap text and AutoFit features to keep your columns narrow. I tell you about Wrap text earlier in this chapter.

AutoFormat

Excel's AutoFormat feature offers a quick way to dress up tabular data in worksheets by applying predefined formats. If you're like me and prefer to leave design for designers, you'll welcome this feature.

To use AutoFormat

1. Select the portion of the worksheet you want to format (**Figure 76**).
2. Choose Format > AutoFormat (**Figure 6**) to display the AutoFormat dialog box (**Figure 77**).
3. Click to choose one of the format samples in the list.
4. Click OK.

   Your worksheet is formatted instantly (**Figure 78**).

✔ Tip

- To pick and choose among the different kinds of formatting automatically applied, click the Options button in the AutoFormat dialog box. The box expands to display check boxes for each type of formatting (**Figure 79**). To exclude a type of change from the AutoFormat process, turn off its check box.

Southwest Division				
First Quarter Sales				
	January	February	March	Total
John	1254	1256	2435	4945
Jean	1865	1736	1905	5506
Joe	1614	1284	2509	5407
Joan	1987	1908	2890	6785
Totals	6720	6184	9739	22643

Figure 76 Select the part of the worksheet that you want to format.

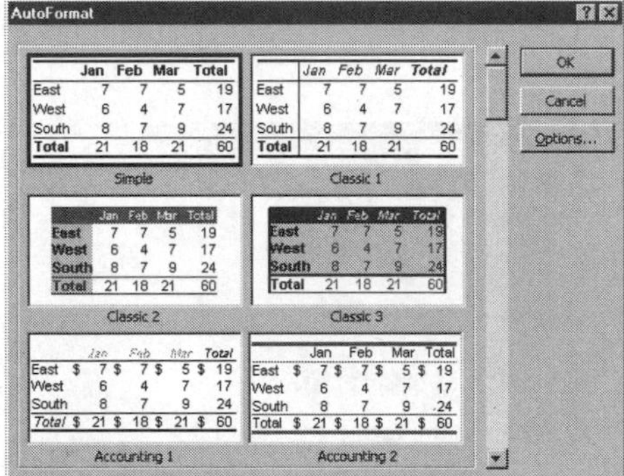

Figure 77 The AutoFormat dialog box.

Southwest Division				
First Quarter Sales				
	January	February	March	Total
John	1254	1256	2435	4945
Jean	1865	1736	1905	5506
Joe	1614	1284	2509	5407
Joan	1987	1908	2890	6785
Totals	6720	6184	9739	22643

Figure 78 The worksheet in **Figure 76** with the Colorful 2 AutoFormat applied.

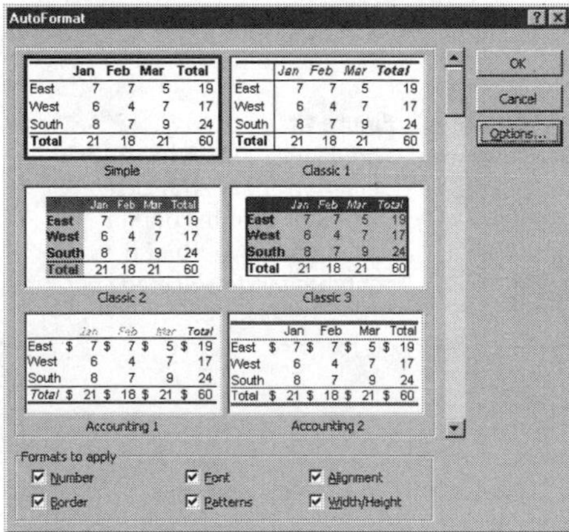

Figure 79 Clicking the Options button expands the AutoFormat dialog box so you can select which parts of the format should be applied.

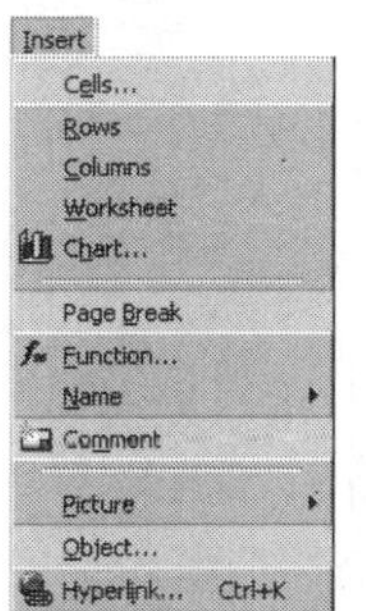

Figure 80 You can find the Comment command on the Insert menu.

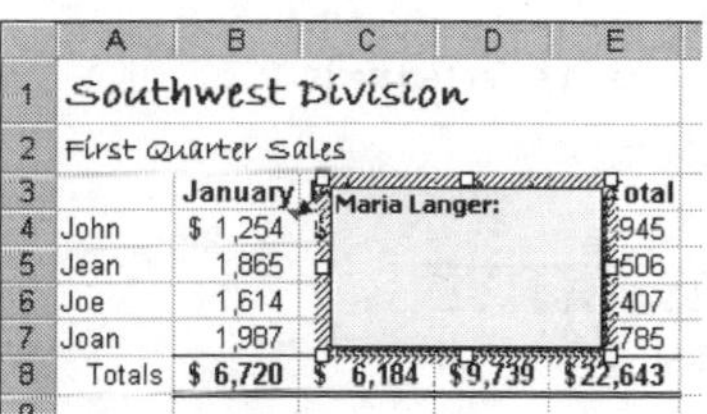

Figure 81 Enter a comment in the comment box.

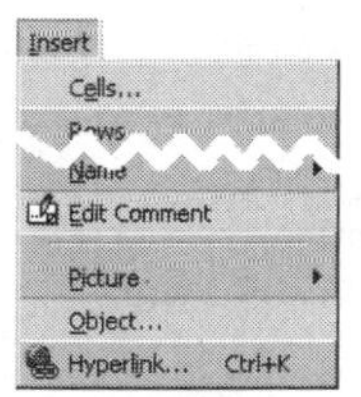

Figure 82 A red mark appears in the corner of a cell containing a comment.

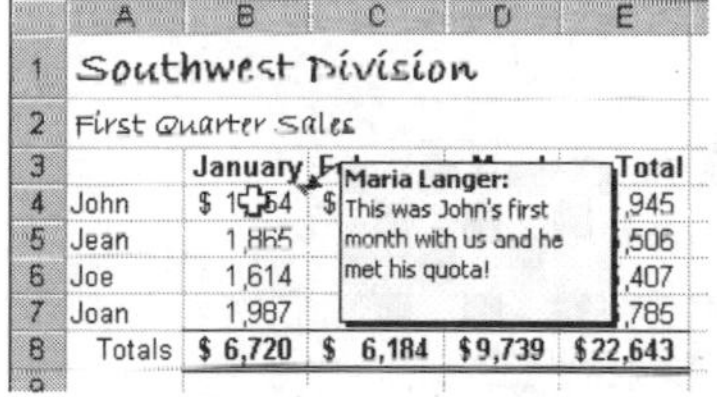

Figure 83 Point to a cell containing a comment to view the comment.

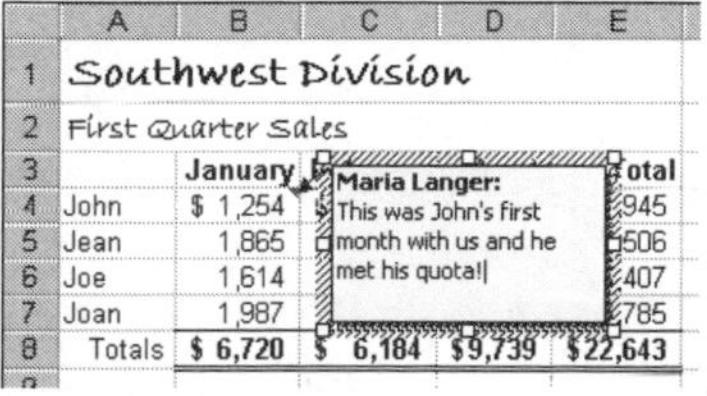

Figure 84 When a cell containing a comment is selected, the Edit Comment command appears under the Insert menu.

Figure 85 You can edit a comment in the comment box.

Cell Comments

Excel lets you add comments to any cell. You can use comments to annotate your worksheets, providing background information for complex calculations or important data.

✔ Tip

- Cell comments are also known as *cell notes*.

To add a cell comment

1. Select the cell to which you want to add a comment.
2. Choose Insert > Comment (**Figure 80**).
3. A yellow comment box with your name in it appears (**Figure 81**). Enter the text for the comment.
4. Click in the worksheet window outside the comment box.

   The box disappears as the comment is saved. A red comment indicator mark appears in the upper-right corner of the selected cell (**Figure 82**).

To view a cell comment

Position the mouse pointer over a cell containing a comment.

An arrow and yellow box containing the comment appear (**Figure 83**).

To edit a comment

1. Select the cell containing the comment you want to edit.
2. Choose Insert > Edit Comment (**Figure 84**).
3. A yellow comment box containing the comment appears (**Figure 85**). Edit the comment as desired.
4. Click in the worksheet window outside the comment box to save your changes.

Removing Formatting & Comments from Cells

You can use options on the Edit menu's Clear submenu (**Figure 86**) to remove only formatting or comments from selected cells. Values or formulas in the cells are not removed.

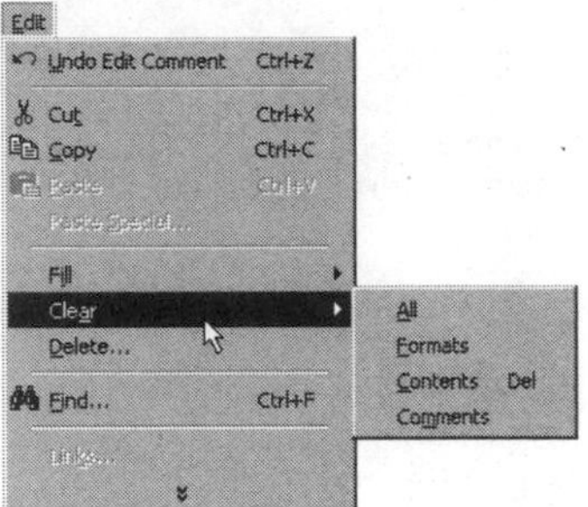

Figure 86 The Clear submenu under the Edit menu enables you to clear just the formats or comments in selected cells.

✔ Tips

- When you remove formats from a cell, you return font formatting to the normal font and number formatting to the General format. You also remove borders or colors added to the cell.
- Removing formatting does not affect column width or row height.

To remove only formatting from cells

1. Select the cell(s) from which you want to remove just the formatting (**Figure 87**).
2. Choose Edit > Clear > Formats (**Figure 86**).

   The formats are removed (**Figure 88**).

	A	B	C	
1	Southwest Division			
2	First Quarter Sales			
3		January	February	M
4	John	$ 1,254	$ 1,256	$2
5	Jean	1,865	1,736	1
6	Joe	1,614	1,284	2
7	Joan	1,987	1,908	2
8	Totals	$ 6,720	$ 6,184	$9

Figure 87 Select the cells from which you want to remove just the formatting.

To remove only comments from cells

1. Select the cell(s) from which you want to remove just the comments.
2. Choose Edit > Clear > Comments (**Figure 86**).

   The comments and red comment indicator marks are removed.

	A	B	C	
1	Southwest Division			
2	First Quarter Sales			
3		January	February	M
4	John	1254	$ 1,256	$2
5	Jean	1865	1,736	1
6	Joe	1614	1,284	2
7	Joan	1987	1,908	2
8	Totals	6720	$ 6,184	$9

Figure 88 All the formatting—but nothing else—is removed from the selected cells.

ADDING GRAPHIC OBJECTS 7

Southwest Division				
First Quarter Sales				
	January	February	March	Total
John	$ 1,254.00	$ 1,256.00	$ 2,435.00	$ 4,945.00
Jean	1,865.00	1,736.00	1,905.00	5,506.00
Joe	1,614.00	1,284.00	2,509.00	5,407.00
Joan	1,987.00	1,908.00	2,890.00	6,785.00
Totals	$ 6,720.00	$ 6,184.00	$ 9,739.00	$ 22,643.00

Figure 1 A formatted worksheet looks fine...

Chase Consulting

Southwest Division				
First Quarter Sales				
	January	February	March	Total
John	$ 1,254.00	$ 1,256.00	$ 2,435.00	$ 4,945.00
Jean	1,865.00	1,736.00	1,906.00	5,508.00
Joe	1,614.00	1,284.00	2,509.00	5,407.00
Joan	1,987.00	1,908.00	2,890.00	6,785.00
Totals	$ 6,720.00	$ 6,184.00	$ 9,739.00	$ 22,643.00

Sales are 57% higher than the previous quarter!

Figure 2 ...but it can have even more impact with the addition of a company logo, callouts, and other graphic objects.

Adding Objects

Formatting, which is covered in **Chapter 6**, offers one way to add impact to your worksheets and make them more visually appealing. Adding graphic objects is another. **Figures 1** and **2** show an example of how the creative use of graphic elements can help communicate information on a worksheet.

Excel enables you to add graphic objects to your worksheets and chart sheets using three methods. You can:

- Use tools on Excel's Drawing toolbar to draw lines and shapes.
- Copy graphics created in other programs and paste them into Excel documents.
- Use commands under Excel's Insert menu to add pictures, such as clip art, graphic files on disk, and WordArt.

This chapter explains how to do all of these things, as well as how to modify the graphic objects you add.

✔ Tip

- All of the techniques covered in this chapter can also be applied to chart sheets. I tell you about creating and formatting chart sheets in **Chapter 8**.

Drawing Objects

Excel's Drawing toolbar (**Figure 4**) includes a wide range of tools you can use to add lines, arrows, shapes, and text boxes to your worksheets and charts. To use these tools, simply click the button to select a tool and drag in the document window to draw a line or shape.

Figure 3 When you display the Drawing toolbar, the Drawing button on the Standard toolbar looks "pushed in."

Figure 4 Excel's Drawing toolbar.

To display the Drawing toolbar

Click the Drawing button on the Standard toolbar. The button turns light gray and looks "pushed in" (**Figure 3**). The Drawing toolbar appears (**Figure 4**).

✔ Tip

- If your Drawing toolbar doesn't look exactly like the one in **Figure 4**, don't panic. Although the Drawing toolbar is docked at the bottom of the screen by default, it may have been floated the last time it was used—Excel remembers the position of all toolbars. I tell you more about floating and docking toolbars in **Chapter 1**.

To hide the Drawing toolbar

Click the Drawing button on the Standard toolbar.

Figure 5 When you click a drawing tool's button, the mouse pointer turns into a crosshairs pointer.

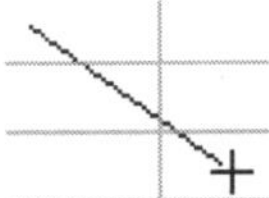

Figure 6 Drag to draw a line or arrow.

Figure 7 A freshly drawn line.

Figure 8 A freshly drawn arrow.

To draw a line or arrow

1. Click the appropriate Drawing toolbar button once to select it:
   - ▲ Use the Line tool to draw straight lines.
   - ▲ Use the Arrow tool to draw straight lines with arrowheads on one or both ends.

   When you click the tool's button the mouse pointer turns into a crosshairs pointer (**Figure 5**).
2. Position the crosshairs where you want to begin drawing the line.
3. Press the mouse button down and drag. As you move the mouse, a line is drawn (**Figure 6**).
4. Release the mouse button to complete the line. The line appears with selection handles on either end (**Figures 7** and **8**). I tell you more about selection handles later in this chapter.

✔ Tips

- To constrain a line to draw at 15° angles from its starting point, hold down Shift in step 3. This also enables you to draw perfectly horizontal or vertical lines.
- To draw multiple lines with the same tool, double-click the tool's button to select it. The tool remains active until you either click the button again, click another button, or press Esc.

To draw a rectangle, square, oval, or circle

1. Click the appropriate Drawing toolbar button once to select it:

   ▲ Use the Rectangle tool to draw rectangles or squares.

   ▲ Use the Oval tool to draw ovals and circles.

   When you click the tool's button the mouse pointer turns into a crosshairs pointer (**Figure 5**).

2. Position the crosshairs where you want to begin drawing the shape.
3. Press the mouse button down and drag. As you move the mouse, the shape begins to take form (**Figure 9**).
4. Release the mouse button to complete the shape. The shape appears with selection handles around it (**Figures 10** and **11**). I tell you more about selection handles later in this chapter.

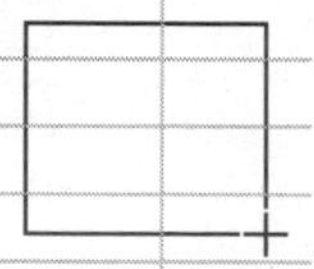

Figure 9 Drag to draw a shape.

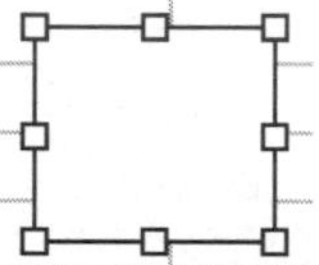

Figure 10 A freshly drawn rectangle.

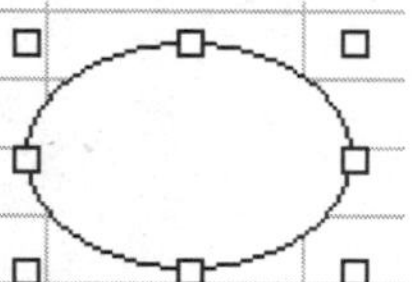

Figure 11 A freshly drawn oval.

✔ Tips

- When you draw with the rectangle or oval tool, you draw from corner to corner.
- To draw a square or a circle, click the Rectangle or Ellipse button, then hold down Shift in step 3. The drawing movements are restricted so only perfectly square or perfectly round shapes can be drawn.
- To draw multiple shapes with the same tool, double-click the tool's button to select it. The tool remains active until you either click the button again, click another button, or press Esc.

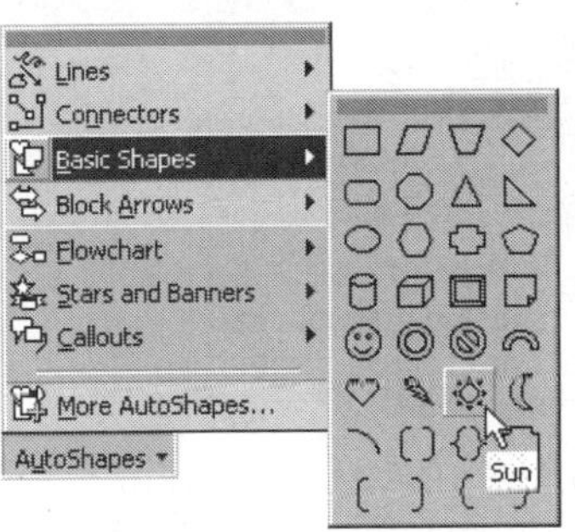

Figure 12 Choose a shape from one of the submenus on the AutoShapes menu.

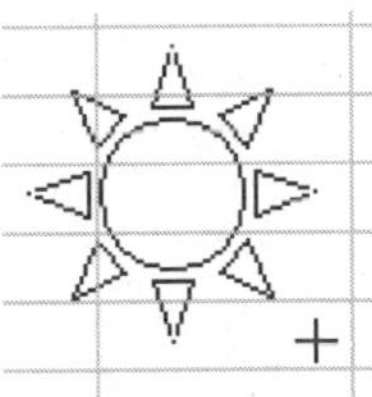

Figure 13 Drag to draw the shape.

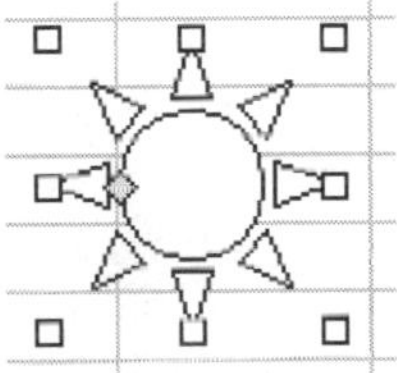

Figure 14 A freshly drawn shape.

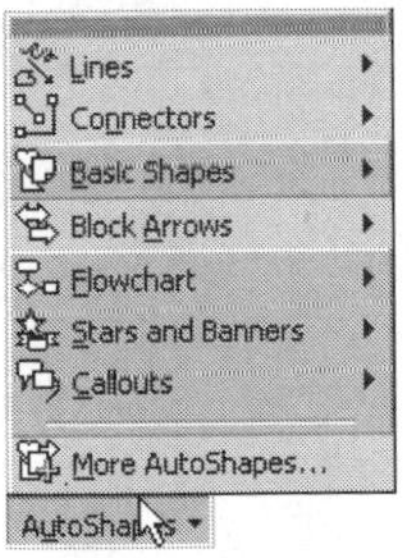

Figure 15 The AutoShapes menu on the Drawing toolbar.

Figure 16 When you drag the AutoShapes menu away from the toolbar, it becomes a floating toolbar.

To draw an AutoShape

1. Choose a shape or line from one of the submenus on the Drawing toolbar's Auto-Shapes menu (**Figure 12**). The mouse pointer turns into a crosshairs pointer (**Figure 5**).
2. Position the crosshairs where you want to begin drawing the shape or line.
3. Press the mouse button down and drag. As you move the mouse, the shape or line begins to take form (**Figure 13**).
4. Release the mouse button to complete the shape. The shape appears with selection handles around it (**Figure 14**). I tell you more about selection handles on the next page.

✔ Tips

- The AutoShapes feature makes it easy to draw complex lines and shapes.
- The Connectors submenu offers options for creating lines that connect two shapes.
- The AutoShapes menu (**Figure 15**) and its submenus (**Figure 12**) can be dragged off the toolbar to create a separate floating toolbar (**Figure 16**).

Selecting Objects

To move or modify a drawn object, you must first select it.

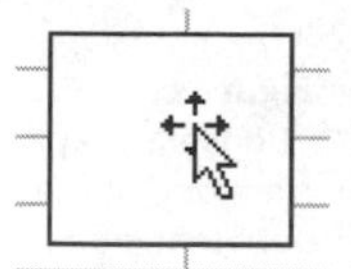

Figure 17 When you position the mouse pointer on an object, the mouse pointer turns into a selection pointer.

To select an object

1. Position the mouse pointer on the object. The mouse pointer turns into a selection pointer (**Figure 17**) rather than the standard worksheet pointer.
2. Click. Selection handles appear around the object (**Figure 10**).

✔ Tips

- If a shape does not have any fill, you must click on its border to select it. I tell you about fill color later in this chapter.
- To change the mouse pointer into a selection pointer so the standard worksheet pointer doesn't appear while you're working with drawing objects, click the Select Objects button on the Drawing toolbar. The button looks "pushed in" and the mouse pointer changes to an arrow. To get the regular pointer back, click the Select Objects button again, double-click any worksheet cell, or press Esc once or twice.

To deselect an object

Click on any other object or anywhere else in the window. The selection handles disappear.

To select multiple objects

1. Follow the instructions on the previous page to select the first object (**Figure 18**).
2. Hold down Shift and continue to select objects until all have been selected (**Figure 19**).

or

1. Click the Select Objects button on the Drawing toolbar to activate the selection pointer.
2. Use the pointer to drag a rectangle that completely surrounds all the objects you want to select (**Figure 20**).

   When you release the mouse button, selection handles appear around each object (**Figure 21**).

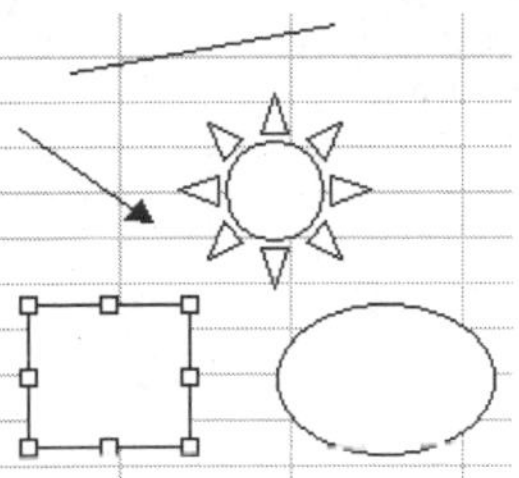

Figure 18 Select the first object.

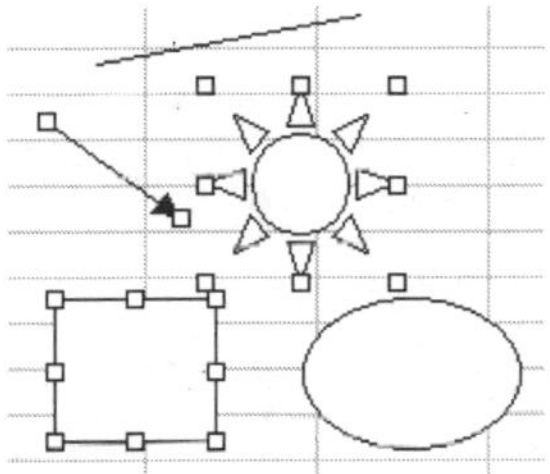

Figure 19 Then hold down Shift and click to select other objects.

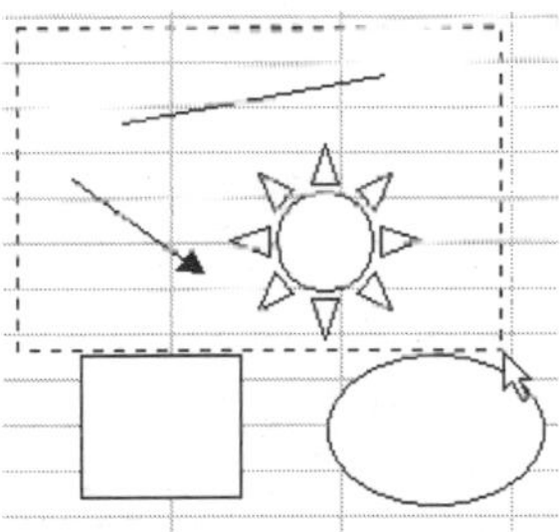

Figure 20 You can use the selection pointer to draw a boundary box that completely surrounds the objects you want to select.

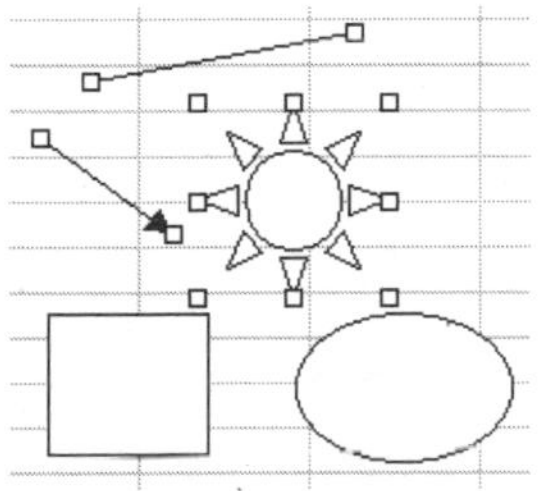

Figure 21 When you release the mouse button, the objects within the boundary are selected.

✔ Tips

- To select all the objects on a worksheet, click the Select Objects button on the Drawing toolbar and press Ctrl A.
- To deselect objects from a multiple selection, hold down Shift while clicking on the objects you want to deselect.

Grouping Objects

To keep multiple objects together, you can group them. This enables you to select, move, and modify all of the objects in the group by clicking any one of them.

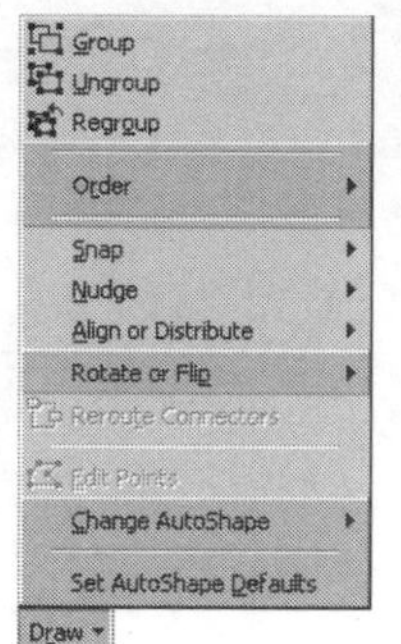

Figure 22 The Drawing toolbar's Draw menu.

To group objects

1. Select all the objects you want to include in the group (**Figure 21**).
2. Choose Group from the Drawing toolbar's Draw menu (**Figure 22**).

   The objects are grouped together, with only one set of selection handles (**Figure 23**).

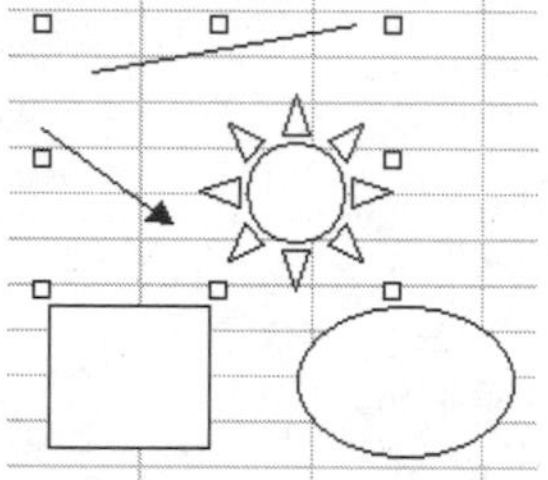

Figure 23 The objects selected in Figure 21 after grouping them.

To ungroup objects

1. Select the grouped objects you want to ungroup (**Figure 23**).
2. Choose Ungroup from the Drawing toolbar's Draw menu (**Figure 22**).

   Separate selection handles appear for each object (**Figure 21**).

✔ Tip

- In addition to grouping individual objects, you can also group groups of objects.

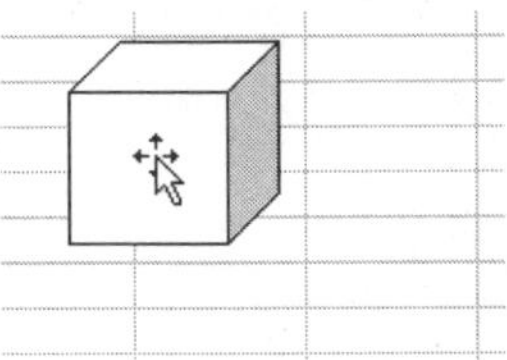

Figure 24 Position the selection pointer on the object.

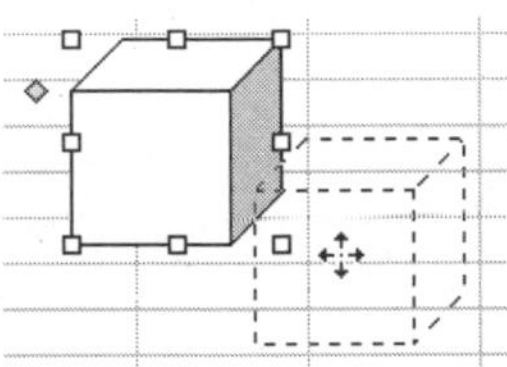

Figure 25 Drag to move the object.

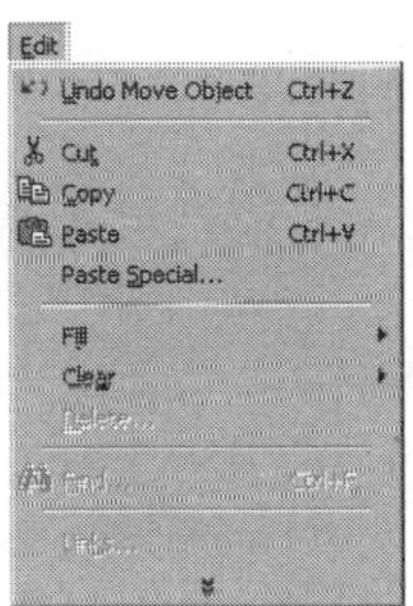

Figure 26 The Edit menu.

Moving, Copying, & Deleting Objects

Objects (or groups of objects) can be moved, copied, or deleted.

To move an object by dragging

1. Position the mouse pointer on the object so that the selection pointer appears (**Figure 24**).
2. Press the mouse button down and drag. An outline of the object moves along with the mouse pointer (**Figure 25**).
3. When the object's outline is in the desired position, release the mouse button. The object moves.

✔ Tip

- To restrict an object's movement so that it moves only horizontally or vertically, hold down Shift while dragging.

To move an object with the Cut & Paste commands

1. Select the object you want to move.
2. Choose Edit > Cut (**Figure 26**), press Ctrl X, or click the Cut button on the Standard toolbar. The object disappears.
3. To paste the object into a different sheet, switch to that sheet.
4. Choose Edit > Paste (**Figure 26**), press Ctrl V, or click the Paste button on the Standard toolbar. The object appears.
5. If necessary, drag the object into the desired position on the sheet.

✔ Tip

- This technique is most useful when moving an object to another sheet.

To copy an object by dragging

1. Position the mouse pointer on the object so that the selection pointer appears (**Figure 24**).
2. While holding down Ctrl, press the mouse button down and drag. An outline of the object moves along with the mouse pointer, which displays a plus sign beside it (**Figure 27**).
3. When you release the mouse button a copy of the object appears at the outline (**Figure 28**).

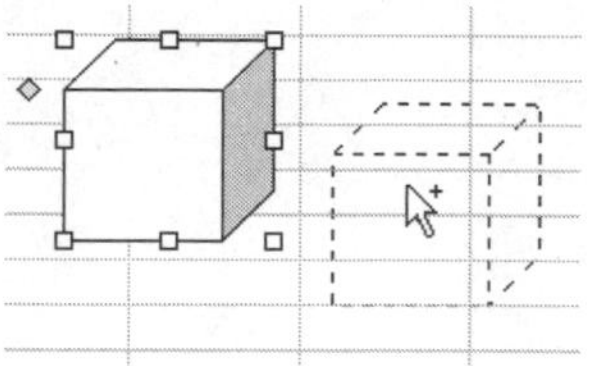

Figure 27 Hold down Ctrl while dragging...

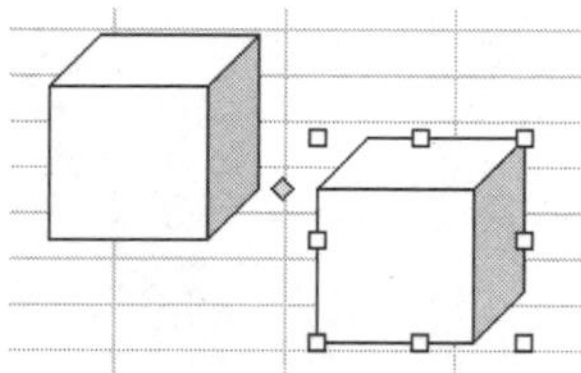

Figure 28 ...to copy an object.

To copy an object with the Copy & Paste commands

1. Select the object you want to copy.
2. Choose Edit > Copy (**Figure 26**), press Ctrl C, or click the Copy button on the Standard toolbar.
3. To paste the object into a different sheet, switch to that sheet.
4. Choose Edit > Paste (**Figure 26**), press Ctrl V, or click the Paste button on the Standard toolbar.

To delete an object

1. Select the object(s) or group of objects you want to delete.
2. Press Backspace or Delete.

   or

   Choose Edit > Clear > All (**Figure 29**).

   The object(s) disappear.

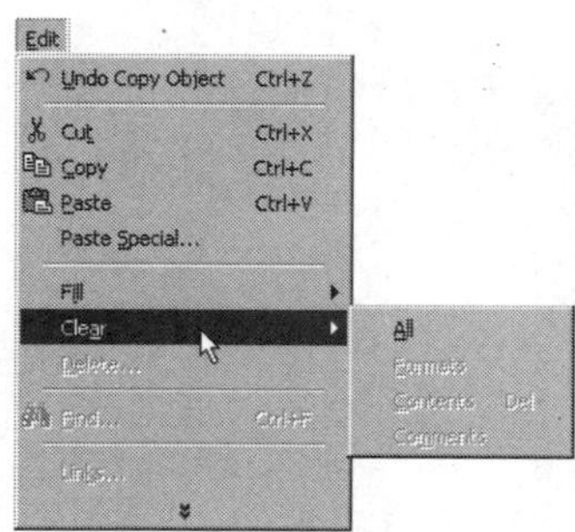

Figure 29 The Clear submenu under the Edit menu when an object is selected.

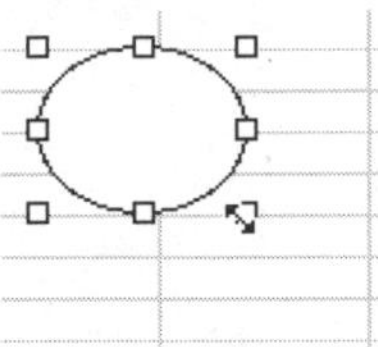

Figure 30 Position the mouse pointer on a selection handle and it turns into a resizing pointer.

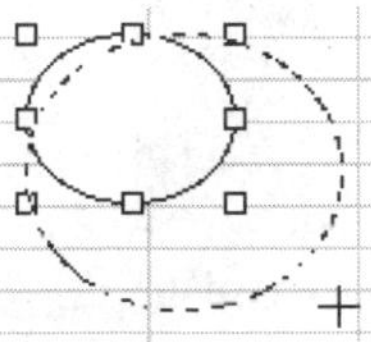

Figure 31 Drag to stretch (or shrink) the object.

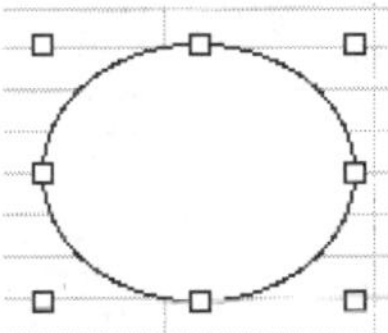

Figure 32 When you release the mouse button, the object resizes.

Modifying Objects

Any object you draw in Excel can be modified to change its size, shape, and formatting.

To resize an object

1. Select the object you want to resize.
2. Position the mouse pointer on a selection handle. The mouse pointer turns into a double-headed arrow (**Figure 30**).
3. Press the mouse button down and drag to stretch or shrink the object. The mouse pointer turns into a crosshairs and an outline of the edge of the object moves with your mouse pointer as you drag (**Figure 31**).
4. When the outline of the object reflects the size you want, release the mouse button. The object is resized (**Figure 32**).

✔ Tips

- To resize an object or group proportionally, hold down Shift while dragging a corner selection handle.
- To resize multiple objects at the same time, select the objects, then resize one of them. All selected objects will stretch or shrink.

To change an AutoShape

1. Select the AutoShape object that you want to change (**Figure 33**).
2. Choose a new shape from one of the Change AutoShape submenus under the Drawing toolbar's Draw menu (**Figure 34**).

   The shape changes (**Figure 35**).

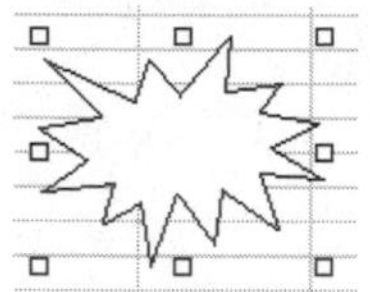

Figure 33 Select the AutoShape that you want to change.

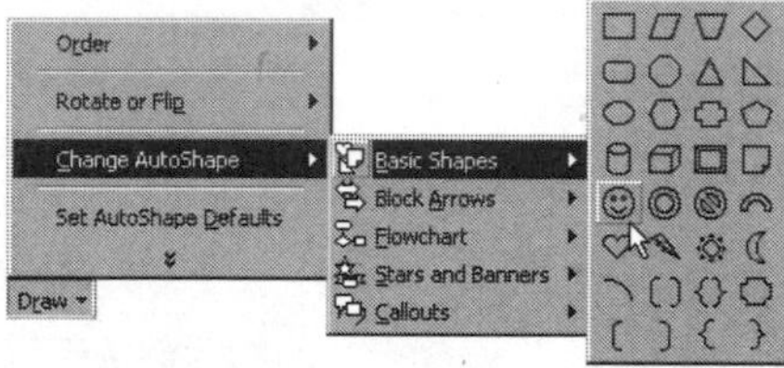

Figure 34 Choose a new shape from one of the Change AutoShape submenus.

✔ Tips

- You cannot change an AutoShape line to an AutoShape shape or change an Auto-Shape shape to an AutoShape line.
- The new shape is the same size as the original shape.

To customize an AutoShape

1. Select the AutoShape object that you want to customize.
2. Position the mouse pointer on the yellow diamond handle. The mouse pointer turns into a hollow white arrowhead pointer.
3. Drag the yellow diamond. As you drag, the outline of the customized shape moves with the mouse pointer (**Figures 36** and **37**).
4. Release the mouse button.

   The shape changes (**Figures 38** and **39**).

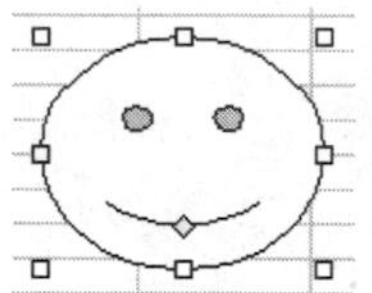

Figure 35 The AutoShape changes to the shape you chose.

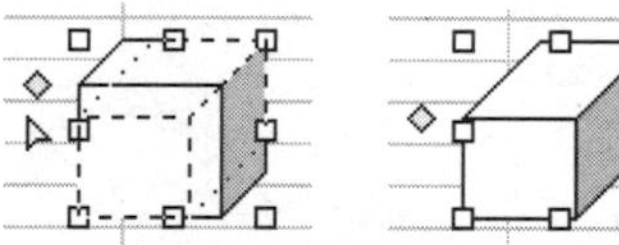

Figures 36 & 37 Drag the yellow diamond (left) to customize the AutoShape (right).

✔ Tip

- This technique can only be used on Auto-Shape lines or shapes that display a yellow diamond when selected.

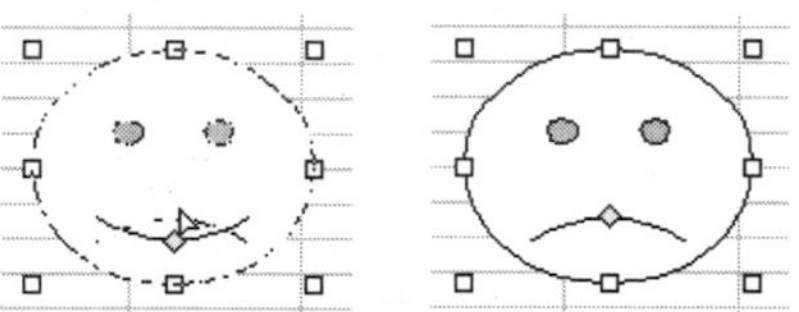

Figures 38 & 39 You can even turn a smile (left) into a frown (right).

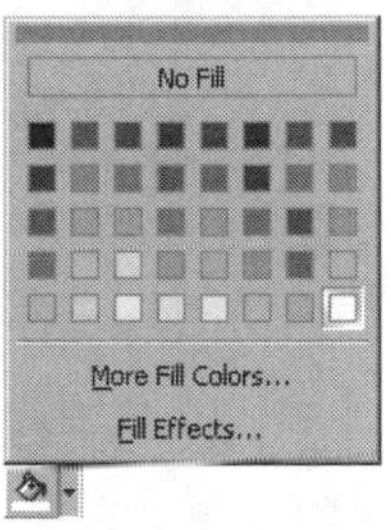

Figure 40 The Fill Color button menu.

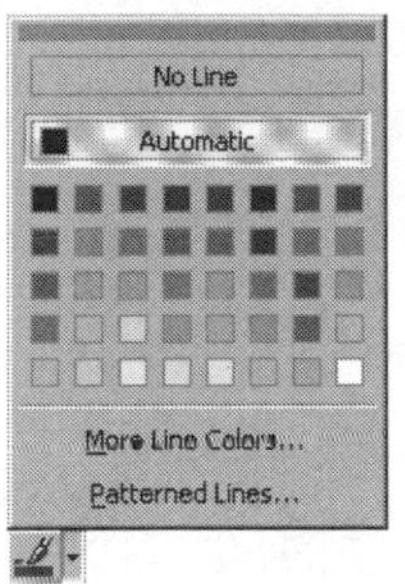

Figure 41 The Line Color button menu.

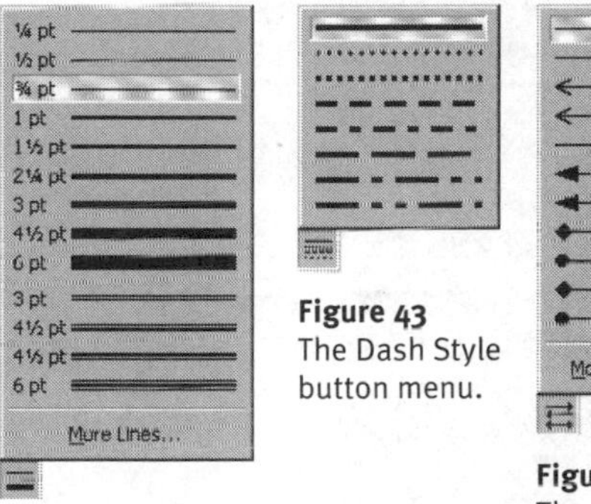

Figure 42 The Line Style button menu.

Figure 43 The Dash Style button menu.

Figure 44 The Arrow Style button menu.

Figure 45 The Shadow button menu.

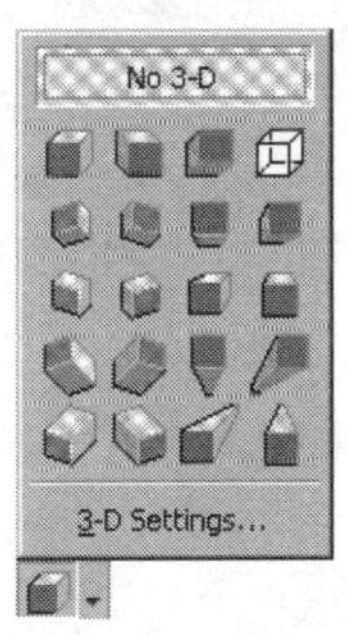

Figure 46 The 3-D button menu.

To format lines & shapes with the Drawing toolbar

1. Select the line or shape you want to format.
2. Use button menus on the Drawing toolbar to format the selected object:
   - ▲ To change the fill color of a shape, choose an option from the Fill Color button menu (**Figure 40**).
   - ▲ To change the line color of a line or shape border, choose an option from the Line Color button menu (**Figure 41**).
   - ▲ To change the line thickness of a line or shape border, choose an option from the Line Style button menu (**Figure 42**).
   - ▲ To change the style of a dashed line or dashed shape border, choose an option from the Dash Style button menu (**Figure 43**).
   - ▲ To add, change, or remove arrow components for a line or arrow, choose an option from the Arrow Style button menu (**Figure 44**).
   - ▲ To add, remove, or change the shadow of a line or shape, choose an option from the Shadow button menu (**Figure 45**).
   - ▲ To add, change, or remove three dimensional effects for a simple shape, choose an option from the 3-D button menu (**Figure 46**).

✔ Tips

- The formatting options that are available depend on the line or shape that is selected.
- You can combine as many formatting options as you like to customize the appearance of lines and shapes.

To format lines & shapes with the Format AutoShape dialog box

1. Select the line or shape you want to format and choose Format > AutoShape (**Figure 47**) or press Ctrl 1.

   or

   Double-click the line or shape you want to format.

2. The Format AutoShape dialog box appears. Click the Colors and Lines tab to display its options (**Figures 48**, **49**, and **50**).

3. Set options as desired:

   ▲ To change the fill color, choose an option from the Color menu in the Fill area of the dialog box (**Figure 48**). The options are the same as those on the Fill Color button's menu (**Figure 40**).

   ▲ To enable objects to be seen through a fill color, turn on the Semitransparent check box in the Fill area of the dialog box (**Figure 48**).

   ▲ To change the line color, choose an option from the Color menu in the Line area of the dialog box (**Figures 48**, **49**, and **50**). The options are the same as those on the Line Color button's menu (**Figure 41**).

   ▲ To change the dashed style, choose an option from the Dashed menu in the Line area of the dialog box (**Figures 48**, **49**, and **50**). The options are the same as those on the Dash Style button's menu (**Figure 43**).

   ▲ To change a connector's style, choose an option from the Connector menu (**Figure 51**) in the Line area of the dialog box (**Figure 50**).

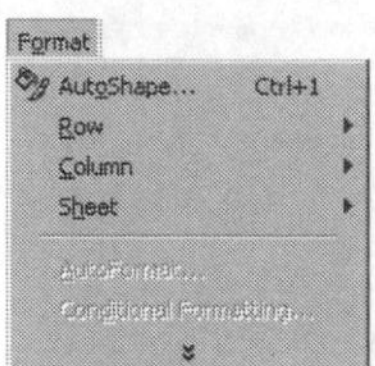

Figure 47 With a line or shape selected, the AutoShape command appears on the Format menu.

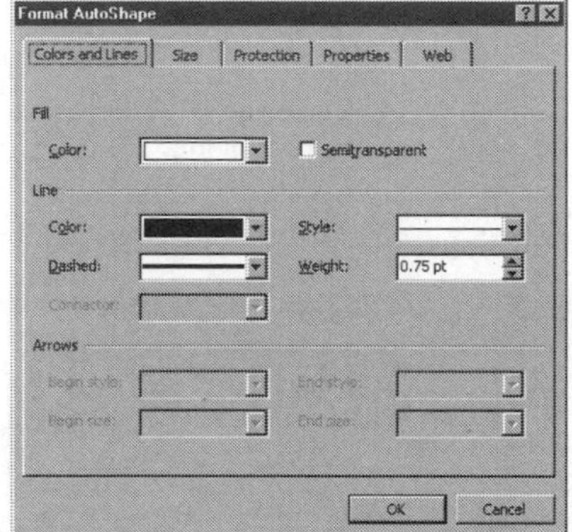

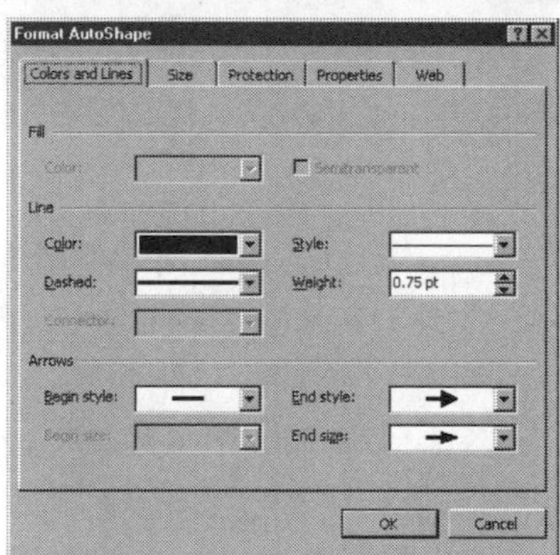

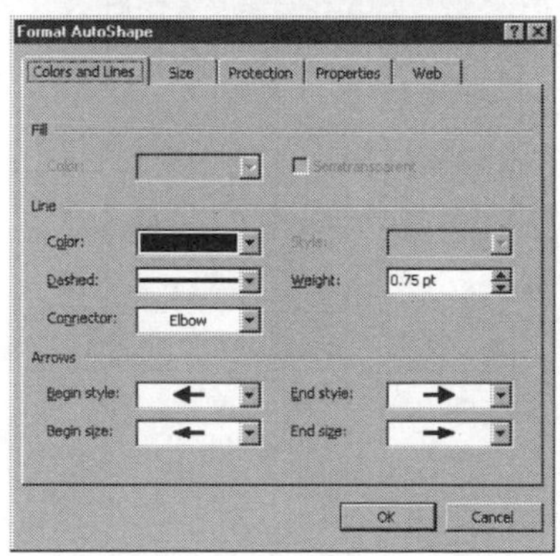

Figures 48, 49, & 50 The Format AutoShape dialog box for a shape (top), line or arrow (middle), and connector (bottom).

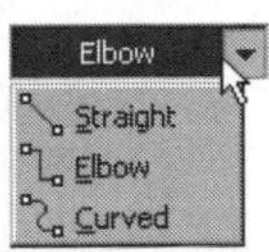

Figure 51
The Connector menu.

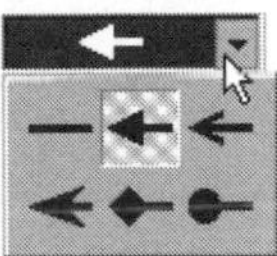

Figure 52
The Begin style menu. The End style menu looks the same, but the arrows point the other way.

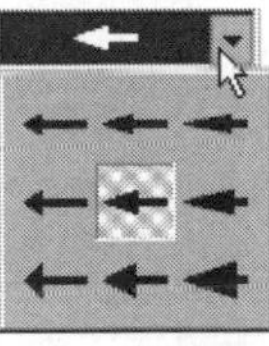

Figure 53
The Begin size menu. The End size menu looks the same, but the arrows point the other way.

- ▲ To change the line style, choose an option from the Style menu in the Line area of the dialog box (**Figure 49**). The options are the same as those on the Line Style button's menu (**Figure 42**).
- ▲ To change the line weight, enter a value in pixels in the Weight edit box in the Line area of the dialog box (**Figures 48**, **49**, and **50**).
- ▲ To change the style of arrowheads on a line or arrow, choose options from the Begin style and End style menus (**Figure 52**) in the Arrows area of the dialog box (**Figures 49** and **50**). When you choose an arrow style, you can also set the arrow size by choosing options from the Begin size and End size menus (**Figure 53**).

4. When you're finished setting options in the dialog box, click OK.

✔ Tips

- As shown in **Figures 48**, **49**, and **50**, the formatting options that are available in the dialog box depend on the line or shape that is selected.
- You can combine as many formatting options as you like to customize the appearance of lines and shapes.

Stacking Order

Each time you draw a shape, Excel puts it on a new drawing layer. When you draw a shape that overlaps another shape, the first shape may be partially obscured by the one "on top" of it (**Figure 54**).

Figure 54 Because each object is drawn in a separate layer, objects can be obscured by other objects "on top" of them.

To change stacking order

1. Select the object(s) you want to move to another layer (**Figure 55**).
2. Choose an option from the Order submenu on the Drawing toolbar's Draw menu (**Figure 56**):
   - ▲ **Bring to Front** moves the object(s) to the top layer (**Figure 57**).
   - ▲ **Send to Back** moves the object(s) to the bottom layer (**Figure 58**).
   - ▲ **Bring Forward** moves the object(s) up one layer.
   - ▲ **Send Backward** moves the object(s) down one layer.

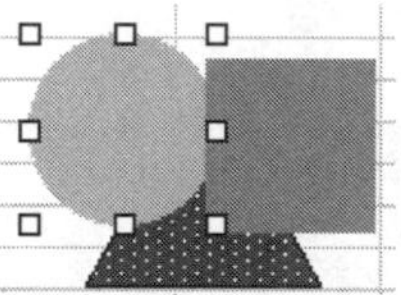

Figure 55 To change an object's layer, begin by selecting it.

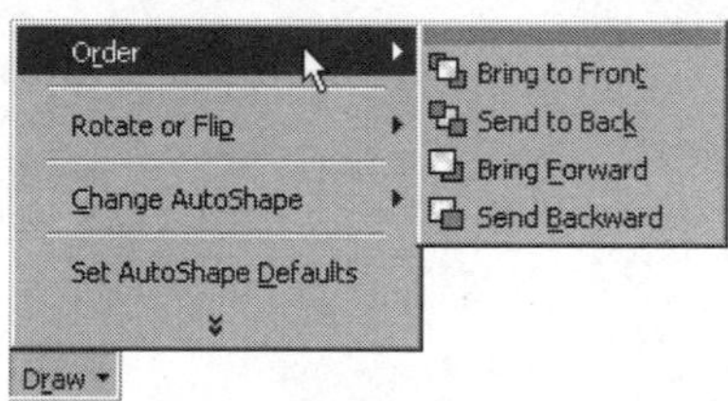

Figure 56 The Order submenu under the Drawing toolbar's Draw menu.

✔ Tips

- Once you have objects in the order you want, consider grouping them so they stay just the way you want them to. I tell you how to group objects earlier in this chapter.
- You cannot move graphic objects behind the worksheet layer.

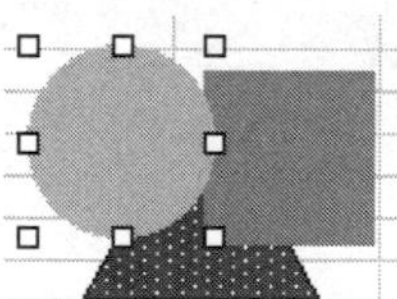

Figure 57 A selected object can be brought to the top layer...

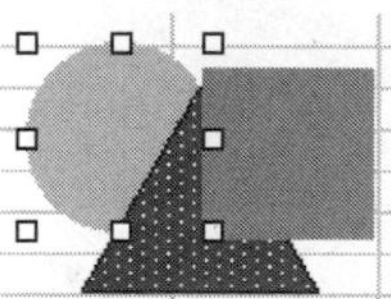

Figure 58 ...or sent to the bottom layer.

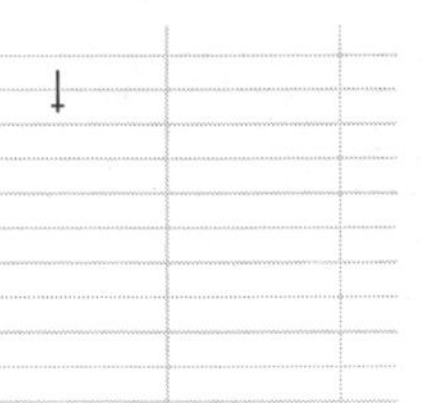

Figure 59 The mouse pointer turns into a crosshairs pointer.

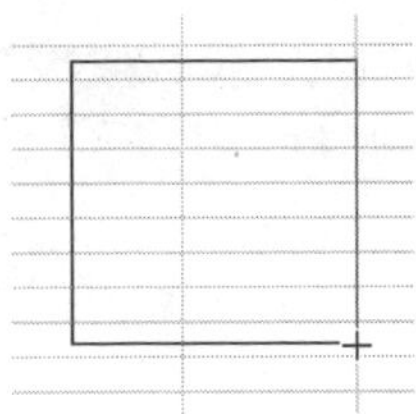

Figure 60 Drag to draw a text box.

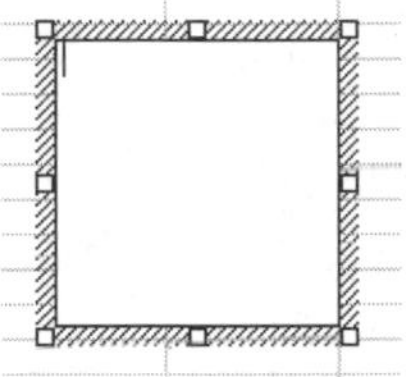

Figure 61 When you release the mouse button, the text box appears with a blinking insertion point inside it.

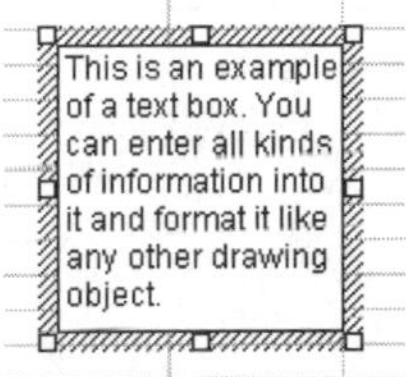

Figure 62 You can type whatever you like in the text box.

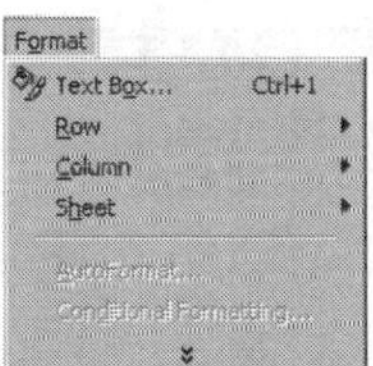

Figure 63 When a text box is selected, the Text Box command appears on the Format menu.

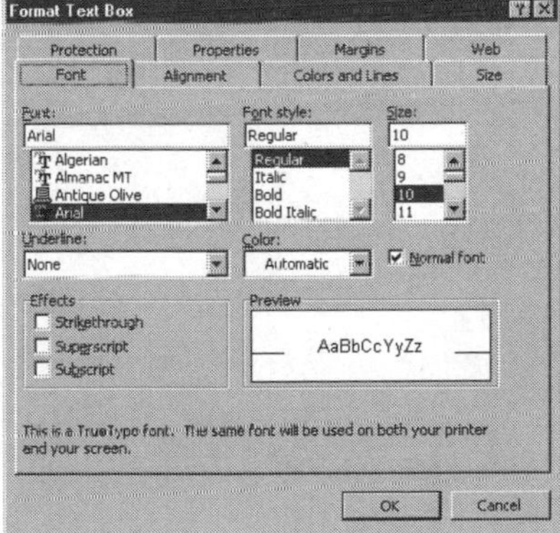

Figure 64 You can use options in the Format Text Box dialog box to format a selected text box or selected text box contents.

Text Boxes

A text box is like a little word processing document within an Excel sheet. Once created, you can enter and format text within it.

✔ Tip

- Text boxes offer more flexibility than worksheet cells when entering long passages of text.

To add a text box

1. Click the Text Box button on the Drawing toolbar. The mouse pointer turns into a special crosshairs pointer (**Figure 59**).
2. Position the crosshairs where you want to begin drawing the text box.
3. Press the mouse button down and drag. As you move the mouse, the text box begins to take form (**Figure 60**).
4. Release the mouse button to complete the text box. An insertion point appears within it (**Figure 61**).
5. Enter the text you want in the text box (**Figure 62**).

✔ Tips

- You can move, copy, resize, and delete a text box just like any other object.
- To edit text in a text box, double-click inside it to select one or more characters. Then use the arrow keys to move the insertion point. Use standard editing techniques to modify text.
- To format a selected text box or selected contents, choose Format > Text Box (**Figure 63**). Then use tabs in the Format Text Box dialog box that appears (**Figure 64**) to set formatting options. Click OK to save your settings.

Other Graphics

You can add graphics created with other programs to your Excel sheets. This enables you to include graphics that are more complex that those you can draw with Excel's drawing tools—like a company logo, stylized text, or clip art.

✔ Tips

- You can move, copy, or resize externally created graphic images like any graphic image created within Excel.
- When an externally created graphic is selected, the Picture toolbar (**Figure 65**) automatically appears. You can use this toolbar to modify the appearance of pictures.

To paste in graphic objects

1. Open the file containing the graphic you want to use.
2. Select the graphic (**Figure 66**).
3. Choose Edit > Copy to copy the object.
4. Switch to the sheet in which you want to paste the object.
5. Choose Edit > Paste (**Figure 26**), press Ctrl V, or click the Paste button on the Standard toolbar. The object appears.
6. Drag the object into the desired position on the sheet (**Figure 67**).

✔ Tip

- How you select a graphic object in step 2 varies depending on the program in which it resides. For more information and specific instructions, consult the documentation that came with the program.

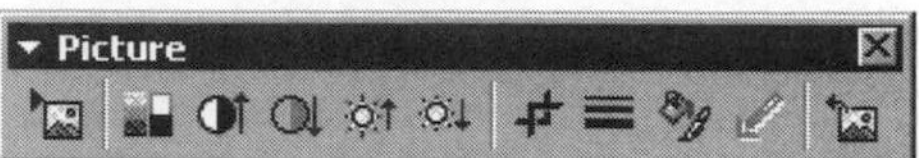

Figure 65 The Picture toolbar appears whenever an externally created graphic object is selected.

Figure 66 Here's a company logo created in Photoshop, selected and ready for copying.

First Quarter Sales

	January	February	March	Total
John	$ 1,254.00	$ 1,256.00	$ 2,435.00	$ 4,945.00
Jean	1,865.00	1,736.00	1,905.00	5,506.00
Joe	1,614.00	1,284.00	2,509.00	5,407.00
Joan	1,987.00	1,908.00	2,890.00	6,785.00
Totals	$ 6,720.00	$ 6,184.00	$ 9,739.00	$ 22,643.00

Figure 67 Here's the same logo pasted into a worksheet to add visual appeal and emphasize corporate identity.

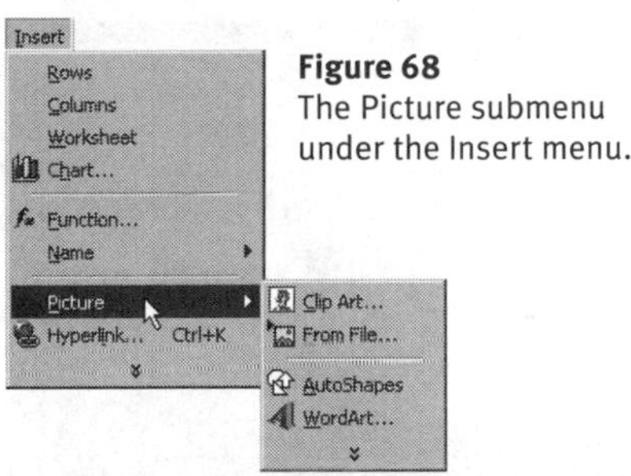

Figure 68 The Picture submenu under the Insert menu.

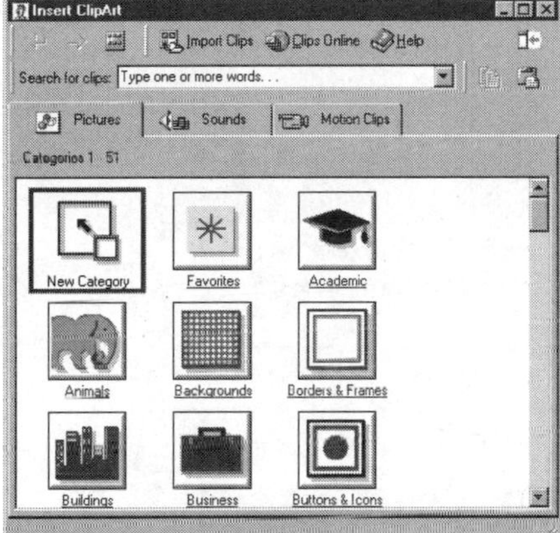

Figure 69 The Insert ClipArt window with the Pictures tab selected.

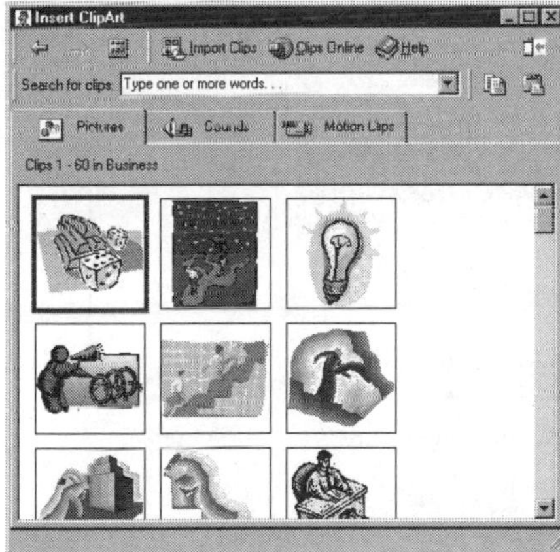

Figure 70 Clicking a category name displays the clips in that category.

Figure 71 Clicking a clip displays a menu of buttons.

To insert clip art

1. Position the insertion point where you want the clip art to appear.
2. Choose Insert > Picture > Clip Art (**Figure 68**) or click the Insert ClipArt button on the Drawing toolbar to display the Insert ClipArt window.
3. Click a tab for a specific type of clip (**Figure 69**).
4. Click a category name or icon to display the clips within that category (**Figure 70**).
5. Click the clip that you want to insert. The clip becomes selected and a menu of buttons appears (**Figure 71**).
6. Click the Insert button .
7. Click the Insert ClipArt window's close button to dismiss it.
8. Drag the clip art picture into the desired position on the sheet.

✔ Tips

- Only the Pictures tab includes content—clips that you can insert into a document. You can add content by clicking the Import Clips button at the top of the dialog box.
- If you used a Typical installation to install Excel or Microsoft Office, Clip Art may not have been installed. If a dialog box offers to install it, do so to access this useful feature.

To insert a picture from a file

1. Position the insertion point where you want the picture to appear.
2. Choose Insert > Picture > From File (**Figure 68**) to display the Insert Picture dialog box (**Figure 72**).
3. Locate and select the file that you want to insert.
4. Click the Insert button. The file is inserted in the document.
5. Drag the object into the desired position on the sheet (**Figure 67**).

✔ Tip

- A preview area on the right side of the Insert Picture dialog box helps identify pictures with cryptic names (**Figure 72**).

To insert WordArt

1. Choose Insert > Picture > WordArt (**Figure 68**) or click the Insert WordArt button on the Drawing toolbar.
2. In the WordArt Gallery dialog box that appears (**Figure 73**), click to select a WordArt style.
3. Click OK.
4. In the Edit WordArt Text dialog box that appears next (**Figure 74**), change the sample text to the text that you want to display. You can also set various font formatting options.
5. Click OK. The WordArt image and WordArt toolbar appear.
6. Drag the WordArt image into the desired position on the sheet (**Figure 75**).

✔ Tip

- To change a WordArt image, double-click it to reopen the Edit WordArt Text dialog box (**Figure 74**). Then follow steps 4 and 5.

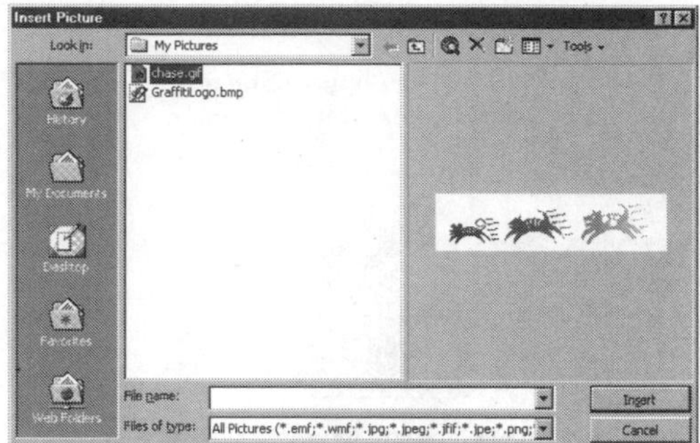

Figure 72 Use the Insert Picture dialog box to locate and insert a picture file on disk.

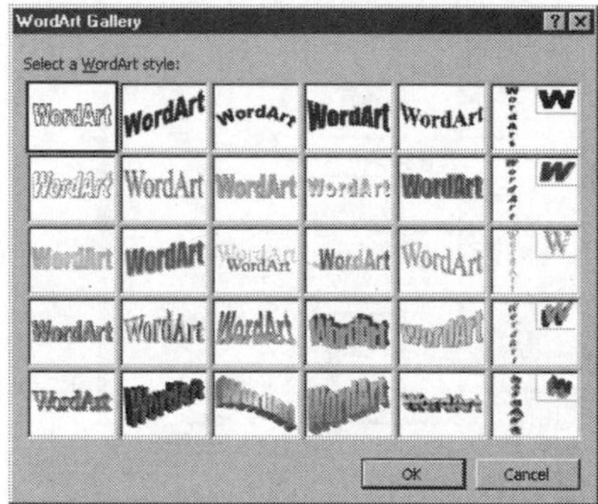

Figure 73 The WordArt Gallery dialog box.

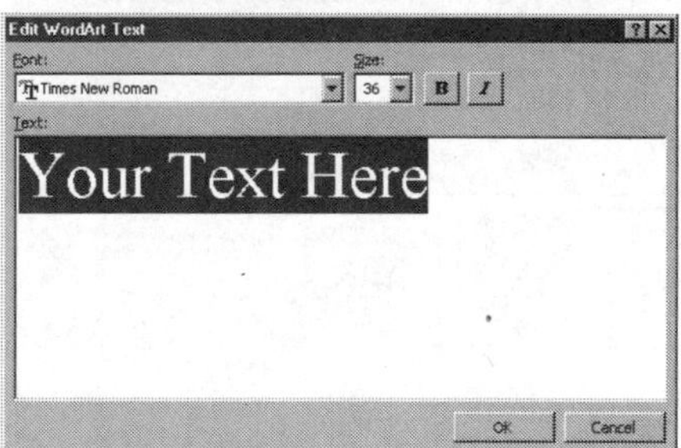

Figure 74 The Edit WordArt Text dialog box.

Figure 75 A WordArt image and the WordArt toolbar.

Creating Charts

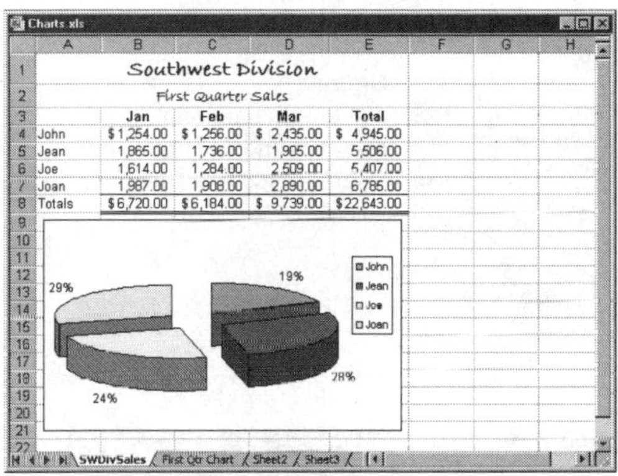

Figure 1 Here's a 3-D pie chart embedded in a worksheet.

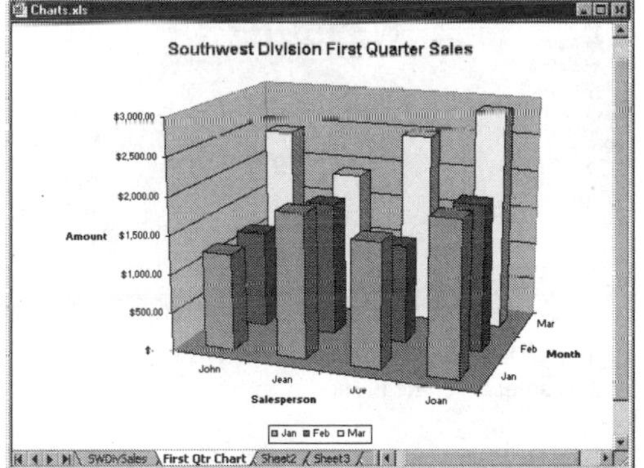

Figure 2 Here's a 3-D column chart on a chart sheet of its own.

Charts

A chart is a graphic representation of data. A chart can be embedded in a worksheet (**Figure 1**) or can be a chart sheet of its own (**Figure 2**).

With Excel, you can create many different types of charts. The 3-D pie chart and 3-D column chart shown here (**Figures 1** and **2**) are only two examples. Since each type of chart has at least one variation and you can customize any chart you create, there's no limit to the number of ways you can present data graphically with Excel.

✔ Tips

- Include charts with worksheets whenever you want to emphasize worksheet results. Charts can often communicate information like trends and comparative results better than numbers alone.
- A skilled chartmaker can, through choice of data, chart format, and scale, get a chart to say almost anything about the data it represents!

The Chart Wizard

Excel's Chart Wizard walks you step-by-step through the creation of a chart. It uses illustrated dialog boxes to prompt you for information. In each step of the Chart Wizard, you get to see what your chart looks like. At any point, you can go back and make changes to selections. When you're finished, your chart appears. You can then use a variety of chart formatting commands and buttons to change the look of your chart.

To use the Chart Wizard

1. Select the data you want to include in the chart (**Figure 3**).
2. Choose Insert > Chart (**Figure 4**) or click the Chart Wizard button on the Standard toolbar.
3. In the Chart Wizard – Chart Type dialog box (**Figure 5**), click to select one of the chart types in the scrolling list. Then click to select one of the chart sub-types on the right side of the dialog box. Click Next.
4. In the Chart Wizard – Chart Source Data dialog box (**Figure 6**), check the contents of the Data Range box to assure that it indicates the data you want to chart. You can see which data range will be charted by clicking the Collapse Dialog button so you can see the sheet behind the dialog box (**Figure 7**). If incorrect, select the correct range. If necessary, click the Expand Dialog button to display the entire dialog box again. You can also select a different Series option to change the way data is charted. Then click Next.

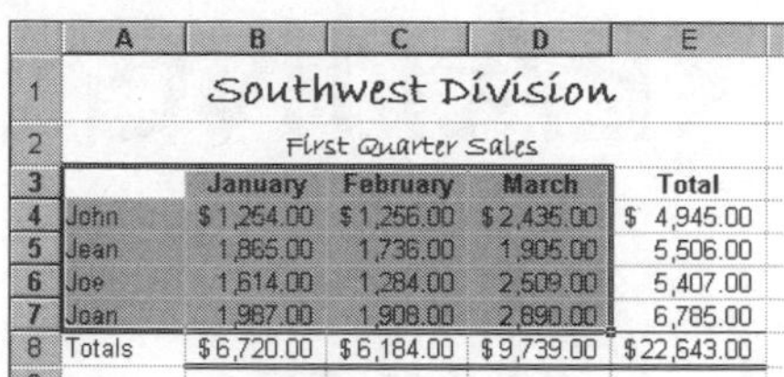

	A	B	C	D	E
1	Southwest Division				
2	First Quarter Sales				
3		January	February	March	Total
4	John	$ 1,254.00	$ 1,256.00	$ 2,435.00	$ 4,945.00
5	Jean	1,865.00	1,736.00	1,905.00	5,506.00
6	Joe	1,614.00	1,284.00	2,509.00	5,407.00
7	Joan	1,987.00	1,908.00	2,890.00	6,785.00
8	Totals	$ 6,720.00	$ 6,184.00	$ 9,739.00	$ 22,643.00

Figure 3 Select the data you want to chart.

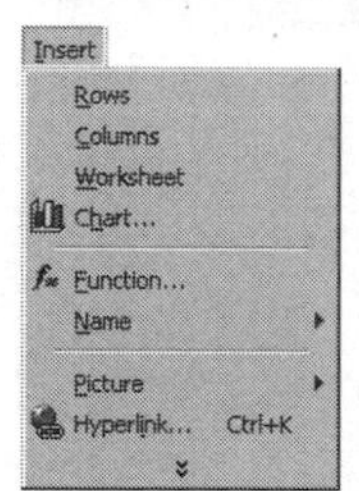

Figure 4
The Chart command can be found on the Insert menu.

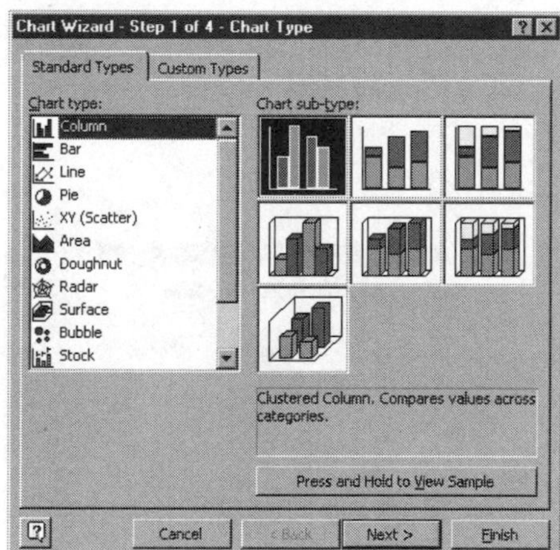

Figure 5 The first step of the Chart Wizard enables you to select a chart type.

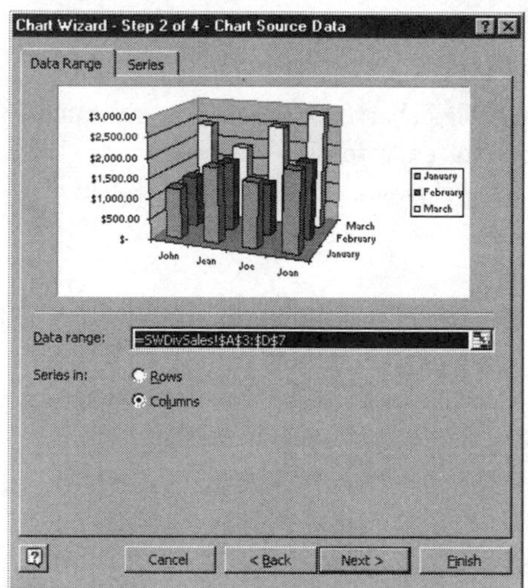

Figure 6 The second step of the Chart Wizard enables you to check and, if necessary, change the range to be charted.

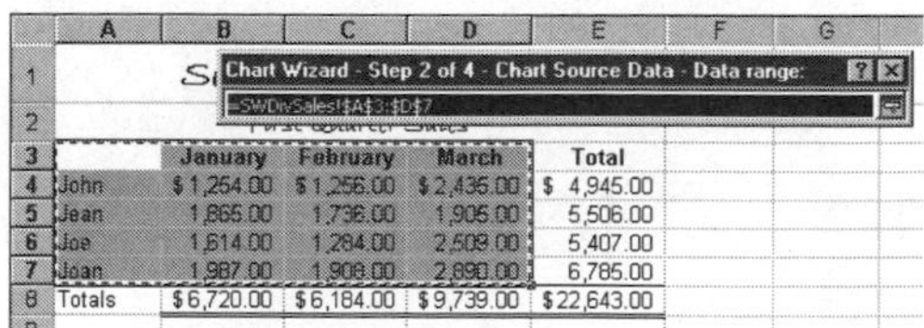

	A	B	C	D	E
3		January	February	March	Total
4	John	$ 1,254.00	$ 1,256.00	$ 2,435.00	$ 4,945.00
5	Jean	1,865.00	1,736.00	1,905.00	5,506.00
6	Joe	1,614.00	1,284.00	2,509.00	5,407.00
7	Joan	1,987.00	1,908.00	2,890.00	6,785.00
8	Totals	$ 6,720.00	$ 6,184.00	$ 9,739.00	$ 22,643.00

Figure 7 You can collapse the Chart Wizard dialog box to see what range is selected.

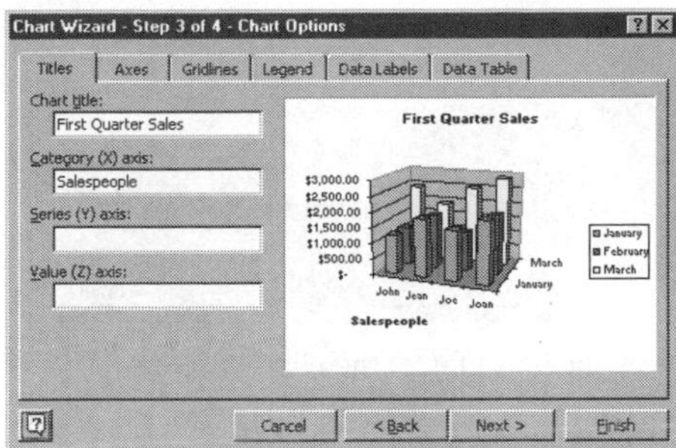

Figure 8 The Chart Wizard Title options.

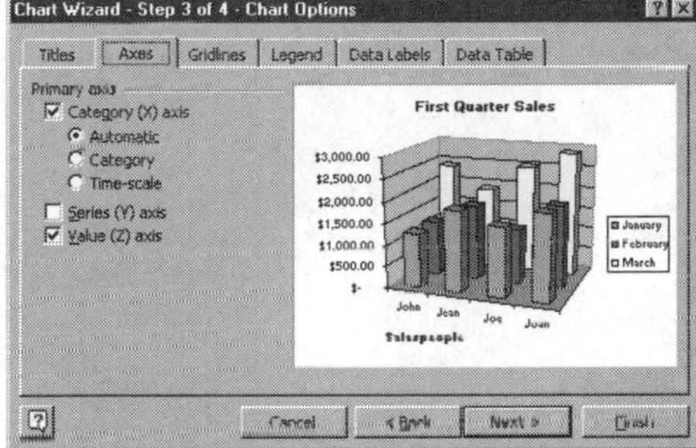

Figure 9 The Chart Wizard Axes options.

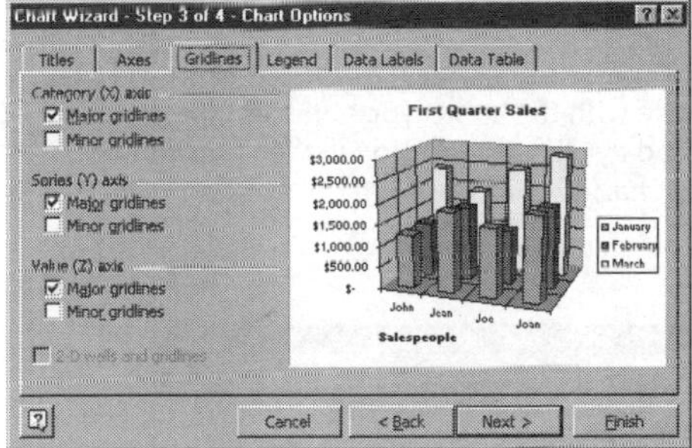

Figure 10 The Chart Wizard Gridlines options.

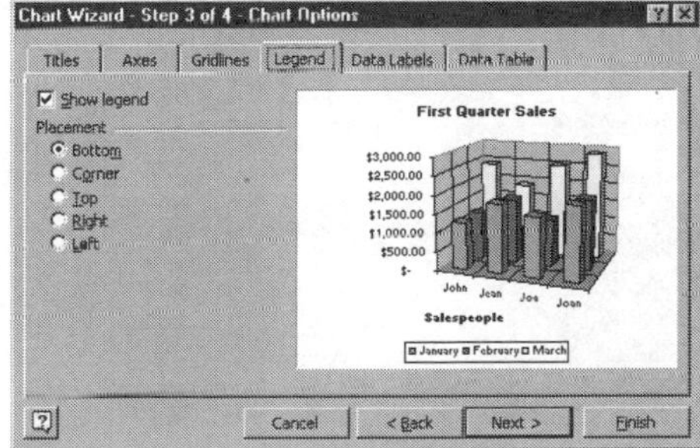

Figure 11 The Chart Wizard Legend options.

5. In the Chart Wizard – Chart Options dialog box, use the tabs at the top of the dialog box to set a variety of formatting options:

   ▲ **Titles (Figure 8)** enables you to set a chart title and axes titles.

   ▲ **Axes (Figure 9)** enables you to select which axes you want to display.

   ▲ **Gridlines (Figure 10)** enables you to select which gridlines to display.

   ▲ **Legend (Figure 11)** enables you to show and position or hide the legend.

   ▲ **Data Labels (Figure 12)** enables you to set the display of data labels.

   ▲ **Data Table (Figure 13)** enables you to include a data table with the chart.

   Set options as desired. When you change a setting, the sample chart changes accordingly. When you are finished, click Next.

Continued on next page...

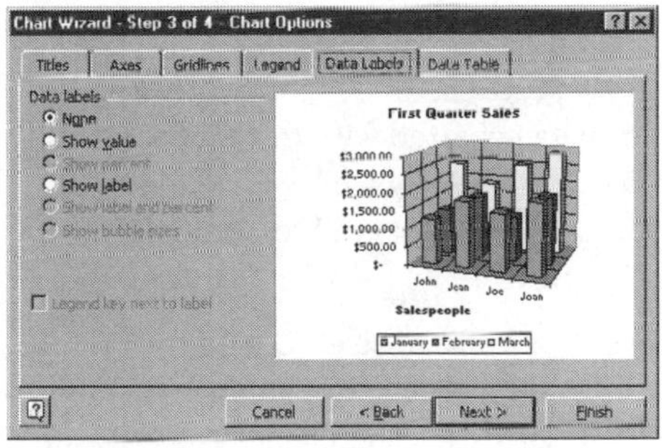

Figure 12 The Chart Wizard Data Labels options.

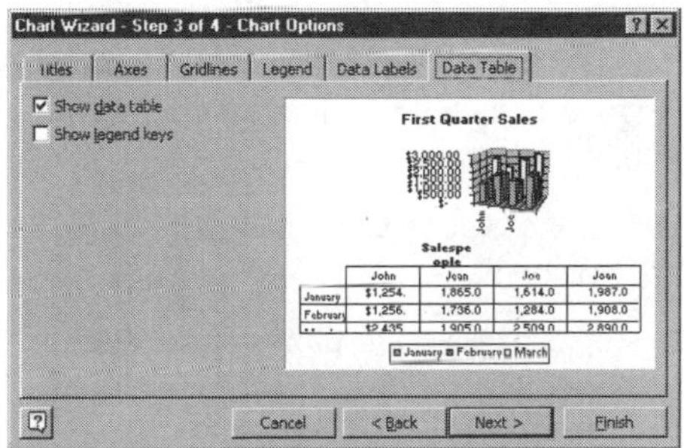

Figure 13 The Chart Wizard Table options.

Continued from previous page.

6. In the Chart Wizard — Chart Location dialog box (**Figure 14**), select the radio button to set the location for the chart:
   - ▲ **As new sheet** puts the chart on a new chart sheet. You can enter a name in the text box to name the new sheet when you create it.
   - ▲ **As object in** puts the chart on another sheet in the workbook. You can use the menu to select the sheet.
7. Click Finish.

   Excel creates and inserts the chart with the settings and in the location you specified.

✔ Tips

- At any time while using the Chart Wizard, you can click the Back button to move to a previous step. Any changes you make in a previous step are carried forward when you continue.
- In step 3, to see what your data would look like when charted with the chart type and sub-type you select, click and hold down the Press and Hold to View Sample button (**Figure 15**).
- In step 3, you can select one of the custom chart types by clicking the Custom Types tab (**Figure 16**). Then follow the instructions in step 3 for that tab.
- In step 4, you can add, modify, or delete data series for the chart in the Series tab (**Figure 17**). I tell you about working with data series later in this chapter.
- I explain all the options in step 5 throughout this book.
- In step 5, axes and gridlines options are only available for charts that have axes or gridlines. Pie charts, for example, have neither axes nor gridlines.

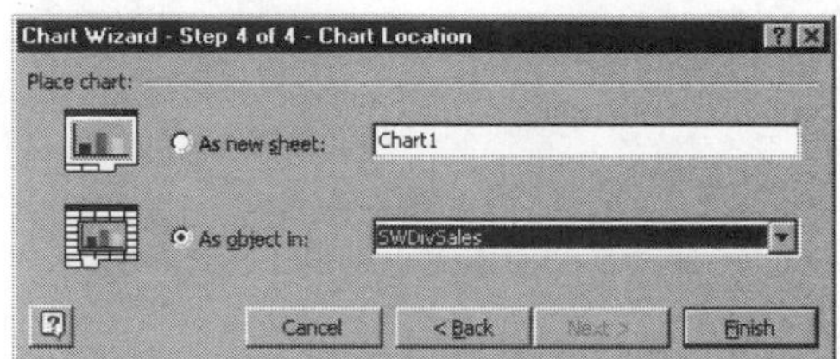

Figure 14 The final step of the Chart Wizard.

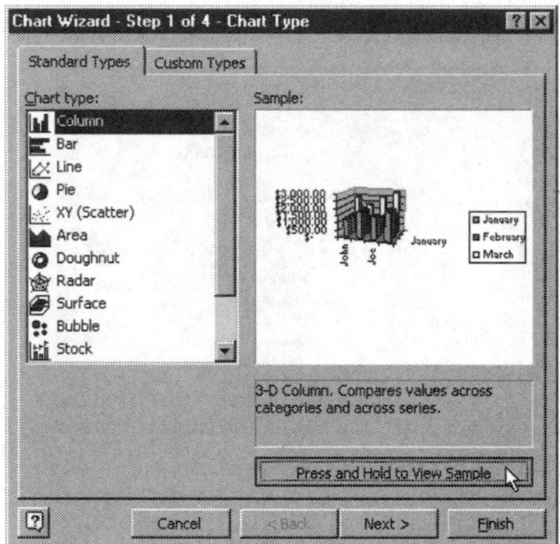

Figure 15 You can preview what your chart will look like with the chart type and sub-type you selected by clicking a button in the first window of the Chart Wizard.

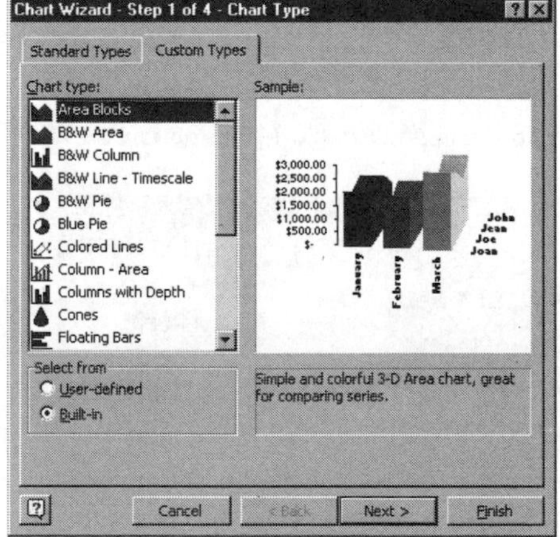

Figure 16 The Chart Wizard also allows you to select some custom chart types from the Chart Gallery.

USING THE CHART WIZARD

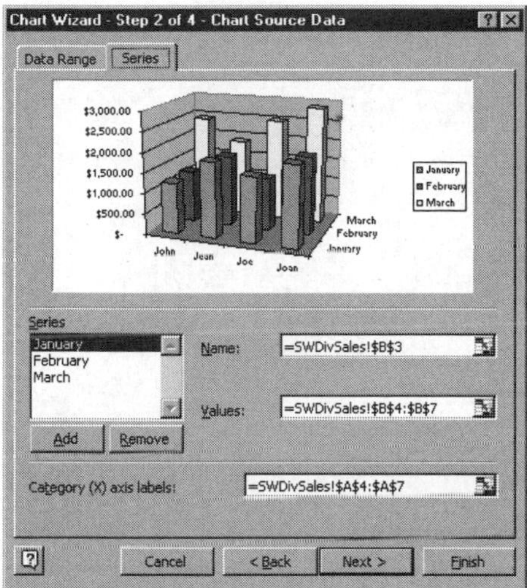

Figure 17 You can also add, modify, or remove data series from a chart within the Chart Wizard.

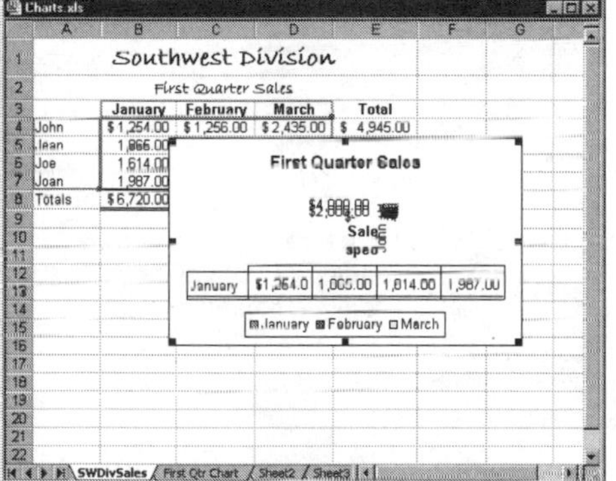

Figure 18 When you create an embedded chart, Excel just plops it on the worksheet.

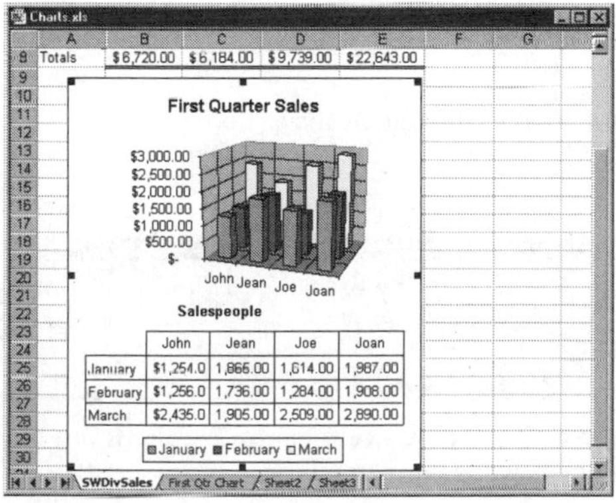

Figure 19 You can move and resize a chart to improve its appearance.

- A chart embedded in a worksheet or a chart sheet is a special kind of graphic. You can move, copy, resize, or delete it just like any other graphic object. I tell you how to work with graphics in **Chapter 7**.
- If an embedded chart is too small to properly display data (**Figure 18**), resize it. The larger the chart, the better it will display (**Figure 19**).
- You can also improve the appearance of an embedded chart by resizing or removing chart elements such as legends, axes labels, and data tables.
- You're not stuck with the formatting you select in the Chart Wizard. I tell you about chart formatting options throughout this chapter.
- Don't be afraid to experiment with the Chart Wizard. Try different options to see what effects you can achieve. You can always delete the chart and start fresh. Deleting a chart does not change data.

To reuse the Chart Wizard

1. Activate the chart by switching to its chart sheet or, if it's an embedded chart, by clicking it.
2. Click the Chart Wizard button on the Standard toolbar.
3. Follow the steps on the previous pages to set or change Chart Wizard options for the chart.

Worksheet & Chart Links

When you create a chart based on worksheet data, the worksheet and chart are linked. Excel knows exactly which worksheet and cells it should look at to plot the chart. If the contents of one of those cells changes, the chart changes accordingly (**Figures 20** and **21**).

✔ Tips

- The link works both ways. With some chart types, you can drag a data point to change the data in the source worksheet (**Figure 22**). This makes a good planning tool for businesses interested in maintaining trends.
- Excel's Range Finder feature places a color-coded box around ranges in a selected chart (**Figure 23**), making them easy to spot.
- You can see (and edit) the links between a chart and a worksheet by activating the chart, selecting one of the data series, and looking at the formula bar. You should see a formula with a SERIES function that specifies the sheet name and absolute cell references for the range making up that series. **Figure 23** shows an example.
- If you delete worksheet data or an entire worksheet that is linked to a chart, Excel may warn you with a dialog box like the one in **Figure 24**. If you removed the data by mistake, choose Edit > Undo Delete, click the Undo button on the Standard toolbar, or press Ctrl Z to get the deleted data back.

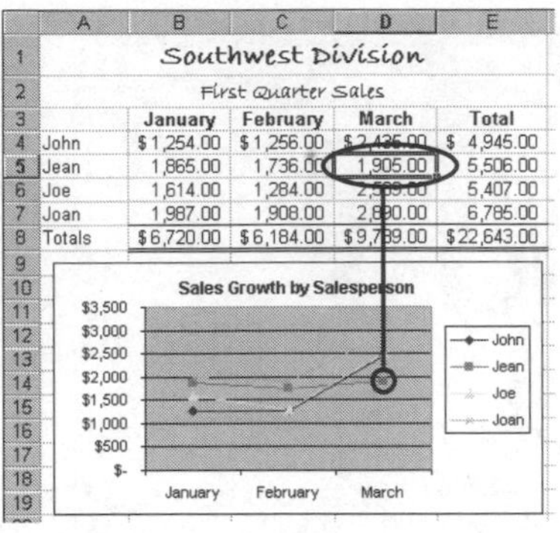

Figure 20 A linked worksheet and chart.

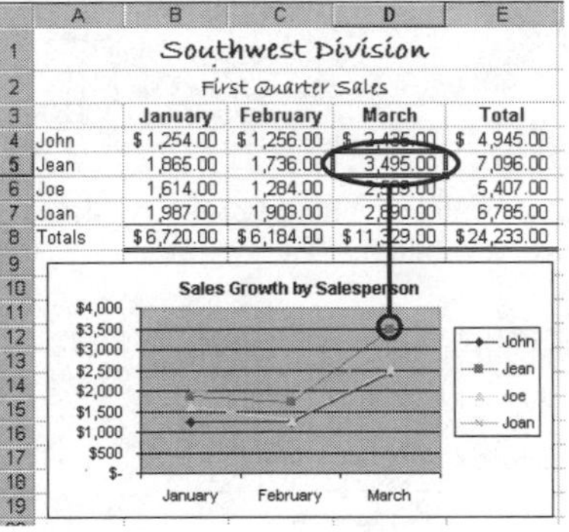

Figure 21 When you change a value, its plotted point, which is linked to the data, changes.

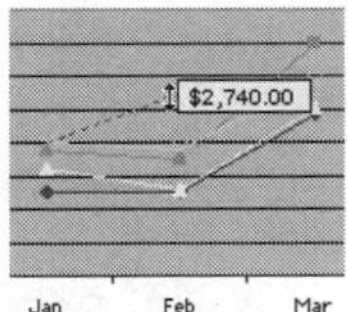

Figure 22 Dragging a data point changes the data in the linked cell.

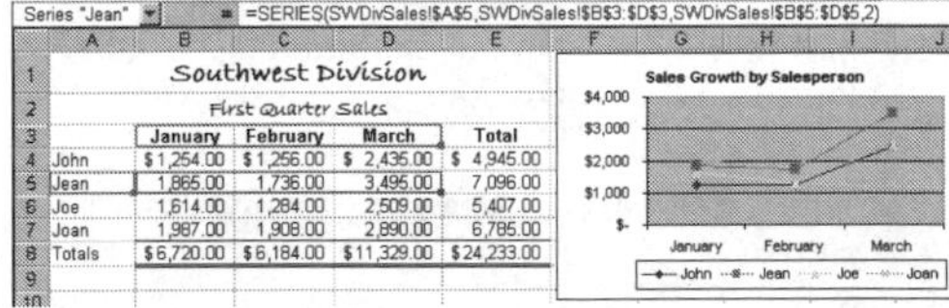

Figure 23 This illustration shows both the Range Finder feature and the SERIES formula.

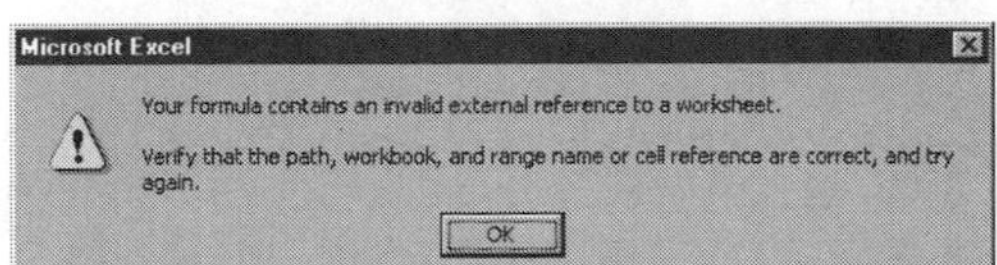

Figure 24 If you delete cells linked to a chart, you may see a dialog box like this.

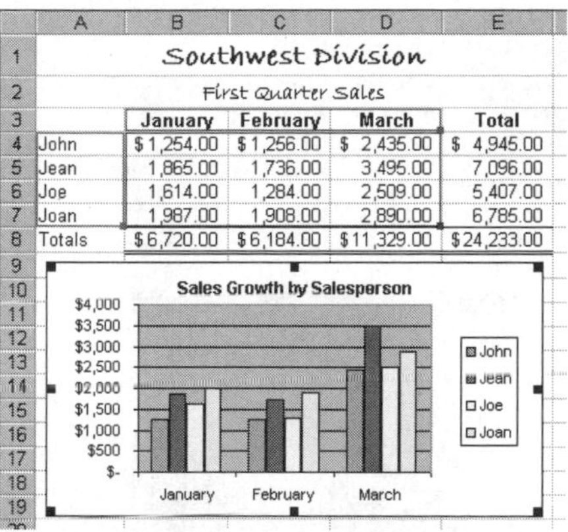

Figure 25 When you activate a chart, Range Finder frames appear around each data series.

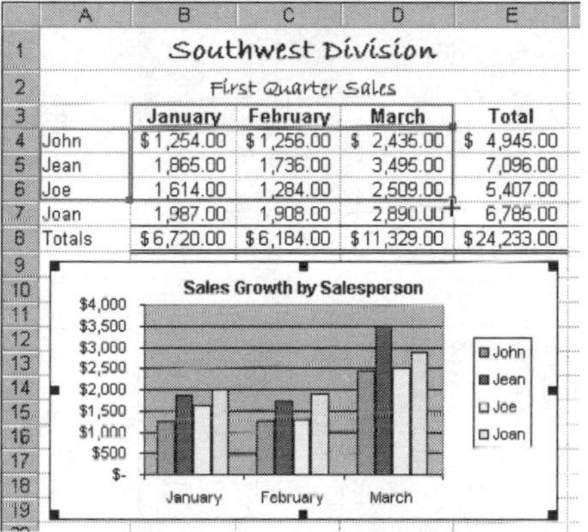

Figure 26 Drag a Range Finder handle to change the size of the series.

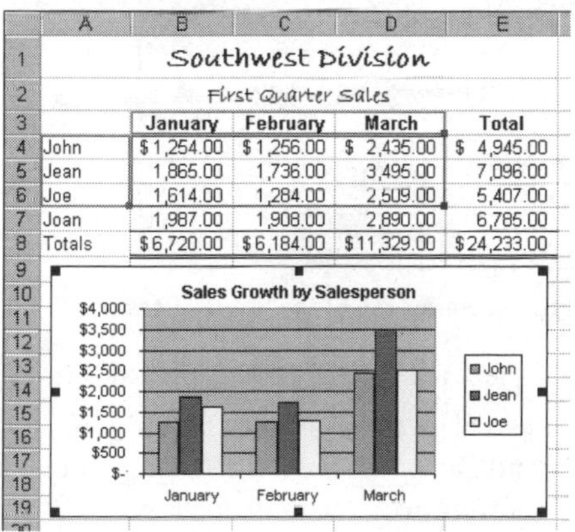

Figure 27 When you release the mouse button, the series—and the chart—changes.

Data Series & Points

A *data series* is a group of related data in a chart. A data series normally corresponds to the values in a linked range of cells in a single column or row of a single worksheet. When plotted on a chart, each data series is assigned its own color or pattern.

Each cell within a data series is called a *data point.* Data points are individually plotted on a chart.

You can change data series included in a chart at any time using four different methods:

- Use Range Finder handles to modify a series in an embedded chart.
- Use the Source Data dialog box to add, modify, or remove a series.
- Use the Copy and Paste commands to paste in a new series.
- Use drag and drop editing to drag in a series.

To modify a data series with Range Finder handles

1. Click the chart to activate it. Range Finder frames with handles appear around each data series (**Figure 25**).
2. Position the mouse pointer on the handle for the series you want to change. The mouse pointer turns into a thick crosshairs pointer.
3. Press the mouse button down, and drag to stretch or shrink the series (**Figure 26**).
4. When you release the mouse button, the series (and any related series) changes, thus changing the information plotted in the chart (**Figure 27**).

✔ Tip

- You can only use this method with an embedded chart.

To modify data series with the Source Data dialog box

1. Activate the chart by switching to its chart sheet or, if it's an embedded chart, by clicking it.
2. Choose Chart > Source Data (**Figure 28**) to display the Source Data dialog box (**Figures 29** and **30**).
3. Click the Data Range tab (**Figure 29**):
   - ▲ To change the range of data plotted in the chart, select a new data range. As you select the range, it is automatically entered in the Data range box for you.
   - ▲ To switch the series from column to row or row to column, select the appropriate Series in option.

   or

   Click the Series tab (**Figure 30**):
   - ▲ To add a data series, click the Add button, then drag in the worksheet to enter a range in the Name and Values boxes.
   - ▲ To modify a data series, select the name of the series you want to change, then drag in the worksheet to modify the range in the Name and/or Values boxes.
   - ▲ To remove a data series, select the name of the series you want to remove and click the Remove button.
4. Consult the sample chart in the dialog box to see the affect of your changes. When the chart shows correct data ranges, click OK.

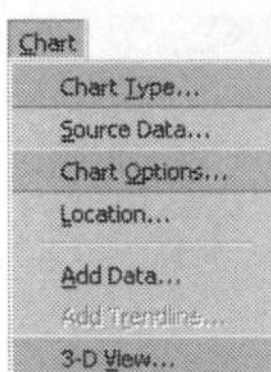

Figure 28 The Chart menu only appears when a chart is active.

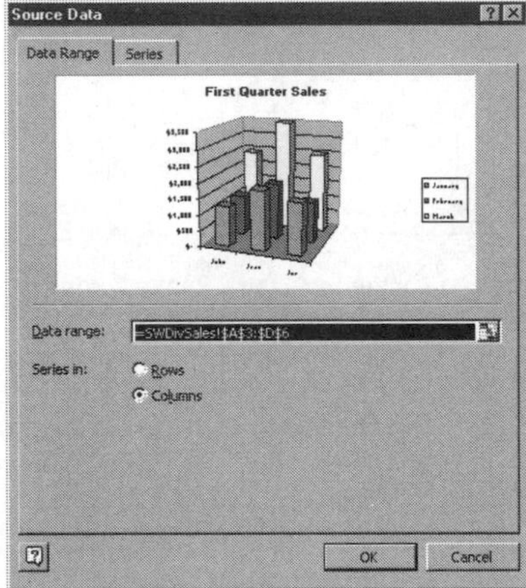

Figure 29 The Data Range tab of the Source Data dialog box.

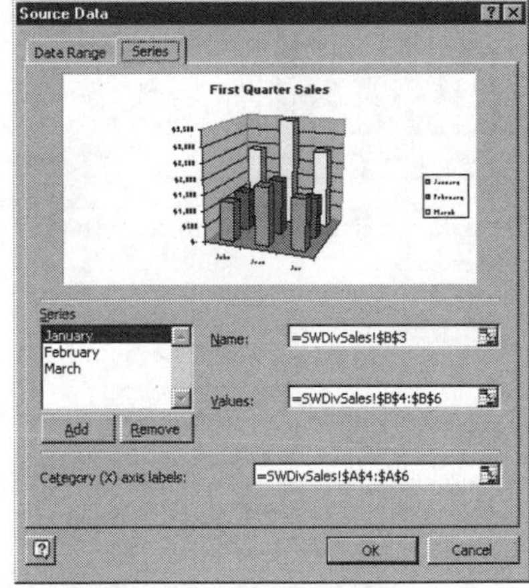

Figure 30 The Series tab of the Source Data dialog box.

✔ Tips

- ■ The Source Data dialog box looks (and works) just like the second step of the Chart Wizard (**Figures 6** and **17**). In fact, you can use the Chart Wizard to make any of the changes discussed on this page.
- ■ You can click the Collapse Dialog or Expand Dialog button to change the size of the Source Data dialog box.
- ■ Removing a data series does not delete data from the source worksheet.

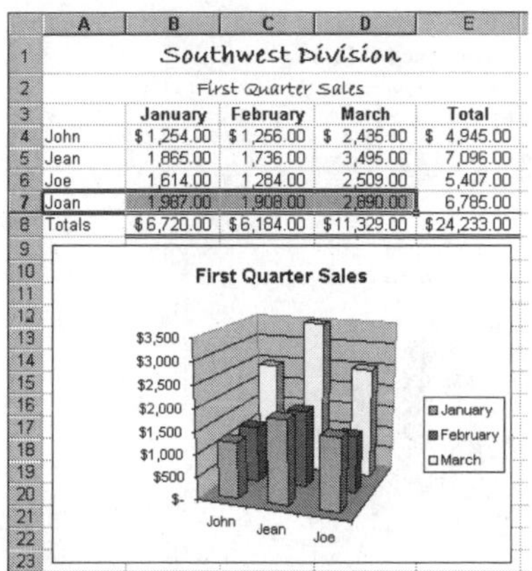

	A	B	C	D	E
1		Southwest Division			
2		First Quarter Sales			
3		January	February	March	Total
4	John	$ 1,254.00	$ 1,256.00	$ 2,435.00	$ 4,945.00
5	Jean	1,865.00	1,736.00	3,495.00	7,096.00
6	Joe	1,614.00	1,284.00	2,509.00	5,407.00
7	Joan	1,987.00	1,908.00	2,890.00	6,785.00
8	Totals	$ 6,720.00	$ 6,184.00	$ 11,329.00	$ 24,233.00

Figure 31 Select the data that you want to add to the chart.

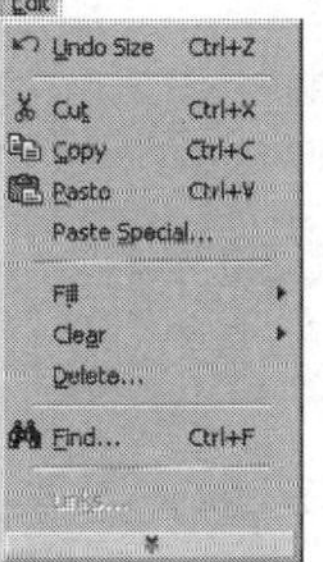

Figure 32 The Edit menu includes the Copy, Paste, and Paste Special commands, which you can use to add data to a chart.

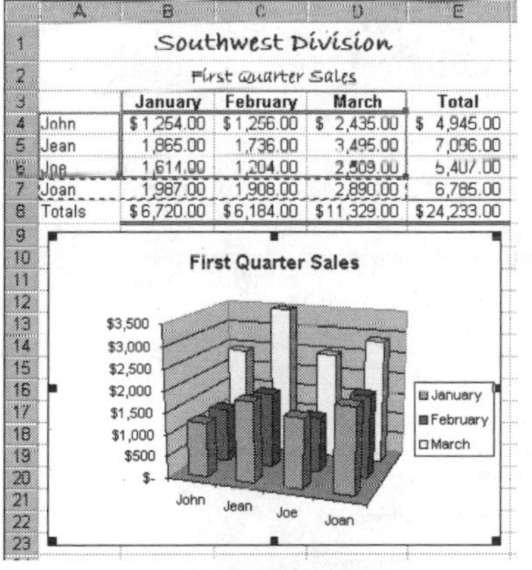

	A	B	C	D	E
1		Southwest Division			
2		First Quarter Sales			
3		January	February	March	Total
4	John	$ 1,254.00	$ 1,256.00	$ 2,435.00	$ 4,945.00
5	Jean	1,865.00	1,736.00	3,495.00	7,096.00
6	Joe	1,614.00	1,284.00	2,509.00	5,407.00
7	Joan	1,987.00	1,908.00	2,890.00	6,785.00
8	Totals	$ 6,720.00	$ 6,184.00	$ 11,329.00	$ 24,233.00

Figure 33 When you paste in the data, the chart changes accordingly.

Paste Special
Add cells as: New series / New point(s)
Values (Y) in: Rows / Columns
OK
Cancel
Series Names (Y Labels) in First Row
Categories (X Labels) in First Column
Replace existing categories

Figure 34 The Paste Special dialog box offers additional options for pasting data into charts.

To add a data series with the Copy & Paste commands

1. In the worksheet, select the data you want to add to the chart (**Figure 31**). Be sure to include column or row headings if they should be included as labels.
2. Choose Edit > Copy (**Figure 32**), press Ctrl C, or click the Copy button on the Standard toolbar.

   A marquee appears around the selected cells.
3. Activate the chart to which you want to add the data by switching to its chart sheet or, if it's an embedded chart, by clicking it.
4. Choose Edit > Paste (**Figure 32**), press Ctrl V, or click the Paste button on the Standard toolbar.

   The chart changes to include the additional data (**Figure 33**).

✔ Tips

- In order for this technique to work properly, the data you add must be the same kind of data originally charted. For example, if you originally plotted totals to create a pie chart, you can't successfully add a series of numbers that aren't totals to the chart.
- For additional control over how data is pasted into a chart, choose Edit > Paste Special (**Figure 32**) in step 4 above. The Paste Special dialog box (**Figure 34**) will sometimes appear on its own when you paste a range into a chart.

To add a data series with drag & drop

1. In the worksheet, select the data you want to add to the chart (**Figure 35**). Be sure to include column or row headings if they should be included as labels.
2. Position the mouse pointer on the border of the selection. The mouse pointer turns into an arrow.
3. Press the mouse button down and drag the selection on top of the chart. The mouse pointer gets a little plus sign next to it and the chart border changes (**Figure 36**).
4. Release the mouse button.

   The chart changes to include the additional data (**Figure 37**).

✔ Tips

- In order for this technique to work properly, the data you add must be the same kind of data originally charted. For example, if you originally plotted totals to create a pie chart, you can't successfully add a series of numbers that aren't totals to the chart.
- This technique only works for charts that are embedded in the worksheet containing the original data.
- To add data contained in noncontiguous ranges, use one of the other methods discussed in this section.

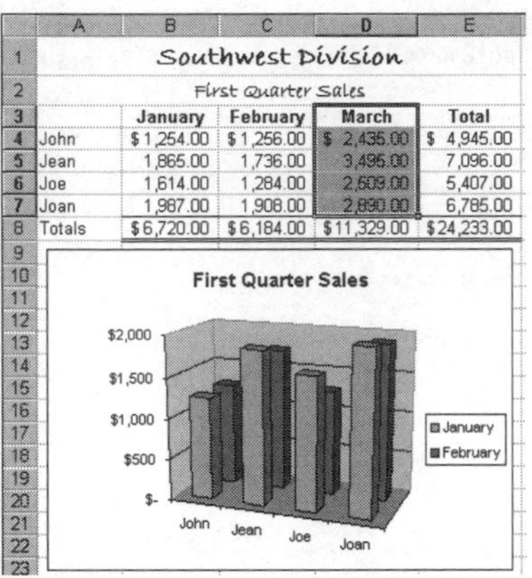

Southwest Division

First Quarter Sales

	January	February	March	Total
John	$1,254.00	$1,256.00	$2,435.00	$4,945.00
Jean	1,865.00	1,736.00	3,495.00	7,096.00
Joe	1,614.00	1,284.00	2,509.00	5,407.00
Joan	1,987.00	1,908.00	2,890.00	6,785.00
Totals	$6,720.00	$6,184.00	$11,329.00	$24,233.00

Figure 35 Select the data you want to add to the chart.

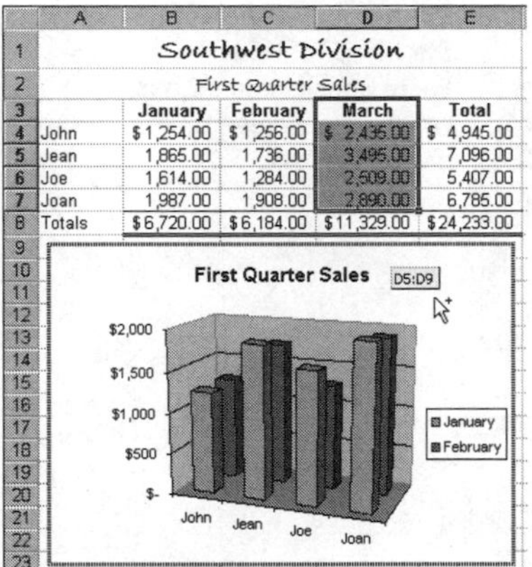

Southwest Division

First Quarter Sales

	January	February	March	Total
John	$1,254.00	$1,256.00	$2,435.00	$4,945.00
Jean	1,865.00	1,736.00	3,495.00	7,096.00
Joe	1,614.00	1,284.00	2,509.00	5,407.00
Joan	1,987.00	1,908.00	2,890.00	6,785.00
Totals	$6,720.00	$6,184.00	$11,329.00	$24,233.00

Figure 36 Drag the selection onto the chart.

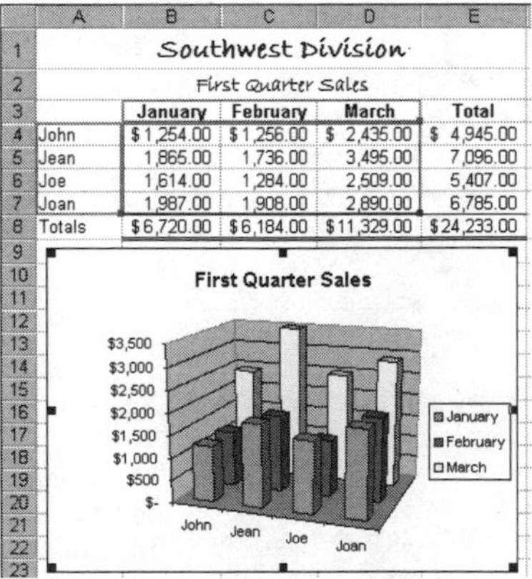

Southwest Division

First Quarter Sales

	January	February	March	Total
John	$1,254.00	$1,256.00	$2,435.00	$4,945.00
Jean	1,865.00	1,736.00	3,495.00	7,096.00
Joe	1,614.00	1,284.00	2,509.00	5,407.00
Joan	1,987.00	1,908.00	2,890.00	6,785.00
Totals	$6,720.00	$6,184.00	$11,329.00	$24,233.00

Figure 37 When you release the mouse button, the data is added to the chart.

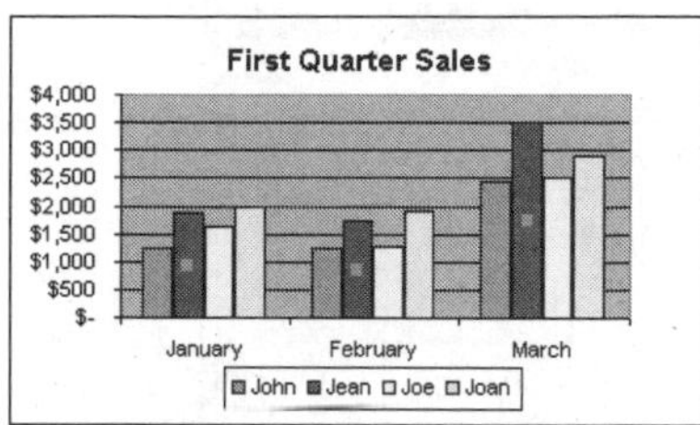

Figure 38 Select the series you want to remove.

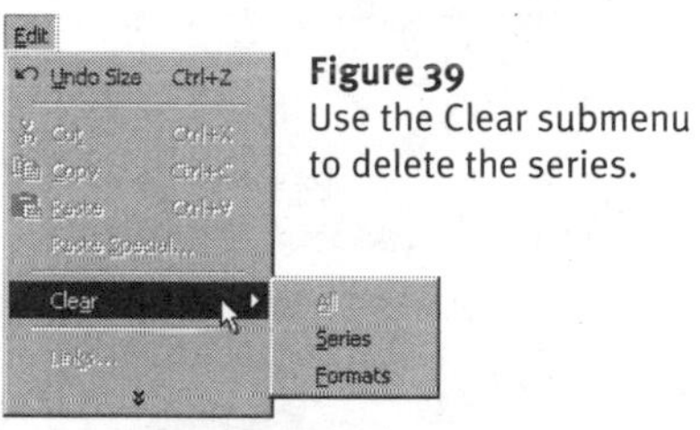

Figure 39 Use the Clear submenu to delete the series.

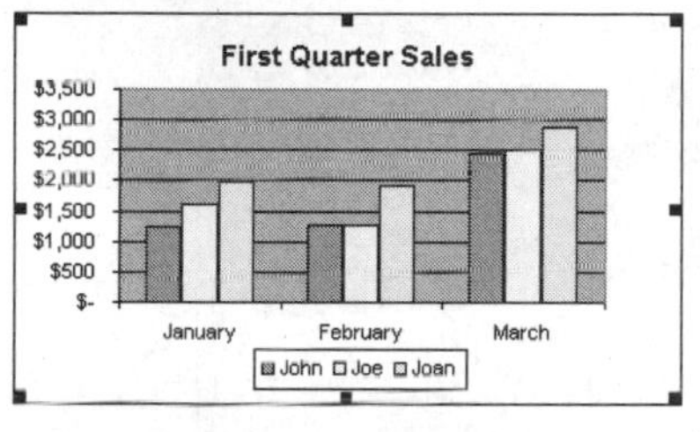

Figure 40 All trace of the series is removed from the chart.

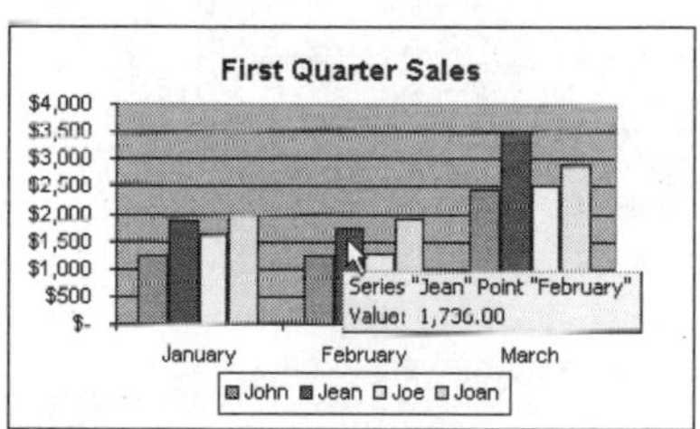

Figure 41 Chart tips identify the chart elements and values you point to.

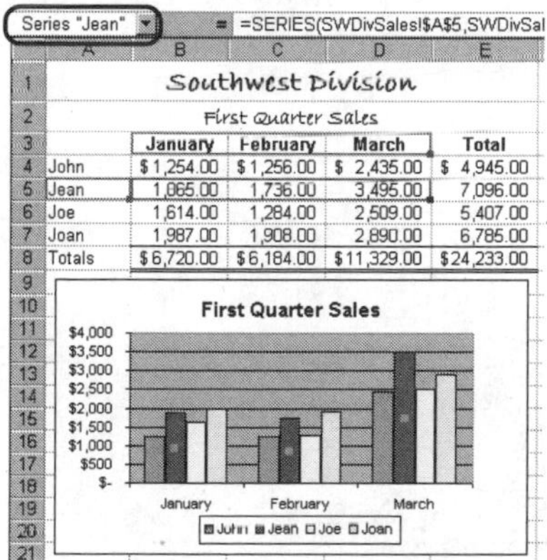

Southwest Division

First Quarter Sales

	January	February	March	Total
John	$1,254.00	$1,256.00	$ 2,435.00	$ 4,945.00
Jean	1,865.00	1,736.00	3,495.00	7,096.00
Joe	1,614.00	1,284.00	2,509.00	5,407.00
Joan	1,987.00	1,908.00	2,890.00	6,785.00
Totals	$6,720.00	$6,184.00	$11,329.00	$24,233.00

Figure 42 The name of a selected element appears in the Name Box on the formula bar.

To remove a data series

1. Click to select the series you want to remove. Selection handles appear at each data point in the series (**Figure 38**).
2. Choose Edit > Clear > Series (**Figure 39**) or press Delete.

   The series disappears (**Figure 40**). If the chart included a legend, it is revised to exclude the deleted data.

✔ Tips

- Removing a series from a chart does not delete data from the source worksheet.
- You can also remove a data series with the Source Data dialog box (**Figure 30**). I tell you how earlier in this chapter.

Chart Elements

Each chart is made up of multiple *elements*, each of which can be selected, then modified or formatted to fine-tune the appearance of a chart.

To identify a chart element

Point to the element you want to identify. Excel displays the name (and values, if appropriate) for the element in a yellow Chart Tip box (**Figure 41**).

To select a chart element

Click the element you want to select. Selection handles or a selection box (or both) appear around it (**Figure 42**).

Chart Type

Excel includes dozens of standard and custom chart types. You select the chart type when you create a chart with the Chart Wizard, but you can change the type at any time. You can also add your formatted charts to the chart gallery so you can use them to create future charts.

To change the chart type

1. Activate the chart by switching to its chart sheet or, if it's an embedded chart, by clicking it.
2. Choose Chart > Chart Type (**Figure 28**) to display the Chart Type dialog box.
3. Click the Standard Types tab (**Figure 43**):
   - ▲ To select a standard chart type, select a Chart type, then select a Chart sub-type.
   - ▲ To apply a chart type to a selected data series, turn on the Apply to selection check box.
   - ▲ To remove formatting you have applied to the chart, turn on the Default formatting check box.

   or

   Click the Custom Types tab:
   - ▲ To select a built-in chart type, select the Built-in option (**Figure 44**), then select a Chart type.
   - ▲ To select a user-defined chart type, select the User-defined option (**Figure 45**), then select a Chart type.
4. Click OK to apply the chart type.

✔ Tip

- The Chart Type dialog box looks (and works) just like the first step of the Chart Wizard (**Figures 5** and **15**). In fact, you can use the Chart Wizard to make any of the changes discussed on this page.

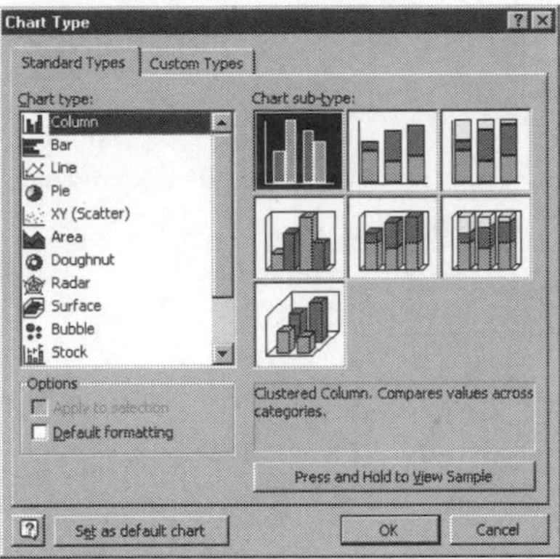

Figure 43 The Standard Types tab of the Chart Type dialog box.

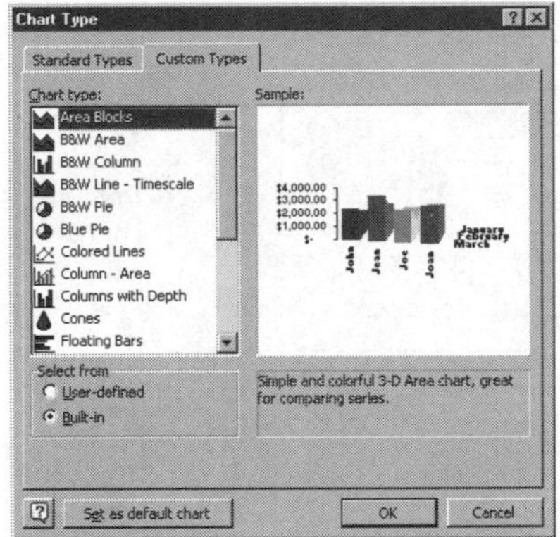

Figure 44 The Custom Types tab of the Chart Type dialog box with Built-in selected.

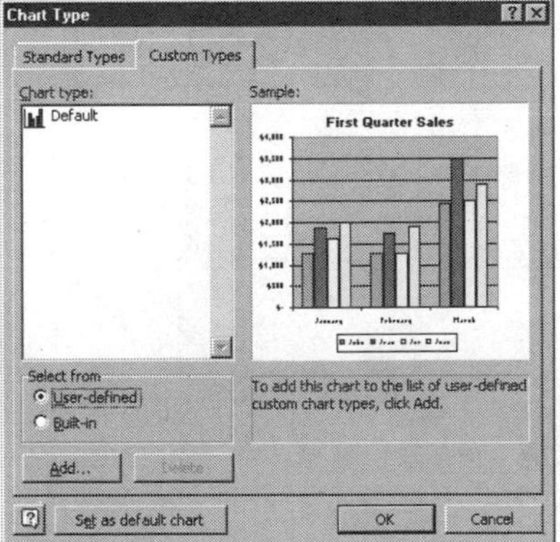

Figure 45 The Custom Types tab of the Chart Type dialog box with User-defined selected.

Changing the Chart Type

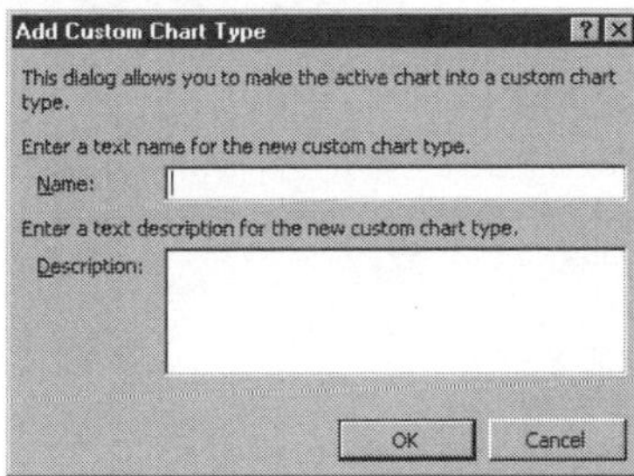

Figure 46 Use the Add Custom Chart Type dialog box to enter a name and description for a chart type.

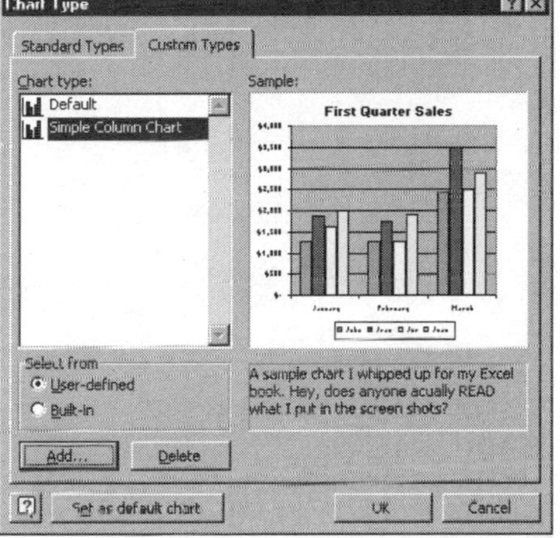

Figure 47 The chart type you added appears in the User-defined Chart type list.

To set the default chart type

1. Choose Chart > Chart Type (**Figure 28**) to display the Chart Type dialog box.
2. Click the Standard Types tab (**Figure 43**).
3. Select the Chart type and sub-type you want to set as the default chart type.
4. Click the Set as default chart button.
5. Click OK.

✔ Tip

- The default chart type is the one automatically selected for creating a new chart.

To add a user-defined chart to the Chart Type dialog box

1. Activate the formatted chart you want to add by switching to its chart sheet or, if it's an embedded chart, by clicking within it.
2. Choose Chart > Chart Type (**Figure 28**) to display the Chart Type dialog box.
3. Click the Custom Types tab.
4. Select the User-defined option (**Figure 45**).
5. Click the Add button.
6. In the Add Custom Chart Type dialog box that appears (**Figure 46**), enter a name and description for the chart in the appropriate text boxes.
7. Click OK.

   The chart appears in the User-defined Chart type list (**Figure 47**).
8. Click OK.

✔ Tip

- This feature makes it easy to create the same basic charts over and over again with different data—like you might have to do for a monthly report.

Chart Options

Chart options refer to the inclusion and basic formatting of chart elements such as titles, axes, gridlines, legend, data labels, and data tables. You set chart options with the Chart Options dialog box.

To use the Chart Options dialog box

1. Activate the chart by switching to its chart sheet or, if it's an embedded chart, by clicking it.
2. Choose Chart > Chart Options (**Figure 28**) to display the Chart Options dialog box (**Figures 48** through **53**).
3. Click the tab for the type of option you want to set.
4. Set options as desired.
5. Repeat steps 3 and 4 for each type of option you want to set.
6. Click OK to apply your settings.

✔ Tips

- I provide details on all options on the following pages.
- The Chart Options dialog box looks (and works) just like the third step of the Chart Wizard (**Figures 8** through **13**). In fact, you can use the Chart Wizard to make any of the changes discussed on this page.
- Each time you make a change in the Chart Options dialog box, the effect of your change is reflected in the chart preview within the dialog box. Use this feature to check your changes before clicking OK to apply them to the chart.
- The options available in the Chart Options dialog box vary based on the type of chart that is selected. If a specific option is not available, it will either not appear or it will appear in gray within the dialog box.

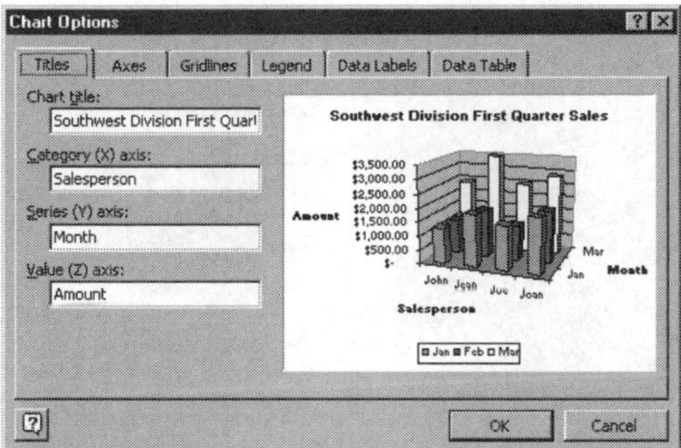

Figure 48 The Titles tab of the Chart Options dialog box for a 3-D column chart. The sample illustration shows all titles set.

Titles

Titles are textual labels that appear in specific locations on the chart.

To set chart titles

1. In the Chart Options dialog box click the Titles tab to display its options (**Figure 48**).
2. Enter titles in the desired text boxes:
   - ▲ **Chart title** is the chart's main title. It appears at the top of the chart.
   - ▲ **Category (X) axis** is the category axis title. Available for most 2-D and 3-D chart types, it appears along the bottom (front) axis.
   - ▲ **Series (Y) axis** is the series axis title. Available for most chart types, it appears down the left side of a 2-D chart and along the bottom (back) axis of a 3-D chart.
   - ▲ **Value (Z) axis** is the value axis title. Available only for 3-D chart types, it appears down the left side of the chart.

To remove a chart title

1. In the Chart Options dialog box click the Titles tab to display its options (**Figure 48**).
2. Clear the text box(es) for the titles you want to remove.

Axes

Axes are the bounding lines of a chart. 2-D charts have two axes: X and Y. 3-D charts have three axes: X, Y, and Z. Pie and doughnut charts do not have axes at all.

✔ Tip

- In case you're wondering, *axes* (pronounced *ax-eez*) is the plural of *axis*. While axes are also tools for chopping wood, you can't chop wood with Excel.

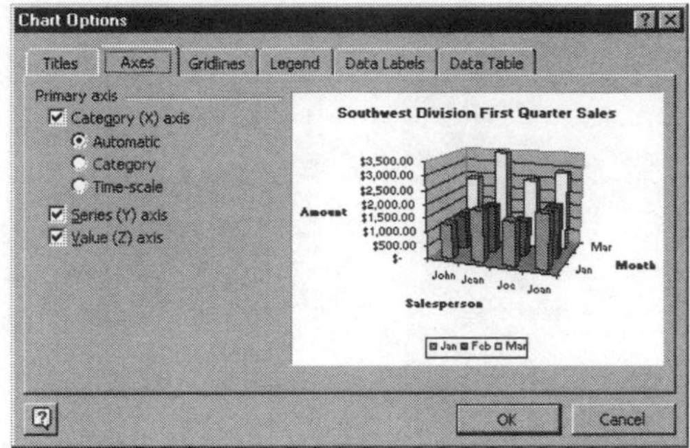

Figure 49 The Axes tab of the Chart Options dialog box for a 3-D column chart. The sample illustration shows all axes displayed.

To set axes options

1. In the Chart Options dialog box click the Axes tab to display its options (**Figure 49**).
2. Turn on the check boxes for the axes you want to display:
   - ▲ **Category (X) axis** appears along the bottom (front) axis.
   - ▲ **Series (Y) axis** appears down the left side of a 2-D chart and along the bottom (back) axis of a 3-D chart.
   - ▲ **Value (Z) axis**, which is available only for 3-D chart types, appears down the left side of the chart.
3. If you turned on the Category (X) axis option in step 2, select one of the formatting option buttons:
   - ▲ **Automatic** instructs Excel to check the formatting of the category data to determine whether it should use time-scale or category formatting.
   - ▲ **Category** instructs Excel to use the category data for the X axis.
   - ▲ **Time-Scale** instructs Excel to create a time scale for the X axis.

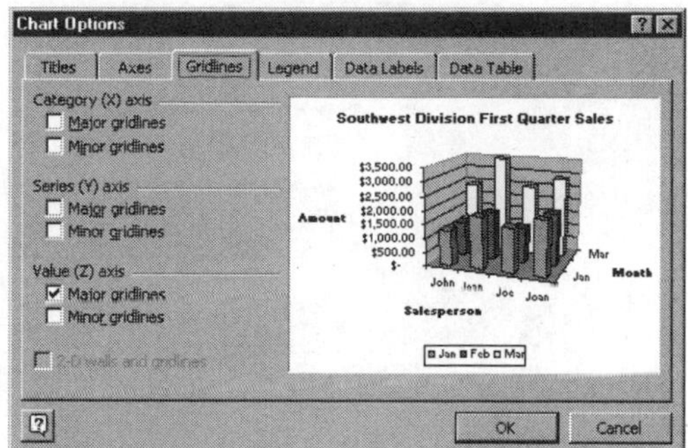

Figure 50 The Gridlines tab of the Chart Options dialog box for a 3-D column chart. The sample illustration shows only the major gridlines for the Value (Z) axis turned on.

Gridlines

Gridlines are lines indicating major and minor scale points along a chart's walls. They can make it easier to follow chart points to corresponding values on a chart axis. Pie and doughnut charts do not have gridlines.

✔ Tip

- Although gridlines can make a chart's data easier to read, too many gridlines can clutter a chart's walls, making data impossible to read.

To set gridlines

1. In the Chart Options dialog box click the Gridlines tab to display its options (**Figure 50**).
2. Turn on the check boxes for the gridlines you want to display on each axis:
   - **Major gridlines** correspond to major tick mark units for the axis scale.
   - **Minor gridlines** correspond to minor tick mark units for the axis scale.
3. To apply a 2-D appearance to 3-D chart walls and gridlines, turn on the 2-D walls and gridlines check box. This option is only available for certain types of charts.

✔ Tips

- *Tick marks* are marks along an axis that correspond to scale values. I explain how to set the scale for an axis later in this chapter.
- I define the three axes on the previous page.

Legend

A legend is a box with color-coded labels identifying a chart's data series. You can turn a legend on or off and set its position within the chart area.

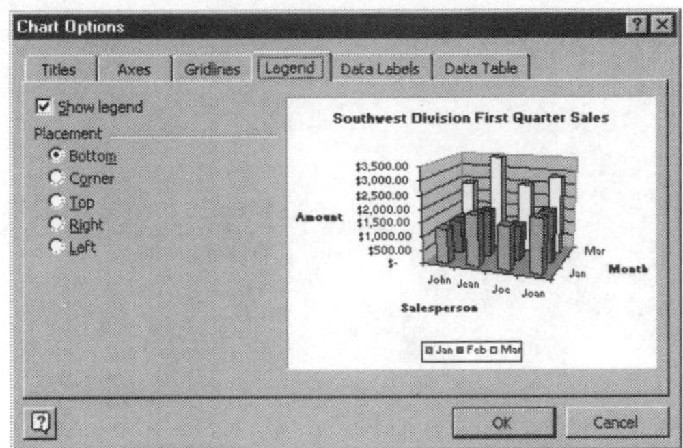

Figure 51 The Legend tab of the Chart Options dialog box for a 3-D column chart. The sample illustration shows a legend placed at the bottom of the chart.

✔ Tip

- Excel creates the legend based on cells selected as part of the data source. That's why it's a good idea to include column and/or row headings in the selected range when you create a chart.

To add a legend

1. In the Chart Options dialog box click the Legend tab to display its options (**Figure 51**).
2. Turn on the Show legend check box.
3. Select one of the options for a legend position:
   - ▲ **Bottom** displays the legend at the bottom-center of the chart.
   - ▲ **Corner** displays the legend at the top-right corner of the chart.
   - ▲ **Top** displays the legend at the top-center of the chart.
   - ▲ **Right** displays the legend at the right-middle of the chart.
   - ▲ **Left** displays the legend at the left-middle of the chart.

✔ Tips

- You can also move a legend by dragging it to a new position within the chart.
- The legend position can affect the size of a chart's plot area.

To remove the legend

1. In the Chart Options dialog box click the Legend tab to display its options (**Figure 51**).
2. Turn off the Show legend check box.

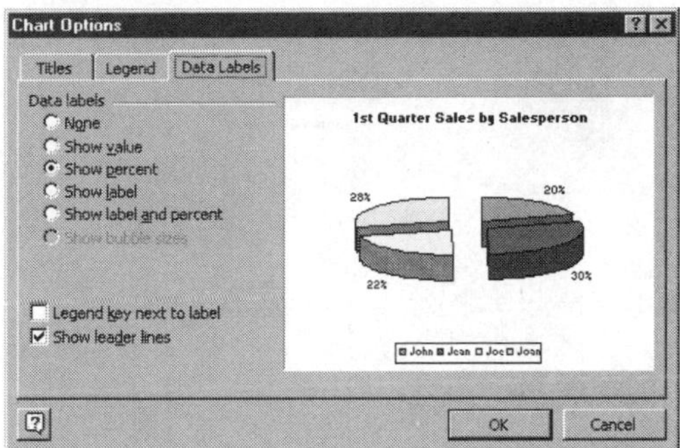

Figure 52 The Data Labels tab of the Chart Options dialog box for a 3-D pie chart. The sample illustration shows percent data labels.

Data Labels

Data labels provide additional information about specific data points.

✔ Tip

- The Chart Options dialog box enables you to set data labels for all chart points. To set data labels for just a single data series or data point, select the series or point, then use the Format dialog box, which I tell you about later in this chapter.

To set data labels

1. In the Chart Options dialog box click the Data Labels tab to display its options (**Figure 52**).
2. Select one of the Data labels options:
   - ▲ **None** removes all data labels.
   - ▲ **Show value** displays the value for each data point.
   - ▲ **Show percent** displays the percentage of the whole for each data point. This option is only available for pie and doughnut charts.
   - ▲ **Show label** displays the legend label for each data point.
   - ▲ **Show label and percent** displays the both the legend label and percentage of the whole for each data point. This option is only available for pie and doughnut charts.
   - ▲ **Show bubble sizes** displays the size of bubbles in a bubble chart.
3. To show the legend color key beside a data label, turn on the Legend key next to label check box.
4. For a pie or doughnut chart, to display a line from the data point to the data label, turn on the Show leader lines check box.

Data Table

A data table is the data plotted on the chart, in tabular format.

✔ Tips

- Data tables are more useful on chart sheets than on embedded charts, since embedded charts can include the worksheet on which the chart is based.
- Data tables are not available for pie and doughnut charts.

To add a data table

1. In the Chart Options dialog box click the Data Table tab to display its options (**Figure 53**).
2. Turn on the Show data table check box.
3. To show the legend color key in the data table, turn on Show legend keys check box.

To remove a data table

1. In the Chart Options dialog box click the Data Table tab to display its options (**Figure 53**).
2. Turn off the Show data table check box.

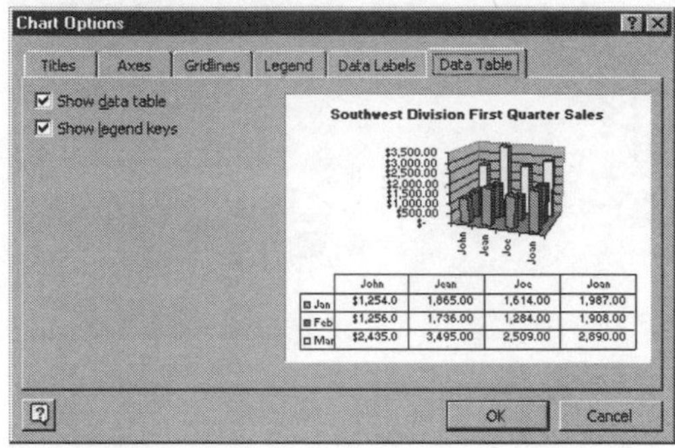

Figure 53 The Data Table tab of the Chart Options dialog box for a 3-D column chart. The sample illustration shows a data table with legend keys turned on.

ADDING & REMOVING DATA TABLES

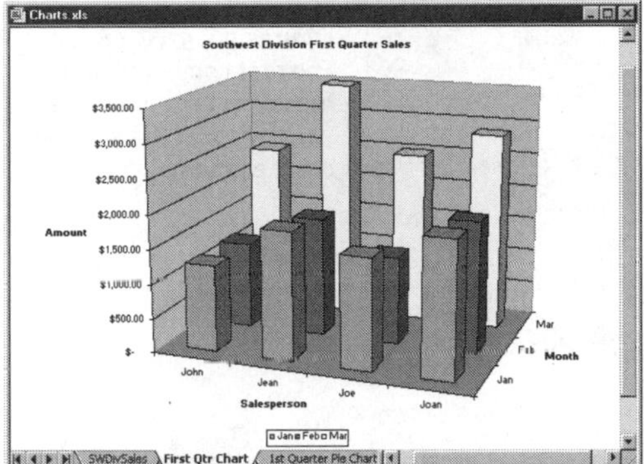

Figure 54 Formatting can make this rather dull default chart...

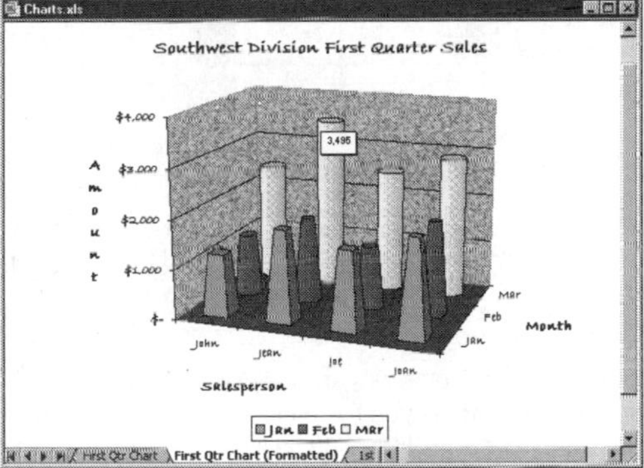

Figure 55 ...look a lot more interesting!

Formatting Chart Elements

You can use the Format dialog box to apply a variety of formatting to chart elements:

- **Font** enables you to change the appearance of an element's font characters.
- **Number** enables you to change the number formatting of values.
- **Alignment** enables you to change the alignment and orientation of text.
- **Patterns** enables you to change an element's color and pattern. It also enables you to set axis tick mark styles.
- **Placement** enables you to set the position for a chart legend.
- **Scale** enables you to change the values that appear on an axis.
- **Shape** enables you to change the shape of data points.
- **Data Labels** enables you to set data labels for a single data series or data point. I discuss these options earlier in this chapter.
- **Series Order** enables you to change the order in which data series appear.
- **Options** enables you to set data series spacing options.

Figures 54 and **55** may give you an idea of what you can do with chart formatting.

In this section, I tell you how chart formatting works and discuss some of the formatting options available just for charts.

✔ Tip

- I discuss pattern, font, number, and alignment formatting in **Chapter 6**. I discuss legend placement and data labels earlier in this chapter.

To use the Format dialog box

1. Select the chart element that you want to format and choose the first command under the Format menu (**Figures 56, 57,** and **58**) or press Ctrl 1.

   or

   Double-click the element that you want to format.
2. In the Format dialog box that appears, click the tab for the type of option you want to set.
3. Set options as desired.
4. Repeat steps 2 and 3 for each type of option you want to set.
5. Click OK to apply the formatting.

✔ Tips

- The exact name of the menu command in step 1 varies depending on the chart element that is selected. You can see this in **Figures 56, 57,** and **58.**
- The exact name of the Format dialog box in step 2 varies depending on the chart element that is selected. You can see this in **Figures 59** and **61.**

To set the data point shape

1. Open the Format Data Series dialog box for a selected data series.
2. Click the Shape tab to display its options (**Figure 59**).
3. Click to select the desired shape.
4. Click OK.

   The shape is applied to the seleted data series (**Figure 60**).

✔ Tip

- This option is only available for certain 3-D charts.

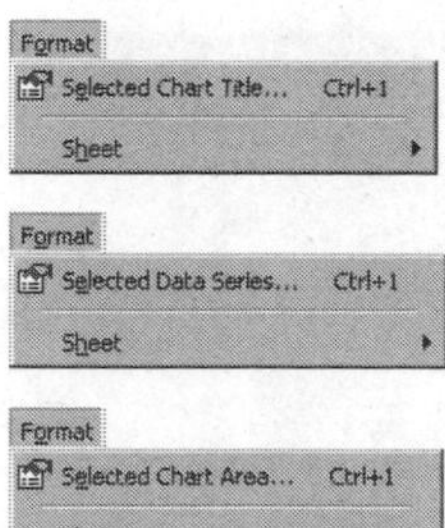

Figures 56, 57, & 58 The first command under the Format menu enables you to format the selected chart element.

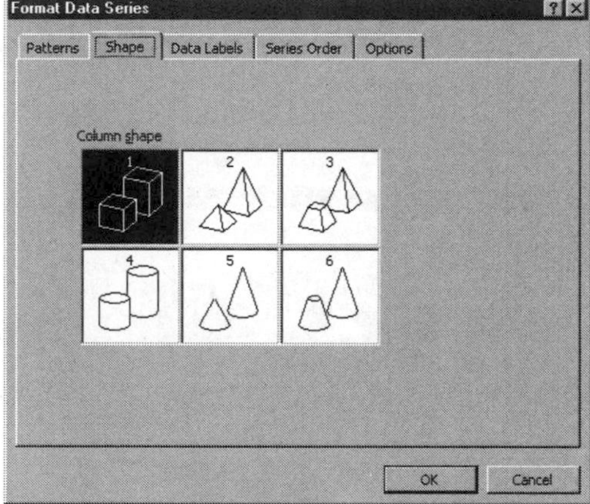

Figure 59 The Shape tab of the Format Data Series dialog box enables you to select a shape to apply to the selected series in a 3-D chart.

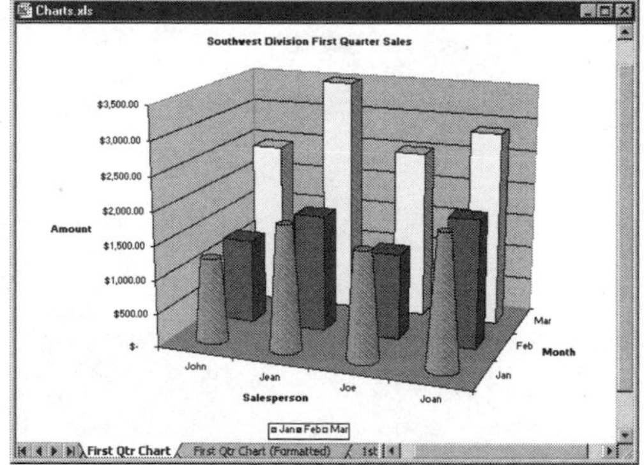

Figure 60 In this example, shape style #6 was applied to one data series.

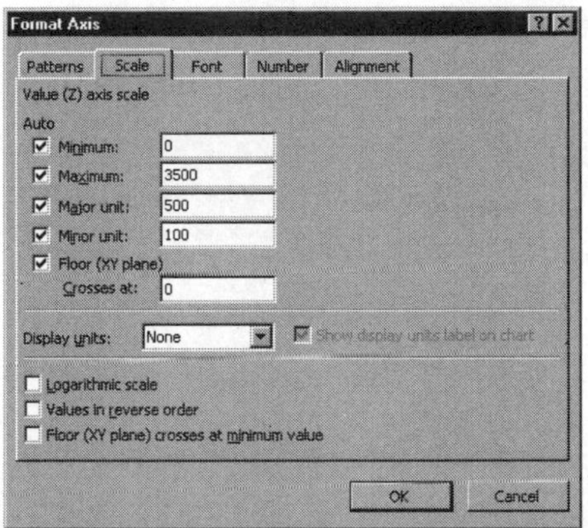

Figure 61 The Scale tab of the Format Axis dialog box.

To set the scale

1. Open the Format Gridlines or Format Axis dialog box for the gridline or axis for which you want to set the scale.
2. Click the Scale tab to display its options (**Figure 61**).
3. Enter the scale values you want to use in the text boxes:
   - **Minimum** is the minimum value on the scale. It is normally set to 0.
   - **Maximum** is the maximum value on the scale. It is normally set to a round number larger than the highest value plotted.
   - **Major unit** is the unit corresponding to major gridlines and tick marks.
   - **Minor unit** is the unit corresponding to minor gridlines and tick marks.
   - **Floor (XY plane) Crosses at** is the value at which the X and Y axes cross each other. It is normally set to 0.
4. Turn on check boxes for special scale options as desired:
   - **Logarithmic scale** recalculates the values in the text boxes as powers of 10.
   - **Values in reverse order** reverses the order in which the scale appears, putting the largest values at the bottom or left side of the axis.
   - **Floor (XY plane) crosses at minimum value** overrides the Floor (XY plane) Crosses at value and sets it to the minimum value.
5. Click OK.

✔ Tip

- When you enter a value in a text box, its corresponding check box should turn itself off automatically; you can turn it back on to use the default setting.

To set tick marks

1. Open the Format Axis dialog box for the axis for which you want to set the tick marks.
2. Click the Patterns tab to display its options (**Figure 62**).
3. Select the option buttons for the desired Major tick mark type and Minor tick mark type:
   - ▲ **None** omits tick marks.
   - ▲ **Inside** displays tick marks inside the plot area.
   - ▲ **Outside** displays tick marks outside the plot area.
   - ▲ **Cross** displays tick marks that cross the axis line.
4. Select the option button for the desired Tick mark labels position:
   - ▲ **None** omits tick mark labels.
   - ▲ **Low** displays tick mark labels at the bottom or to the right of the plot area.
   - ▲ **High** displays tick mark labels at the top or to the left of the plot area.
   - ▲ **Next to axis** displays tick mark labels next to the selected axis. This is the default option.
5. If desired, use options in the Axis area to modify the appearance of the Axis.
6. Click OK.

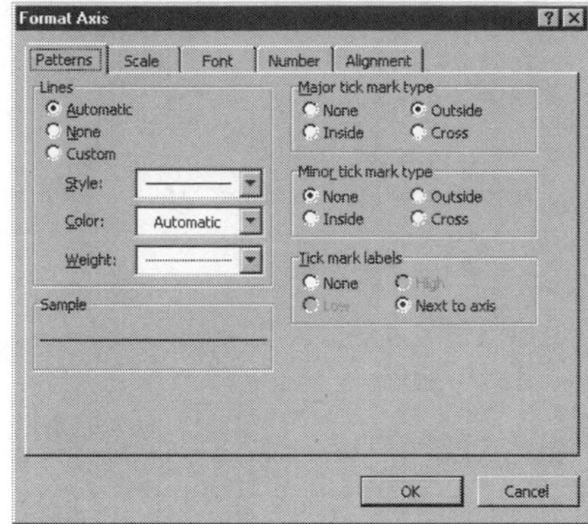

Figure 62 The Patterns tab of the Format Axis dialog box.

Figure 63 To move a chart element, drag it to its new position.

Figure 64 When you release the mouse button, it moves.

Other Formatting Options

In addition to formatting individual chart elements, you can modify the appearance of a chart in other ways. Here are a few additional options you may find handy.

To move a chart element

1. Click the element to select it.
2. Position the mouse pointer on the element, press the mouse button down, and drag. As you drag, an outline of the element moves with the mouse pointer (**Figure 63**).
3. Release the mouse button. The element moves (**Figure 64**).

✔ Tip

- You can use this technique with most chart elements.

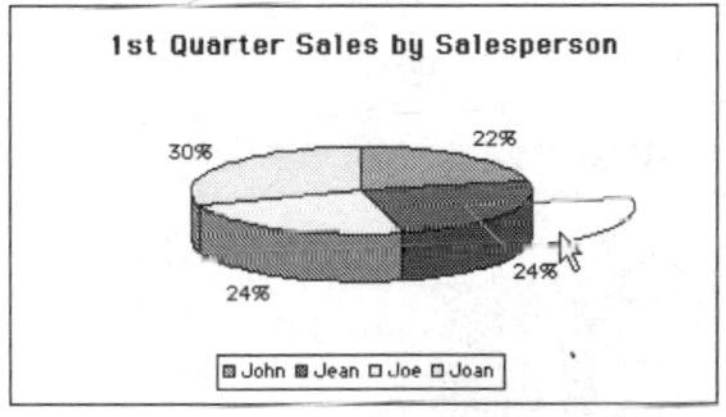

Figure 65 When you move a piece of a pie chart away from the rest of the pie...

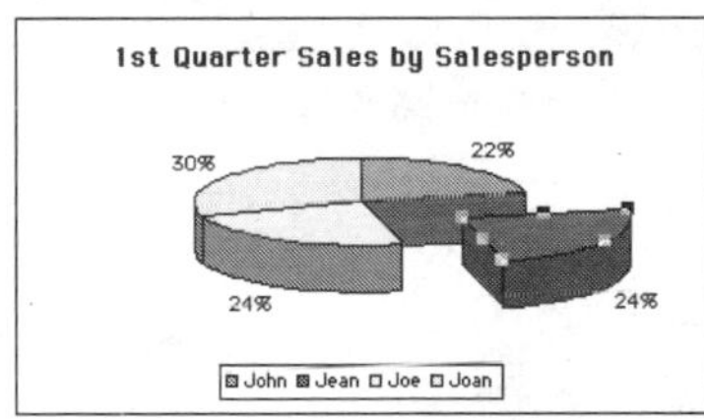

Figure 66 ...you get an "exploded" effect.

To "explode" a pie chart

1. Select the data point for the pie piece you want to move.
2. Drag the pie piece away from the pie (**Figure 65**).
3. Release the mouse button. The piece moves away from the pie (**Figure 66**).

✔ Tip

- If desired, you can drag more than one piece away from the pie.

To rotate a 3-D chart

1. Activate the chart you want to rotate (**Figure 67**).
2. Choose Chart > 3-D View (**Figure 28**).
3. In the 3-D View dialog box (**Figure 68**), click the Elevation, Rotation, and Perspective buttons to change the view of the chart.
4. When you're finished making changes, click OK. The chart rotates (**Figure 69**).

✓ Tips

- You can click the Apply button in the 3-D View dialog box (**Figure 68**) to get a first-hand look at the modified chart without closing the dialog box. You may have to drag the Format 3-D View dialog box out of the way to see your chart.
- You can click the Default button in the 3-D View dialog box to return the chart to its default rotation.
- Some changes in the 3-D View dialog box may change the size of the chart.

To resize a chart element

1. Click the element to select it.
2. Position the mouse pointer on one of the resizing handles for the element, press the mouse button down, and drag. As you drag, the border of the element moves with the mouse pointer (**Figure 70**).
3. Release the mouse button. The element resizes (**Figure 71**).

✓ Tip

- You can use this technique with most chart elements.

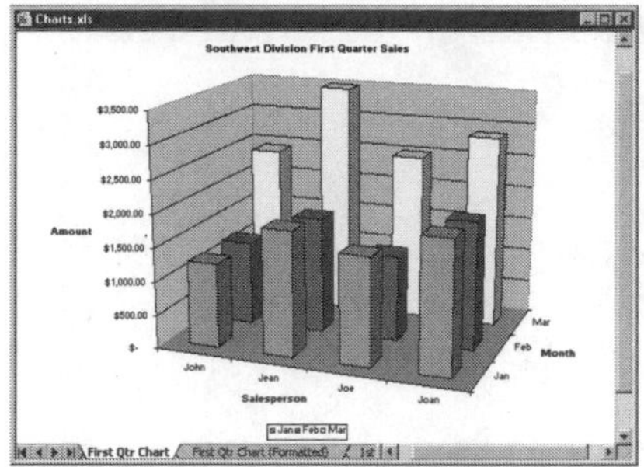

Figure 67 A chart before rotation.

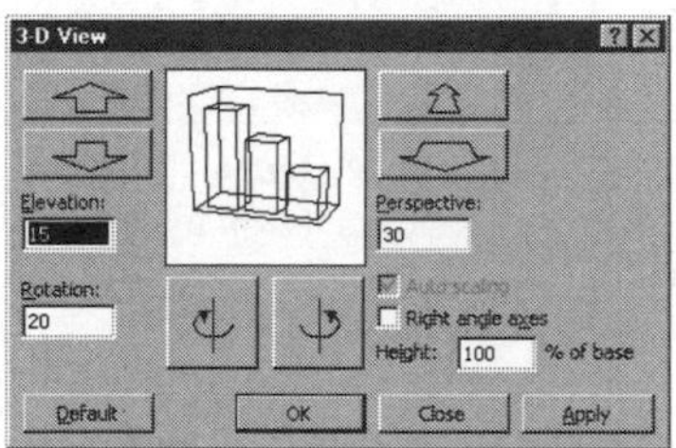

Figure 68 The 3-D View dialog box.

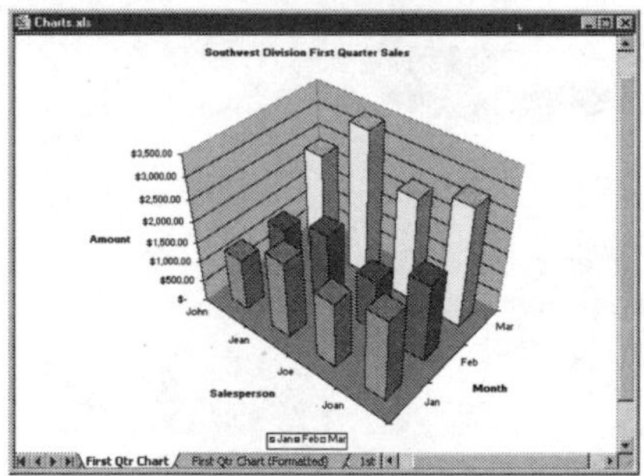

Figure 69 The chart from **Figure 67** after rotation.

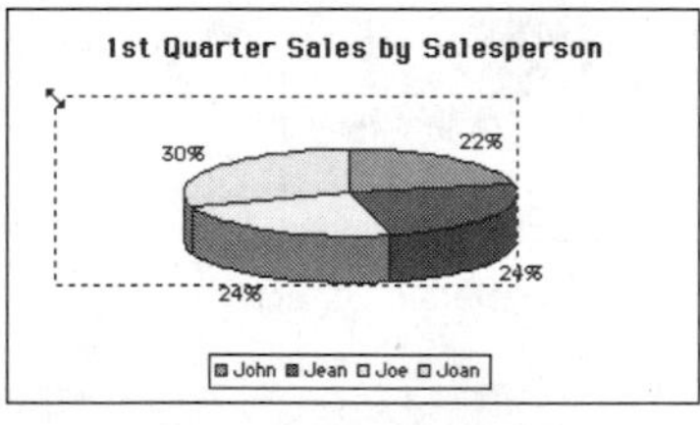

Figure 70 Drag a selection handle...

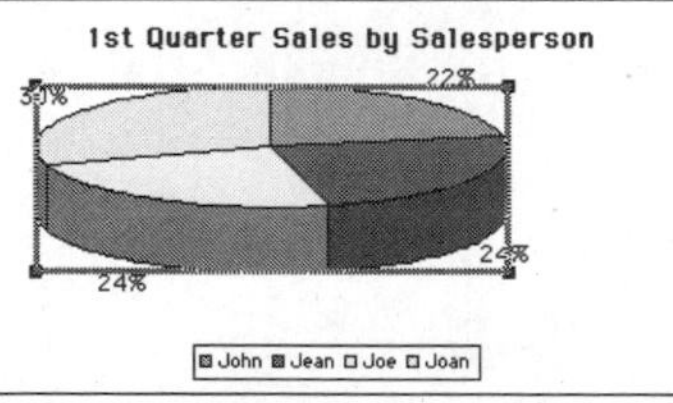

Figure 71 ...to resize almost any chart element.

PRINTING

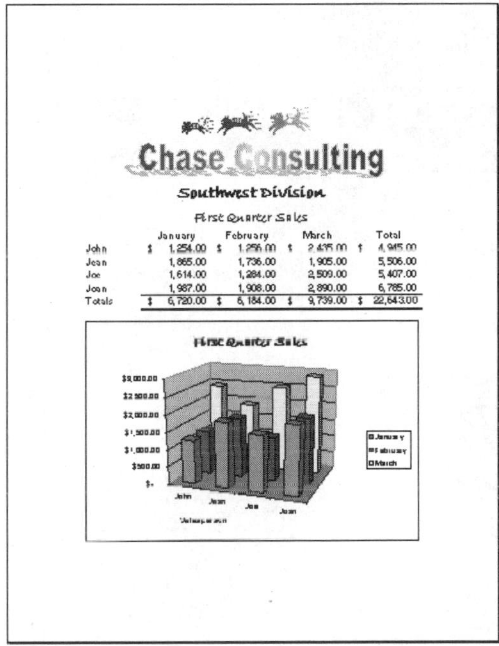

Figure 1 Print Preview lets you see reports before you commit them to paper.

Printing

In most cases, when you create a worksheet or chart, you'll want to print it. With Excel, you can print all or part of a sheet, multiple sheets, or an entire workbook—all at once. Excel gives you control over page size, margins, headers, footers, page breaks, orientation, scaling, page order, and content. Its Print Preview feature (**Figure 1**) shows you what your report will look like when printed, so you can avoid wasteful, time-consuming reprints.

Printing is basically a three-step process:

1. Use the Page Setup dialog box to set up your report for printing. You can skip this step if you set the report up the last time you printed it and don't need to change the setup.
2. Use the Print Preview feature to take a look at your report before committing it to paper. You can skip this step if you already know what the report will look like.
3. Use the Print command to send the desired number of copies to the printer for printing.

In this chapter, I tell you about each of these steps.

✔ Tip

- When you save a document, Excel saves many Page Setup and Print options with it.

The Page Setup Dialog Box

The Page Setup dialog box lets you set up a document for printing. Setup options are organized under the following tabs:

- **Page** (**Figure 3**) lets you set the orientation, scaling, first page number, paper size, and print quality.
- **Margins** (**Figures 6** and **7**) lets you set the page margins, the distance the header and footer should be from the edge of the paper, and the positioning of the document on the paper.
- **Header/Footer** (**Figure 8**) lets you select a standard header and footer or create custom ones.
- **Sheet** (**Figure 14**) lets you specify the print area, print titles, items to print, and page order. If a chart sheet is active when you choose Page Setup, you'll see a Chart tab (**Figure 21**) rather than a Sheet tab. Use it to specify the printed chart size and print quality.

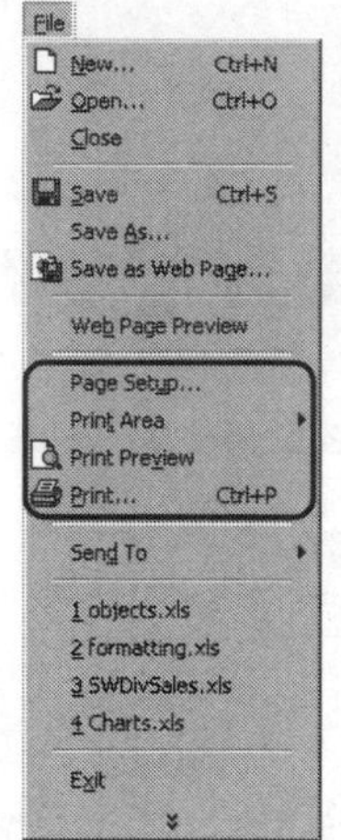

Figure 2
The File menu offers a number of printing-related commands.

To open the Page Setup dialog box

Choose File > Page Setup (**Figure 2**).

or

Click the Setup button in the Print Preview window (**Figure 22**).

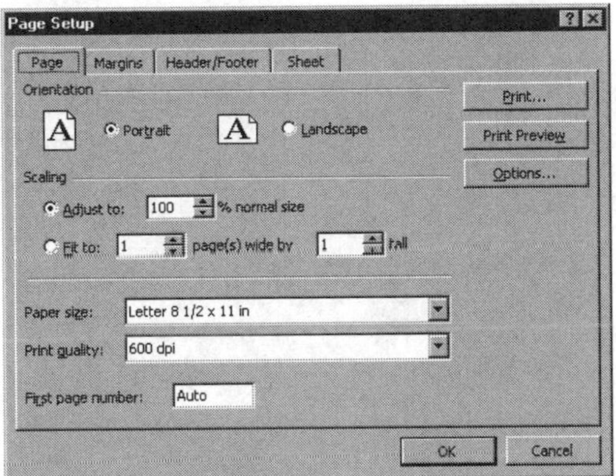

Figure 3 The Page tab of the Page Setup dialog box.

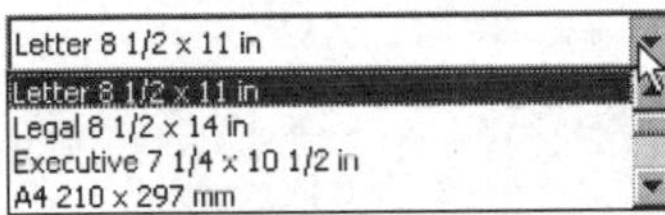

Figure 4 The Paper size menu.

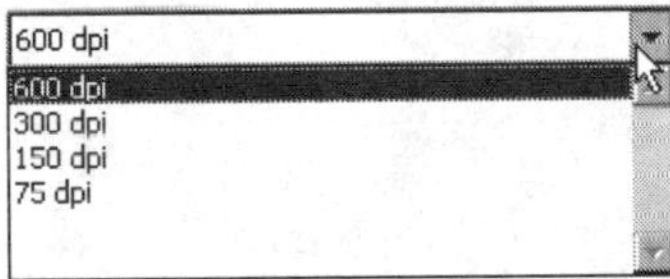

Figure 5 The Print quality menu. Options may vary depending on your printer.

To set page options

1. Click the Page tab in the Page Setup dialog box to display its options (**Figure 3**).
2. In the Orientation area, select the desired orientation option:
   - ▲ **Portrait**, the default option for worksheets, prints vertically down the page.
   - ▲ **Landscape**, the default option for chart sheets, prints horizontally across the page.
3. For a worksheet only, in the Scaling area, select the desired scaling radio button:
   - ▲ **Adjust to** enables you to specify a percentage of the normal size for printing. Be sure to enter a value in the text box. This option is selected by default with 100 in the text box.
   - ▲ **Fit to** instructs Excel to shrink the report so it fits on the number of pages you specify. Be sure to enter values in the two text boxes.
4. Choose a paper size from the Paper size menu (**Figure 4**).
5. Choose an option from the Print quality menu (**Figure 5**).
6. If desired, in the First page number box, enter a value that should be used as the page number on the first page of the report. This enables you to start page numbering at a value other than 1.
7. Click OK to save your settings.

✔ Tip

- Neither scaling option is available for chart sheets. You can change the scaling for a chart sheet on the Chart tab of the Page Setup dialog box, which I discuss later in this chapter.

To set margins & centering options

1. Click the Margins tab in the Page Setup dialog box to display its options (**Figure 6** or 7).
2. Enter values in the Top, Left, Right, and Bottom text boxes to set the amount of space between the edge of the paper and the report content.
3. Enter values in the Header and Footer text boxes to set the amount of space between the edge of the paper and the header and footer content.
4. For a worksheet only, turn on the desired Center on page check boxes:
   - ▲ **Horizontally** centers the report content between the left and right margins.
   - ▲ **Vertically** centers the report content between the top and bottom margins.
5. Click OK to save your settings.

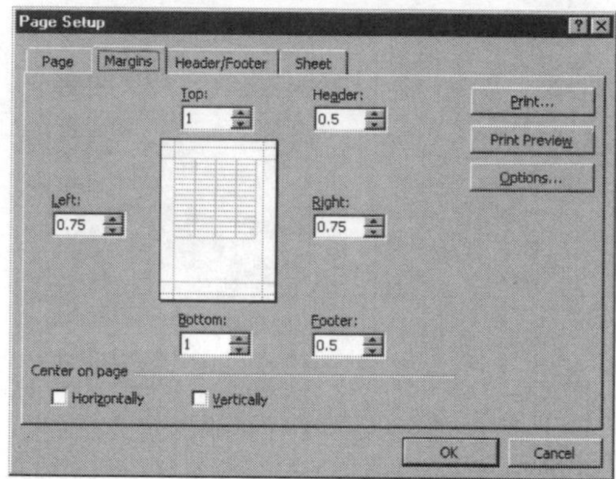

Figure 6 The Margins tab of the Page Setup dialog box for a worksheet...

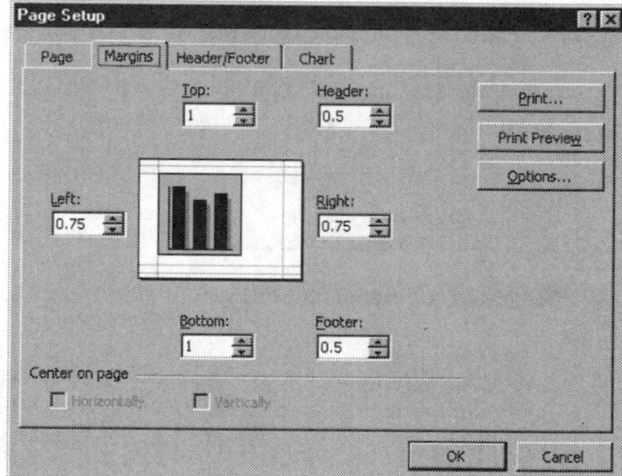

Figure 7 ...and for a chart sheet.

✔ Tips

- As you make changes in this window, the preview area changes accordingly. This helps you get an idea of what the document will look like when previewed or printed.
- You can also set margins in the Print Preview window. I tell you how later in this chapter.
- Do not set margins to smaller values than the Header and Footer values or Excel may print your report over the header or footer.
- Some printers cannot print close to the edge of the paper. If part of your report is cut off when printed, increase the margin, header, and footer values.

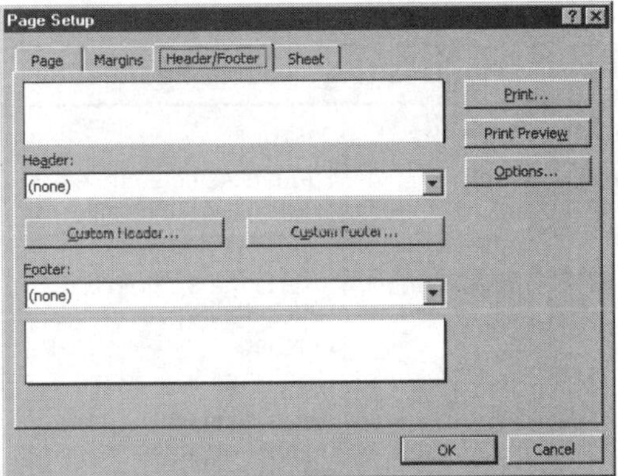

Figure 8 The Header/Footer tab of the Page Setup dialog box.

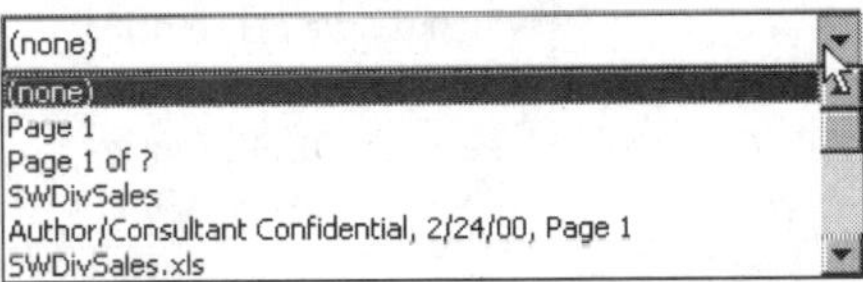

Figure 9 The Header and Footer menus offer a number of predefined headers and footers.

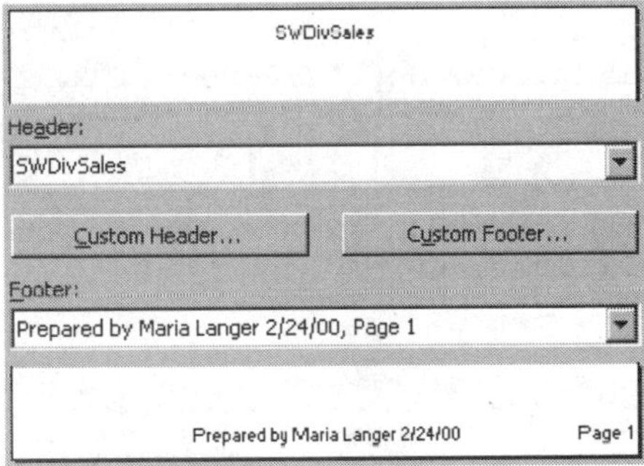

Figure 10 The header and footer you select appear in the sample areas of the dialog box.

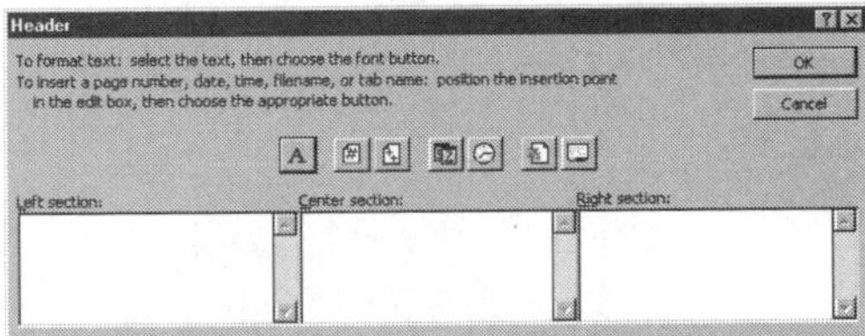

Figure 11 The Header dialog box. The Footer dialog box looks and works just like it.

To add built-in headers & footers

1. Click the Header/Footer tab in the Page Setup dialog box to display its options (**Figure 8**).
2. Choose options from the Header and Footer menus (**Figure 9**).

   The option(s) you selected appear in the sample area(s) in the dialog box (**Figure 10**).
3. Click OK to save your settings.

✔ Tips

- The menu for Footer is identical to the one for Header.
- Excel gets your name and company name from entries you made when you installed Excel. You can change the name by choosing Tools > Options, entering a new User name in the General tab of the Options dialog box, and clicking OK. You cannot change the company name without reinstalling Excel.
- To change the formatting of text in the header or footer, you need to use the Custom Header or Custom Footer button in the Header/Footer tab of the Page Setup dialog box (see below).

To add custom headers & footers

1. Click the Header/Footer tab in the Page Setup dialog box to display its options (**Figure 8**).
2. To add a header, click the Custom Header button to display the Header dialog box (**Figure 11**).
3. Enter the text or codes that you want to appear in the header in the Left section, Center section, and Right section text boxes. You can use the buttons in **Table 1** to format selected text or insert codes for

Continued on next page...

Continued from previous page.

dynamic information. **Figure 12** shows an example.

4. Click OK to save your settings.

   The settings appear in the Page Setup dialog box (**Figure 13**).

5. To add a footer, click the Custom Footer button. This displays the Footer dialog box, which looks and works just like the Header dialog box.
6. Repeat steps 3 and 4 for the footer.
7. Click OK in the Page Setup dialog box to save your settings.

✔ Tips

- In step 3, to enter an ampersand (&) character in a header or footer, type *&&* where you want it to appear.
- To specify the starting page number to be printed in the header or footer, enter a value in the First page number text box of the Page tab of the Page Setup dialog box (**Figure 3**).
- Dynamic information is information that changes automatically. For example the page number changes automatically for each page and the print date changes automatically each day you print the file. Using the buttons or codes for dynamic information (**Table 1**) ensures header and footer contents are accurate.

To remove headers & footers

1. Click the Header/Footer tab in the Page Setup dialog box to display its options (**Figure 8**).
2. Choose (none) from the Header and Footer menus (**Figure 9**). The header and footer disappear from the dialog box.
3. Click OK to save your settings.

Table 1

Buttons for Inserting Dynamic Information

Button	Button Name	Description
A	Font	Formats selected text. I tell you how to format text in **Chapter 6**.
	Page Number	Inserts the *&[Page]* code, which displays the page number.
	Total Pages	Inserts the *&[Pages]* code, which displays the total number of pages.
	Date	Inserts the *&[Date]* code, which displays the print date.
	Time	Inserts the *&[Time]* code, which displays the print time.
	File Name	Inserts the *&[File]* code, which displays the name of the file.
	Sheet Name	Inserts the *&[Sheet]* code, which displays the name of the sheet.

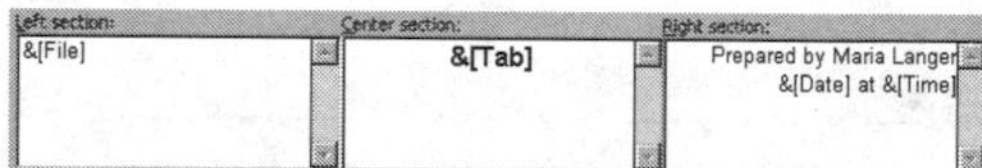

Figure 12 An example of a custom header entered into the Header dialog box.

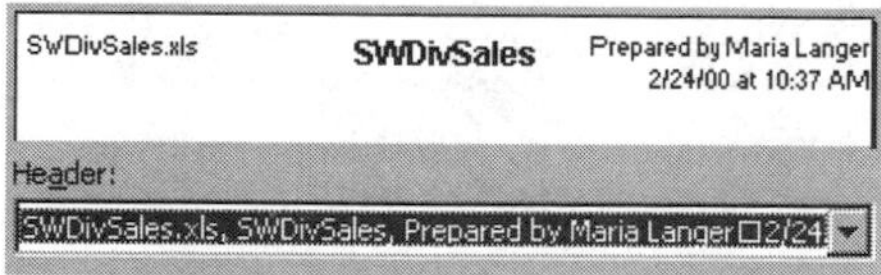

Figure 13 Here's the header from **Figure 12** in the Page Setup dialog box.

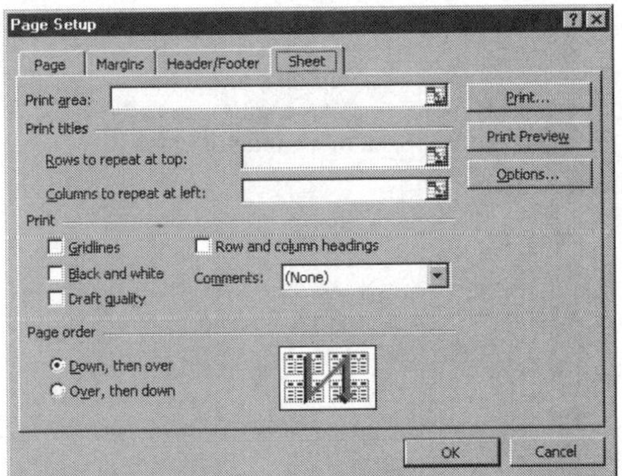

Figure 14 The Sheet tab of the Page Setup dialog box. This tab is only available when a sheet is active.

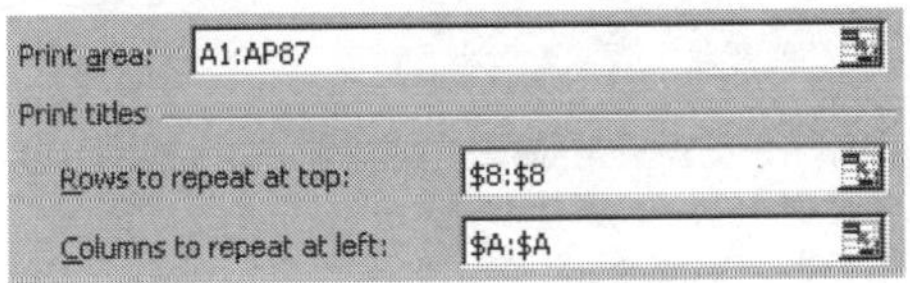

Figure 15 This example shows the proper way to enter ranges for the Print area and Print titles.

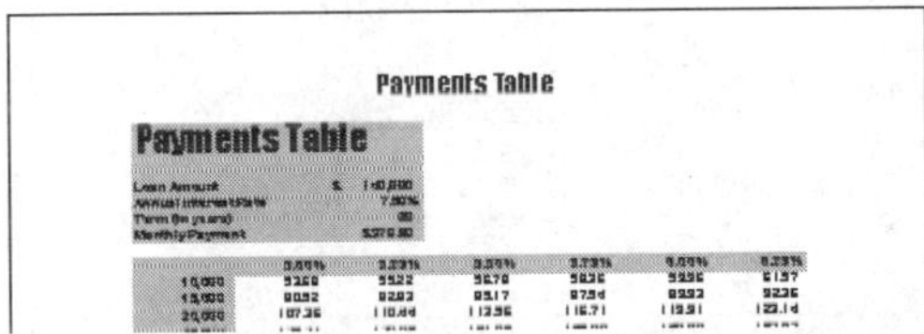

Figure 16 Here's the first page of a lengthy report.

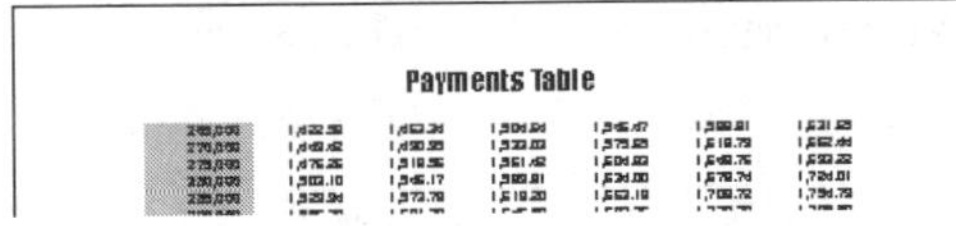

Figure 17 Without page titles, the headings don't appear on subsequent pages.

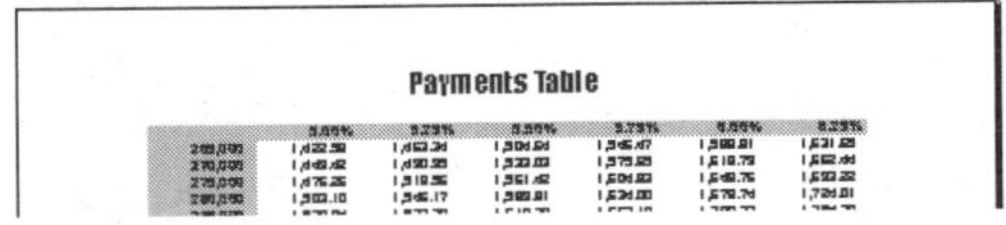

Figure 18 But with page titles set as they are in **Figure 15**, headings appear on every page.

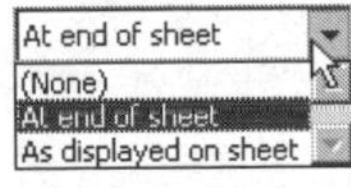

Figure 19 The Comments menu.

To set sheet options

1. Click the Sheet tab in the Page Setup dialog box to display its options (**Figure 14**).
2. To print less than the entire worksheet, enter a range in the Print area text box (**Figure 15**).
3. To display column or row titles on all pages of a lengthy report, enter row or column (or both) ranges in the Rows to repeat at top or Columns to repeat at left text boxes (**Figure 15**). **Figures 16** through **18** show how this affects the printout.
4. Turn on check boxes in the center of the dialog box to set additional print options as desired:
   - ▲ **Gridlines** prints the worksheet gridlines.
   - ▲ **Black and white** prints the worksheet in black and white. This can save time if you print on a color printer.
   - ▲ **Draft quality** reduces printing time by omitting gridlines and most graphics.
   - ▲ **Row and column headings** prints the column letters and row numbers with the worksheet.
5. To print worksheet comments (which I cover in **Chapter 6**), choose an option other than (None) from the Comments menu (**Figure 19**).
6. Select a Page order option for a long or wide worksheet:
   - ▲ **Down, then over** prints all rows of the first few columns first, then prints rows from subsequent columns.
   - ▲ **Over, then down** prints all columns of the first bunch of rows first, then prints columns from subsequent rows.
7. Click OK to save your settings.

Continued on next page...

Continued from previous page.

✔ Tips

- In steps 2 and 3, you can enter each range manually by typing it into the text box or have Excel enter it automatically for you by clicking in the text box, then selecting the range in the worksheet window.
- You can use the Collapse Dialog button to collapse the dialog box so you can see the worksheet behind it. You can then use the Expand Dialog button to restore the dialog box so you can continue working with it.
- You can also specify the range of cells to print by selecting the range in the worksheet, then choosing File > Print Area > Set Print Area (**Figure 20**). The Clear Print Area command clears any previously set print area.

To set chart options

1. Click the Chart tab in the Page Setup dialog box to display its options (**Figure 21**).
2. Select one of the Printed chart size options:
   - ▲ **Use full page** expands the chart so it fills the page. The size of chart objects may change, relative to each other.
   - ▲ **Scale to fit page** expands the chart proportionally until it fills the space between one set of opposite margins.
   - ▲ **Custom** prints the chart in the size you specified by stretching or shrinking it in the chart window.
3. To omit graphics from a chart sheet and reduce memory requirements for printing, turn on the Draft quality check box.
4. To print the chart in black and white with patterns replacing colors, turn on the Print in black and white check box.
5. Click OK to save your settings.

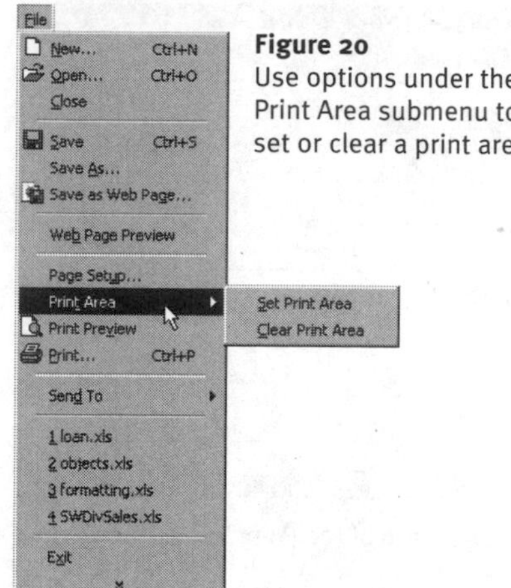

Figure 20 Use options under the Print Area submenu to set or clear a print area.

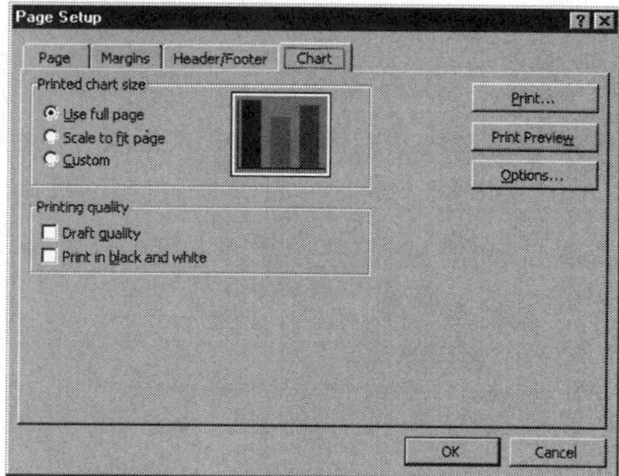

Figure 21 The Chart tab of the Page Setup dialog box. This tab is only available when a chart is active.

✔ Tip

- For the largest possible image, make sure Landscape is the selected orientation in the Page tab of the Page Setup dialog box (**Figure 3**). I tell you about orientation earlier in this chapter.

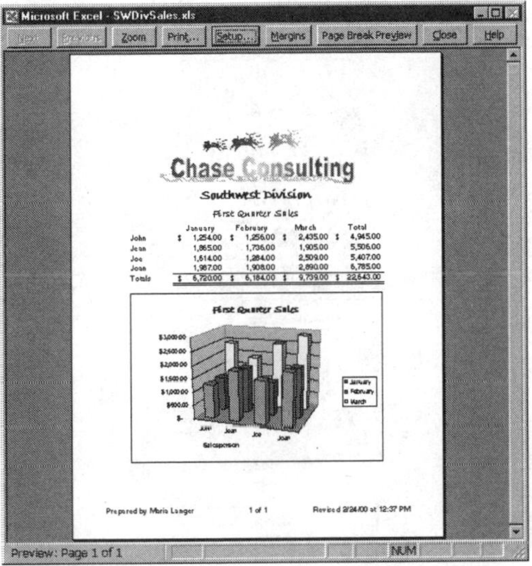

Figure 22 A worksheet with embedded chart in Print Preview.

Print Preview

Excel's Print Preview feature lets you see what a report will look like before you print it. If a report doesn't look perfect, you can use Setup, Margins, and Page Break Preview buttons right inside the Print Preview dialog box to make adjustments. When you're ready to print, click the Print button.

To preview a report

Choose File > Print Preview (**Figure 2**).

or

Click the Print Preview button on the Standard toolbar.

or

Click the Print Preview button in the Page Setup or Print dialog box.

A preview of the current sheet appears (**Figure 22**). It reflects all Page Setup dialog box settings.

✔ Tips

- To view the other pages of the report, click the Next or Previous button.
- To zoom in to see report detail, click the Zoom button or click the mouse pointer (a magnifying glass) on the area you want to magnify.
- To open the Print dialog box and print, click the Print button. I tell you about the Print dialog box later in this chapter.
- To change Page Setup dialog box options, click the Setup button.
- To close the Print Preview dialog box, click the Close button.

To change margin options & column widths

1. In the Print Preview window, click the Margins button. Handles for margins, header and footer locations, and column widths appear around the report preview (**Figure 23**).
2. Position the mouse pointer over the handle or guideline for the margin, header, footer, or column you want to change. The mouse pointer turns into a line with two arrows coming out of it (**Figure 24**).
3. Press down the mouse button and drag to make the change. A measurement for your change appears in the status bar as you drag.
4. Release the mouse button to complete the change. The report reformats automatically.

Figure 23 When you click the Margins button, handles for margins, header, footer, and columns appear.

Figure 24 Position the mouse pointer on a handle and drag to change the measurement.

✔ Tips

- The changes you make by dragging handles in the Print Preview dialog box will be reflected in the appropriate text boxes of the Page Setup dialog box.
- I explain how to change margins and header and footer locations with the Page Setup dialog box earlier in this chapter. I tell you how to change column widths in the worksheet window or with the Column Width dialog box in **Chapter 6**.

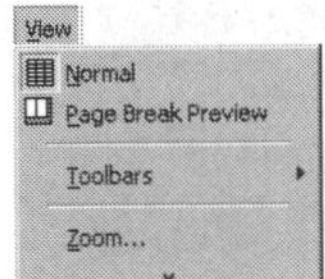

Figure 25 The View menu.

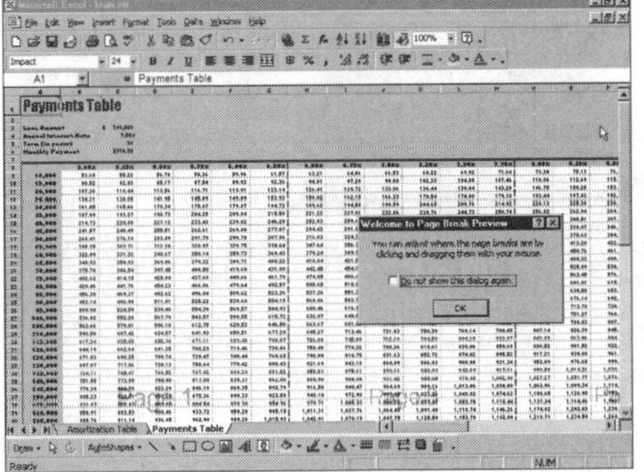

Figure 26 Page Break Preview view, with its instruction dialog box.

Figure 27 Drag a page break to change it.

Figure 28 When you move one page break, the ones beyond it move, too.

To set page breaks

1. In normal view, choose View > Page Break Preview (**Figure 25**).

   or

   In the Print Preview window (**Figure 22**), click the Page Break Preview button.

   The sheet appears in Page Break Preview view (**Figure 26**).

2. Position the mouse pointer over one of the dashed, blue page break lines. The mouse pointer turns into a line with two arrows coming out of it.

3. Press down the mouse button and drag to make the change. A dark line moves with the mouse pointer (**Figure 27**).

4. Release the mouse button.

   The page break shifts to the new position and turns into a solid blue line. Any automatic page break to its right or below it also shifts (**Figure 28**).

5. To return to Normal view, choose View > Normal (**Figure 25**).

   or

   To return to Print Preview, choose File > Print Preview (**Figure 2**) or click the Print Preview button on the Standard toolbar.

✔ Tips

- The first time you use the Page Break Preview feature, a dialog box with instructions appears (**Figure 26**). You must click OK to dismiss the dialog box before you can drag page breaks. Turn on the check box within the dialog box if you don't want to see it again.
- You may need to scroll within the window to see all the page breaks for a very large worksheet.
- You can use this feature to change both vertical and horizontal page breaks.

The Print Dialog Box

You use the Print dialog box (**Figure 29**) to set a number of options for the print job, including the printer to which you want to print, the part of the file you want to print, and the number of copies you want to print. After setting options, clicking the Print button sends the document to the printer.

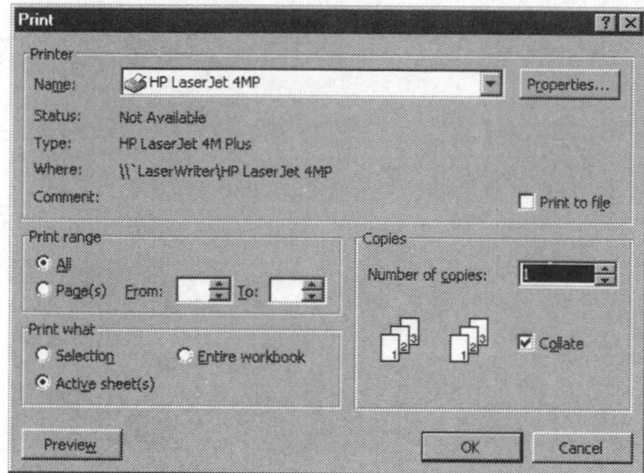

Figure 29 The Print dialog box.

✔ Tip

- The options offered in the Print dialog box may vary depending on your printer. For more information about options not covered here, check the manual that came with your printer.

To set print options

1. Choose File > Print (**Figure 2**), press Ctrl P, or click the Print button in the Page Setup dialog box or Print Preview window (**Figure 22**) to display the Print dialog box (**Figure 29**).
2. Choose a printer from the Name menu.
3. Select a Print range option:
   - ▲ **All** prints all pages.
   - ▲ **Pages** enables you to enter a page range. Enter the first and last page to print in the From and To text boxes.
4. Select a Print what option:
   - ▲ **Selection** prints the currently selected cells, sheet, or object.
   - ▲ **Active sheet(s)** prints the currently selected sheets.
   - ▲ **Entire workbook** prints all nonblank sheets in the workbook file.
5. Enter the number of copies to print in the Number of copies text box.

✔ Tips

- Clicking the Print button on the Standard toolbar sends the document to the printer without displaying the Print dialog box.
- If printing multiple copies, you can turn on the Collate check box to automatically collate the copies.

Figure 30 The Print To File dialog box enables you to specify a name and location for a .PRN file created from an Excel worksheet.

To print

Click the OK button in the Print dialog box (**Figure 29**). This prints the document using the settings in the dialog box.

or

Click the Print button on the Standard toolbar. This prints the document using the default print options or those set the last time the document was printed using the Print dialog box.

To print to a .PRN file

1. Choose File > Print (**Figure 2**), press Ctrl P, or click the Print button in the Page Setup dialog box or Print Preview window (**Figure 22**) to display the Print dialog box (**Figure 29**).
2. Turn on the Print to file check box.
3. Click OK.
4. Use the Print To File dialog box that appears (**Figure 30**) to enter a name and specify a location for the .PRN file.
5. Click OK. The document is saved as a .PRN file on disk.

✔ Tip

- A .PRN file is a plain text file that includes all the information that would normally be printed. .PRN files are sometimes used to share worksheet information with DOS computer programs or to print worksheets from DOS.

WORKING WITH DATABASES

Databases

Excel's database features and functions help make it a flexible tool for creating, maintaining, and reporting data. With Excel, you can use a form to enter data into a list, filter information, sort records, and automatically generate subtotals. You can also use Excel's calculating, formatting, charting, and printing features on your database.

In Excel, a database is any list of information with unique labels in the first row. You don't need to do anything special to identify a database—Excel is smart enough to know one when it sees it (**Figure 1**).

A database is organized into fields and records. A *field* is a category of information. In **Figure 1**, *Product Code*, *Department*, and *Cost* are the first three fields. A *record* is a collection of fields for one thing. In **Figure 1**, *row 2* shows the record for the item with product code *BOB159G* and *row 3* shows the record for *MQA2210N*.

✔ Tip

- Fields are always in columns; records are aways in rows.

	A	B	C	D	E	F	G	H	I
1	Product Code	Department	Cost	Sale Price	Reorder Point	Qty on Hand	Time to Order?	Resale Value	Markup
2	BOB159G	Women's Clothes	21.32	42.99	130	181		7,781	202%
3	MQA2210N	Toys	24.42	79.99	40	300		23,997	328%
4	HJM248H	Big & Tall Men's Cloth	4.33	22.99	90	377		8,667	531%
5	ZEN1612P	Pets	12.96	28.99	120	165		4,783	224%
6	TAE1414G	Housewares	18.21	38.99	200	223		8,695	214%
7	CEY186Z	Boy's Clothes	2.58	3.99	100	12	Reorder Now!	48	155%
8	HNY2514O	Big & Tall Men's Cloth	7.06	10.99	180	437		4,803	156%
9	NCL817S	Hardware	7.14	27.99	120	108	Reorder Now!	3,023	392%

Figure 1 The first few rows of a list that Excel can automatically recognize as a database.

To create a list

1. In a worksheet window, enter unique column titles for each of the fields in your list (**Figure 2**). These will be the field names.
2. Beginning with the row immediately below the one containing the column titles, enter the data for each record (**Figure 3**). Be sure to put the proper information in each column.

✔ Tips

- Use only one cell for each column title. If the field name is too long to fit in the cell, use the Alignment tab in the Font dialog box to wrap text in the cell (**Figure 4**). I tell you about alignment options in **Chapter 6**.
- Do not skip rows when entering information. A blank row indicates the end of the database above it.
- If the first few characters that you type into a cell match an existing entry in the same column, Excel automatically fills in the remaining characters for you (**Figure 5**). To accept the entry, press Enter. To type something else, continue typing.
- You can format your list any way you like (**Figure 4**). The formatting will not affect the way Excel recognizes and works with the list data.
- Your list can include formulas. Excel treats the results of the formulas like any other field.

	A	B	C
1	First Name	Last Name	Phone Number
2			

Figure 2 Enter unique field names in the first row of the list.

	A	B	C
1	First Name	Last Name	Phone Number
2	Nancy	Drew	555-2354
3	Sherlock	Holmes	555-1452
4	Lew	Archer	555-4813
5	Sam	Spade	555-7365
6	Peter	Whimsey	555-9842
7	Jessica	Fletcher	555-6584
8	John	Aabbott	555-3215

Figure 3 Enter the data, one record per row.

	A	B	C
1	**First Name**	**Last Name**	**Phone Number**
2	Nancy	Drew	555-2354
3	Sherlock	Holmes	555-1452
4	Lew	Archer	555-4813
5	Sam	Spade	555-7365
6	Peter	Whimsey	555-9842
7	Jessica	Fletcher	555-6584
8	John	Aabbott	555-3215

Figure 4 Formatting a list doesn't affect the way Excel works with data.

QVD248Q	Bed & Bath
ZBE125G	Pets
VAQ512W	Electronics
HHL92K	Big & Tall Men's Cloth
FOX112Y	Misses Clothes
ZBY983G	Pets

Figure 5 When the first few characters you type match an existing entry in the column, Excel fills in the remaining characters for you.

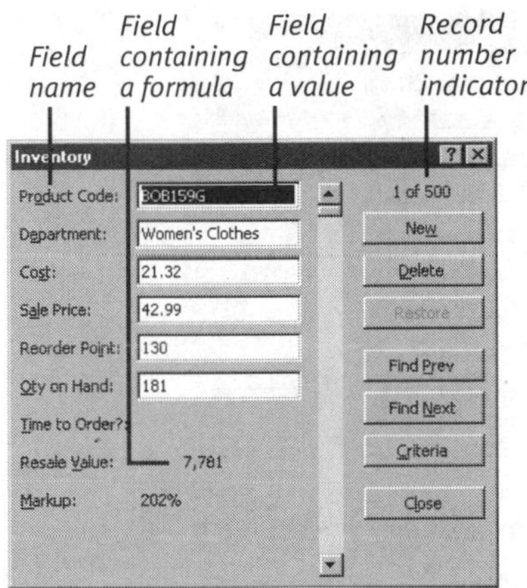

Figure 6 The data form offers another way to enter, edit, delete, and find records.

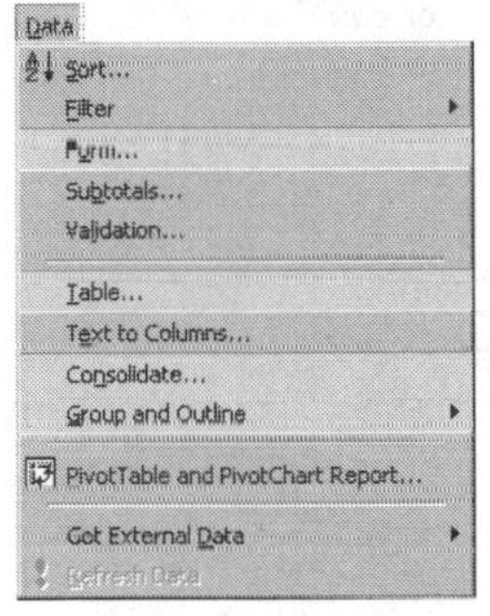

Figure 7 The Data menu includes a number of commands for working with lists.

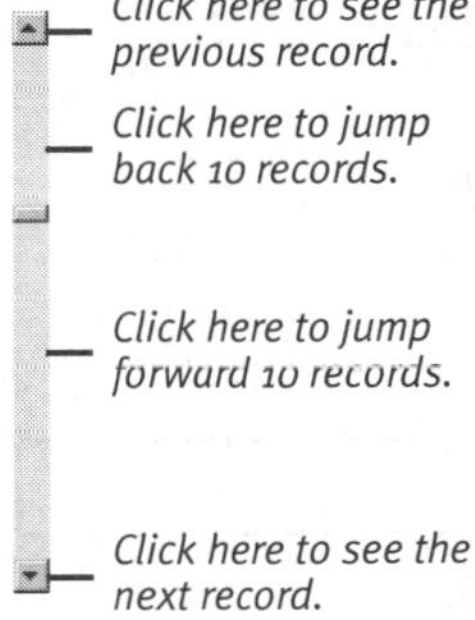

Figure 8 Use the scroll bar in the data form to browse records.

Using the Data Form

Excel's data form feature creates a dialog box with custom text boxes for fields (**Figure 6**). You can use this dialog box to enter, edit, delete, and find records in a database.

To open the data form

1. Select any cell in the list.
2. Choose Data > Form (**Figure 7**).

To browse records

Use the scroll bar (**Figure 8**) as follows:

- To see the next record, click the down arrow on the scroll bar.
- To see the previous record, click the up arrow on the scroll bar.
- To jump ahead 10 records, click the scroll bar beneath the scroll box.
- To jump back 10 records, click the scroll bar above the scroll box.

To enter, edit, and delete data

To create a new record, click the New button (**Figure 6**) and enter the information into the empty text boxes for each field.

or

To edit a record, locate the record you want to edit and make changes in the appropriate text boxes (**Figure 6**).

or

To delete a record, locate the record you want to delete and click the Delete button (**Figure 6**).

✔ Tips

- Excel records your changes when you move to another record or click the Close button to close the form.
- If a field contains a formula, Excel carries the formula forward from the previous record and performs the calculation.

USING THE DATA FORM

To find records

1. In the data form, click the Criteria button. A criteria form appears (**Figure 9**).
2. Enter search criteria in the field(s) in which you expect to find a match (**Figure 10**).
3. Click the Find Next button to move forward through the list for records that match the criteria.

   or

   Click the Find Prev button to move backward through the list for records that match the criteria.

   Excel beeps when it reaches the end or beginning of the matches.

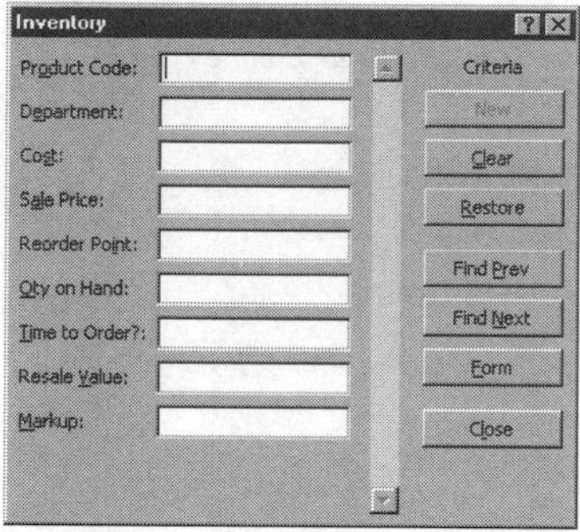

Figure 9 The data form turns into a criteria form when you click the Criteria button.

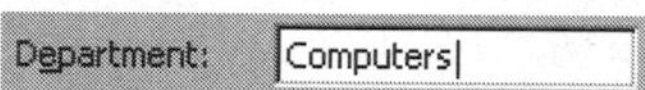

Figure 10 Enter the search criteria in the field in which you expect to find a match.

✔ Tips

- You can enter criteria in any combination of fields. If you enter criteria into multiple fields, Excel looks for records that match all criteria.
- The more fields you enter data into, the more specific you make the search and the fewer matches you'll find.
- You can use comparison operators (**Table 1**) and wildcard characters (**Table 2**) in conjunction with criteria. For example, *>100* finds records with values greater than 100 and *P** finds records with values that begin with the letter P.
- You can also use Excel's AutoFilter feature to quickly locate and display all records that match search criteria. I tell you how next.

Table 1

Comparison Operators

Operator	Meaning
=	Equal To
<>	Not Equal To
>	Greater Than
>=	Greater Than or Equal To
<	Less Than
<=	Less Than or Equal To

Table 2

Wildcard Characters

Character	Meaning
?	Any single character
*	Any group of characters

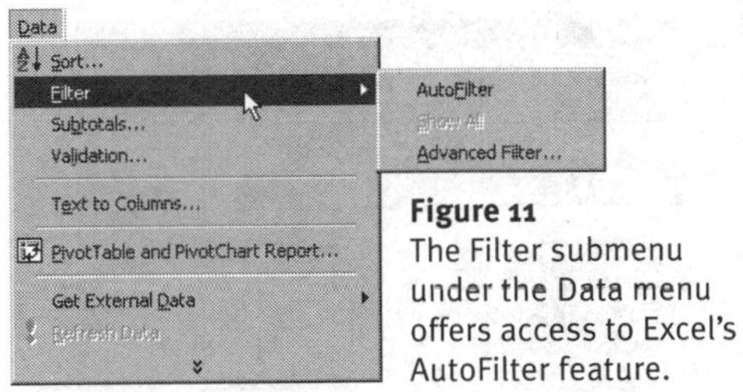

Figure 11 The Filter submenu under the Data menu offers access to Excel's AutoFilter feature.

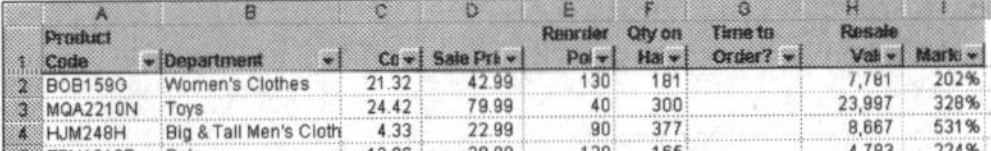

	A	B	C	D	E	F	G	H	I
1	Product Code	Department	Co	Sale Pri	Reorder Poi	Qty on Ha	Time to Order?	Resale Val	Mark
2	BOB159G	Women's Clothes	21.32	42.99	130	181		7,781	202%
3	MQA2210N	Toys	24.42	79.99	40	300		23,997	328%
4	HJM248H	Big & Tall Men's Cloth	4.33	22.99	90	377		8,667	531%

Figure 12 The AutoFilter feature creates menus for each field.

Figure 13 Choose search criteria from a menu...

	A	B	C	D	E	F	G	H	I
1	Product Code	Department	Co	Sale Pri	Reorder Poi	Qty on Ha	Time to Order?	Resale Val	Mark
[illegible]	OYG1512M	Automotive	3.08	16.99	30	152		2,582	552%
[illegible]	OBW212Q	Automotive	22.00	68.00	160	143	Reorder Now!	[illegible]	[illegible]
[illegible]	ODA522R	Automotive	14.38	60.99	50	371		22,627	424%
[illegible]	OZE2010J	Automotive	11.71	67.99	150	494		33,587	581%
[illegible]	OYM66B	Automotive	12.79	69.99	60	105		7,349	547%
163	OJJ42I	Automotive	1.96	11.99	80	283		3,393	612%
187	OPL2222H	Automotive	24.53	144.99	100	160		23,198	591%
221	OGI2316B	Automotive	4.78	18.99	10	199		3,779	397%
235	OXN516D	Automotive	1.21	4.99	10	152		758	412%
309	OZW228W	Automotive	12.01	59.99	40	189		11,338	500%
412	OFQ2613L	Automotive	7.66	35.99	120	414		14,900	470%
458	OHZ1214D	Automotive	0.74	3.99	110	179		714	539%
474	OYP418Q	Automotive	0.80	3.99	20	15	Reorder Now!	60	499%
475	OIO911Z	Automotive	4.20	15.99	130	458		7,323	381%

Figure 14 ...to display only the records that match the criteria you chose.

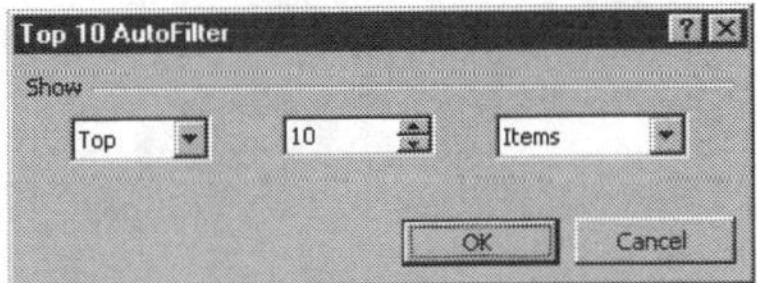

Figure 15 Use the Top 10 AutoFilter dialog box to find the top or bottom number or percent of items.

Using AutoFilter

The AutoFilter feature puts menus in the titles of each column (**Figure 12**). You can use these menus to choose criteria in the column and display only those records that match the criteria.

To display AutoFilter menus

1. Select any cell in the list.
2. Choose Data > Filter > AutoFilter (**Figure 11**).

   Excel scans the data and creates menus for each field (**Figure 12**).

To find records with AutoFilter

1. Display the AutoFilter menus (**Figure 12**).
2. Use a menu to select criteria in a specific field (**Figure 13**).

   Only the records matching the criteria you selected are displayed (**Figure 14**).

✔ Tip

- To display all of the records again, choose Data > Filter > Show All (**Figure 11**) or choose (All) from the menu you used to filter the data (**Figure 13**).

To use the Top 10 AutoFilter

1. Display the AutoFilter menus (**Figure 12**).
2. Choose (Top 10...) from the menu for the field by which you want to filter information.
3. In the Top 10 AutoFilter dialog box (**Figure 15**), set options to locate the top or bottom number or percent of items based on the field you selected. Click OK.

   Excel filters the database and displays only the records that match the settings you entered.

To set a custom AutoFilter

1. Choose (Custom...) from the menu for the field for which you want to set criteria (**Figure 13**). The Custom AutoFilter dialog box (**Figure 16**) appears.
2. Use the menus (**Figure 17**) to choose one or two comparison operators.
3. Use the menus or text boxes to enter one or two criteria.
4. Select the And or Or option to tell Excel whether it should match both criteria (And) or either criteria (Or).
5. Click OK.

   Only the records matching the criteria you entered are displayed (**Figure 18**).

✔ Tip

- Criteria can include wildcard characters (**Table 2**).

To use multiple AutoFilters

Choose filters from the menus for each of the fields for which you want to set criteria. Excel will display only the records that match all of the filters (**Figure 19**).

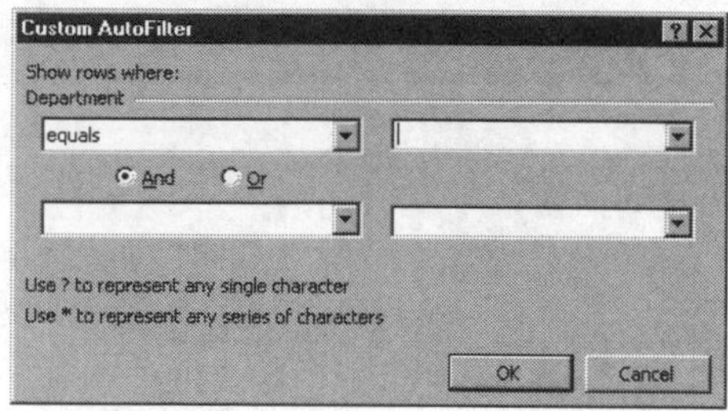

Figure 16 The Custom AutoFilter dialog box.

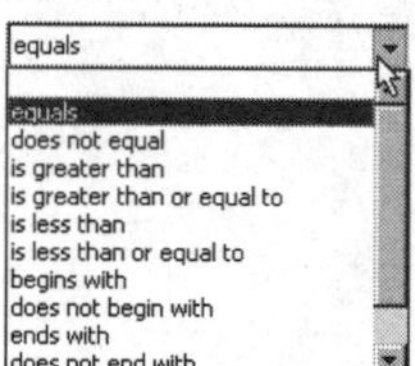

Figure 17 Use this menu to choose a comparison operator.

	A	B	C	D	E	F	G	H	I
1	Product Code	Department	Cc	Sale Pri	Reorder Poi	Qty on Ha	Time to Order?	Resale Val	Mark
15	GTL103G	Junior Clothes	0.63	1.99	190	329		655	316%
44	FLC611M	Misses Clothes	24.63	68.99	20	61		4,208	280%
49	GII1423R	Junior Clothes	5.32	18.99	60	94		1,785	357%
58	GKS255F	Junior Clothes	0.98	1.99	160	455		905	203%
67	FTQ914Y	Misses Clothes	22.00	93.99	50	50		4,700	427%
83	GIJ1117G	Junior Clothes	9.70	46.99	150	268		12,593	484%
94	GZA157Z	Junior Clothes	3.22	7.99	60	370		2,956	248%
110	FEU2113N	Misses Clothes	11.60	13.99	100	286		4,001	121%
122	GZG126P	Junior Clothes	23.90	88.99	110	286		25,451	372%
139	GHP710T	Junior Clothes	9.99	42.99	80	113		4,858	430%
166	GYM29L	Junior Clothes	15.46	64.99	160	77	Reorder Now!	5,004	420%
214	FCV423R	Misses Clothes	4.69	13.99	130	233		3,260	298%
239	GNA141H	Junior Clothes	6.42	8.99	50	113		1,016	140%
250	FZX1916K	Misses Clothes	8.58	46.99	100	280		13,157	548%
258	GRZ2010Y	Junior Clothes	24.89	53.99	70	338		18,249	217%
276	GXE1419E	Junior Clothes	4.76	11.99	30	68		815	252%
289	GRC2213T	Junior Clothes	20.07	59.99	190	394		23,636	299%
329	GHY173K	Junior Clothes	17.88	31.99	40	31	Reorder Now!	992	179%
342	GBV921Z	Junior Clothes	12.70	16.99	130	308		5,233	134%
346	FFW1919R	Misses Clothes	3.41	9.99	40	437		4,366	293%
361	FQP1615H	Misses Clothes	2.39	12.99	140	157		2,039	544%

Figure 18 In this example, the Custom AutoFilter was used to find all inventory items in the Junior Clothes or Misses Clothes department.

	A	B	C	D	E	F	G	H	I
1	Product Code	Department	Cc	Sale Pri	Reorder Poi	Qty on Ha	Time to Order?	Resale Val	Mark
15	GTL103G	Junior Clothes	0.63	1.99	190	329		655	316%
58	GKS255F	Junior Clothes	0.98	1.99	160	455		905	203%
94	GZA157Z	Junior Clothes	3.22	7.99	60	370		2,956	248%
239	GNA141H	Junior Clothes	6.42	8.99	50	113		1,016	140%
346	FFW1919R	Misses Clothes	3.41	9.99	40	437		4,366	293%
364	FPK813O	Misses Clothes	0.85	1.99	40	356		708	234%
444	FUZ1426A	Misses Clothes	2.88	5.99	190	18	Reorder Now!	108	208%

Figure 19 This example narrows down the search by adding another filter: Sale Price<10.

	K	L
1	Department	Markup
2	Automotive	>250%
3	Electronics	>250%
4	Hardware	>250%

Figure 20 Create a criteria range with field names and values that you want to match.

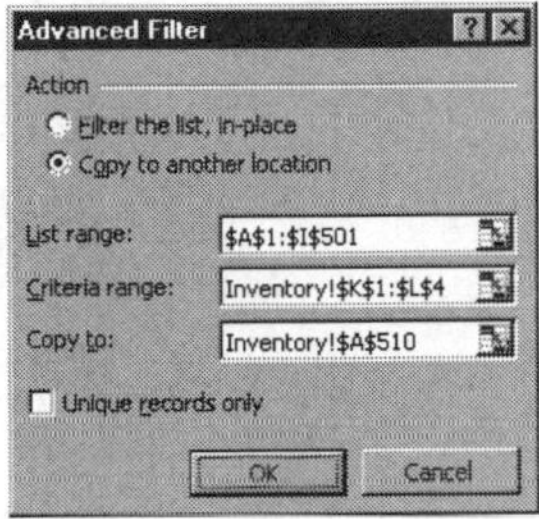

Figure 21 The Advanced Filter dialog box, all set up to filter a list.

	A	B	C	D	E	F	G	H	I
510	Product Code	Department	Cost	Sale Price	Reorder Point	Qty on Hand	Time to Order?	Resale Value	Markup
511	NAK415A	Hardware	19.46	79.99	50	245		19,598	411%
512	OXN516D	Automotive	1.21	4.99	10	152		758	412%
513	NPW820D	Hardware	17.79	76.99	30	459		35,338	433%
514	VBU1124H	Electronics	24.27	90.99	10	487		47,234	400%
515	OIO911Z	Automotive	4.20	15.99	130	458		7,323	381%
516	VNU29D	Electronics	1.42	5.99	140	53	Reorder Now!	317	422%
517	VYZ2116O	Electronics	10.97	57.99	200	299		17,339	529%
518	NTL2314V	Hardware	6.98	30.99	150	261		8,088	444%
519	OFQ2613L	Automotive	7.66	35.99	120	414		14,000	470%
520	NHW93O	Hardware	2.15	10.99	200	16	Reorder Now!	176	511%
521	NER1613Z	Hardware	23.72	109.99	0	303		33,327	464%
522	NUJ418L	Hardware	24.95	68.99	110	484		33,391	277%
523	NVP264B	Hardware	23.54	108.99	0	427		46,630	462%
524	NGH83K	Hardware	19.30	70.99	40	267		18,954	368%
525	OJJ42I	Automotive	1.96	11.99	80	283		3,393	612%
526	VWF119X	Electronics	18.80	95.99	0	243		23,326	511%
527	NYW1123P	Hardware	0.32	1.99	40	174		346	622%
528	NGY610N	Hardware	24.93	86.99	100	290		25,227	349%
529	OPL2222H	Automotive	24.53	144.99	100	160		23,198	591%
530	NES2620O	Hardware	13.76	67.99	60	286		19,445	494%
531	OYP418Q	Automotive	0.80	3.99	20	15	Reorder Now!	60	499%
532	NAR517M	Hardware	13.26	37.99	130	374		14,208	287%
533	NDL106X	Hardware	3.21	11.99	160	72	Reorder Now!	876	374%

Figure 22 The criteria in **Figure 21** found these records.

Advanced Filters

Advanced filters enable you to specify even more criteria than you can with AutoFilters. First set up a criteria range, then use the Advanced Filter dialog box to perform the search.

To use advanced filters

1. Create a criteria range by copying the data labels in the list to a blank area of the worksheet and then entering the criteria in the cells beneath it (**Figure 20**).
2. Choose Data > Filter > Advanced Filter (**Figure 11**).
3. In the Advanced Filter dialog box (**Figure 21**), select an option to specify whether the matches should replace the original list (Filter the list, in-place) or be created elsewhere (Copy to another location).
4. In the List range box, confirm that the correct cell references for your list have been entered.
5. In the Criteria range box, enter the cell references for the range containing your criteria (including the field labels).
6. If you selected the Copy option in step 3, enter a cell reference for the first cell of the new list in the Copy to box.
7. To omit duplicate records from the results, turn on the Unique records only check box.
8. Click OK.

   Excel searches for records that match the criteria and either replaces the original list or creates a new list with the matches (**Figure 22**).

✔ Tip

- You can enter a range into any of the text boxes in the Advanced Filter dialog box (**Figure 21**) by clicking in the box and then dragging in the worksheet to select a range.

Sorting

You can sort lists by any column(s). Excel will quickly put database information in the order you specify.

To sort a list

1. Select any cell in the list.
2. Choose Data > Sort (**Figure 7**) to display the Sort dialog box (**Figure 23**).
3. Choose a primary sort field from the Sort by menu (**Figure 24**).
4. Select a sort order option:
   - ▲ **Ascending** is lowest to highest.
   - ▲ **Descending** is highest to lowest.
5. If desired, repeat steps 3 and 4 for a secondary and tertiary sort field using options in the Then by areas.
6. If the list has column titles, select the Header row option; otherwise, select the No header row option.
7. Click OK.

   Excel sorts the list as you specified (**Figure 25**).

or

1. Select a cell in the column for the field by which you want to sort.
2. Click the Sort Ascending button to sort from lowest to highest value or the Sort Descending button to sort from highest to lowest value. (Both buttons are on the Standard toolbar.)

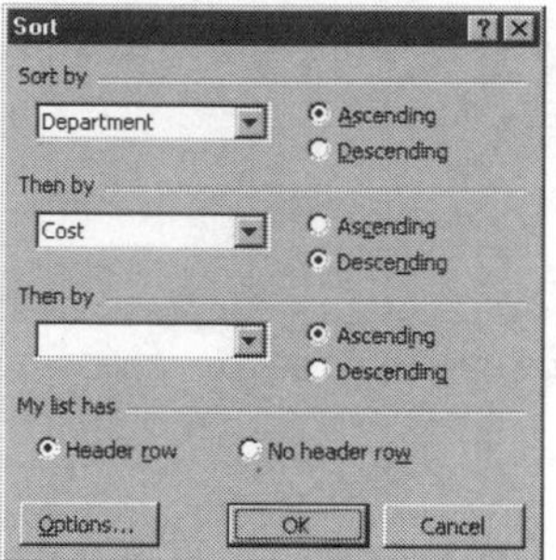

Figure 23 The Sort dialog box, with a primary and secondary sort set up.

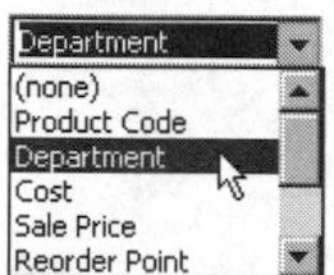

Figure 24 The Sort by (or Then by) menu lists all database fields.

	A	B	C	D	E	F	G	H	I
1	Product Code	Department	Cost	Sale Price	Reorder Point	Qty on Hand	Time to Order?	Resale Value	Markup
2	RAO228O	Appliances	23.91	104.99	100	68	Reorder Now!	7,139	439%
3	RPB2024Q	Appliances	13.41	41.99	110	140		5,879	313%
4	RLA1020I	Appliances	12.60	31.99	150	136	Reorder Now!	4,351	254%
5	RUR1313N	Appliances	7.20	16.99	110	421		7,153	236%
6	RYD818Y	Appliances	6.08	34.99	200	498		17,425	575%
7	RHK915B	Appliances	3.43	20.99	70	137		2,876	612%
8	RPY424R	Appliances	3.06	12.99	90	40	Reorder Now!	520	425%
9	RFB2113N	Appliances	1.40	5.99	150	327		1,959	428%
10	OPL2222H	Automotive	24.53	144.99	100	160		23,198	591%
11	OBW212Q	Automotive	22.08	58.99	160	143	Reorder Now!	8,436	267%
12	ODA522R	Automotive	14.38	60.99	50	371		22,627	424%
13	OYM66B	Automotive	12.79	69.99	60	105		7,349	547%
14	OZW228W	Automotive	12.01	59.99	40	189		11,338	500%
15	OZE2010J	Automotive	11.71	67.99	150	494		33,587	581%
16	OFQ2613L	Automotive	7.66	35.99	120	414		14,900	470%
17	OGI2316B	Automotive	4.78	18.99	10	199		3,779	397%
18	OIO911Z	Automotive	4.20	15.99	130	458		7,323	381%
19	OYG1512M	Automotive	3.08	16.99	30	152		2,582	552%
20	OJJ42I	Automotive	1.96	11.99	80	283		3,393	612%
21	OXN516D	Automotive	1.21	4.99	10	152		758	412%
22	OYP418Q	Automotive	0.80	3.99	20	15	Reorder Now!	60	499%
23	OHZ1214D	Automotive	0.74	3.99	110	179		714	539%

Figure 25 The beginning of a list sorted using the sort orders shown in **Figure 23**.

SORTING

✔ Tips

- You can sort an entire list, a filtered list, or a list created with the Advanced Filter dialog box.
- The two Then by fields in the Sort dialog box are "tie-breakers" and are only used if the primary sort field has more than one record with the same value. **Figures 23** and **25** show how they can be used.
- If the results of a sort are not what you expected, choose Edit > Undo Sort, press Ctrl Z, or click the Undo button on the Standard toolbar to restore the original sort order.
- If you make the wrong selection in the "My list has" area at the bottom of the dialog box, you could sort column titles along with the rest of the list. Undo the sort and try again.
- If you select a cell in the column by which you want to sort, that column is automatically referenced in the Sort dialog box when you open it.
- To sort by more than three columns, sort by the least important columns first, then by the most important ones. For example, to sort a list by columns A, B, C, D, and E, you'd sort first by columns D and E, then by columns A, B, and C.
- In order to use Excel's Subtotal feature, you must first sort the data by the column for which you want subtotals. I tell you about the Subtotal feature next.

Subtotals

Excel's Subtotal feature enters formulas with the SUBTOTAL function in sorted database lists. The SUBTOTAL function (**Figure 28**) returns a subtotal for a sorted list. It uses the following syntax:

SUBTOTAL(*function_num,ref***)**

The function_num argument is a number that specifies which function to use. **Table 3** shows the valid values. (I tell you about most of these functions in **Chapter 5**.) The ref argument is the range of cells to subtotal.

To subtotal a list

1. Sort the list by the field(s) for which you want subtotals and activate any cell in the list (**Figure 25**).
2. Choose Data > Subtotals (**Figure 7**) to display the Subtotal dialog box (**Figure 26**).
3. Choose the name of the field to be grouped for subtotaling from the At each change in menu. The field you select will probably be one of the fields you sorted by.
4. Choose a function from the Use function menu (**Figure 27**).
5. In the Add subtotal to scrolling list, use the check boxes to choose the field(s) to subtotal.
6. If desired, use the check boxes at the bottom of the dialog box to set other options.
7. Click OK.

   Excel turns the list into an outline and enters row titles and subtotals (**Figure 28**).

✔ Tips

- To remove subtotals, click the Remove All button in the Subtotal dialog box (**Figure 26**).
- Excel's outline feature groups information into different levels. You can show or hide information based on its level.

Table 3

Valid *function_num* Values for SUBTOTAL

Number	Function Name
1	AVERAGE
2	COUNT
3	COUNTA
4	MAX
5	MIN
6	PRODUCT
7	STDEV
8	STDEVP
9	SUM
10	VAR
11	VARP

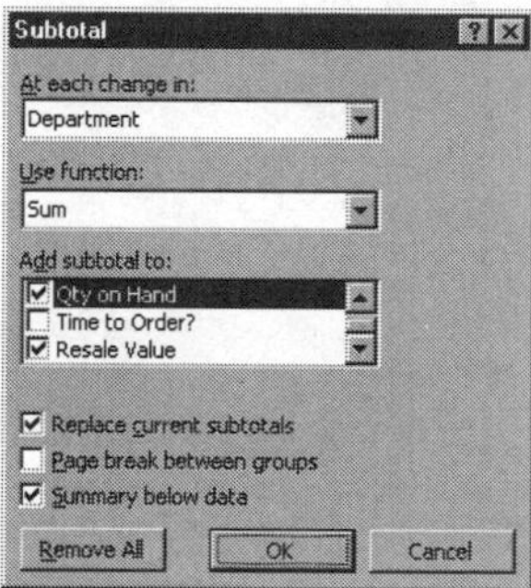

Figure 26 The Subtotal dialog box.

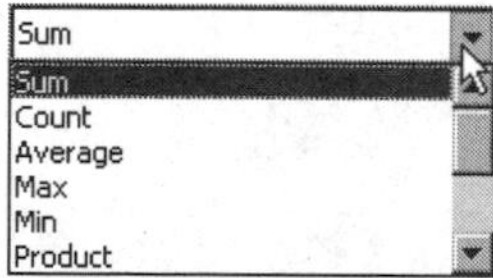

Figure 27 Use this menu to choose a function for the Subtotal. In most cases, you'll choose Sum.

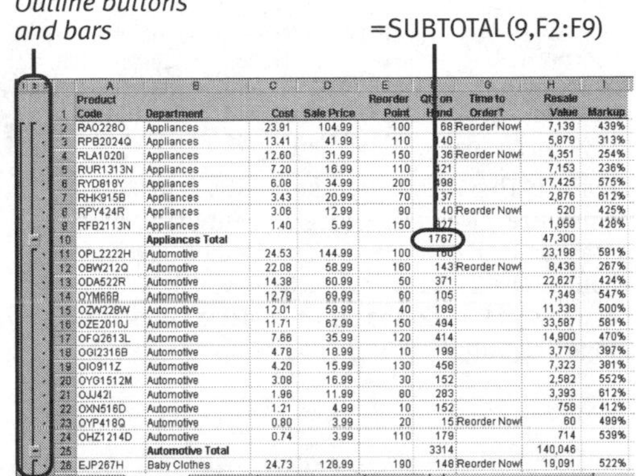

	A	B	C	D	E	F	G	H	I
1	Product Code	Department	Cost	Sale Price	Reorder Point	Qty on Hand	Time to Order?	Resale Value	Markup
2	RAO228O	Appliances	23.91	104.99	100	68	Reorder Now!	7,139	439%
3	RPB2024Q	Appliances	13.41	41.99	110	40		5,879	313%
4	RLA1020I	Appliances	12.60	31.99	150	36	Reorder Now!	4,351	254%
5	RUR1313N	Appliances	7.20	16.99	110	21		7,153	236%
6	RYD818Y	Appliances	6.08	34.99	200	98		17,425	575%
7	RHK915B	Appliances	3.43	20.99	70	37		2,876	612%
8	RPY424R	Appliances	3.06	12.99	90	40	Reorder Now!	520	425%
9	RFB2113N	Appliances	1.40	5.99	150	27		1,959	428%
10		**Appliances Total**				1767		47,300	
11	OPL2222H	Automotive	24.53	144.99	100	[illegible]		23,198	591%
12	OBW212Q	Automotive	22.08	58.99	160	143	Reorder Now!	8,436	267%
13	ODA522R	Automotive	14.38	60.99	50	371		22,627	424%
14	OYM66B	Automotive	12.79	69.99	60	105		7,349	547%
15	OZW228W	Automotive	12.01	59.99	40	189		11,338	500%
16	OZE2010J	Automotive	11.71	67.99	150	494		33,587	581%
17	OFQ2613L	Automotive	7.66	35.99	120	414		14,900	470%
18	OGI2316B	Automotive	4.78	18.99	10	199		3,779	397%
19	OIO911Z	Automotive	4.20	15.99	130	458		7,323	381%
20	OYG1512M	Automotive	3.08	16.99	30	152		2,582	552%
21	OJJ42I	Automotive	1.96	11.99	80	283		3,393	612%
22	OXN516D	Automotive	1.21	4.99	10	152		758	412%
23	OYP418Q	Automotive	0.80	3.99	20	15	Reorder Now!	60	499%
24	OHZ1214D	Automotive	0.74	3.99	110	179		714	539%
25		**Automotive Total**				3314		140,046	
26	EJP267H	Baby Clothes	24.73	128.99	190	148	Reorder Now!	19,091	522%

Figure 28 Here's part of the list in **Figure 25** with subtotals.

	A	B	C	D	E	F	G	H	I
1	Product Code	Department	Cost	Sale Price	Reorder Point	Qty on Hand	Time to Order?	Resale Value	Markup
10		**Appliances Total**				1767		47,300	
25		**Automotive Total**				3314		140,046	
44		**Baby Clothes Total**				3114		158,781	
45	QCI1326D	Bed & Bath	23.93	51.99	20	96		4,991	217%
46	QPS2015W	Bed & Bath	23.71	95.99	70	349		33,501	405%
47	QFT1524E	Bed & Bath	22.33	125.99	190	151	Reorder Now!	19,024	564%
48	QNY1313Q	Bed & Bath	20.65	59.99	0	484		29,035	291%
49	QYD217J	Bed & Bath	20.49	115.99	20	428		49,844	588%
50	QDW2422J	Bed & Bath	20.13	49.99	180	394		19,696	248%
51	QNT1920P	Bed & Bath	19.08	114.99	10	120		14,719	603%
52	QWP1616R	Bed & Bath	16.83	93.99	110	346		32,521	558%
53	QXG2613N	Bed & Bath	16.20	23.99	140	312		7,485	148%
54	QOO1424Z	Bed & Bath	16.00	67.99	130	65	Reorder Now!	4,419	425%
55	QGD1320E	Bed & Bath	15.14	20.99	40	437		9,173	139%
56	QUV77I	Bed & Bath	14.88	47.99	130	291		13,965	323%
57	QVD248Q	Bed & Bath	13.76	52.99	90	337		17,858	385%
58	QVH173G	Bed & Bath	13.38	71.99	0	252		18,141	538%
59	QBO38A	Bed & Bath	12.04	27.99	110	303		10,720	210%
60	QRI817L	Bed & Bath	10.86	18.99	50	16	Reorder Now!	304	175%
61	QCU1025Y	Bed & Bath	10.04	15.99	130	459		7,339	159%
62	QOM2011Z	Bed & Bath	3.47	6.99	80	102		713	201%
63	QSA2517X	Bed & Bath	1.59	4.99	60	52	Reorder Now!	259	314%
64		**Bed & Bath Total**				5082		293,507	
80		**Big & Tall Men's Clothes Total**				4847		202,517	
100		**Books Total**				5644		217,820	

Database | Inventory | Calculations | Database Functions

Figure 29 Here's the outline from **Figure 28** with some of the detail hidden.

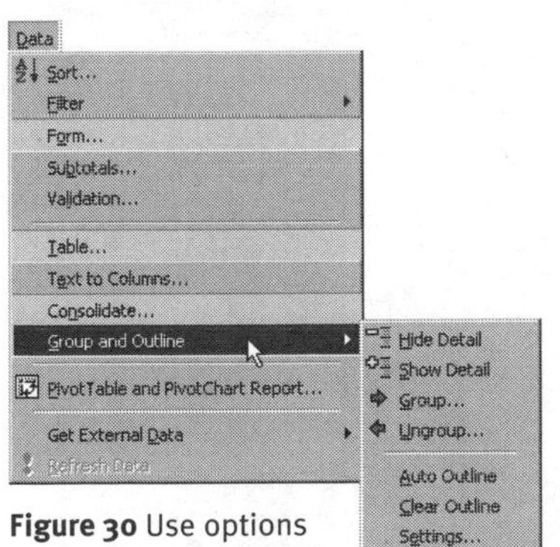

Figure 30 Use options on the Group and Outline submenu under the Data menu to experiment with Excel's outline feature on your own.

To work with a subtotal outline

Click outline buttons on the left side of the window to display or hide detail:

- Click a minus sign button to collapse the outline for that section.
- Click a plus sign button to expand the outline for that section.
- Click one of the outline level numbers to collapse or expand the entire outline to that level.

Figure 29 shows an outline created by the Subtotal command partially collapsed. Note how the outline buttons and bars to the left of the data are set.

✔ Tip

- You can create an outline for virtually any spreadsheet data. Although manually creating outlines is beyond the scope of this book, here's a hint to get you started if you decide to explore this feature: Use commands on the Group and Outline submenu under the Data menu (**Figure 30**) to create and clear groups and outlines.

Database Functions

Excel includes several database and list management functions. (SUBTOTAL, which I discuss on the previous two pages, is one of them.) Here are a few of the most commonly used ones, along with their syntax:

DSUM(*database,field,criteria***)**

DAVERAGE(*database,field,criteria***)**

DCOUNT(*database,field,criteria***)**

DCOUNTA(*database,field,criteria***)**

DMAX(*database,field,criteria***)**

DMIN(*database,field,criteria***)**

The database argument is the cell references for a range containing the database or list. The field argument is the name of the field you want to summarize. The criteria argument is either the data you want to match or a range containing the data you want to match.

Figure 31 shows an example of these database functions in action, using the criteria range in **Figure 20**.

✔ Tips

- Each database function corresponds to a mathematical or statistical function and performs the same kind of calculation—but on records matching criteria only. I tell you about other functions in **Chapter 5**.
- You can enter database functions with the Formula Palette. I tell you how to use the Formula Palette in **Chapter 5**.

DSUM	595.05	=DSUM(A1:I501,"Cost",K1:L4)
DAVERAGE	12.396875	=DAVERAGE(A1:I501,"Cost",K1:L4)
DCOUNT	48	=DCOUNT(A1:I501,"Cost",K1:L4)
DCOUNTA	48	=DCOUNTA(A1:I501,"Cost",K1:L4)
DMAX	24.95	=DMAX(A1:I501,"Cost",K1:L4)
DMIN	0.11	=DMIN(A1:I501,"Cost",K1:L4)

Figure 31 These formulas use database functions to summarize information based on criteria. The database is the 500-record list used throughout this chapter. The field is the Cost field, which is found in column *C* of the database. The criteria range is the range illustrated in **Figure 20**.

ADVANCED TECHNIQUES

	A	B	C	D	E
1	Southwest Division				
2	First Quarter Sales				
3		Jan	Feb	Mar	Total
4	John	$1,254.00	$1,256.00	$ 2,435.00	$ 4,945.00
5	Jean	1,865.00	1,736.00	1,905.00	5,506.00
6	Joe	1,614.00	1,284.00	2,509.00	5,407.00
7	Joan	1,987.00	1,908.00	2,890.00	6,785.00
8	Totals	$6,720.00	$6,184.00	$ 9,739.00	$22,643.00

Figure 1 The reference to the selected range would be a lot easier to remember if it had a name like *FirstQtrSales* rather than just *A4:D7*.

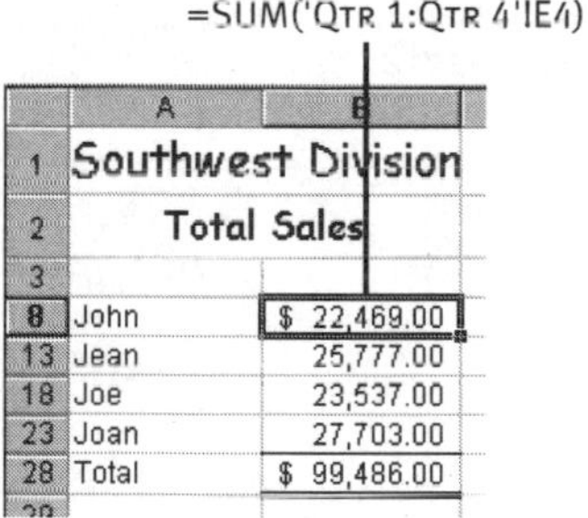

Figure 2 3-D cell references make it possible to link information from different worksheets or workbooks.

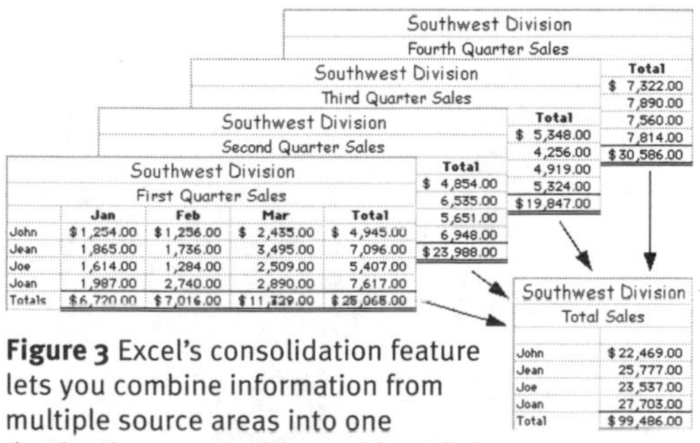

Figure 3 Excel's consolidation feature lets you combine information from multiple source areas into one destination area—with or without links.

Advanced Techniques

Excel has many advanced features that you can use to tap into Excel's real power. In this chapter, I tell you about some of the advanced techniques I think you'll find most useful in your day-to-day work with Excel:

- **Names (Figure 1)** let you name cells or ranges. You can then use the names in place of cell references in formulas.
- **3-D cell references (Figure 2)** let you write formulas with links to other worksheets and workbooks.
- **Consolidations (Figure 3)** let you summarize information from several sources in one destination, with or without live links.
- **Custom views** let you create predefined views of workbook contents.
- **Macros** let you automate repetitive tasks.

✔ Tips

- The information in this chapter builds on information in previous chapters of this book. It's a good idea to have a solid understanding of the information covered up to this point in this book before exploring the features in this chapter.
- Through the use of Excel's built-in Visual Basic programming language, the macro feature also enables you to create highly customized workbook files, complete with special dialog boxes, menus, and commands. This, however, is far beyond the scope of this book.

Names

The trouble with using cell references in formulas is that they're difficult to remember. To make matters worse, cell references can change if cells above or to the left of them are inserted or deleted.

Excel's names feature eliminates both problems by letting you assign easy-to-remember names to individual cells or ranges of cells in your workbooks. The names, which you can use in formulas, don't change, no matter how much worksheet editing you do.

✔ Tips

- Excel can automatically recognize many column and row labels as cell or range names. I tell you about this feature on the next page.
- Names can be up to 255 characters long and can include letters, numbers, periods, question marks, and underscore characters (_). The first character must be a letter. Names cannot contain spaces or "look" like cell references.
- If you enter an incorrect name reference in a formula, one of two things happens:
  - ▲ Excel's Formula AutoCorrect feature offers to fix it (**Figure 4**)—if Excel can "guess" what name you meant to type.
  - ▲ A *#NAME?* error value appears in the cell (**Figure 5**).

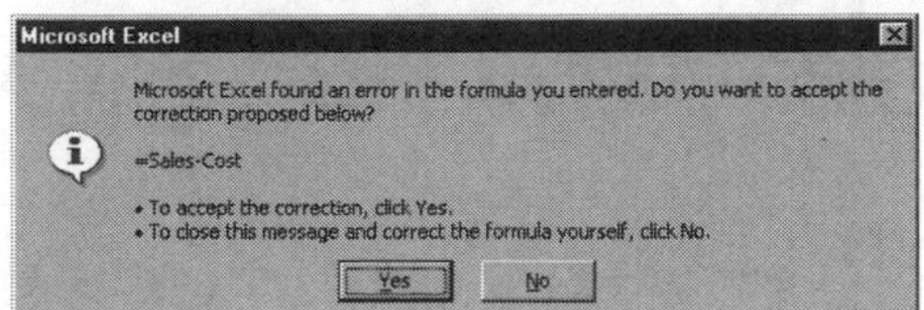

Figure 4 The Formula AutoCorrect feature can sometimes help you fix incorrectly entered name references.

B3 = =Sales-Costs

	A	B	C	D
1	Sales	1000		
2	Cost	400		
3	Profit	#NAME?		

Figure 5 If a name reference in a formula is not correct, a *#NAME?* error appears in the cell.

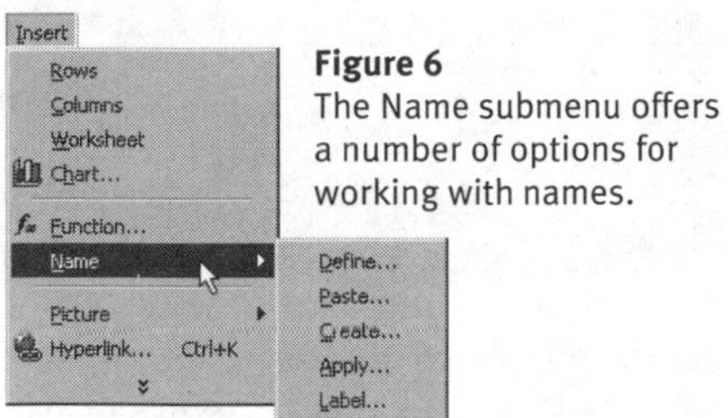

Figure 6 The Name submenu offers a number of options for working with names.

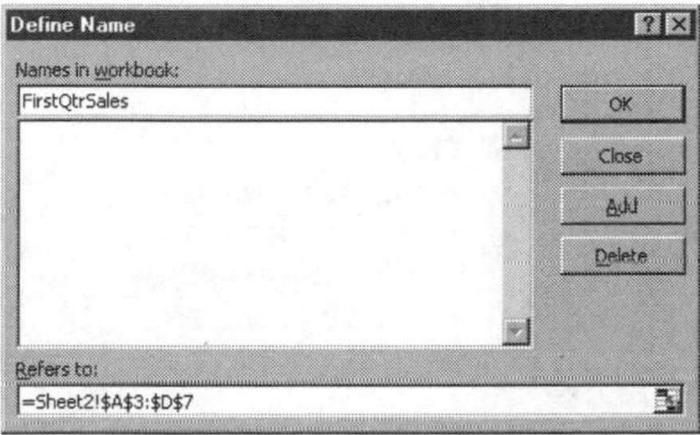

Figure 7 Use the Define Name dialog box to set a name for one or more cells. As you can see, the name of the worksheet is part of the cell reference.

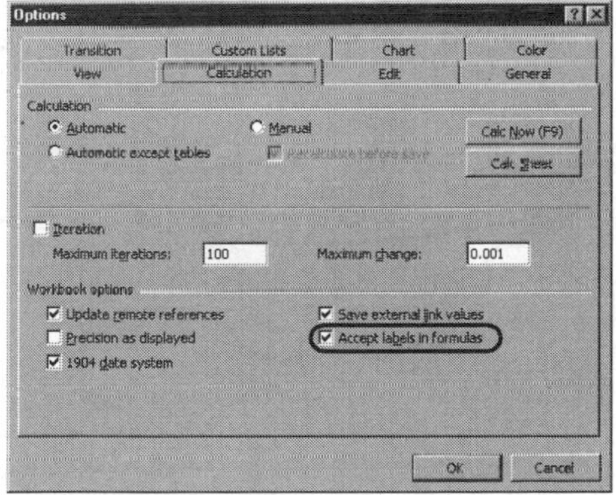

Figure 8 To use labels as names, make sure the Accept labels in formulas check box is turned on.

Jan *Jean* *Mar Joan*

	A	B	C	D
1	**Southwest Division**			
2	**First Quarter Sales**			
3		**Jan**	**Feb**	**Mar**
4	John	1254	1256	2435
5	Jean	1865	1736	1905
6	Joe	1614	1204	2509
7	Joan	1987	1908	2890

Figure 9 Examples of labels automatically recognized as range and cell names.

To define a name

1. Select the cell(s) you want to name (**Figure 1**).
2. Choose Insert > Name > Define (**Figure 6**).
3. In the Define Name dialog box that appears, Excel may suggest a name in the Names in workbook box. You can enter a name you prefer (**Figure 7**).
4. The cell reference in the Refers to box should reflect the range you selected in step 1. To enter a different range, delete the range that appears in the box and either type in a new range or reselect the cell(s) in the worksheet window.
5. Click OK.

✔ Tip

- To define more than one name, follow the above steps for the first name but click the Add button in step 5. Then repeat steps 3 through 5 for each name you want to define. When you're finished, click OK.

To use labels as names

Make sure the Accept labels in formulas check box is turned on in the Calculation tab of the Options dialog box (**Figure 8**). (See **Chapter 13** for more information about setting options.)

✔ Tips

- The Accept labels in formulas option is turned off by default.
- Here's how Excel applies labels to ranges and cells (**Figure 9**):
  - ▲ To refer to a column, use the label at the top of the column.
  - ▲ To refer to a row, use the label at the left end of the row.
  - ▲ To refer to a cell, use the label at the top of the column and the label at the left end of the row.

To create names

1. Select the cells containing the ranges you want to name as well as labels in adjoining cells that you want to use as names (**Figure 10**).
2. Choose Insert > Name > Create (**Figure 6**).
3. In the Create Names dialog box (**Figure 11**), turn on the check box(es) for the cells that contain the labels you want to use as names.
4. Click OK.

   Excel uses the text in the cells you indicated as names for the adjoining cells. You can see the results if you open the Define Name dialog box (**Figure 12**).

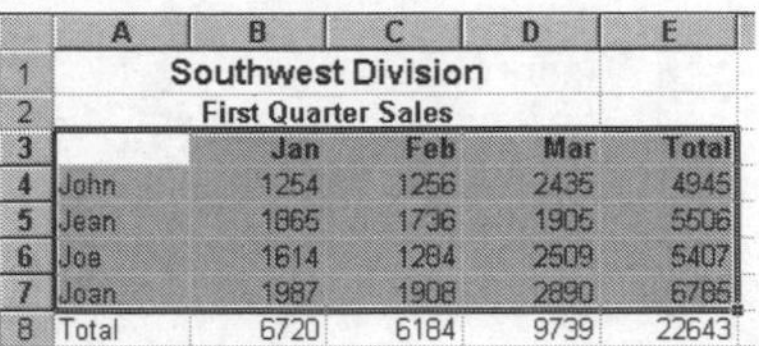

	A	B	C	D	E
1	Southwest Division				
2	First Quarter Sales				
3		Jan	Feb	Mar	Total
4	John	1254	1256	2435	4945
5	Jean	1865	1736	1905	5506
6	Joe	1614	1284	2509	5407
7	Joan	1987	1908	2890	6785
8	Total	6720	6184	9739	22643

Figure 10 To use the Create Names dialog box, you must first select the cells you want to name, as well as the adjoining cells with text you want to use as names.

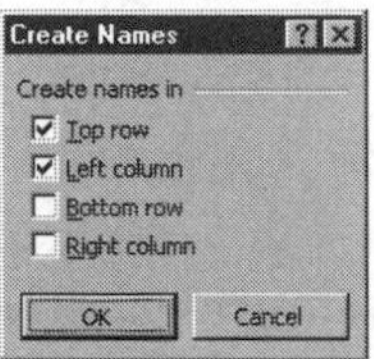

Figure 11 In the Create Names dialog box, tell Excel which cells contain the text for names.

✔ Tips

- This is a quick way to create a lot of names all at once.
- Use this feature to name ranges based on labels if you decide to keep the Accept labels in formulas option (discussed on the previous page) turned off.

To delete a name

1. Choose Insert > Name > Define (**Figure 4**).
2. In the Define Name dialog box (**Figure 12**), click to select the name you want to delete.
3. Click the Delete button. The name is removed from the list.
4. Repeat steps 2 and 3 to delete other names as desired.
5. Click OK to dismiss the Define Name dialog box.

Figure 12 Look in the Define Name dialog box to see how many names were added.

✔ Tip

- Deleting a name does not delete the cells to which the name refers.

	A	B
1		Southwest
2		First Quarte
3		Jan
4	John	1254
5	Jean	1865
6	Joe	1614
7	Joan	1987
8	Total	=SUM(Jan)

Figure 13 Type the formula using names instead of references.

	A	B
1		Southwest
2		First Quart
3		Jan
4	John	1254
5	Jean	1865
6	Joe	1614
7	Joan	1987
8	Total	6720

Figure 14 When you complete the formula, the result appears in the cell.

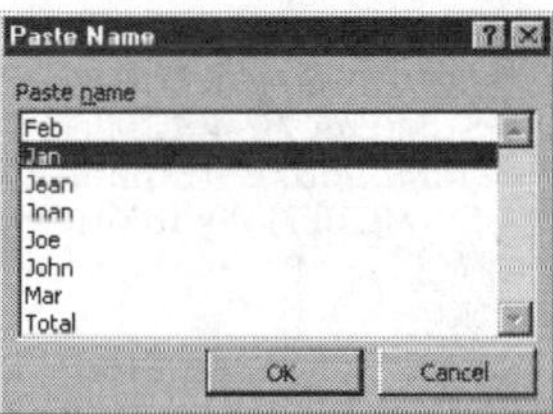

Figure 15 Use the Paste Name dialog box to select and paste in a name.

To enter names in a formula

1. Activate the cell in which you want to enter the formula.
2. Type in the formula, using cell or range names rather than references (**Figure 13**).
3. Complete the entry by pressing [Enter] or clicking the Enter button ✓ on the formula bar (**Figure 14**).

✔ Tips

- You can use the Paste Name command to enter a name for you. Follow the steps above, but when it's time to type in the name, choose Insert > Name > Paste (**Figure 6**). Use the Paste Name dialog box that appears (**Figure 15**) to select and paste in the name you want. The Paste Name command even works when you use the Formula Palette to write formulas. I tell you about using the Formula Palette in **Chapter 5**.
- When you delete a name, Excel responds with a *#NAME?* error in each cell that contains a formula referring to that name (**Figure 5**). These formulas must be rewritten.

To apply names to existing formulas

1. Select the cells containing formulas for which you want to apply names. If you want to apply names throughout the worksheet, click any single cell.
2. Choose Insert > Name > Apply (**Figure 6**).
3. In the Apply Names dialog box (**Figure 16**), select the names that you want to use in place of the cell reference. To select or deselect a name, click on it.
4. Click OK.

   Excel rewrites the formulas with the appropriate names from those you selected. **Figure 17** shows an example of formulas changed by selecting *Jan, Feb, Mar,* and *Total* in **Figure 16**.

✔ Tips

- If only one cell is selected, Excel applies names based on your selection(s) in the Apply Names dialog box, not the selected cell.
- If you turn off the Ignore Relative/Absolute check box in the Apply Names dialog box (**Figure 16**), Excel matches the type of reference. I explain the difference between relative and absolute references in **Chapter 3**.

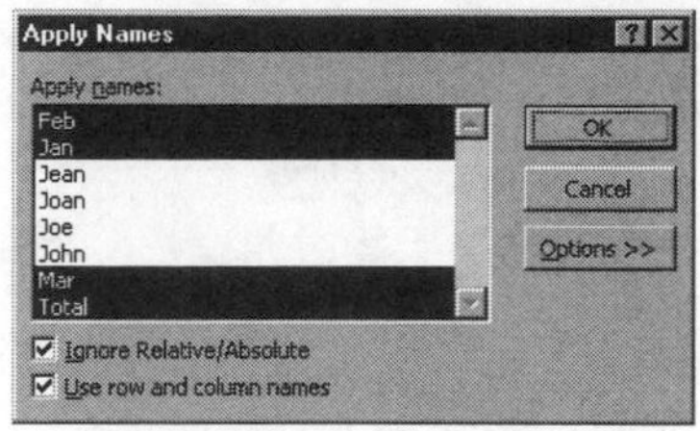

Figure 16 Select the names that you want to apply to formulas in your worksheet.

	A	B	C	D	E
1		Southwest Division			
2		First Quarter Sales			
3		Jan	Feb	Mar	Total
4	John	1254	1256	2435	4945
5	Jean	1865	1736	1905	5506
6	Joe	1614	1284	2509	5407
7	Joan	1987	1908	2890	6785
8	Total	6720	6184	9739	22643

Figure 17 Excel applies the names that you selected to the formulas that reference their ranges.

Cell:	Before:	After:
B8	=SUM(B4:B7)	=SUM(Jan)
C8	=SUM(C4:C7)	=SUM(Feb)
D8	=SUM(D4:D7)	=SUM(Mar)
E8	=SUM(E4:E7)	=SUM(Total)

To select named cells

Choose the name of the cell(s) you want to select from the Name menu on the far-left end of the formula bar (**Figure 18**).

or

1. Click the Name box at the far-left end of the formula bar to select it.
2. Type in the name of the cells you want to select (**Figure 19**).
3. Press Enter.

or

1. Choose Edit > Go To (**Figure 20**) or press Ctrl G or F5.
2. In the Go To dialog box (**Figure 21**), click to select the name of the cell(s) you want to select in the Go to list.
3. Click OK.

✔ Tip

- When named cells are selected, the name appears in the cell reference area at the far-left end of the formula bar.

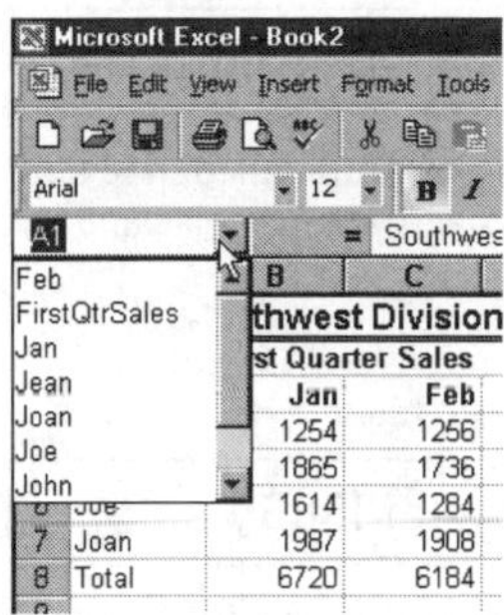

Figure 18 The Name menu on the far-left end of the formula bar lets you select named ranges quickly.

Figure 19 If you prefer, you can type in a name and press Enter to select it.

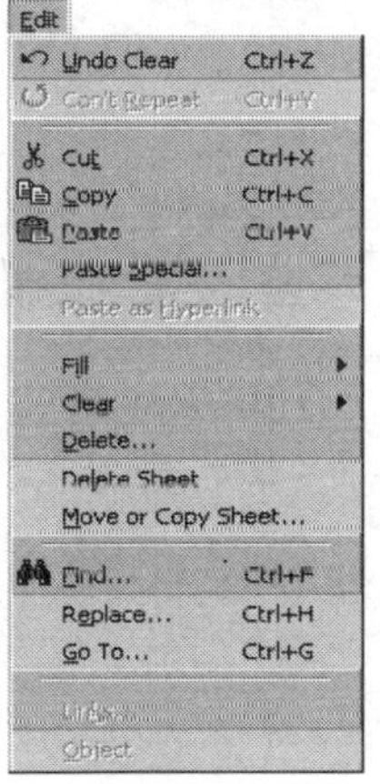

Figure 20 You can choose the Go To command under the Edit menu...

Figure 21 ...then select the name of the cell(s) you want.

3-D References

3-D cell references let you write formulas that reference cells in other worksheets or workbooks. The links are live—when a cell's contents change, the results of formulas in cells that reference it change.

Excel offers several ways to write formulas with 3-D cell references:

- **Use cell names.** I tell you about cell names in the first part of this chapter. **Figure 22** shows an example.
- **Type them in.** When you type in a 3-D cell reference, you must include the name of the sheet (in single quotes, if the name contains a space), followed by an exclamation point (!) and cell reference. If the reference is for a cell in another workbook, you must also include the workbook name, in brackets. **Figures 23**, **24**, and **25** show examples.
- **Click on them.** You'll get the same results as if you had typed the references, but Excel does all the typing for you.
- **Use the Paste Special command.** The Paste Link button in the Paste Special dialog box lets you paste a link between cells in different sheets of a workbook or different workbooks.

✔ Tips

- When you delete a cell, Excel displays a #REF! error in any cells that referred to it. The cells containing these errors must be revised to remove the error.
- Do not make references to an unsaved file. If you do and you close the file with the reference before saving (and naming) the file it refers to, Excel won't be able to update the link.

```
=SUM(John,Joan,Joe,Jean)
```

Figure 22 This example uses the SUM function to add the contents of the cells named *John*, *Joan*, *Joe*, and *Jean* in the same workbook.

```
='Results for Year'!$B$9
```

Figure 23 This example refers to cell *B9* in a worksheet called *Results for Year* in the same workbook.

```
=SUM('Qtr 1:Qtr 4'!E9)
```

Figure 24 This example uses the SUM function to add the contents of cell *E9* in worksheets starting with *Qtr 1* and ending with *Qtr 4* in the same workbook.

```
=[Sales]'Results for Year'!$B$9
```

Figure 25 This example refers to cell *B9* in a worksheet called *Results for Year* in a workbook called *Sales*.

3-D REFERENCES

Figures 26 & 27 Two examples of 3-D references utilizing names. The first example refers to a name in the same workbook. The second example refers to a name in a different workbook.

SUM =Qtr 1'!E8

consolid.xls

	A	B	C	D	E
1		Southwest Division			
2		First Quarter Sales			
3		Jan	Feb	Mar	Total
4	John	$ 1,254.00	$ 1,256.00	$ 2,435.00	$ 4,945.00
5	Jean	1,865.00	1,736.00	3,495.00	7,096.00
6	Joe	1,614.00	1,284.00	2,509.00	5,407.00
7	Joan	1,987.00	2,740.00	2,890.00	7,617.00
8	Totals	$ 6,720.00	$ 7,016.00	$ 11,329.00	$ 25,065.00
9					

Qtr 1 / Qtr 2 / Qtr 3 / Qtr 4 / Cons

Figure 28 After typing an equal sign in the cell in which you want the reference to go, you can select the cell(s) you want to reference.

To reference a named cell or range in another worksheet

1. Select the cell in which you want to enter the reference.
2. Type an equal sign (=).
3. If the sheet containing the cells you want to reference is in another workbook, type the name of the workbook (within single quotes, if the name contains a space) followed by an exclamation point (!).
4. Type the name of the cell(s) you want to reference (**Figures 26** and **27**).
5. Press Enter or click the Enter button on the formula bar.

✔ Tip

- If the name you want to reference is in the same workbook, you can paste it in by choosing Insert > Name > Paste (**Figure 6**). I explain how to use the Paste Name dialog box earlier in this chapter.

To reference a cell or range in another worksheet by clicking

1. Select the cell in which you want to enter the reference.
2. Type an equal sign (=).
3. If the sheet containing the cells you want to reference is in another workbook, switch to that workbook.
4. Click on the sheet tab for the worksheet containing the cell you want to reference.
5. Select the cell(s) you want to reference (**Figure 28**).
6. Press Enter or click the Enter button on the formula bar.

To reference a cell or range in another worksheet by typing

1. Select the cell in which you want to enter the reference.
2. Type an equal sign (=).
3. If the sheet containing the cells you want to reference is in another workbook, type the name of the workbook within brackets ([ ]).
4. Type the name of the sheet followed by an exclamation point (!).
5. Type the cell reference for the cell(s) you want to reference.
6. Press Enter or click the Enter button on the formula bar.

✔ Tip

- If the name of the sheet includes a space character, it must be enclosed within single quotes in the reference. See **Figures 23**, **24**, and **25** for examples.

To reference a cell with the Paste Special command

1. Select the cell you want to reference.
2. Choose Edit > Copy (**Figure 20**), press Ctrl C, or click the Copy button on the Standard toolbar.
3. Switch to the worksheet in which you want to put the reference.
4. Select the cell in which you want the reference to go.
5. Choose Edit > Paste Special (**Figure 20**).
6. In the Paste Special dialog box (**Figure 29**), click the Paste Link button.

Figure 29 You can click the Paste Link button in the Paste Special dialog box to paste a reference to cells you copied.

✔ Tips

- Do not press Enter after using the Paste Special command! Doing so pastes the copied cell or range into the cell, thus overwriting the link.
- Using the Paste Link button to paste a range of cells creates a special range called an *array*. Each cell in an array shares the same cell reference and cannot be changed unless all cells in the array are changed.

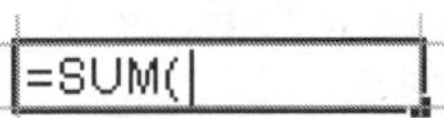

Figure 30 Type the beginning of a formula with the SUM function...

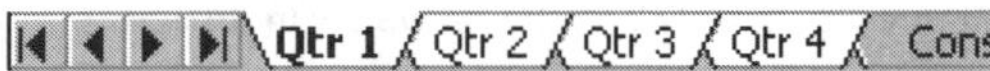

Figure 31 ...then select all of the tabs for sheets that contain the cells you want to sum...

=sum('Qtr 1:Qtr 4'!

Figure 32 ...so the sheet names are appended as a range in the formula bar.

To write a formula with 3-D references

1. Select the cell in which you want to enter the formula.
2. Type an equal sign (=).
3. Use any combination of the following techniques until the formula is complete.
   - ▲ To enter a function, use the Formula Palette or type in the function. I tell you how to use the Formula Palette in **Chapter 5**.
   - ▲ To enter an operator, type it in. I tell you about using operators in **Chapter 2**.
   - ▲ To enter a cell reference, select the cell(s) you want to reference or type the reference in. If typing the reference, be sure to include single quotes, brackets, and exclamation points as discussed on the previous page.
4. Press Enter or click the Enter button ✓ on the formula bar.

To write a formula that adds the same cell on multiple, adjacent sheets

1. Select the cell in which you want to enter the formula.
2. Type *=SUM(* (**Figure 30**).
3. If the cells you want to add are in another workbook, switch to that workbook.
4. Click the sheet tab for the first worksheet containing the cell you want to sum.
5. Hold down Shift and click on the sheet tab for the last sheet containing the cell you want to sum. All tabs from the first to the last become selected (**Figure 31**). The formula in the formula bar should look something like the one in **Figure 32**.

Continued on next page...

Continued from previous page.

6. Click the cell you want to sum (**Figure 33**). The cell reference is added to the formula (**Figure 34**).
7. Type *)*.
8. Press Enter or click the Enter button on the formula bar.

✔ Tips

- Use this technique to link cells of identically arranged worksheets. This results in a "3-D worksheet" effect.
- Although you can use this technique to consolidate data, the Consolidate command, which I begin discussing on the next page, automates consolidations with or without links.

Opening Worksheets with Links

When you open a worksheet that has a link to another workbook file, a dialog box like the one in **Figure 35** appears.

- If you click Yes, Excel checks the other file and updates linked information. If Excel can't find the other workbook, it displays a dialog box you can use to find it.
- If you click No, Excel does not check the data in the other file.

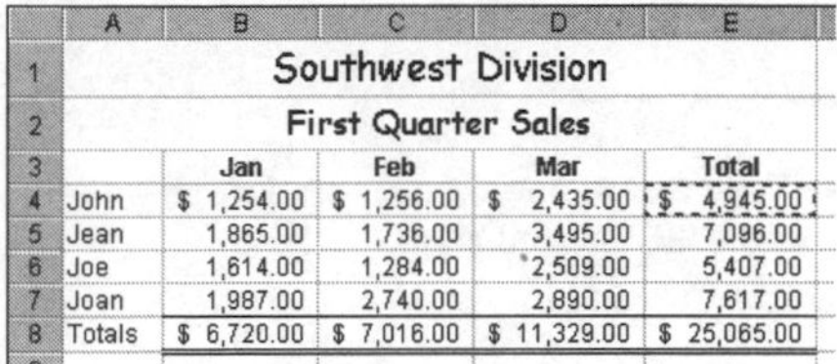

	A	B	C	D	E
1	Southwest Division				
2	First Quarter Sales				
3		Jan	Feb	Mar	Total
4	John	$ 1,254.00	$ 1,256.00	$ 2,435.00	$ 4,945.00
5	Jean	1,865.00	1,736.00	3,495.00	7,096.00
6	Joe	1,614.00	1,284.00	2,509.00	5,407.00
7	Joan	1,987.00	2,740.00	2,890.00	7,617.00
8	Totals	$ 6,720.00	$ 7,016.00	$ 11,329.00	$ 25,065.00

Figure 33 Then click on the cell you want to add...

=SUM('Qtr 1:Qtr 4'!E4

Figure 34 ...so its reference is appended to the formula in the formula bar.

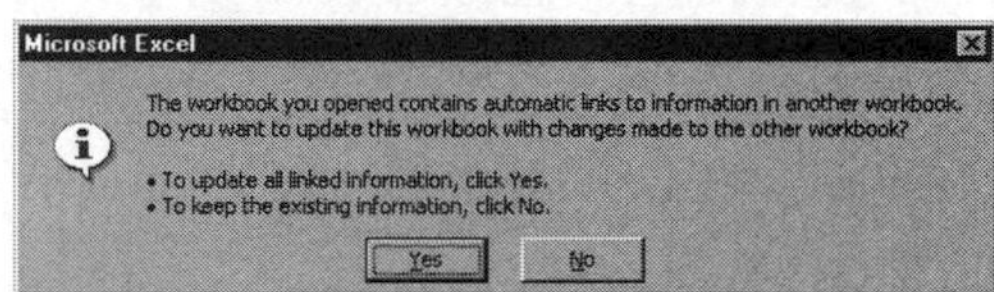

Figure 35 This dialog box appears if you open a workbook that contains links to another workbook.

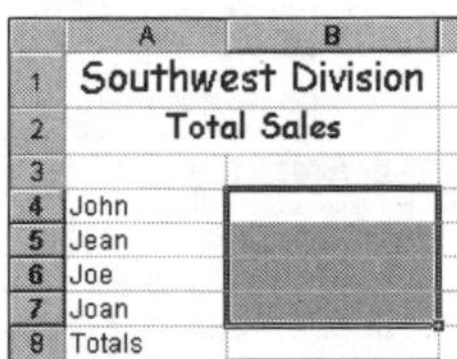

	A	B
1	Southwest Division	
2	Total Sales	
3		
4	John	
5	Jean	
6	Joe	
7	Joan	
8	Totals	

Figure 36 Select the cells in which you want the consolidated data to go.

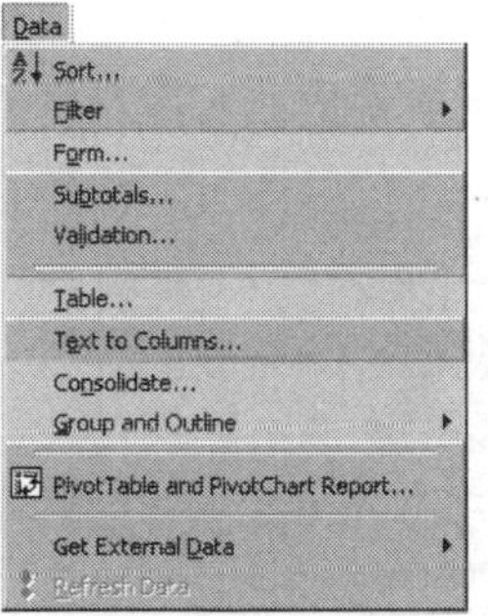

Figure 37 Choose Consolidate from the Data menu.

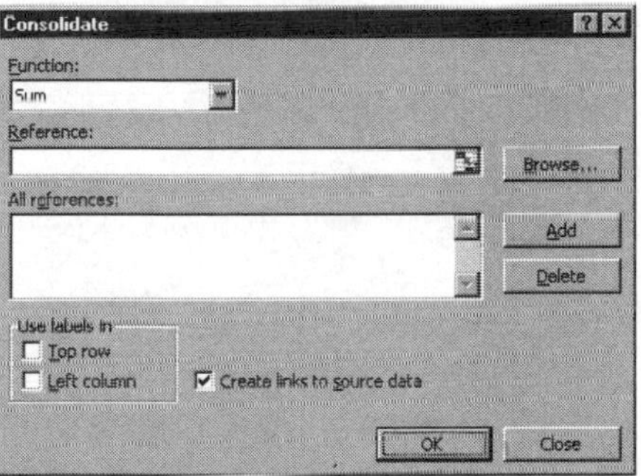

Figure 38 Use the Consolidate dialog box to identify the cells you want to combine and set other options.

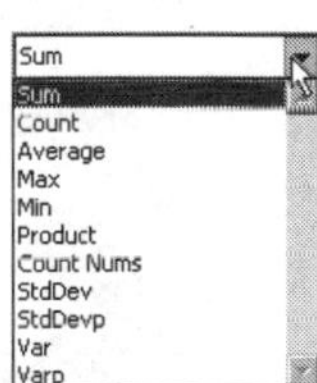

Figure 39 Choose a function for the consolidation from the Function menu.

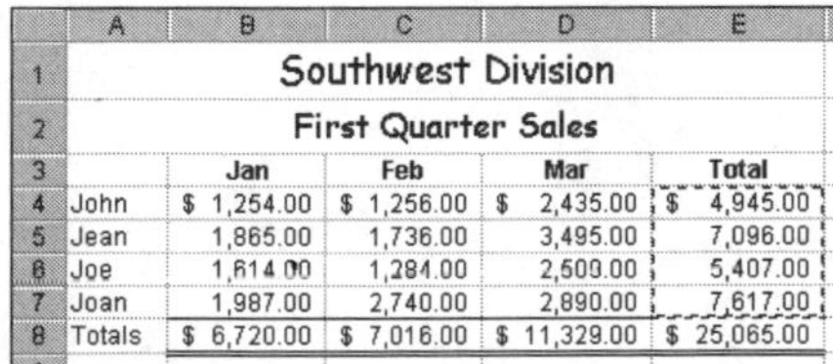

	A	B	C	D	E
1	Southwest Division				
2	First Quarter Sales				
3		Jan	Feb	Mar	Total
4	John	$ 1,254.00	$ 1,256.00	$ 2,435.00	$ 4,945.00
5	Jean	1,865.00	1,736.00	3,495.00	7,096.00
6	Joe	1,614.00	1,284.00	2,509.00	5,407.00
7	Joan	1,987.00	2,740.00	2,890.00	7,617.00
8	Totals	$ 6,720.00	$ 7,016.00	$ 11,329.00	$ 25,065.00

Figure 40 Enter references for cells in the Consolidate dialog box by selecting them.

Consolidations

The Consolidate command lets you combine data from multiple sources. Excel lets you do this in two ways:

- **Consolidate based on the arrangement of data.** This is useful when data occupies the same number of cells in the same arrangement in multiple locations (**Figure 3**).
- **Consolidate based on identifying labels or categories.** This is useful when the arrangement of data varies from one source to the next.

✔ Tip

- With either method, Excel can create links to the source information so the consolidation changes automatically when linked data changes.

To consolidate based on the arrangement of data

1. Select the cell(s) where you want the consolidated information to go (**Figure 36**).
2. Choose Data > Consolidate (**Figure 37**).
3. In the Consolidate dialog box (**Figure 38**), choose a function from the Function menu (**Figure 39**).
4. Switch to the worksheet containing the first cell(s) to be included in the consolidation. The reference is entered into the Reference box.
5. Select the cell(s) you want to include in the consolidation (**Figure 40**). The reference is entered into the Reference box.
6. Click Add.

Continued on next page...

Continued from previous page.

7. Repeat steps 4, 5, and 6 for all of the cells that you want to include in the consolidation. When you're finished, the All references list in the Consolidate dialog box might look something like **Figure 41**.
8. To create links between the source data and destination cell(s), turn on the Create links to source data check box.
9. Click OK.

   Excel consolidates the information in the originally selected cell(s) (**Figure 42**).

✔ Tips

- For this technique to work, each source range must have the same number of cells with data arranged in the same way.
- If the Consolidate dialog box contains references when you open it, you can clear them by selecting each one and clicking the Delete button.
- If you turn on the Create links to source data check box, Excel creates an outline with links to all source cells (**Figure 42**). You can expand or collapse the outline by clicking the outline buttons. I tell you a little more about outlines in **Chapter 10**.

Figure 41 The cells you want to consolidate are listed in the All references list in the Consolidate dialog box.

	A	B
1	Southwest Division	
2	Total Sales	
3		
8	John	$ 22,469.00
13	Jean	25,777.00
18	Joe	23,537.00
23	Joan	27,703.00
24	Totals	

Figure 42 Excel combines the data in the cell(s) you originally selected.

Figure 43 Select the destination cell(s).

	A	B
1		Widgets
2	John	$ 1,254.00
3	Jean	1,865.00
4	Joe	1,614.00
5	Joan	1,987.00
6	Total	$ 6,720.00

	A	B
1		Screw Balls
2	John	$ 1,254.00
3	Jason	$ 2,745.00
4	Jean	1,865.00
5	Joe	1,614.00
6	Jack	2,412.00
7	Joan	1,987.00
8	Total	$ 11,877.00

	A	B
1		Wing Nuts
2	John	$ 1,254.00
3	Jean	1,865.00
4	Jerry	1,984.00
5	Joe	1,614.00
6	Jack	1,420.00
7	Joan	1,987.00
8	Total	$ 10,124.00

Figures 44, 45, & 46 Select the cells you want to include in the consolidation.

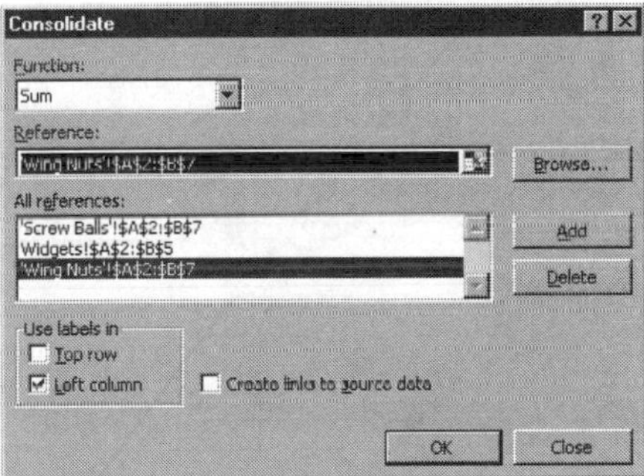

Figure 47 The Consolidate dialog box records all selections and enables you to specify where the data labels are.

	A	B
1	John	$ 3,762.00
2	Jason	$ 2,745.00
3	Jean	5,595.00
4	Jerry	1,984.00
5	Joe	4,842.00
6	Jack	3,832.00
7	Joan	5,961.00

Figure 48 The final consolidation accounts for all data.

To consolidate based on labels

1. Select the cell(s) in which you want the consolidated information to go. As shown in **Figure 43**, you can select just a single starting cell.
2. Choose Consolidate from the Data menu (**Figure 37**).
3. In the Consolidate dialog box (**Figure 38**), choose a function from the Function menu (**Figure 39**).
4. Switch to the worksheet containing the first cell(s) to be included in the consolidation. The reference is entered into the Reference box.
5. Select the cell(s) you want to include in the consolidation, including any text that identifies data (**Figure 44**). The text must be in cells adjacent to the data. The reference is entered into the Reference box.
6. Click Add.
7. Repeat steps 4, 5, and 6 for all cells you want to include in the consolidation. **Figures 45** and **46** show the other two ranges included for the example. When you're finished, the Consolidate dialog box might look something like **Figure 47**.
8. Turn on the appropriate check box(es) in the Use labels in area to tell Excel where identifying labels for the data are.
9. Click OK.

   Excel consolidates the information in the originally selected cell(s) (**Figure 48**).

Custom Views

Excel's custom views feature lets you create multiple *views* of a workbook file. A view includes the window size and position, the active cell, the zoom percentage, hidden columns and rows, and print settings. Once you set up a view, you can select it from a dialog box to see it quickly.

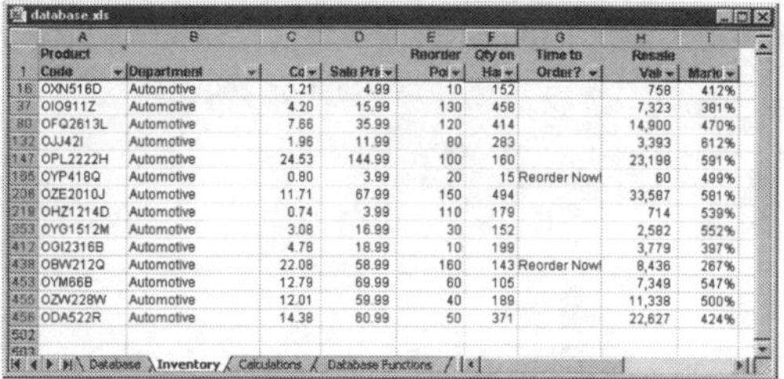

database.xls

	A	B	C	D	E	F	G	H	I
1	Product Code	Department	Co	Sale Pri	Reorder Poi	Qty on Ha	Time to Order?	Resale Val	Marku
16	OXN516D	Automotive	1.21	4.99	10	152		758	412%
37	OIO911Z	Automotive	4.20	15.99	130	458		7,323	381%
80	OFQ2613L	Automotive	7.66	35.99	120	414		14,900	470%
132	OJJ42I	Automotive	1.96	11.99	80	283		3,393	612%
147	OPL2222H	Automotive	24.53	144.99	100	160		23,198	591%
195	OYP418Q	Automotive	0.80	3.99	20	15	Reorder Now!	60	499%
208	OZE2010J	Automotive	11.71	67.99	150	494		33,587	581%
219	OHZ1214D	Automotive	0.74	3.99	110	179		714	539%
353	OYG1512M	Automotive	3.08	16.99	30	152		2,582	552%
412	OGI2316B	Automotive	4.78	18.99	10	199		3,779	397%
438	OBW212Q	Automotive	22.08	58.99	160	143	Reorder Now!	8,436	267%
453	OYM66B	Automotive	12.79	69.99	60	105		7,349	547%
455	OZW228W	Automotive	12.01	59.99	40	189		11,338	500%
458	ODA522R	Automotive	14.38	60.99	50	371		22,627	424%
502									
503									

Database | Inventory | Calculations | Database Functions

Figure 49 Create a view you'd like to save.

✔ Tip

- Including print settings in views makes it possible to create and save multiple custom reports for printing.

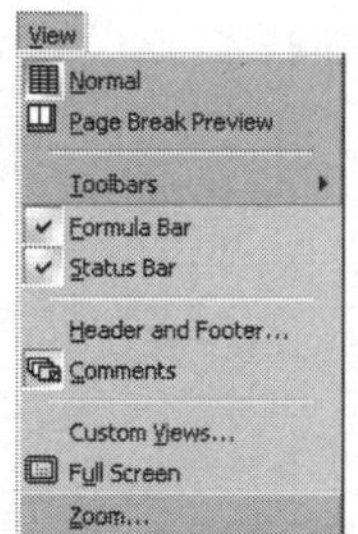

Figure 50 Choose Custom Views from the View menu.

To add a custom view

1. Create the view you want to save. **Figure 49** shows an example.
2. Choose View > Custom Views (**Figure 50**).
3. In the Custom Views dialog box (**Figure 51**), click the Add button.
4. In the Add View dialog box (**Figure 52**), enter a name for the view in the Name box.
5. Turn on the appropriate Include in view check boxes:
   - ▲ **Print settings** includes current Page Setup and other printing options in the view.
   - ▲ **Hidden rows, columns and filter settings** includes current settings for hidden columns and rows, as well as filter selections.
6. Click OK.

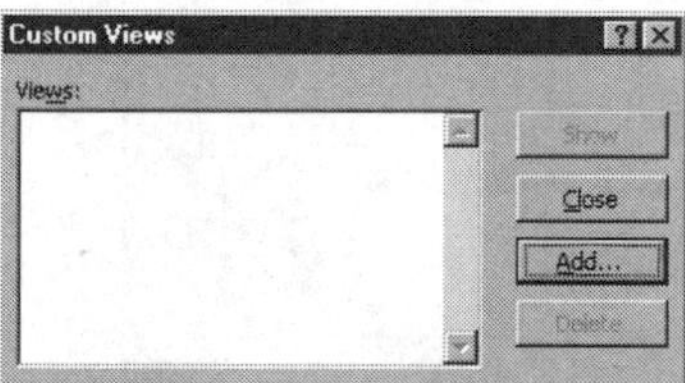

Figure 51 The Custom Views dialog box.

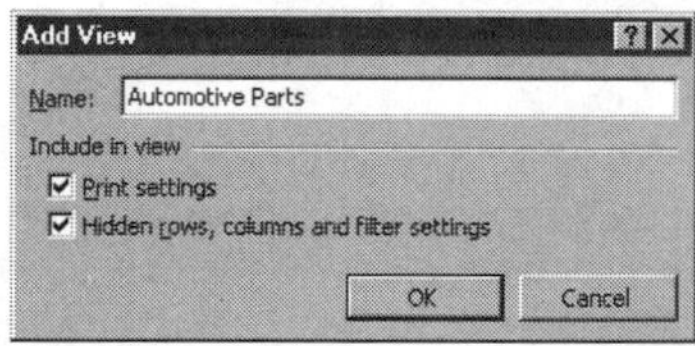

Figure 52 Use the Add View dialog box to name and set options for a view.

Adding Custom Views

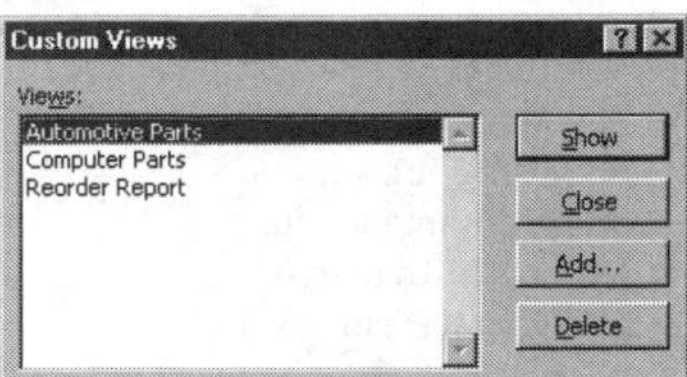

Figure 53 To see or delete a view, select the name of the view in the Custom Views dialog box, then click Show or Delete.

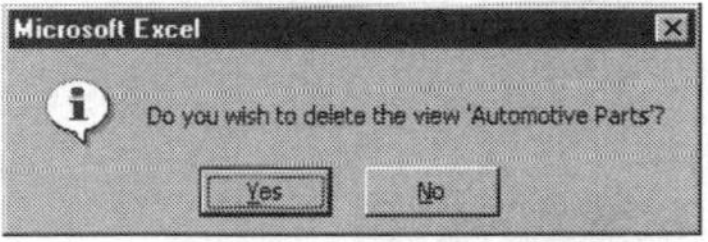

Figure 54 When you click the Delete button in the Custom Views dialog box to delete a view, Excel asks you to confirm that you really do want to delete it.

To switch to a view

1. Switch to the sheet containing the view you want to see.
2. Choose View > Custom Views (**Figure 50**).
3. In the Views list of the Custom Views dialog box (**Figure 53**), select the view you want to see.
4. Click Show.

   Excel changes the window so it looks just like it did when you created the view.

To delete a view

1. Switch to the sheet containing the view you want to delete.
2. Choose View > Custom Views (**Figure 50**).
3. In the Views list of the Custom Views dialog box (**Figure 53**), select the view you want to delete.
4. Click Delete.
5. In the confirmation dialog box that appears (**Figure 54**), click Yes.
6. Follow steps 3 through 5 to delete other views if desired.
7. Click Close to dismiss the Custom Views dialog box without changing the view.

✔ Tip

- Deleting a view does not delete the information contained in the view. It simply removes the reference to the information from the Views list in the Custom Views dialog box (**Figure 53**).

Macros

A macro is a series of commands that Excel can perform automatically. You can create simple macros to automate repetitive tasks, like entering data or formatting cells.

Although macros are created with Excel's built-in Visual Basic programming language, you don't need to be a programmer to create them. Excel's Macro Recorder will record your keystrokes, menu choices, and dialog box settings as you make them and will write the programming code for you. This makes macros useful for all Excel users, even raw beginners.

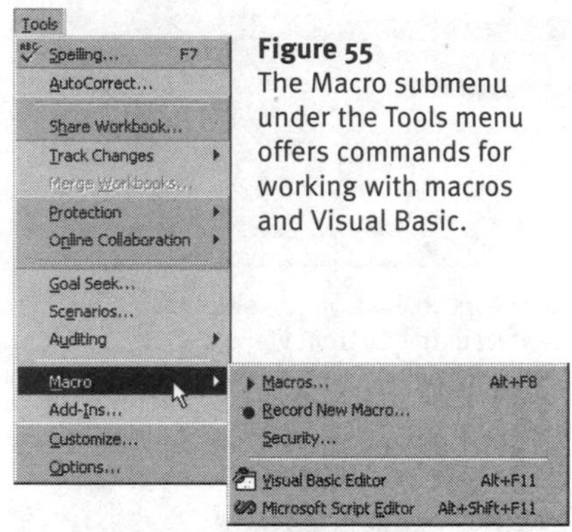

Figure 55 The Macro submenu under the Tools menu offers commands for working with macros and Visual Basic.

To record a macro with the Macro Recorder

1. Choose Tools > Macro > Record New Macro (**Figure 55**) to display the Record Macro dialog box (**Figure 56**).
2. Enter a name for the macro in the Macro name box.
3. If desired, enter a keystroke to use as a shortcut key in the Ctrl+ box.
4. If desired, edit the description that was automatically entered in the Description box.
5. Click OK.
6. Perform all the steps you want to include in your macro. Excel records them all—even the mistakes—so be careful!
7. When you're finished recording macro steps, click the Stop Recording button on the tiny Stop Recording toolbar (**Figure 57**).

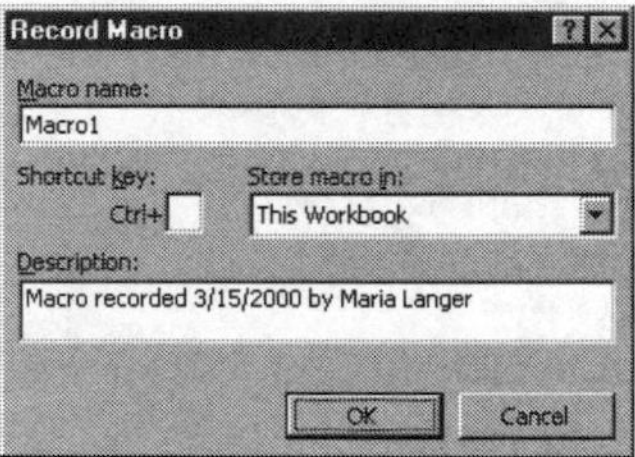

Figure 56 The Record Macro dialog box.

Figure 57 When you're finished recording macro steps, click the Stop Recording button on the tiny Stop Recording toolbar.

✔ Tips

- In step 3, if you enter a keystroke that is already used by Excel for a shortcut key, the shortcut key will no longer function. Instead, it will invoke the macro.
- If you make a mistake when recording a macro, you can click the Stop Recording button to stop recording the macro, then start over, following the instructions above.

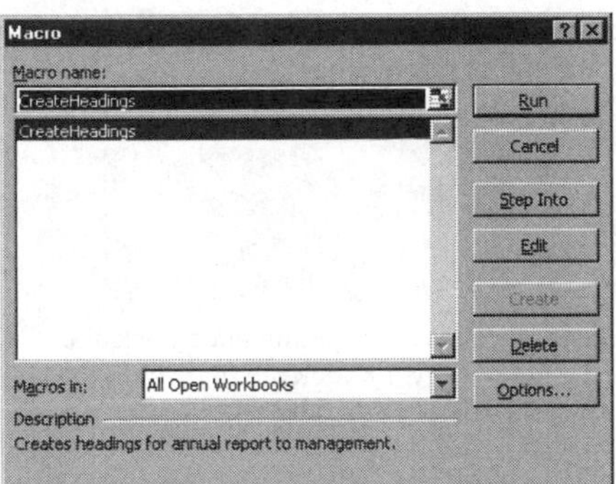

Figure 58 The Macro dialog box enables you to run, edit, and delete macros.

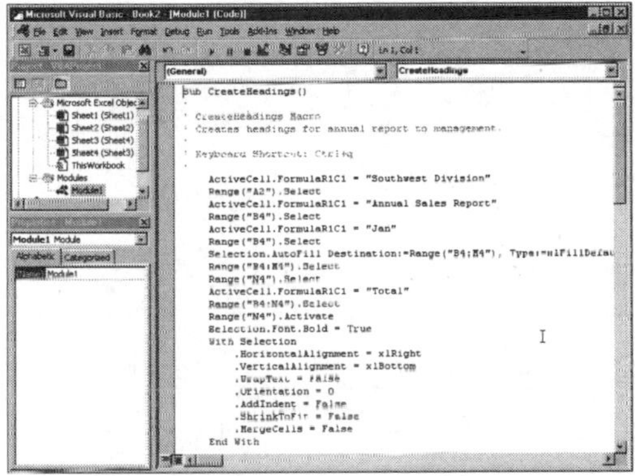

Figure 59 Clicking the Edit button in the Macro dialog box displays the macro in Excel's Visual Basic editing environment. Editing a macro requires knowledge of Visual Basic.

To run a macro

Press the keystroke you specified as a shortcut key for the macro when you created it.

or

1. Choose Macros from the Macro submenu under the Tools menu (**Figure 55**).
2. In the Macro dialog box (**Figure 58**), select the macro you want to run.
3. Click Run.

Excel performs each macro step, just the way you recorded it.

✔ Tips

- Save your workbook *before* running a macro for the first time. You may be surprised by the results and need to revert the file to the way it was before you ran the macro. Excel's Undo command cannot undo the steps of a macro, so reverting to the last saved version of the file is the only way to reverse macro steps.
- Excel stores each macro as a *module*. View and edit a macro by selecting it in the Macro dialog box and clicking the Edit button. **Figure 59** shows an example. I don't recommend editing macro code unless you have at least a general understanding of Visual Basic!
- More advanced uses of macros include the creation of custom functions and applications that work within Excel.

Macro Virus Protection

Excel's macro virus protection feature displays a warning dialog box like the one in **Figure 60** when you open an Excel workbook file that contains macros or customized toolbars, menus, or shortcut keys. (These features could contain Excel macro viruses.) When this dialog box appears, you have three options:

- **Enable Macros** opens the file the normal way. The macros will function as intended. If the file contains a macro virus, your Excel files may become infected. Use this option only if you are certain that the file does not contain any viruses.
- **Disable Macros** opens the file with the macros disabled. This prevents the macros from operating as intended. Your Excel files cannot become infected if the file contains a macro virus.
- **More Info** provides more information about Excel macro viruses.

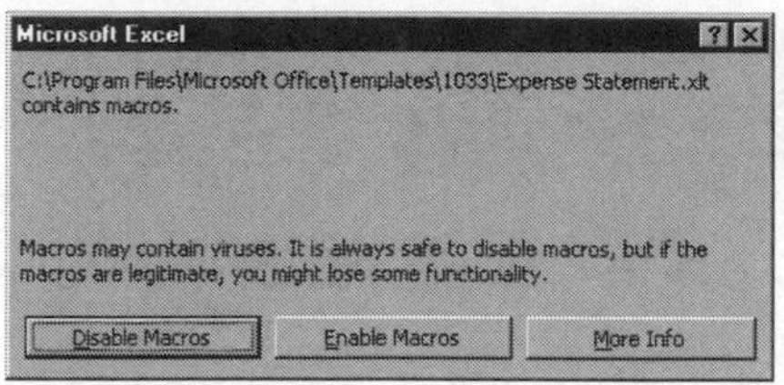

Figure 60 Excel displays a warning dialog box like this when you open a workbook file that contains macros or other Visual Basic modules.

✔ Tip

- Excel's macro virus protection feature cannot be disabled.

Web Publishing

12

Web Publishing

The World Wide Web has had a bigger impact on publishing than any other communication medium introduced in the past fifty years. Web pages, which can include text, graphics, and hyperlinks, can be published on the Internet or an intranet, making them available to audiences 24 hours a day, 7 days a week. They can provide information quickly and inexpensively to anyone who needs it.

This chapter explains how you can publish and interact with Excel worksheets and charts on the Web. It also tells you how you can include hyperlinks in all of your Excel documents.

✔ Tips

- This chapter explains how to create Web pages from Excel documents. Modifying the HTML underlying those pages is beyond the scope of this book.
- *HTML (or HyperText Markup Language)* is a system of codes for defining Web pages.
- To learn more about the World Wide Web, Web publishing, and HTML, check these Peachpit Press books:
  - *The Little Web Book* by Alfred and Emily Glossbrenner.
  - *Home Sweet Home Page* by Robin Williams.
  - *The Non-Designer's Web Book* by Robin Williams and John Tollett.
  - *HTML 4 for the World Wide Web: Visual QuickStart Guide* by Elizabeth Castro.
- Web pages are normally viewed with a special kind of software called a *Web browser*. Microsoft Internet Explorer and Netscape Navigator are two examples of Web browsers.
- To access the Internet, you need an Internet connection, either through an organizational network or dial-up connection. Setting up a connection is beyond the scope of this book; consult the documentation that came with your System or Internet access software for more information.
- To publish a Web page, you need access to a Web server. Contact your organization's Network Administrator or your Internet Service Provider (ISP) for more information.

Creating Web Pages

Excel 2000 has built-in Web publishing features that make it easy to publish Excel data on the Web:

- Save Excel documents as standard Web pages (**Figure 1**). This enables you to publish formatted worksheets and charts on the Web so the information can be shared with others.
- Publish Excel documents as interactive Web pages (**Figure 2**). This enables you to publish spreadsheet solutions on the Web in a format that allows the information to be edited and formatted by others who access it with a Web browser.

✔ Tips

- The interactive features of a spreadsheet published on the Web with Excel are only available when the spreadsheet is accessed with Microsoft Internet Explorer 4.01 or later with the Microsoft Office Web Components installed.
- When you publish an Excel document as an interactive Web page, some features—such as graphics, text boxes, patterns, and other formatting options—do not appear on the Web.

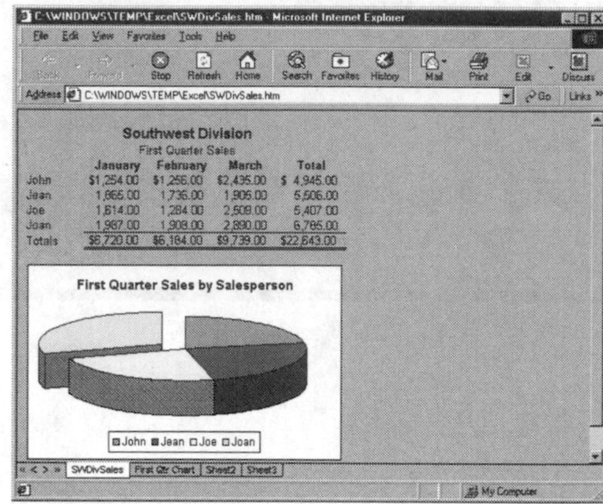

Figure 1 Here's an example of an Excel workbook file saved as a Web page...

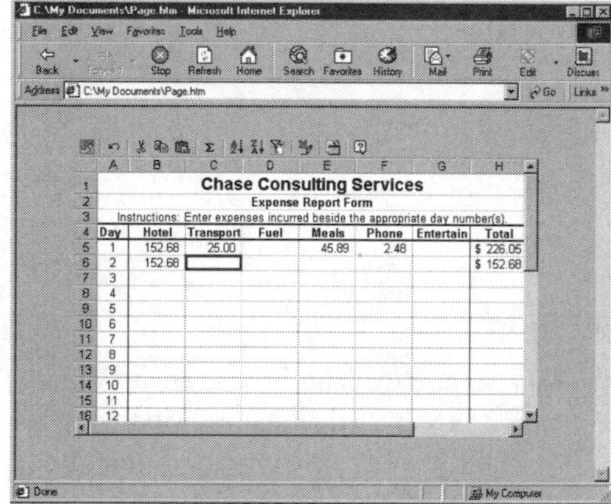

Figure 2 ...and here's an example of an Excel spreadsheet published as an interactive Web page. As you can see, when you enter data into cells, formulas in other cells immediate calculate results.

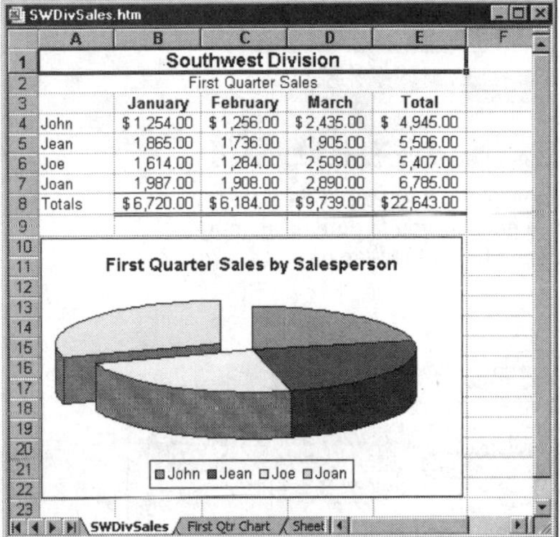

Figure 3 Here's a simple workbook, all ready to be saved as a Web page.

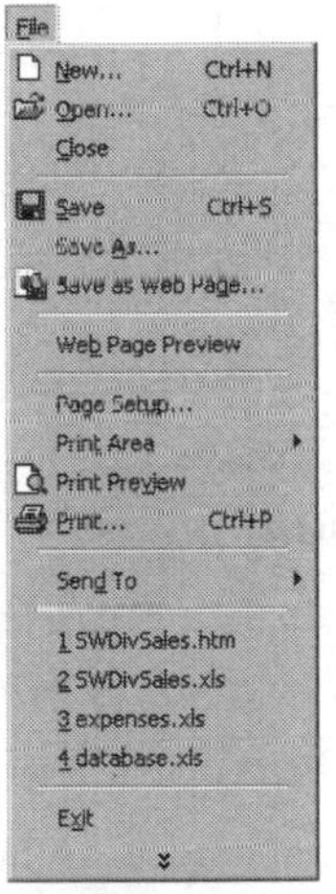

Figure 4 The File menu includes commands for working with Web pages.

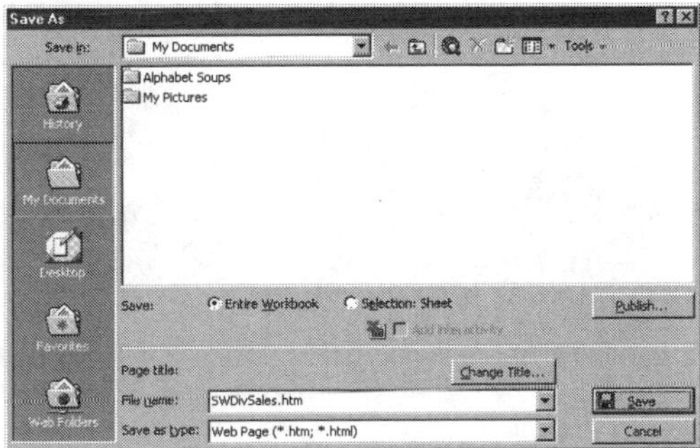

Figure 5 The Save As dialog box that appears when you choose the Save as Web Page command.

To save a document as a Web page

1. Open or activate the workbook that you want to save as a Web page (**Figure 3**).
2. If you want to publish fewer than all sheets in the workbook, select the tabs for the sheets you want to publish.

   or

   If you want to publish only a range of cells in the worksheet, select the cells.
3. Choose File > Save as Web Page (**Figure 4**) to display a special Save As dialog box (**Figure 5**).
4. Use the Save in menu and Places Bar buttons in the dialog box to locate and open the folder in which you want to save the Web page.
5. Select a Save option button:
   - ▲ **Entire workbook** saves all sheets in the workbook as a Web page.
   - ▲ **Selection** saves only the selection (sheets or cells determined in step 2) as a Web page.
6. To enter a title for the Web page, click the Change Title button. Then enter a new title in the Set Page Title dialog box that appears (**Figure 6**) and click OK.
7. Enter a name for the Web page file in the File name box. Be sure to follow the naming rules required by your Web server.
8. Confirm that Web Page is chosen from the Save as type menu.
9. Click Save.

The document (or selected portions of it) is saved as a standard HTML document in the location you specified.

Continued on next page...

Continued from previous page.

✔ Tips

- To see what a workbook file would look like on the Web without actually saving it as a Web page, choose File > Web Page Preview (**Figure 4**). Excel creates a temporary file for the Web page, runs your default Web browser, and displays the page in the Web browser window (**Figure 1**).
- In step 4, you can click the Web Folders button to open a folder accessible on an intranet or the Internet.
- A page title is what appears in the title bar at the top of the Web browser window. It's not the same as the name of the file.
- You can get more information about HTML document file naming rules from your organization's Network Administrator or your ISP.
- When you save a file as a Web page, Excel creates a folder in the same folder as the page (**Figure 7**), to store converted graphics that appear on the page. When moving a Web page from one disk location to another in Windows Explorer, it's vital that the Web page and the support files folder be moved together. Otherwise, page components will not appear properly.

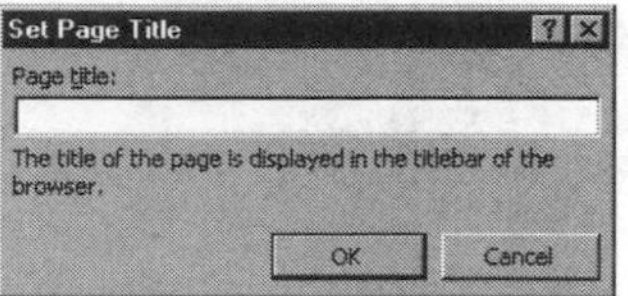

Figure 6 The Set Page Title dialog box enables you to enter a custom page title for the Web page.

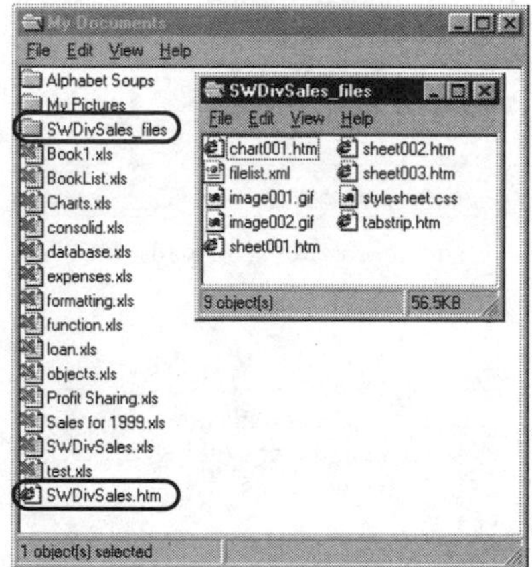

Figure 7 I saved the Web page in the My Documents folder on my hard disk. Excel created a folder in the same location and stored all graphics files within it. You can see the contents of the folder in the open *SWDivSales_files* window.

To view an Excel document saved as a standard Web page

1. Use your favorite Web browser to open the Web page file (**Figure 1**).
2. If more than one sheet was saved as part of the Web page, use the tabs at the bottom of the Web page document to switch from one sheet to another (just like in Excel).

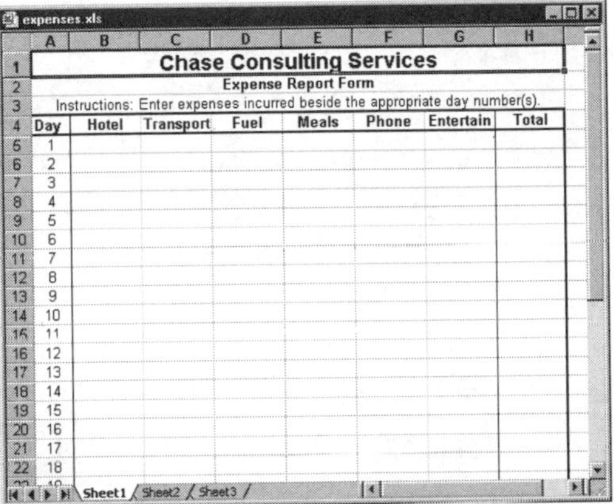

Figure 8 Here's a simple worksheet containing blank cells and formulas, all ready to publish as an interactive Web-based form.

Figure 9 Select Selection, then turn on the Add interactivity check box.

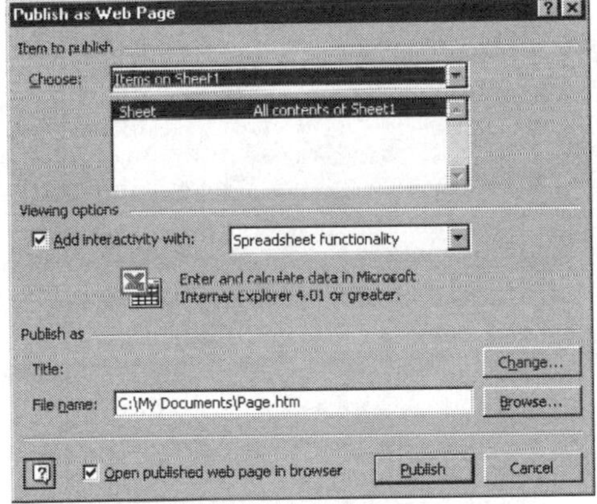

Figure 10 Use the Publish as Web Page dialog box to set options for interactive Web publishing.

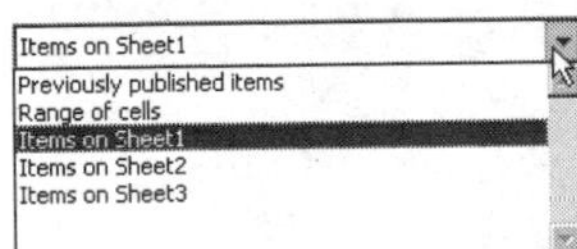

Figure 11 The Choose menu lists several options, including each sheet in the workbook.

To publish an Excel document as an interactive Web page

1. Open or activate the workbook that you want to publish as an interactive Web page (**Figure 8**).
2. Activate the sheet you want to publish.
3. Choose File > Save as Web Page (**Figure 4**) to display a special Save As dialog box (**Figure 5**).
4. Use the Save in menu and Places Bar buttons in the dialog box to locate and open the folder in which you want to save the Web page.
5. Select the Save option button for Selection, and then turn on the Add interactivity check box (**Figure 9**).
6. To enter a title for the Web page, click the Change Title button. Then enter a new title in the Set Page Title dialog box that appears (**Figure 6**) and click OK.
7. Enter a name for the Web page file in the File name box. Be sure to follow the naming rules required by your Web server.
8. Click the Publish button to display the Publish as Web Page dialog box (**Figure 10**).
9. Choose an option from the Choose menu (**Figure 11**):
   - ▲ **Previously published items** displays a list of items in the workbook that have already been published (**Figure 12**). This enables you to update or republish these items. If you choose this option, be sure to select the desired item.
   - ▲ **Range of cells** enables you to enter a range of cells to publish. Use this option when you want to publish less than an entire sheet. If you choose this option, enter the desired range of cells in the box beneath the menu (**Figure 13**).

Continued on next page...

Continued from previous page.

- ▲ **Items on *SheetN*** enables you to select a specific sheet if you did not do so in step 2.

10. Confirm that the Add interactivity with check box is turned on. Then choose an option from the menu beside it:

- ▲ **Spreadsheet functionality** makes the sheet work like a regular worksheet file.
- ▲ **PivotTable functionality** makes the sheet work like a PivotTable.
- ▲ **Chart functionality** makes the sheet work like a chart. This option is automatically selected when you publish a chart sheet or a chart embedded on a worksheet.

11. To preview the page after it is saved, turn on the Open published Web page in browser check box.

12. Click the Publish button.

The sheet (or a selected portion of it) is saved as an interactive Web page in the location you specified. If you turned on the Open published web page in browser check box in step 11, the page is displayed in a Web browser window (**Figures 2** and **14**).

✔ Tips

- In step 9, if you chose Range of cells from the Choose menu, you can click in the box beneath the menu and then select the range of cells you want to publish. This is usually easier than entering the cell references for a range.
- PivotTables are an advanced feature of Excel that is beyond the scope of this book.
- As you can see in **Figure 14**, Excel includes the data underlying a chart when you publish a chart as an interactive Web page.

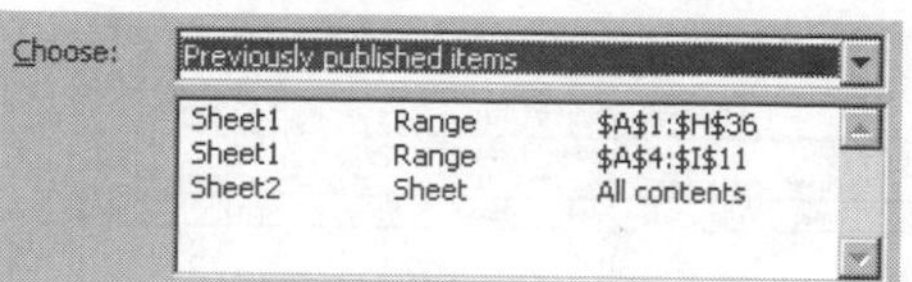

Figure 12 When you choose Previously published items, a list of items you've already published appears.

Figure 13 When you choose Range of cells, you can enter the desired range in a box below the menu.

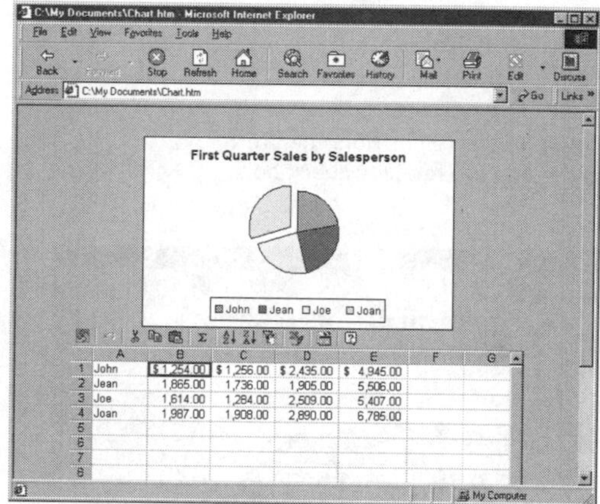

	A	B	C	D	E
1	John	$ 1,254.00	$ 1,256.00	$ 2,435.00	$ 4,945.00
2	Jean	1,865.00	1,736.00	1,905.00	5,506.00
3	Joe	1,614.00	1,284.00	2,509.00	5,407.00
4	Joan	1,987.00	1,908.00	2,890.00	6,785.00

Figure 14 Here's the chart from **Figure 3** published as an interactive Web page.

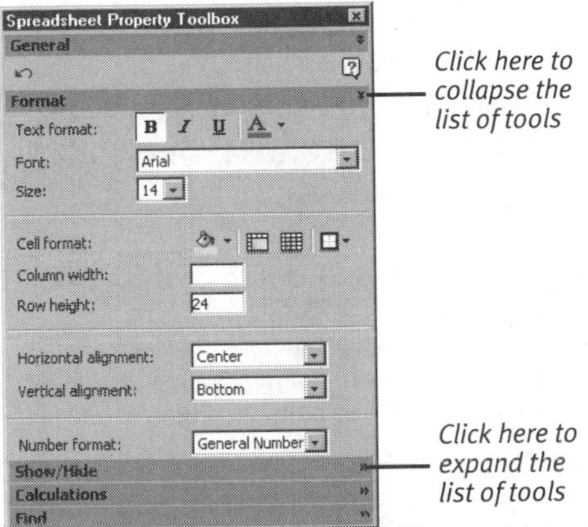

Figure 15 Clicking the Property Toolbox button in an interactively published worksheet window displays additional options for working with the sheet.

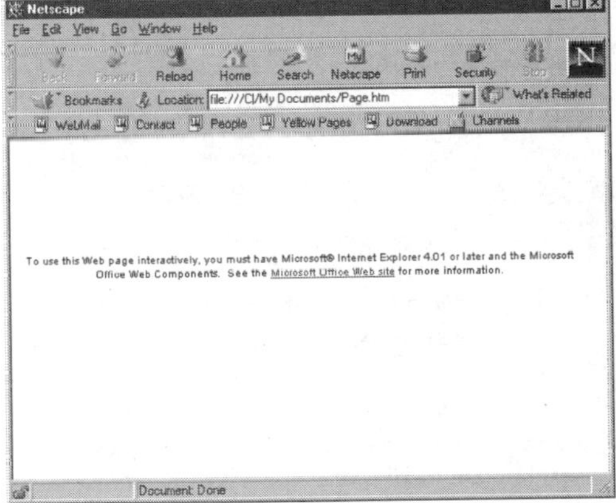

Figure 16 Incompatible browsers can't display interactively published Excel documents.

To work with an Excel document saved as an interactive Web page

1. Use Internet Explorer version 4.01 or later to open the Web page file (**Figures 2** and **14**).
2. Work with the document as desired:
   - ▲ Enter or edit data in cells. Any formula that references a cell you change will recalculate results immediately.
   - ▲ Use buttons on the toolbar above the worksheet data to modify the sheet. Most of these buttons are the same ones you'd find on Excel's Standard toolbar.
   - ▲ Click the Property Toolbox button on the toolbar above the worksheet data to display a palette of tools (**Figure 15**) that you can use to work with the sheet.
   - ▲ Click the Export to Excel button on the toolbar above the worksheet data to open the sheet in Excel as a read-only document. You can continue to work with it there and, if desired, use Excel's save command to save the file to disk.

✔ Tips

- ■ To access the interactive features of a sheet published with Excel, you must have Microsoft Internet Explorer 4.01 or later and the Microsoft Office Web Components installed on your computer. These programs come with Office 2000 and are automatically installed when you do a Typical Office installation. **Figure 16** shows what an interactive Web page looks like when opened with Netscape Navigator 4.0. Other incompatible browsers will display similar messages.
- ■ The changes you make to an interactive Web page are not saved. The page looks the same each time it is opened unless it is updated or republished with different data.

Hyperlinks

A hyperlink is text or a graphic that, when clicked, displays other information. Excel enables you to create two kinds of hyperlinks:

- A link to a *URL* (*Uniform Resource Locator*), which is the address of a document or individual on the Internet. There are three main types of URLs:
  - ▲ **http://** links to a Web page on a Web server.
  - ▲ **ftp://** links to a downloadable file on an FTP server.
  - ▲ **mailto:** links to an e-mail address.
- A link to another document on your hard disk or network.

By default, hyperlinks appear as blue, underlined text (**Figure 17**).

✔ Tips

- Excel can automatically format URLs as hyperlinks. Simply type the complete URL in a cell. When you press Enter or click the Enter button ✓ to complete the entry, Excel turns the URL into a hyperlink.
- You can put a hyperlink in any Excel document—not just one that you plan to publish on the Web.

Figure 17 Hyperlinks usually appear as blue, underlined text. When you point to a hyperlink, the mouse pointer turns into a pointing finger.

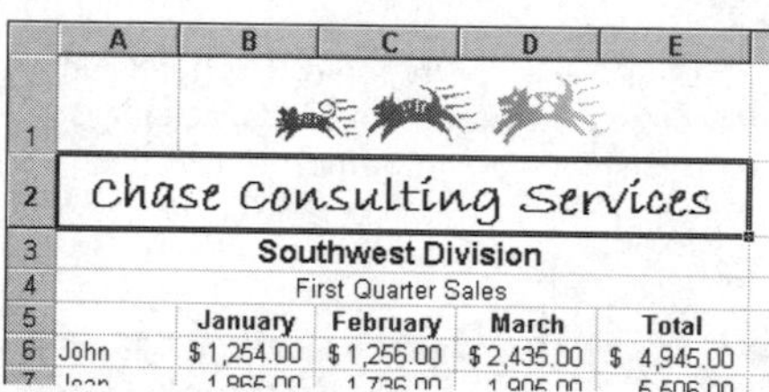

Figure 18 Select a cell...

Figure 19 ...or select a picture that you want to convert into a hyperlink.

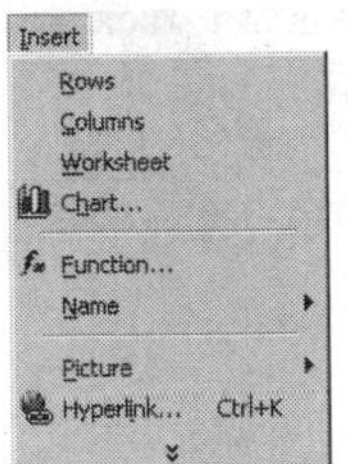

Figure 20 The Hyperlink command is on the Insert menu.

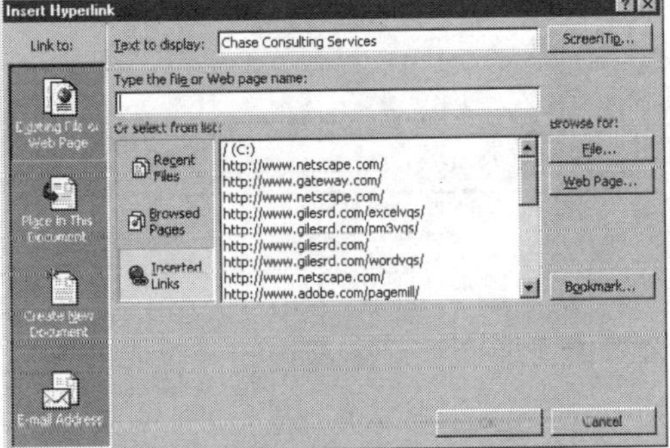

Figure 21 The Insert Hyperlink dialog box. This illustration shows a list of recently inserted links.

Figure 22 Enter the URL for the link location.

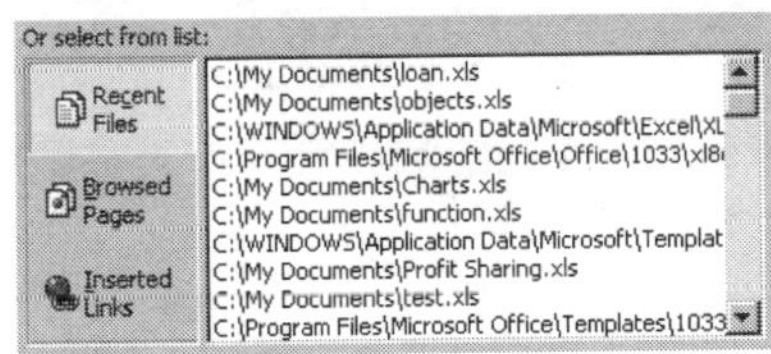

Figure 23 Excel keeps track of recently opened files...

Figure 24 ...as well as recently browsed Web pages.

To insert a hyperlink

1. Select the cell in which you want the hyperlink to appear (**Figure 18**).

   or

   Select the picture that you want to convert to a hyperlink (**Figure 19**).

2. Choose Insert > Hyperlink (**Figure 20**), press Ctrl K, or click the Insert Hyperlink button on the Standard toolbar.

   The Insert Hyperlink dialog box appears (**Figure 21**).

3. If necessary, enter the text that you want to appear as a link in the Text to display box.

4. Enter the complete URL or pathname for the Web page, e-mail address, or file to which you want to link in the Type the file or Web page name box (**Figure 22**).

   or

   Click one of the buttons along the left side of the URL or file list to display a list of Recent Files (**Figure 23**), Browsed Pages (**Figure 24**), or Inserted Links (**Figure 21**). Click to select one of the listed items.

   or

   Click the File button and use the Link to File dialog box that appears to locate and select a file on disk or accessible via network.

   or

   Click the Web Page button and use Internet Explorer to locate and select a Web page file on an intranet or the Internet.

5. Click OK to save your settings and dismiss the Insert Hyperlink dialog box.

   The hyperlink is inserted (**Figure 17**).

To follow a hyperlink

1. Position the mouse pointer on the hyperlink. The mouse pointer turns into a pointing finger (**Figure 17**).
2. Click once.

   If the hyperlink points to an Internet URL, Excel launches your Web browser, connects to the Internet, and displays the URL.

   or

   If the hyperlink points to a file on your hard disk or another computer on the network, the file opens.

✔ Tip

- The Web toolbar appears when you follow a link (**Figure 25**). You can use this toolbar to navigate to linked pages on your computer, your local area network, or the Web.

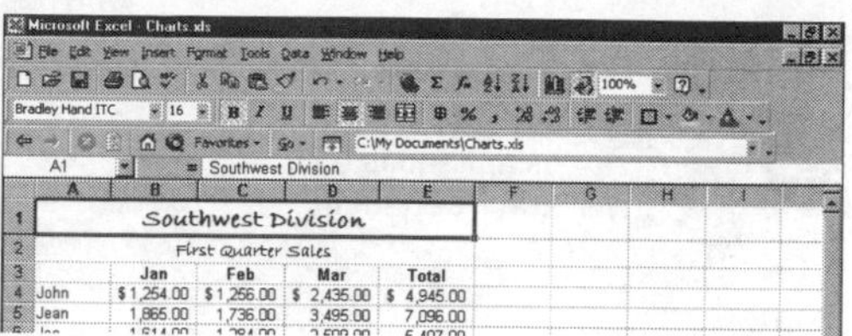

Figure 25 When you follow a hyperlink, the Web toolbar appears beneath the Formatting toolbar.

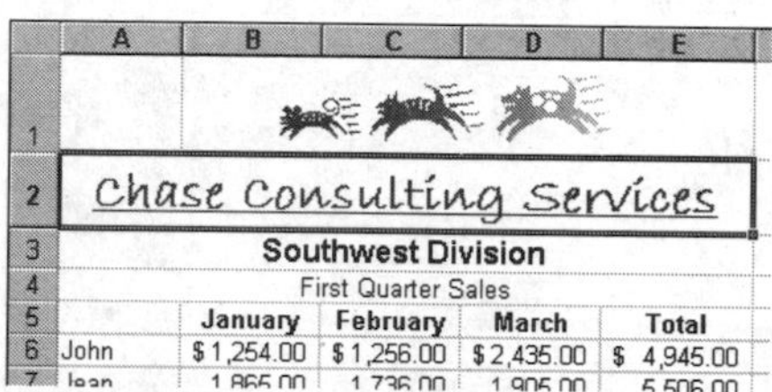

Figure 26 Select the cell containing the link.

To modify or remove a hyperlink

1. Select the cell or picture containing the hyperlink (**Figure 26**).
2. Choose Insert > Hyperlink (**Figure 20**), press Ctrl K, or click the Insert Hyperlink button on the Standard toolbar to display the Edit Hyperlink dialog box (**Figure 27**).
3. To modify the link, enter a new URL or pathname as instructed in step 4 on the previous page.

   or

   To remove the link, click the Remove Link button.
4. Click OK.

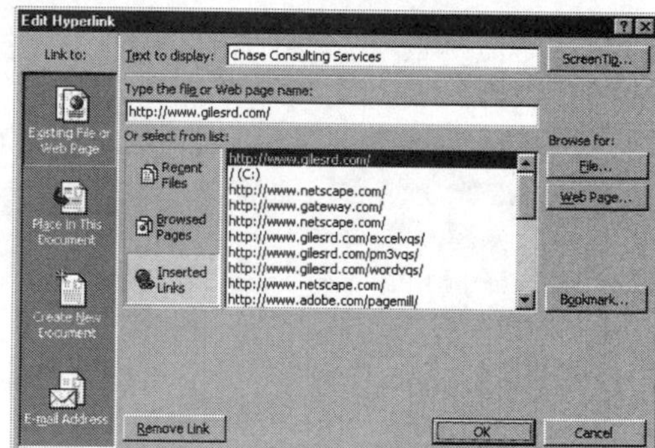

Figure 27 You can use the Edit Hyperlink dialog box to modify or remove a link.

✔ Tip

- Removing a hyperlink does not delete the text or image that appears in the document window—just the link.

SETTING OPTIONS

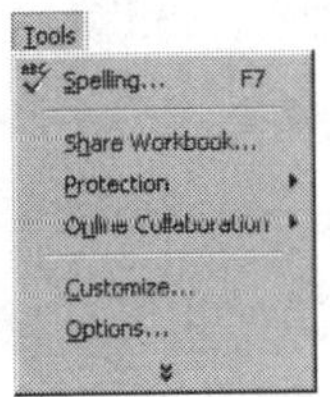

Figure 1
Choose Options from the Tools menu.

The Options Dialog Box

Excel's Options dialog box offers eight categories of settings that customize the way Excel works for you:

- **View** options control Excel's on-screen appearance.
- **Calculation** options control the way Excel calculates formulas.
- **Edit** options control editing.
- **General** options control general operations.
- **Transition** options control settings for Excel users who also work with other spreadsheet programs.
- **Custom Lists** options enable you to create or modify series lists.
- **Chart** options control the active chart and chart tips.
- **Color** options control standard, chart fill, and chart line colors.

✔ Tip

- Excel's default options settings are discussed and illustrated throughout this book.

To open the Options dialog box

Choose Tools > Options (**Figure 1**).

The Options dialog box appears, displaying its most recently accessed tab (**Figure 2**).

View Options

The View tab of the Options dialog box (**Figure 2**) offers options in four categories: Show, Comments, Objects, and Window options.

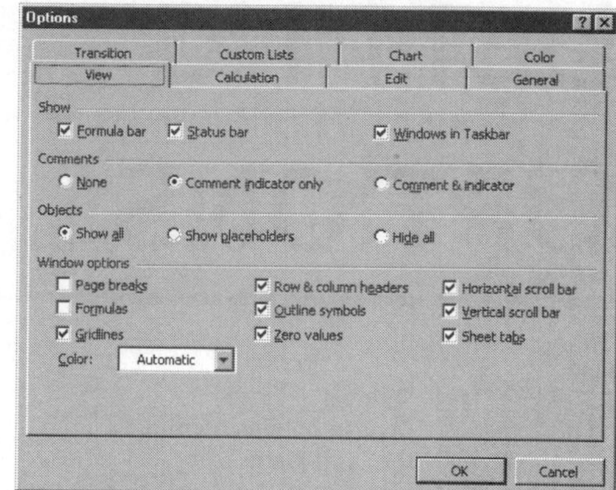

Figure 2 The default options in the View tab of the Options dialog box. Some of the Window options are not available when a chart sheet is active.

✔ Tip

- The available options in the View tab vary depending on the type of sheet that is active when you open the Options dialog box. When a chart sheet is active, many of the Window options are gray.

Show

Show options determine which Excel elements appear on screen:

- **Formula bar** displays the formula bar above the document window.
- **Status bar** displays the status bar at the bottom of the screen.
- **Windows in Taskbar** displays a separate icon in the Windows Taskbar for each open Excel document.

Comments

The Comments area enables you to select one of three options for displaying comments:

- **None** does not display comments or comment indicators.
- **Comment indicator only** displays a small red triangle in the upper-right corner of a cell containing a comment. When you point to the cell, the comment appears in a yellow box.
- **Comment & indicator** displays cell comments in yellow boxes as well as a small red triangle in the upper-right corner of each cell containing a comment.

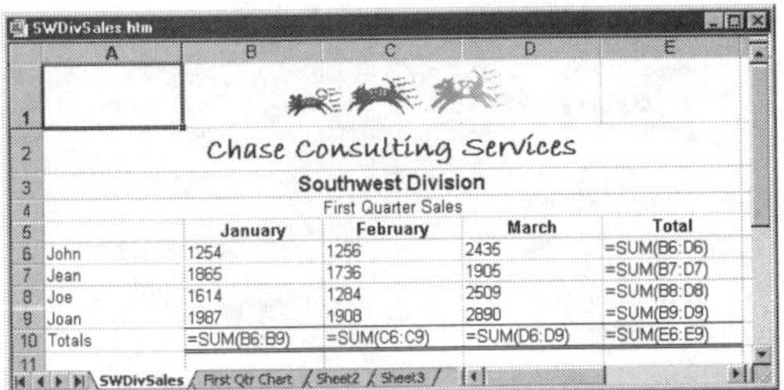

Figure 3 If desired, you can display formulas rather than their results.

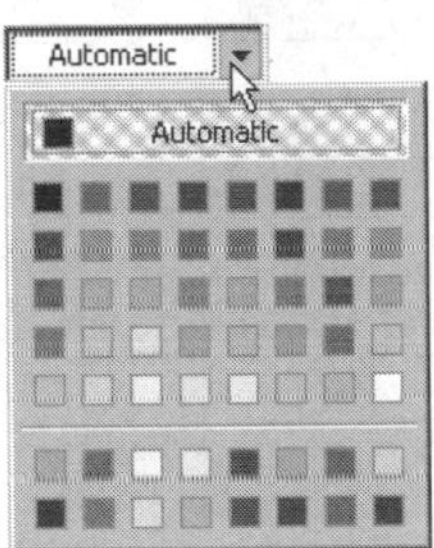

Figure 4
Use the Color menu to select a color for the gridlines that appear in a worksheet window.

Objects

The Objects area enables you to select one of three options for displaying graphic objects, buttons, text boxes, drawn objects, and pictures:

- **Show all** displays all objects.
- **Show placeholders** displays gray rectangles as placeholders for pictures and charts. This may speed up scrolling in windows with many graphic objects.
- **Hide all** does not display (or print) any objects.

Window options

Window options determine how various Excel elements are displayed in the active window.

- **Page breaks** displays horizontal and vertical page breaks.
- **Formulas** displays formulas instead of formula results (**Figure 3**). This feature is useful to document worksheets.
- **Gridlines** displays the boundaries of cells as gray lines.
- **Color** offers a menu (**Figure 4**) for selecting a gridline color. Automatic (the default option) displays gridlines in gray.
- **Row & column headings** displays the numeric row headings and alphabetical column headings.
- **Outline symbols** displays outline symbols when the worksheet includes an outline.
- **Zero values** displays a 0 (zero) in cells that contain zero values. Turn off this check box to leave cells containing zero values blank.
- **Horizontal scroll bar** displays a scroll bar along the bottom of the window.
- **Vertical scroll bar** displays a scroll bar along the right side of the window.
- **Sheet tabs** displays tabs at the bottom of the window for each sheet in the workbook.

Calculation Options

Calculation options (**Figure 5**) control the way formulas are calculated (or recalculated) in a worksheet. There are several groups of options: Calculation, Iteration, Calc buttons, and Workbook options.

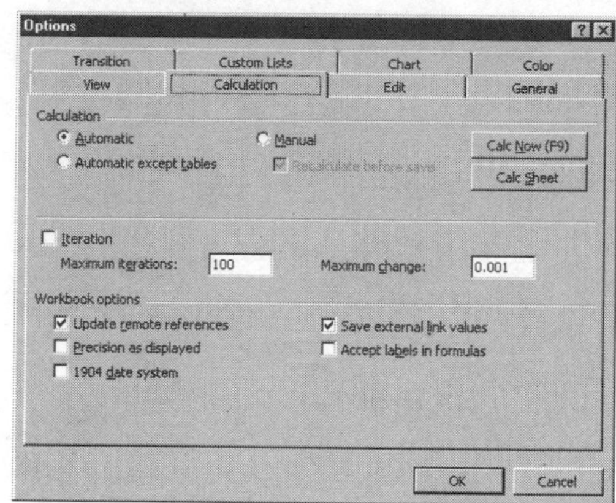

Figure 5 The default settings in the Calculation tab of the Options dialog box.

Calculation

The Calculation area enables you to select one of three options for specifying how formulas should be calculated:

- **Automatic** tells Excel to recalculate all dependent formulas whenever you change a value, formula, or name.
- **Automatic except tables** is the same as Automatic, but does not recalculate data tables. With this option selected, you must click the Calc Now button or press F9 to recalculate data tables.
- **Manual** recalculates formulas only when you click the Calc Now button or press F9. With this option selected, you can turn on the Recalculate before save check box to ensure that the worksheet is recalculated each time you save it.

Iteration

The Iteration check box enables you to set limits for the number of times Excel tries to resolve circular references or complete goal seeking calculations. To use this advanced option, turn on the check box, then enter values in the two edit boxes below it:

- **Maximum iterations** is the maximum number of times Excel should try to resolve circular references or solve goal seeking problems.
- **Maximum change** is the maximum amount of result change below which iteration stops.

Calc buttons

Two buttons enable you to calculate formulas on demand:

- **Calc Now (F9)** recalculates all open worksheets and updates all open chart sheets. You can also access this option by pressing F9.
- **Calc Sheet** recalculates the active worksheet and updates linked charts or updates the active chart sheet.

Workbook options

Workbook options control calculation in the active workbook file.

- **Update remote references** calculates formulas with references to documents created with other applications.
- **Precision as displayed** permanently changes values stored in cells from 15-digit precision to the precision of the applied formatting. This may result in rounding.
- **1904 date system** changes the starting date from which all dates are calculated to January 2, 1904, which is the date system used on Macintosh computers. (Wintel computers begin dates at January 1, 1900.) Turning on this option enhances compatibility with Mac OS system spreadsheet programs.
- **Save external link values** saves copies of values from linked documents within the workbook file. If many values are linked, storing them can increase the file size; turning off this option can reduce the file size.
- **Accept labels in formulas** allows you to use column and row headings to identify ranges of cells when writing formulas.

Edit Options

Edit options (**Figure 6**) control the way certain editing tasks work:

- **Edit directly in cell** enables you to edit a cell's value or formula by double-clicking the cell. With this option turned off, you must edit a cell's contents in the formula bar.
- **Allow cell drag and drop** enables you to copy or move cells by dragging them to a new location. With this option turned on, you can also turn on the **Alert before overwriting cells** check box to have Excel warn you if a drag-and-drop operation will overwrite the contents of destination cells.
- **Move selection after Enter** tells Excel to move the cellpointer when you press Enter. With this option turned on, you can use the **Direction** menu (**Figure 7**) to choose a direction: Down, Right, Up, or Left.
- **Fixed decimal** instructs Excel to automatically place a decimal point when you enter a value. Turn on the check box and enter a value in the **Places** edit box. A positive value moves the decimal to the left; a negative value moves the decimal to the right.
- **Cut, copy, and sort objects with cells** keeps objects with cells that you cut, copy, filter, or sort.
- **Ask to update automatic links** prompts you to update links when you open a workbook containing links to other files.
- **Provide feedback with Animation** displays worksheet movement when you insert or delete cells. Turning on this option may slow Excel's performance on some systems.
- **Enable AutoComplete for cell values** turns on the AutoComplete feature for entering values in cells based on entries in the same column.

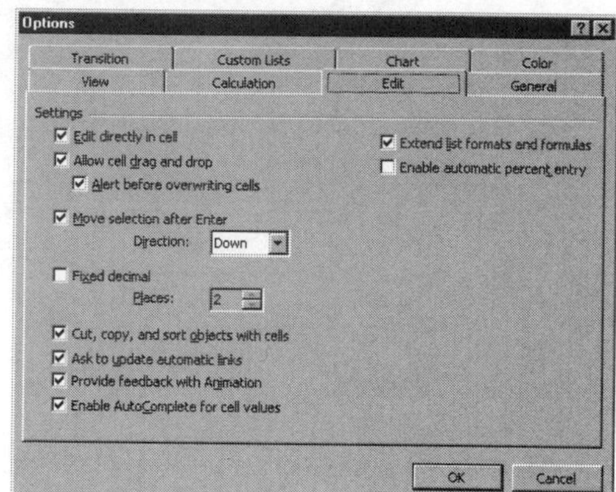

Figure 6 The default settings in the Edit tab of the Options dialog box.

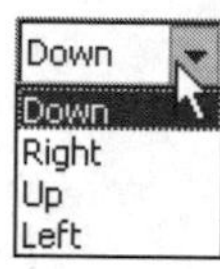

Figure 7 The Direction menu.

- **Extend list formats and formulas** tells Excel to automatically format and copy repeated formulas to new items added at the end of a list.
- **Enable automatic percent entry** tells Excel to multiply by 100 all numbers less than 1 that you enter in cells formatted with a Percentage format.

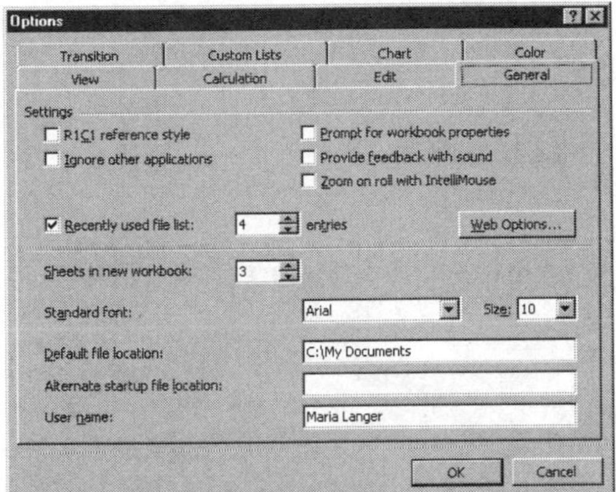

Figure 8 The default settings in the General tab of the Options dialog box.

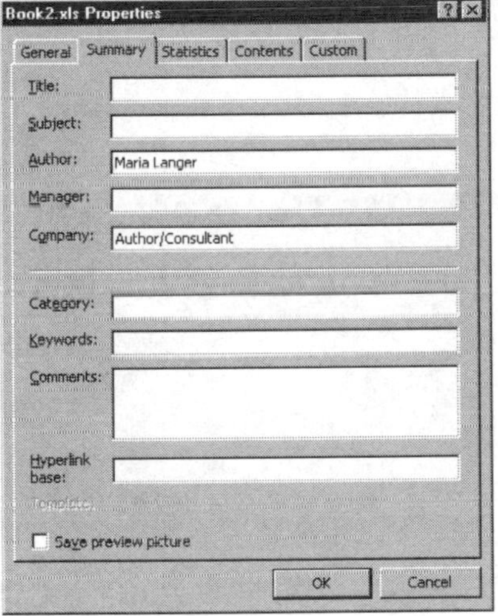

Figure 9 You can use the Summary tab of the Properties dialog box to enter information about the file the first time you save it. You can also open this dialog box by choosing Properties from the File menu.

General Options

General options (**Figure 8**) control the general operation of Excel. There are two main groups of options—Settings and other options—and a button to access additional Web-related options.

Settings

The Settings area offers check boxes to set a variety of options:

- **R1C1 reference style** changes the style of cell references so both rows and columns have numbers.
- **Ignore other applications** prevents the exchange of data with other applications that use Dynamic Data Exchange (DDE).
- **Recently used file list** enables you to specify the number of recently opened files that should appear near the bottom of the File menu. Turn on the check box and enter a value in the **entries** text box. This feature is handy for quickly reopening recently accessed files.
- **Prompt for workbook properties** displays the Properties dialog box (**Figure 9**) the first time you save a file. You can use this dialog box to enter summary information about a file.
- **Provide feedback with sound** plays sounds at certain events, such as opening, saving, and printing files and displaying error messages. If this option is turned on in one Microsoft Office application, it is automatically turned on in all Office applications.
- **Zoom on roll with IntelliMouse** sets the wheel button to zoom instead of scroll on Microsoft IntelliMouse pointing devices.

Other options

The bottom half of the dialog box lets you set a variety of other workbook options:

- **Sheets in new workbook** enables you to specify the number of worksheets that should be included in each new workbook you create. Enter a value in the text box.
- **Standard font** (**Figure 10**) enables you to select the default font for worksheets and charts.
- **Default file location** allows you to specify the default location in which new workbook files should be saved.
- **Alternate startup file location** lets you specify a secondary startup folder in which Excel should look for files when it launches.
- **User name** is the name that appears when Excel displays a user name.

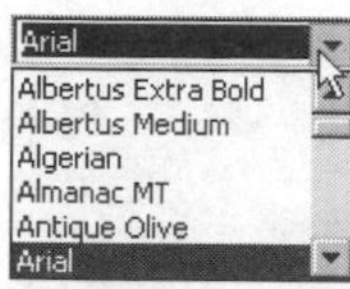

Figure 10 Use the Standard font menu to choose a default font for worksheet files.

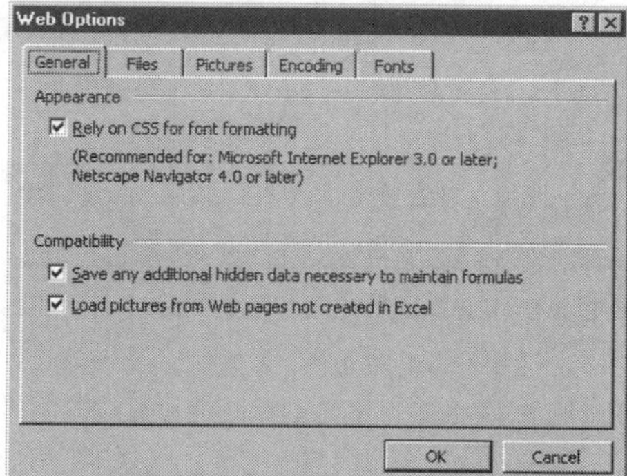

Figure 11 The General tab of the Web Options dialog box.

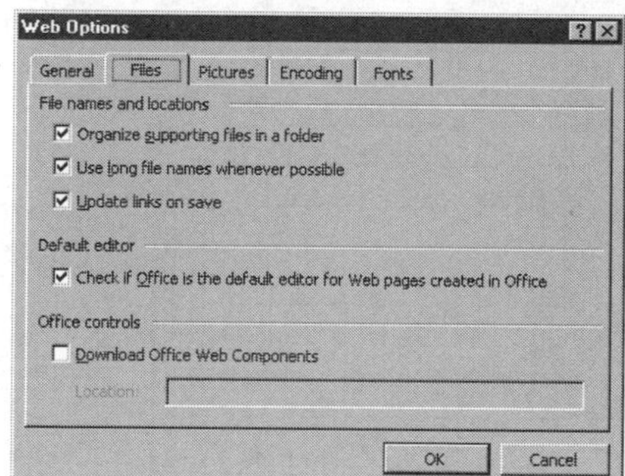

Figure 12 The Files tab of the Web Options dialog box.

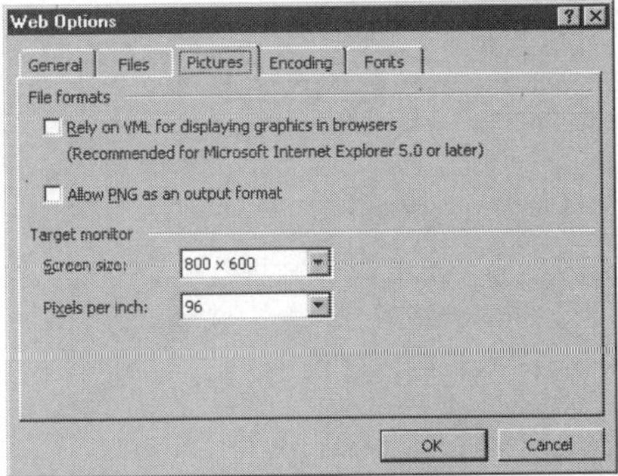

Figure 13 The Pictures tab of the Web Options dialog box.

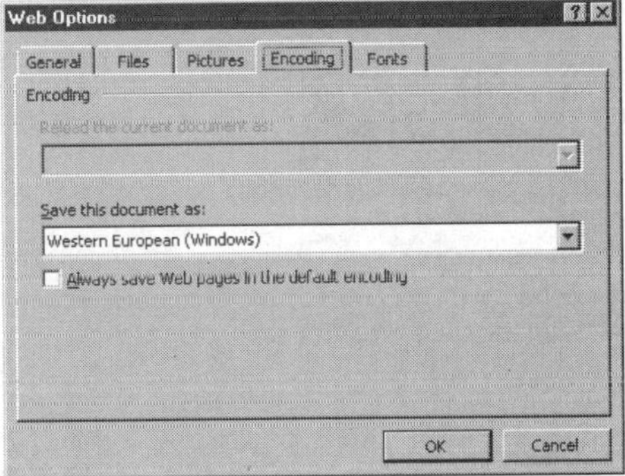

Figure 14 The Encoding tab of the Web Options dialog box.

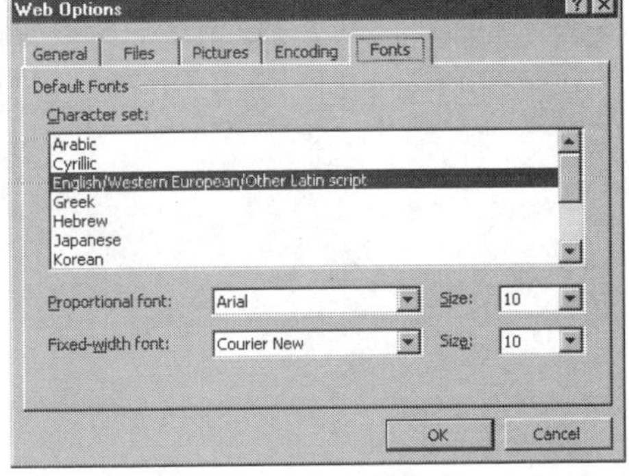

Figure 15 The Fonts tab of the Web Options dialog box.

Web Options

Clicking the Web Options button displays the Web Options dialog box (**Figures 11** through **15**), which has five different tabs of options relating to the Web. Although these options are advanced and far beyond the scope of this book, here's a quick overview of each tab:

- **General** options (**Figure 11**) control the coding and appearance of Web pages you create and view with Excel.
- **Files** options (**Figure 12**) control file naming and locations and the default editor for Web pages.
- **Pictures** options (**Figure 13**) control the file formats of images and the resolution of the target monitor.
- **Encoding** options (**Figure 14**) control how a Web page is coded when saved.
- **Fonts** options (**Figure 15**) control the character set and default fonts.

Transition Options

Transition options (**Figure 16**) offer settings to help you transition between Excel and other spreadsheet software packages, such as Lotus 1-2-3.

- **Save Excel files as** enables you to specify the default file format for every Excel file you save. Choose an option from the menu (**Figure 17**). The option you select will automatically appear in the Save As dialog box. You can override this choice if desired when you save a file. This option is useful if you often share the Excel files you create with people who use a different version of Excel or some other spreadsheet or database application.
- **Microsoft Excel menu or help key** allows you to specify the keyboard key that will activate Excel's menu bar or start Help for Lotus 1-2-3 users.
- **Transition formula evaluation** instructs Excel to evaluate Lotus 1-2-3 formulas without changing them. This option may be extremely helpful if you often open files created with Lotus 1-2-3.
- **Transition formula entry** converts formulas entered in Lotus 1-2-3 release 2.2 syntax to Excel syntax and changes the behavior of Excel-defined names to Lotus-defined names. This makes it possible for a Lotus 1-2-3 user to use Excel with less retraining.

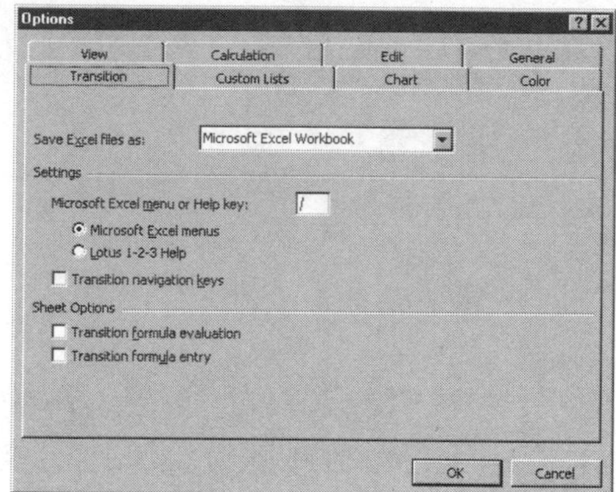

Figure 16 The default settings in the Transition tab of the Options dialog box.

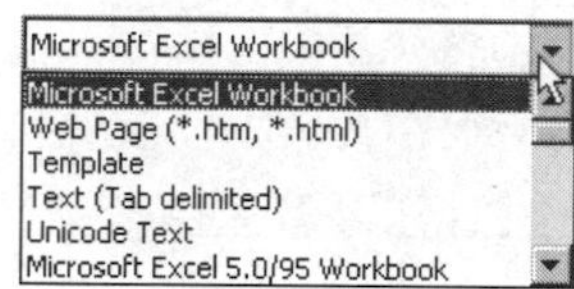

Figure 17 The Save Excel files as menu enables you to choose a default file format for saving Excel files.

Custom Lists Options

The Custom Lists options (**Figure 18**) enable you to create, modify, and delete custom lists. Once created, you can use the AutoFill feature I discuss in **Chapter 3** to enter list contents into cells.

✔ Tip

- You cannot modify or delete the predefined Custom lists (**Figure 18**).

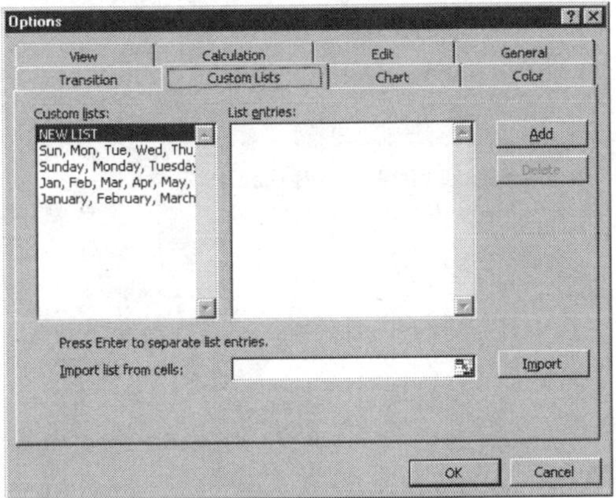

Figure 18 The default settings in the Custom Lists tab of the Options dialog box.

To create a custom list

1. In the Custom Lists tab of the Options dialog box, select NEW LIST (**Figure 18**).
2. Enter the list contents in the List entries area (**Figure 19**). Be sure to press Enter after each item.
3. Click Add.

   The list appears in the Custom lists list (**Figure 20**).

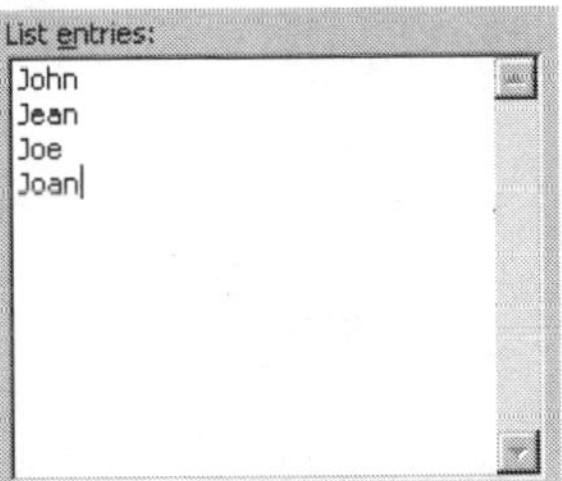

Figure 19 Enter the values you want to include in the list, one per line.

To import cell contents as a custom list

1. In the Custom Lists tab of the Options dialog box, select NEW LIST (**Figure 18**).
2. Click in the Import list from cells box.
3. In the worksheet window, drag to select the cells containing the values you want to use as a custom list (**Figure 21**).
4. Click Import.

   The list appears in the Custom lists list (**Figure 20**).

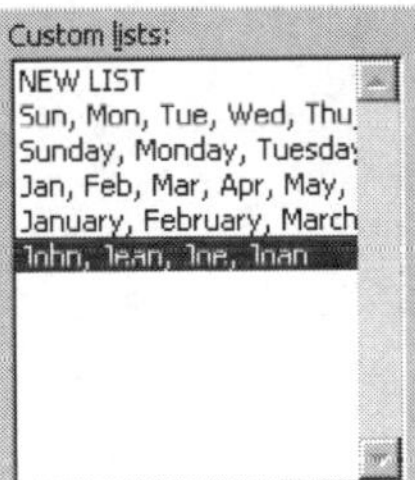

Figure 20 The list appears in the Custom lists list.

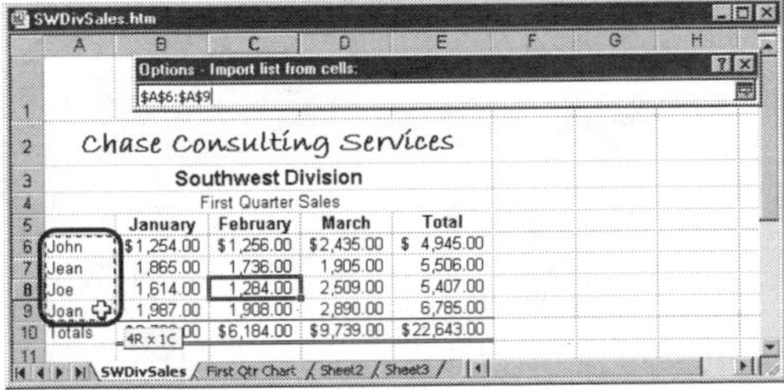

Figure 21 Select the cells containing the values you want to appear in the custom list.

To modify a custom list

1. In the Custom Lists tab of the Options dialog box, select the list you want to modify.
2. Edit the list contents as desired in the List entries area.
3. Click Add.

   The custom list changes.

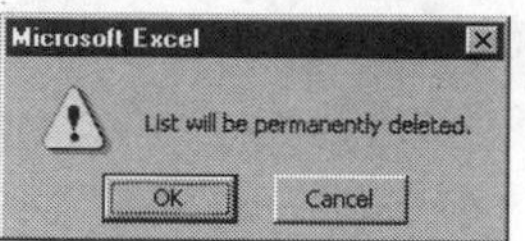

Figure 22 Excel displays this dialog box when you delete a custom list.

To delete a custom list

1. In the Custom Lists tab of the Options dialog box, select the list you want to delete.
2. Click Delete.
3. A confirmation dialog box like the one in **Figure 22** appears. Click OK.

   The list disappears from the Custom list list.

✔ Tip

- Deleting a custom list does not delete any data from your workbook files. It simply removes the list from the Custom Lists tab of the Options dialog box so you can no longer use it with the AutoFill feature.

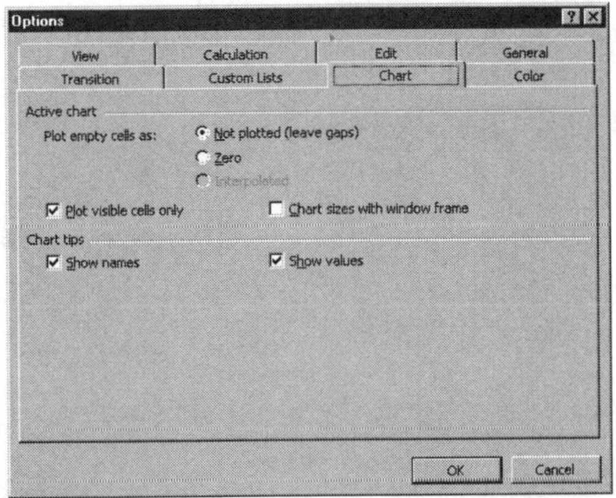

Figure 23 The default settings in the Chart tab of the Options dialog box.

Chart Options

Chart options (**Figure 23**) let you set preferences for the active chart and chart tips.

Active chart

Active chart options affect the active chart only. Be sure to activate the chart for which you want to set these options before opening the Options dialog box.

- **Plot empty cells as** enables you to select one of two or three options to specify how Excel should plot empty cells on the chart:
  - ▲ **Not plotted (leave gaps)** tells Excel not to plot the cell values at all. This leaves gaps in the chart.
  - ▲ **Zero** tells Excel to plot empty cells as zeros, thus including a zero data point for each empty cell.
  - ▲ **Interpolated** tells Excel to interpolate data points for blank cells and fill in the chart gaps with connecting lines. This option is not available for all chart types.
- **Plot visible cells only** tells Excel to plot only the cells that are displayed on the worksheet. If one or more cells are in hidden columns or rows, they are not plotted.
- **Chart sizes with window frame** resizes the chart in a chart sheet window so it fills the window, no matter how the window is sized. This option is not available for charts embedded in worksheets.

Chart tips

Chart tips options enable you to specify what displays in chart tips.

- **Show names** displays the names of data points.
- **Show values** displays the values of data points.

Color Options

The Color tab of the Options dialog box (**Figure 24**) enables you to set the color palettes used within the Excel workbook file.

- **Standard colors** are the colors that appear in color menus throughout Excel.
- **Chart fills** are the first eight colors Excel uses as chart fills.
- **Chart lines** are the first eight colors Excel uses as chart lines.

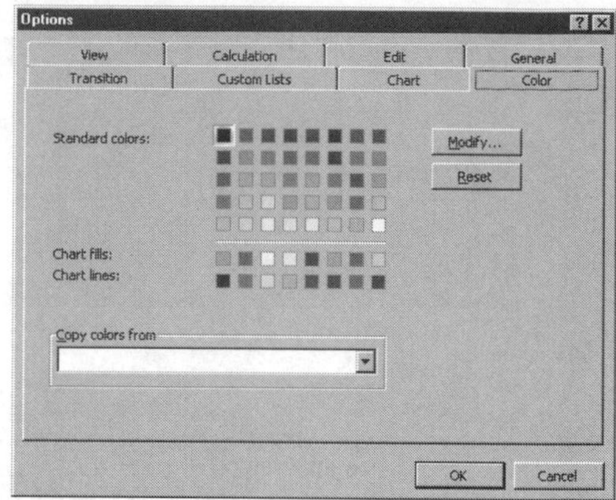

Figure 24 The default settings in the Color tab of the Options dialog box.

To modify the color palette

1. Click the color that you want to change to select it.
2. Click the Modify button.
3. In the Standard (**Figure 25**) or Custom tab of the Colors dialog box, click to select a color.
4. Click OK. The selected color changes.
5. Repeat steps 1 through 4 for each color you want to change.

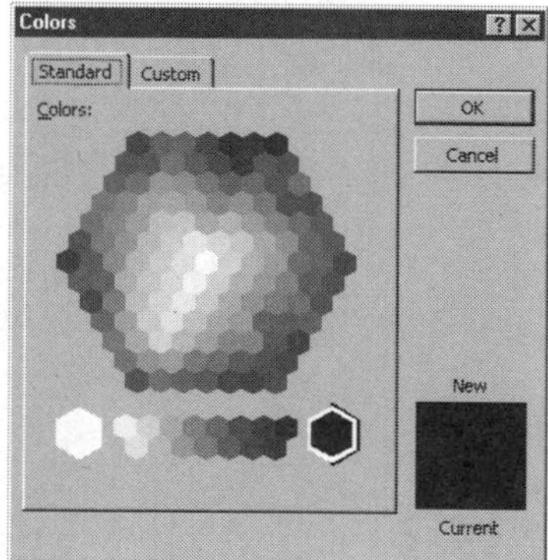

Figure 25 The Standard tab of the Colors dialog box.

To copy colors from another workbook file

1. Before opening the Options dialog box, open the workbook file from which you want to copy colors.
2. Open the Color tab of the Options dialog box.
3. From the Copy colors from menu (**Figure 26**), choose the workbook file from which you want to copy colors.

   The palette changes to reflect the colors from the other workbook file.

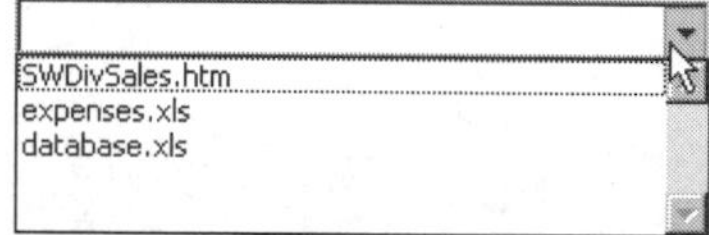

Figure 26 You can copy the color palette from another open workbook file by choosing it from the Copy colors from menu.

To reset the color palette

Click the Reset button. The colors change back to the default colors.

Menus & Shortcut Keys

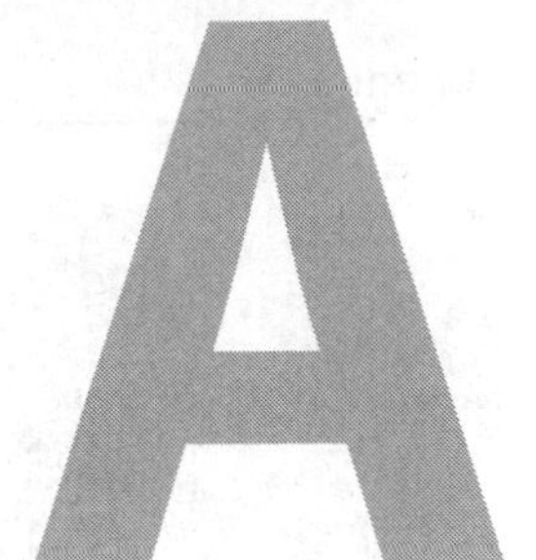

Menus & Shortcut Keys

This appendix illustrates all of Excel's full menus and provides a list of shortcut keys.

To use a shortcut key, hold down the modifier key (usually Ctrl) and press the keyboard key corresponding to the command. For example, to use the Save command's shortcut key, hold down Ctrl and press S.

✔ Tips

- I tell you all about using menus and shortcut keys in **Chapter 1**.
- Throughout this Appendix, when a menu or submenu has a different appearance for a worksheet and chart, both are illustrated.

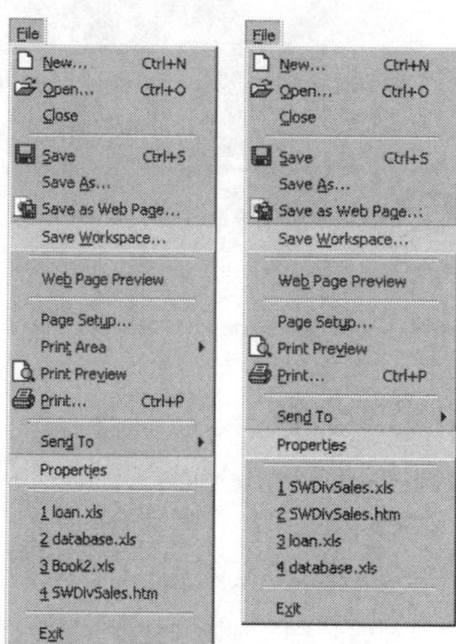

File Menu

Ctrl N	New
Ctrl O	Open
Ctrl S	Save
Ctrl P	Print

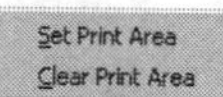

Print Area submenu (worksheet only)

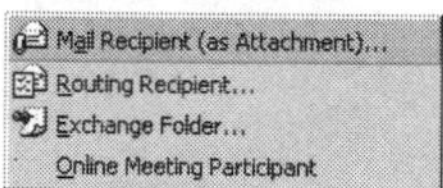

Send To submenu

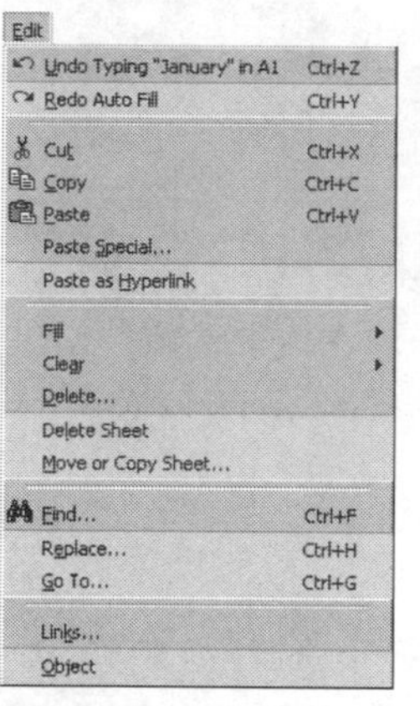

Edit Menu

Ctrl Z	Undo
Ctrl Y	Repeat
Ctrl Y	Redo
Ctrl X	Cut
Ctrl C	Copy
Ctrl V	Paste
Ctrl A	Select All
Ctrl F	Find
Ctrl H	Replace
Ctrl G	Go To

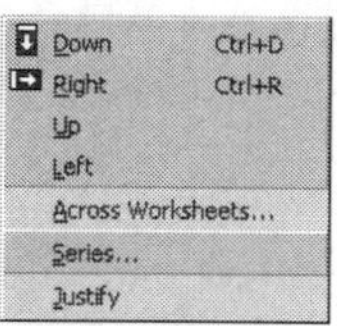

Fill submenu (worksheet only)

Ctrl D	Down
Ctrl R	Right

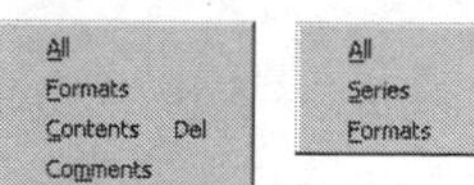

Fill submenu

Delete	Contents

FILE & EDIT MENUS

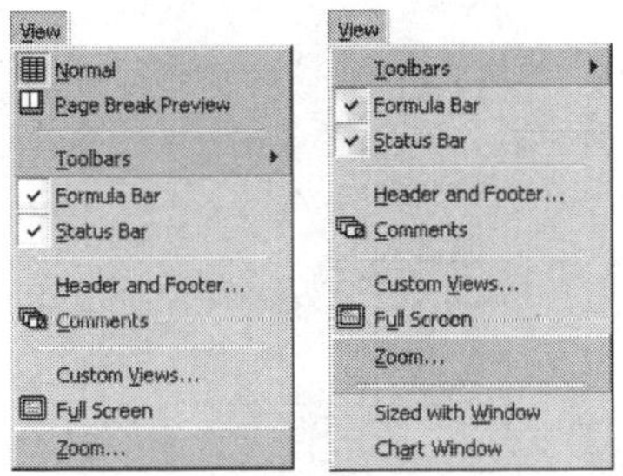

View Menu

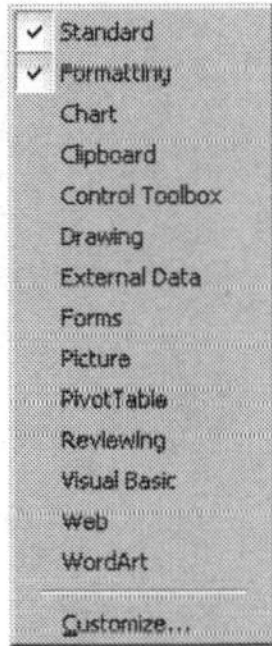

Toolbars submenu

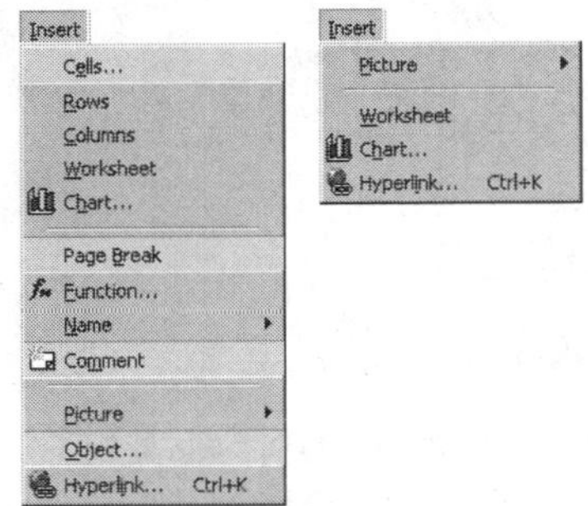

Insert Menu

Ctrl K Hyperlink

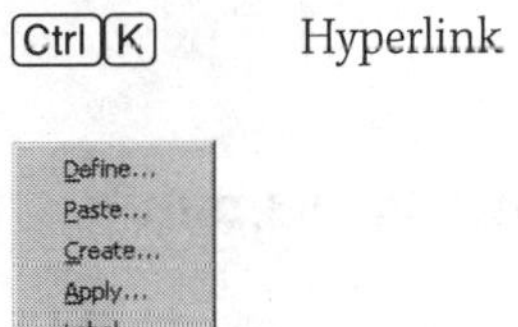

Name submenu (worksheet only)

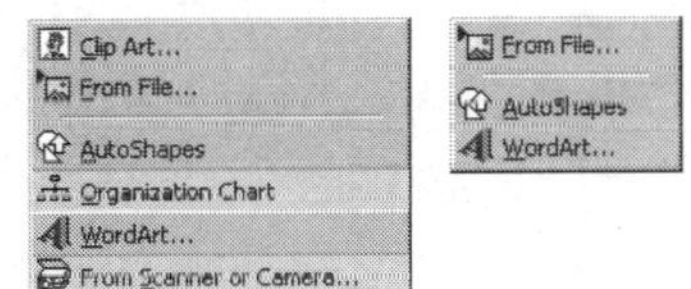

Picture submenu

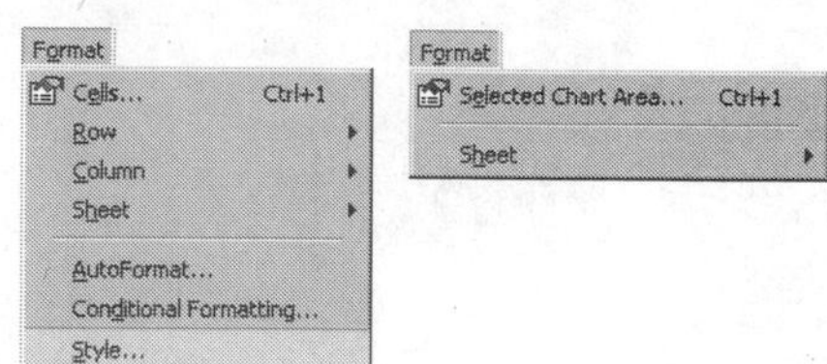

Format Menu

Ctrl 1 — Cells (worksheet) or Selection (Chart sheet or object)

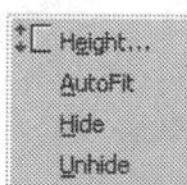

Row submenu (worksheets only)

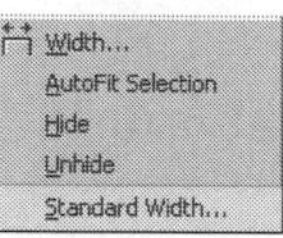

Column submenu (worksheets only)

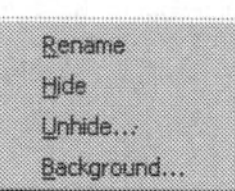

Sheet submenu

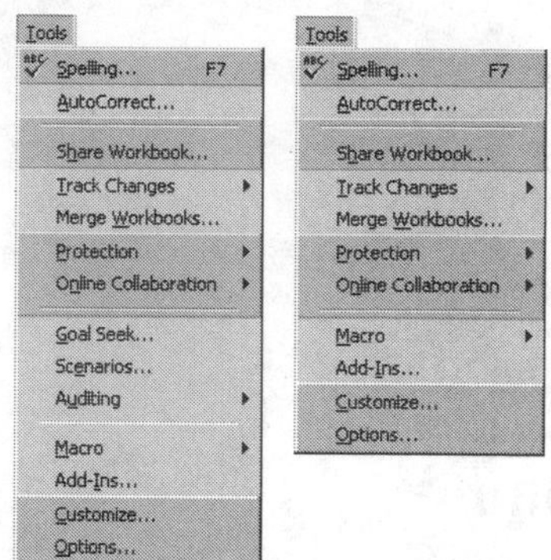

Tools Menu

F7 — Spelling

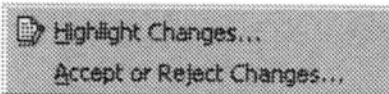

Track Changes submenu

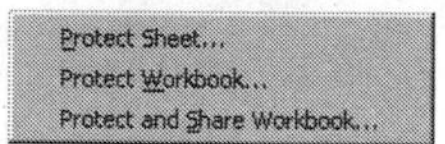

Protection submenu

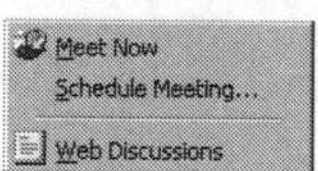

Online Collaboration submenu

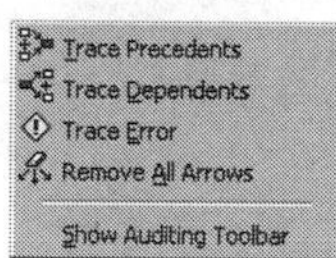

Auditing submenu (worksheets only)

Macro submenu

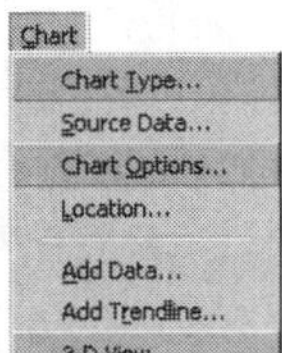

Chart Menu (charts only)

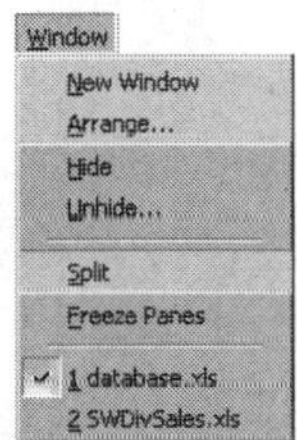

Window Menu

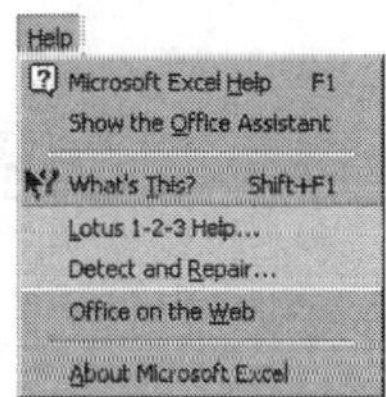

Help Menu

F1	Microsoft Excel Help
Shift F1	What's This?

FUNCTION REFERENCE

Functions

Functions are predefined formulas for making specific kinds of calculations. Functions make it quicker and easier to write formulas. I tell you about functions in **Chapter 5**. In this appendix, I provide a complete list of every function installed as part of a standard installation of Excel 2000, along with its arguments and a brief description of what it does.

Financial Functions

Function	Description
DB(cost,salvage,life,period,month)	Returns the depreciation of an asset for a specified period using the fixed-declining balance method.
DDB(cost,salvage,life,period,factor)	Returns the depreciation of an asset for a specified period using the double-declining balance method or some other method you specify.
FV(rate,nper,pmt,pv,type)	Returns the future value of an investment.
IPMT(rate,per,nper,pv,fv,type)	Returns the interest payment for an investment for a given period.
IRR(values,guess)	Returns the internal rate of return for a series of cash flows.
MIRR(values,finance_rate,reinvest_rate)	Returns the internal rate of return where positive and negative cash flows are financed at different rates.
NPER(rate,pmt,pv,fv,type)	Returns the number of periods for an investment.
NPV(rate,value1,value2,...)	Returns the net present value of an investment based on a series of periodic cash flows and a discount rate.
PMT(rate,nper,pv,fv,type)	Returns the period payment for an annuity.
PPMT(rate,per,nper,pv,fv,type)	Returns the payment on the principal for an investment for a given period.
PV(rate,nper,pmt,fv,type)	Returns the present value of an investment.

RATE(nper,pmt,pv,fv,type,guess)	Returns the interest rate per period of an annuity.
SLN(cost,salvage,life)	Returns the straight-line depreciation of an asset for one period.
SYD(cost,salvage,life,per)	Returns the sum-of-years'-digits depreciation of an asset for a specified period.
VDB(cost,salvage,life,start_period,end_period,factor,...)	Returns the depreciation of an asset for a specified or partial period using a declining balance method.

Date & Time Functions

DATE(year,month,day)	Returns the serial number of a particular date.
DATEVALUE(date_text)	Converts a date in the form of text to a serial number.
DAY(serial_number)	Converts a serial number to a day of the month.
DAYS360(start_date,end_date,method)	Calculates the number of days between two dates based on a 360-day year.
HOUR(serial_number)	Converts a serial number to an hour.
MINUTE(serial_number)	Converts a serial number to a minute.
MONTH(serial_number)	Converts a serial number to a month.
NOW()	Returns the serial number of the current date and time.
SECOND(serial_number)	Converts a serial number to a second.
TIME(hour,minute,second)	Returns the serial number of a particular time.
TIMEVALUE(time_text)	Converts a time in the form of text to a serial number.
TODAY()	Returns the serial number of today's date.
WEEKDAY(serial_number,return_type)	Converts a serial number to a day of the week.
YEAR(serial_number)	Converts a serial number to a year.

Math & Trig Functions

ABS(number)	Returns the absolute value of a number.
ACOS(number)	Returns the arccosine of a number.
ACOSH(number)	Returns the inverse hyperbolic cosine of a number.
ASIN(number)	Returns the arcsine of a number.
ASINH(number)	Returns the inverse hyperbolic sine of a number.
ATAN(number)	Returns the arctangent of a number.
ATAN2(x_num,y_num)	Returns the arctangent from x- and y-coordinates.
ATANH(number)	Returns the inverse hyperbolic tangent of a number.
CEILING(number,significance)	Rounds a number to the nearest whole number or to the nearest multiple of significance.

COMBIN(number,number_chosen)	Returns the number of combinations for a given number of objects.
COS(number)	Returns the cosine of a number.
COSH(number)	Returns the hyperbolic cosine of a number.
DEGREES(angle)	Converts radians to degrees.
EVEN(number)	Rounds a number up to the nearest even whole number.
EXP(number)	Returns e raised to the power of a given number.
FACT(number)	Returns the factorial of a number.
FLOOR(number, significance)	Rounds a number down, toward 0.
INT(number)	Rounds a number down to the nearest whole number.
LN(number)	Returns the natural logarithm of a number.
LOG(number,base)	Returns the logarithm of a number to a specified base.
LOG10(number)	Returns the base-10 logarithm of a number.
MDETERM(array)	Returns the matrix determinant of an array.
MINVERSE(array)	Returns the matrix inverse of an array.
MMULT(array1,array2)	Returns the matrix product of two arrays.
MOD(number,divisor)	Returns the remainder from division.
ODD(number)	Rounds a number up to the nearest odd whole number.
PI()	Returns the value of pi.
POWER(number,power)	Returns the result of a number raised to a power.
PRODUCT(number 1,number2,...)	Multiplies its arguments.
RADIANS(angle)	Converts degrees to radians.
RAND()	Returns a random number between 0 and 1.
ROMAN(number,form)	Converts an Arabic numeral to a Roman numeral, as text.
ROUND(number,num_digits)	Rounds a number to a specified number of digits.
ROUNDDOWN(number,num_digits)	Rounds a number down, toward 0.
ROUNDUP(number,num_digits)	Rounds a number up, away from 0.
SIGN(number)	Returns the sign of a number.
SIN(number)	Returns the sine of a number.
SINH(number)	Returns the hyperbolic sine of a number.
SQRT(number)	Returns a positive square root.
SUBTOTAL(function_num,ref1,...)	Returns a subtotal in a list or database.
SUM(number1,number2,...)	Adds its arguments.
SUMIF(range,criteria, sum_range)	Adds the cells specified by a given criteria.

SUMPRODUCT(array1,array2,array3,...)	Returns the sum of the products of corresponding array components.
SUMSQ(number1,number2,...)	Returns the sum of the squares of its arguments.
SUMX2MY2(array_x,array_y)	Returns the sum of the difference of squares of corresponding values in two arrays.
SUMX2PY2(array_x,array_y)	Returns the sum of the sum of squares of corresponding values in two arrays.
SUMXMY2(array_x,array_y)	Returns the sum of squares of differences of corresponding values in two arrays.
TAN(number)	Returns the tangent of a number.
TANH(number)	Returns the hyperbolic tangent of a number.
TRUNC(number,num_digits)	Truncates a number to a whole number.

Statistical Functions

AVEDEV(number1,number2,...)	Returns the average of the absolute deviations of data points from their mean.
AVERAGE(number1,number2,...)	Returns the average of its arguments.
AVERAGEA(value1,value2,...)	Returns the average of its arguments, including text and logical values.
BETADIST(x,alpha,beta,A,B)	Returns the cumulative beta probability density function.
BETAINV(probability,alpha,beta,A,B)	Returns the inverse of the cumulative beta probability density function.
BINOMDIST(number_s,trials,probability_s,cumulative)	Returns the individual term binomial distribution probability.
CHIDIST(x,degrees_freedom)	Returns the one-tailed probability of the chi-squared distribution.
CHIINV(probability,degrees_freedom)	Returns the inverse of the one-tailed probability of the chi-squared distribution.
CHITEST(actual_range,expected_range)	Returns the test for independence.
CONFIDENCE(alpha,standard_dev,size)	Returns the confidence interval for a population mean.
CORREL(array1,array2)	Returns the correlation coefficient between two data sets.
COUNT(value1,value2,...)	Counts how many numbers are in the list of arguments.
COUNTA(value2,value2,...)	Counts how many values are in the list of arguments.
COUNTBLANK(range)	Counts the number of blank cells within a range.

COUNTIF(range,criteria)	Counts the number of non-blank cells within a range which meet the given criteria.
COVAR(array1,array2)	Returns covariance, the average of the products of paired deviations.
CRITBINOM(trials,probability_s,alpha)	Returns the smallest value for which the cumulative binomial distribution is greater than or equal to a criterian value.
DEVSQ(number1,number2,...)	Returns the sum of squares of deviations.
EXPONDIST(x,lambda,cumulative)	Returns the exponential distribution.
FDIST(x,degrees_freedom1,degrees_freedom2)	Returns the F probability distribution.
FINV(probability,degrees_freedom1,degrees_freedom2)	Returns the inverse of the F probability distribution.
FISHER(x)	Returns the Fisher transformation.
FISHERINV(y)	Returns the inverse of the Fisher transformation.
FORECAST(x,known_y's,known_x's)	Returns a value along a linear trend.
FREQUENCY(data_array,bins_array)	Returns a frequency distribution as a vertical array.
FTEST(array1,array2)	Returns the result of an F-test.
GAMMADIST(x,alpha,beta,cumulative)	Returns the gamma distribution.
GAMMAINV(probability,alpha,beta)	Returns the inverse of the gamma cumulative distribution.
GAMMALN(x)	Returns the natural logarithm of the gamma function.
GEOMEAN(number1,number2,...)	Returns the geometric mean.
GROWTH(knowy_y's,known_x's,new_x's,const)	Returns values along an exponential trend.
HARMEAN(number1,number2,...)	Returns the harmonic mean.
HYPGEOMDIST(sample_s,number_sample,population_s,...)	Returns the hypergeometric distribution.
INTERCEPT(known_y's,known_x's)	Returns the intercept of the linear regression line.
KURT(number1,number2,...)	Returns the kurtosis of a data set.
LARGE(array,k)	Returns the k-th largest value in a data set.
LINEST(known_y's,known_x's,const,stats)	Returns the parameters of a linear trend.
LOGEST(known_y's,known_x's,const,stats)	Returns the parameters of an exponential trend.
LOGINV(probability,mean,standard_dev)	Returns the inverse of the lognormal distribution.
LOGNORMDIST(x,mean,standard_dev)	Returns the cumulative lognormal distribution.
MAX(number1,number2,...)	Returns the maximum value in a list of arguments.
MAXA(value1,value2,...)	Returns the maximum value in a list of arguments, including text and logical values.
MEDIAN(number1,number2,...)	Returns the median of the given numbers.

MIN(number1,number2,...) Returns the minimum value in a list of arguments.

MINA(value1,value2,...) Returns the minimum value in a list of arguments, including text and logical values.

MODE(number1,number2,...) Returns the most common value in a data set.

NEGBINOMDIST(number_f,number_s,probability_s) Returns the negative binomial distribution.

NORMDIST(x,mean,standard_dev,cumulative) Returns the normal cumulative distribution.

NORMINV(probability,mean,standard_dev) Returns the inverse of the normal cumulative distribution.

NORMSDIST(z) Returns the standard normal cumulative distribution.

NORSINV(probability) Returns the inverse of the standard normal cumulative distribution.

PEARSON(array1,array2) Returns the Pearson product moment correlation coefficient.

PERCENTILE(array,k) Returns the k-th percentile of values in a range.

PERCENTRANK(array,x,significance) Returns the percentage rank of a value in a data set.

PERMUT(number,number_chosen) Returns the number of permutations for a given number of objects.

POISSON(x,mean,cumulative) Returns the Poisson distribution.

PROB(x_range,prob_range,lower_limit,upper_limit) Returns the probability that values in a range are between two limits.

QUARTILE(array,quart) Returns the quartile of a data set.

RANK(number,ref,order) Returns the rank of a number in a list of numbers.

RSQ(known_y's,known_x's) Returns the square of the Pearson product moment correlation coefficient. If you know what that means, I hope you're making a lot of money.

SKEW(number1,number2,...) Returns the skewness of a distribution.

SLOPE(known_y's,known_x's) Returns the slope of the linear regression line.

SMALL(array,k) Returns the k-th smallest value in a data set.

STANDARDIZE(x,mean,standard_dev) Returns a normalized value.

STDEV(number1,number2,...) Estimates standard deviation based on a sample.

STDEVA(value1,value2,...) Estimates standard deviation based on a sample, including text and logical values.

STDEVP(number1,number2,...) Calculates standard deviation based on the entire population.

STDEVPA(value1,value2,...) Calculates standard deviation based on the entire population, including text and logical values.

STEYX(known_y's,known_x's)	Returns the standard error of the predicted y-value for each x in the regression.
TDIST(x,degrees_freedom,tails)	Returns the Student's t-distribution.
TINV(probability,degrees_freedom)	Returns the inverse of the Student's t-distribution.
TREND(known_y's,known_x's,new_x's,const)	Returns values along a linear trend.
TRIMMEAN(array,percent)	Returns the mean of the interior of a data set.
TTEST(array1,array2,tails,type)	Returns the probability associated with a Student's t-test.
VAR(number1,number2,...)	Estimates variance based on a sample.
VARA(value1,value2,...)	Estimates variance based on a sample, including text and logical values.
VARP(number1,number2,...)	Calculates variance based on the entire population.
VARPA(value1,value2,...)	Calculates variance based on the entire population, including text and logical values.
WEIBULL(x,alpha,beta,cumulative)	Returns the Weibull distribution.
ZTEST(array,x,sigma)	Returns the two-tailed P-value of a z-test. Really.

Lookup & Reference Functions

ADDRESS(row_num,column_num,abs_num,a1,sheet_text)	Returns a reference as text to a single cell in a worksheet.
AREAS(reference)	Returns the number of areas in a reference.
CHOOSE(index_num,value1,value2,...)	Chooses a value from a list of values.
COLUMN(reference)	Returns the column number of a reference.
COLUMNS(array)	Returns the number of columns in a reference.
HLOOKUP(lookup_value,table_array,row_index_num,...)	Looks in the top row of a table and returns the value of the indicated cell.
HYPERLINK(link_location,friendly_name)	Creates a shortcut that opens a document stored on a network computer or the Internet.
INDEX(...)	Uses an index to choose a value from a reference or array.
INDIRECT(ref_text,a1)	Returns a reference indicated by a text value.
LOOKUP(...)	Looks up values in a vector or array.
MATCH(lookup_value,lookup_array,match_type)	Looks up values in a reference or array.
OFFSET(reference,rows,cols,height,width)	Returns a reference offset from a given reference.
ROW(reference)	Returns the row number of a reference.

ROWS(array)	Returns the number of rows in a reference.
TRANSPOSE(array)	Returns the transpose of an array.
VLOOKUP(lookup_value,table_array,col_index_num,...)	Looks in the first column of a table and moves across the row to return the value of a cell.

Database Functions

DAVERAGE(database,field,criteria)	Returns the average of selected database entries.
DCOUNT(database,field,criteria)	Counts the cells containing numbers from a specified database and criteria.
DCOUNTA(database,field,criteria)	Counts nonblank cells from a specified database and criteria.
DGET(database,field,criteria)	Extracts from a database a single record that matches the specified criteria.
DMAX(database,field,criteria)	Returns the maximum value from selected database entries.
DMIN(database,field,criteria)	Returns the minimum value from selected database entries.
DPRODUCT(database,field,criteria)	Multiplies the values in a particular field of records that match the criteria in a database.
DSTDEV(database,field,criteria)	Estimates the standard deviation based on a sample of selected database entries.
DSTDEVP(database,field,criteria)	Calculates the standard deviation based on the entire population of selected database entries.
DSUM(database,field,criteria)	Adds the numbers in the field column of records in the database that match the criteria.
DVAR(database,field,criteria)	Estimates the variance based on a sample from selected database entries.
DVARP(database,field,criteria)	Calculates variance based on the entire population of selected database entries.

Text Functions

CHAR(number)	Returns the character specified by the code number.
CLEAN(text)	Removes all nonprintable characters from text.
CODE(text)	Returns a numeric code for the first character in a text string.
CONCATENATE(text1,text2,...)	Joins several text items into one text item.
DOLLAR(number,decimals)	Converts a number to text, using currency format.
EXACT(text1,text2)	Checks to see if two text values are identical.

FIND(find_text,within_text,start_num)	Finds one text value within another. This function is case-sensitive.
FIXED(number,decimals,no_commas)	Formats a number as text with a fixed number of decimals.
LEFT(text,num_chars)	Returns the leftmost characters from a text value.
LEN(text)	Returns the number of characters in a text string.
LOWER(text)	Converts text to lowercase.
MID(text,start_num,num_chars)	Returns a specific number of characters from a text string.
PROPER(text)	Capitalizes the first letter in each word of a text value.
REPLACE(old_text,start_num,num_chars,new_text)	Replaces characters within text.
REPT(text,number_times)	Repeats text a given number of times.
RIGHT(text,num_chars)	Returns the rightmost characters from a text value.
SEARCH(find_text,within_text,start_num)	Finds one text value within another. This function is not case-sensitive.
SUBSTITUTE(text,old_text,new_text,instance_num)	Substitutes new text for old text in a text string.
T(value)	Converts its arguments to text.
TEXT(value,format_text)	Formats a number and converts it to text.
TRIM(text)	Removes spaces from text.
UPPER(text)	Converts text to uppercase.
VALUE(text)	Converts a text argument to a number.

Logical Functions

AND(logical1,logical2,...)	Returns TRUE if all of its arguments are TRUE.
FALSE()	Returns the logical value FALSE.
IF(logical_test,value_if_true,value_if_false)	Specifies a logical test to perform and the value to return based on a TRUE or FALSE result.
NOT(logical)	Reverses the logic of its argument.
OR(logical1,logical2,...)	Returns TRUE if any argument is TRUE.
TRUE()	Returns the logical value TRUE.

Information Functions

CELL(info_type,reference)	Returns information about the formatting, location, or contents of a cell.
ERROR.TYPE(error_val)	Returns a number corresponding to an error value.

INFO(type_text)	Returns information about the current operating environment.
ISBLANK(value)	Returns TRUE if the value is blank.
ISERR(value)	Returns TRUE if the value is any error value except #N/A.
ISERROR(value)	Returns TRUE if the value is any error value.
ISLOGICAL(value)	Returns TRUE if the value is a logical value.
ISNA(value)	Returns TRUE if the value is the #N/A error value.
ISNONTEXT(value)	Returns TRUE if the value is not text.
ISNUMBER(value)	Returns TRUE if the value is a number.
ISREF(value)	Returns TRUE if the value is a reference.
ISTECT(value)	Returns TRUE if the value is text.
N(value)	Returns a value converted to a number.
NA()	Returns the error value #N/A.
TYPE(value)	Returns a number indicating the data type of a value.

INDEX

D

INDEX

E

F

G

H

I

J

K

L

T

U

INDEX

Other Books for Microsoft Office 2000 Users

Word 2000 for Windows: Visual QuickStart Guide

Maria Langer

Microsoft Word has long been the most versatile, powerful, word processor available. Users who appreciate its speed, reliability, and ease of use are in for a treat with Word 2000. An important component of Office 2000, Word boasts impressive tools for increased collaboration and communication with other Office applications and with the Internet. Producing and posting a Web page in Word will be as simple as creating and saving any document. Easier access to synonyms, improved table editing capabilities, and the new Click and Type feature are also among the highlights of Word 2000.

The *Word 2000 for Windows: Visual QuickStart Guide* will introduce new and experienced Word users alike to the host of new features and improved Web integration and functionality. Using concise steps and numerous illustrations, the book covers everything from word processing basics and formatting fundamentals to desktop and Webtop publishing techniques. This is a comprehensive introduction to the powerful capabilities of Word 2000.

272 pages • ISBN 0-201-35428-4 • $17.99

PowerPoint 2000/98 for Windows and Macintosh: Visual QuickStart Guide

Rebecca Altman

Most professionals turn to Microsoft PowerPoint to make their presentations come alive. The latest version, PowerPoint 2000, promises to attract a legion of new converts, lured by its full integration with the other Office 2000 apps and its new and improved formatting and Web features. *PowerPoint 2000/98 for Windows and Macintosh: Visual QuickStart Guide* is the quickest, easiest way to learn how to add slides, movie clips, sound, animation—even Web pages—to your presentations using this powerful package.

Thanks to the book's straightforward, task-oriented format, you can go directly to the information you need. Like the other titles in Peachpit's *Visual QuickStart Guide* series, *PowerPoint 2000/98: VQS* uses hundreds of screenshots and step-by-step instructions to explain the most popular features of PowerPoint, and it covers both the Windows 2000 and Macintosh 98 platforms. Whether you use it as a tutorial or a reference guide, you'll be putting together impressive presentations in no time.

336 pages • ISBN 0-201-35441-1 • $17.99

To order these and other Peachpit Press books, visit our Web site at http://www.peachpit.com/
or call toll-free 1-800-283-9444

About Giles Road Press

Giles Road Press is a small Web publishing organization that provides the following information for Macintosh and Windows users:

- **Companion Web sites for recent books by Maria Langer.** These sites include information about books, sample chapters, sample files used throughout the book, corrections and clarifications, tips and tricks, and news links of interest to book readers.
- **Discounts and special offers on books and software.** Giles Road Press offers all recent books by Maria Langer at a discount to site visitors. You can even get an autographed copy! Links to other computer and non-computer books available through Amazon.com make it easy to find books that interest you without dealing with cryptic search engines. Occasionally, visitors will also find special offers on clearance and other items offered by Giles Road Press's Web partners.
- **Macintosh Tips & Tricks.** This newsletter, which is issued periodically, provides a wealth of information for Macintosh users. Recent issues covered topics such as HFS+ and choosing an Internet service provider (ISP).
- **Links to other sites.** The Giles Road Press site includes links to other sites of interest to Macintosh and Windows users and writers.

There is no charge for accessing the Giles Road Press Web site or any of its information. No membership or registration is required.

Get On Our Mailing List!

To get on the Giles Road Press mailing list and learn about major changes to the site and special offers, send an e-mail message to **info@gilesrd.com** with the word **ADD** in the subject line. (You will receive confirmation that you have been added, along with instructions for being removed from the list.) The Giles Road Press mailing list seldom sends out more than 4 messages in a month and is not shared with any other organization.

For more information about Giles Road Press, including information on how you can become a site sponsor, visit the site or send an e-mail message to **info@gilesrd.com**.

Visit Giles Road Press at http://www.gilesrd.com/